Acknowledgements

To our families:

Dorothy, Matthew and Teagan and
Karen, Adrian and Ellena

for their love, support and understanding.

We would like to pay special thanks to Mark Lewis, Steve Snyder and Meredith Payne Stotzner for their advice and editorial input and to David Albon and Lisa Jones at Focal Press for their hard work in getting this book to press.

Picture credits

Paul Allister; Craig Banks; Magdalena Bors; Andrew Boyle: Haydn Cattach; Abhijit Chattaraj; Dorothy Connop; Catherine Dorsen; Haydn Cattach; Samantha Everton; Serena Galante; Rory Gardiner; Shari Gleeson; Morten Haugen; John Hay; Eeyong Heng; Kane Hibberd; Paulina Hryniewiecka; Jakub Kazmierczak; Anitra Keogh; Jeff Ko; Bronek Kozka; Michelle Lee; Seok-Jin Lee; Anica Meehan; Chris Mollison; Shane Monopoli; Chris Neylon; Serap Osman; Rod Owen; Ed Purnomo; Craig Shell; Daniel Stainsby; Jennifer Stephens; Victoria Verdon Roe; Rahel Weiss.

Also our thanks go to www.iStockphoto.com for supporting this venture by supplying various images.

All other images and illustrations by the authors.

Contents

foundation module

Contents

5. Digital Printing

Digital Basics – DVD Chapter 1   DVD1

Digital Darkroom – DVD Chapter 2   DVD27

digital basics - dvd chapter

photoshop photoshop photoshop photoshop photoshop photoshop photo

Contents

- Introduction
- Channels and modes
- Levels
- Hue, Saturation and Brightness
- Color and light overview
- Bit depth
- File size
- File formats
- Image compression
- Resolution
- Image size
- Interpolation

Serap Osman

Mark Galer
Philip Andrews

Photoshop CS5
essential skills

Note >

Click on a heading from the contents to go straight to that topic, or use the navigation arrows at the bottom of each page to move forward or back through the document.

➤

Contents

advanced skills module

Contents

Contents

imaging projects module

imaging

Contents

projects

Contents DVD

The DVD is a veritable treasure trove of supporting files for the projects in this book as well as a resource for your own creative projects. The images and movies on the DVD are divided into their respective chapters and can be accessed via Bridge (see *Bridge* > page 45). Most of the images in the Foundation and Advanced Skills modules of the book can be found on the DVD together with all of the images from the Imaging Projects module. The movies are an invaluable resource, allowing you to start, stop and rewind so that the skills can be quickly and easily acquired at your own pace. The DVD also contains multi-layered image files (PSDs) of the completed projects, TIFF files with saved selections and Camera Raw files. Loadable Actions and Presets are also available to enhance your software, together with a rich stock library of royalty-free images.

Contents

Introduction

Photoshop has helped revolutionize how photographers capture, edit and prepare their images for viewing. Most of what we now see in print has been edited and prepared using the Adobe software. The image-editing process extends from basic retouching and sizing of images, to the highly manipulated and preconceived photographic montages that are commonly used by the advertising industry. This book is intended for photographers and designers who wish to use the 'digital darkroom' rather than the traditional darkroom for creative photographic illustration. The information, activities and assignments contained in this book provide the essential skills necessary for competent and creative image editing. The subject guides offer a comprehensive and highly structured learning approach, giving comprehensive support to guide Photoshop users through each editing process. An emphasis on useful (essential) practical advice and activities maximizes the opportunities for creative image production.

Anitra Keogh

Acquisition of skills

The first section of this book is a foundation module designed to help the user establish an effective working environment and act as a guide for successful navigation through the image-editing process from capture to print. Emphasis is placed on the essential techniques and skills whilst the terminology is kept as simple as possible, using only those terms in common usage.

Application of skills

The subsequent modules extend and build on the basic skills to provide the user with the essential techniques to enable creative and skilful image editing. The guides explore creative applications including advanced retouching, photomontage, vector graphics, special effects and preparing images for the web. Creative practical tasks, using a fully illustrated and simple step-by-step approach, are undertaken in each of the guides to allow the user to explore the creative possibilities and potential for each of the skills being offered.

A structured learning approach

The study guides contained in this book offer a structured learning approach and an independent learning resource that will give the user a framework for the techniques of digital imaging as well as the essential skills for personal creativity and communication.

The skills

To acquire the essential skills to communicate effectively and creatively takes time and motivation. Those skills should be practised repeatedly so that they become practical working knowledge rather than just basic understanding. Become familiar with the skills introduced in one study guide and apply them to each of the following guides wherever appropriate.

The DVD has images and movies available to support and guide the learning process.

Supporting DVD

A supporting DVD and dedicated web log (blog) have been set up to enable users to access current information. The address for the blog site is: **www.photoshopessentialskills.com**
The supporting files can be accessed through the Bridge interface (Computer > CS5_DVD).

Research and resources

You will only realize your full creative potential by looking at a variety of images from different sources. Artists and designers find inspiration in many different ways, but most find that they are influenced by other work they have seen and admired.

Essential information

The basic equipment required to complete this course is access to a computer with Adobe Photoshop CS5 (CS4 would suffice for many of the projects contained in the book). The photographic and design industries have traditionally used Apple Macintosh computers but many people now choose 'Windows'-based PCs as a more cost-effective alternative. When Photoshop is open there are minor differences in the interface, but all of the features and tools are identical. It is possible to use this book with either Windows-based or Apple Macintosh computers.

Storage

Due to the large file sizes involved with digital imaging it is advisable that you have a high-capacity, removable storage device attached to the computer or use a CD or DVD writer to archive your images.

Commands

Computer commands which allow the user to modify digital files can be accessed via menus and submenus. The commands used in the study guides are listed as a hierarchy, with the main menu indicated first and the submenu or command second, e.g. Main menu > Command or Submenu > Command. For example, the command for opening the Image Size dialog box would be indicated as follows: Edit > Image Adjustments > Image Size.

Keyboard shortcuts

Many commands that can be accessed via the menus and submenus can also be accessed via keyboard '**shortcuts**'. A shortcut is the action of pressing two or more keys on the keyboard to carry out a command (rather than clicking a command or option in a menu). Shortcuts speed up digital image processing enormously and it is worth learning the examples given in the study guides. If in doubt use the menu (the shortcut will be indicated next to the command) until you become more familiar with the key combinations.

Note > The keyboard shortcuts indicate both the Mac and PC equivalents.

Example: The shortcut for pasting objects and text in most applications uses the key combination Command/Ctrl + V. The Macintosh requires the Command key (next to the spacebar) and the V key to be pressed in sequence whilst a PC requires the Control key (Ctrl) and the V key to be pressed.

what's new for CS5

Ed Purnomo

essential skills

- Overview of the new and changed features in Photoshop CS5.

'New and revised' for CS5

With some releases of Photoshop, the spread of new tools and features on offer seem to cater for the broader user community, rather than photographers specifically, but happily this is not the case for CS5. A quick glance at the top features list will reassure you that there is much here for the digital shooter and I can safely say that this is the strongest release for photographers for quite a while.

Two CS5 flavors

As with the last few releases of the product, the CS5 release includes two versions of the program — Photoshop CS5 and Photoshop CS5 Extended. Photoshop CS5 contains the lion's share of the new tools and features, with the Extended version adding new and improved 3D options (see the table on the next page). Photoshop CS5 Extended ships with most Creative Suite packages and, as more and more photographers are seeing the value of buying these suites, many of you will be getting 'Extended' without having to make a decision about if you need the extra 3D imaging power. But more on this later.

More editing power to you

Photoshop has always provided photographers with a plethora of controls aimed at giving them tools needed for the precise enhancement of their images. CS5 continues this tradition with a very important update of Adobe Camera Raw (ACR6) featuring a complete rewriting of the demosaicing engine to produce higher quality raw conversions, a quantum leap forward in noise reduction, better sharpening, and more control of post-crop vignetting. The changes here are so good that it has me reworking raw files I have already processed, just so that I can take advantage of the quality gains offered by ACR6.

The new Merge To HDR Pro dialog offers substantially more creative control and precision over the processing and styling of High Dynamic Range photos and the lens correction features (available as a filter in Photoshop, in ACR6, and via batch processing) provide customized correction of key lens aberrations.

Creative control as well

Alongside editing precision, Photoshop CS5 also delivers new tools and features to help you achieve your creative photographic vision. In a massive shake-up of Photoshop's painting abilities, the program now includes the new Mixer Brush and Bristle Tips, which enable you to realistically blend colors and paint with naturalistic strokes. Don't feel like you have the artistic ability to create masterpieces from scratch? No problem. Simply start the painting process with a photo original. Use the incredible new Puppet Warp tool to easily reposition an image element and employ the almost 'magical' powers of Content-Aware Fill to intelligently recreate missing picture content.

Terrific as these new options are, many might say the true 'killer-feature' of this release is the new selection technology. The changes made to the Refine Edge dialog box include great tools and controls that help you make complex selections of difficult subjects such as hair and foliage more quickly and easily than ever before.

64-bit is here...

If you are sitting in the Windows camp, then this news is a little less exciting than if you are a Mac user. Why? Well Windows got a 64-bit optimized version of Photoshop last time around. With CS5, now Mac users can also take advantage of the better performance that native 64-bit support yields.

Expect to see real gains when working with large image files in particular.

Photoshop CS5 is further enhanced with dozens of time-saving features suggested by Photoshop users like you. The engineering team put aside time in their busy development cycle to address a bunch of improvements that, although not ground breaking, will make their impact felt immediately in your day-to-day workflow.

These improvements include the ability to save to unsupported bit depths, easily reverse clone sources images, save layer style presets, more easily straighten crooked photos, create masks from the transparent area of a layer and heaps more. Check our complete list later in this chapter.

	Photoshop CS5	Photoshop CS5 Ext.
Mixer Brush and Bristle Tips	✓	✓
Adobe Camera Raw 6 plug-in with support for more than 275 camera models	✓	✓
Re-engineered noise removal and additive grain	✓	✓
Enhanced post-crop vignetting	✓	✓
Enhanced sharpening	✓	✓
Automated lens correction	✓	✓
HDR Pro for high dynamic range imaging	✓	✓
HDR Toning	✓	✓
Puppet Warp	✓	✓
Content-Aware Fill	✓	✓
LAB B&W Action	✓	✓
New black-and-white presets	✓	✓
Intelligent edge-selection technology	✓	✓
Color decontamination	✓	✓
Refine Radius and Erase Refinements tools	✓	✓
Adobe Bridge CS5 and Adobe Mini Bridge	✓	✓
Cross-platform 64-bit support	✓	✓
More flexible custom panels	✓	✓
Workspace Switcher and Live Workspaces	✓	✓
More powerful printing options	✓	✓
GPU-accelerated Crop Guides, on-screen Color Picker, Eyedropper and color sampler ring	✓	✓
Broader file format support	✓	✓
More than three dozen customer-inspired features and enhancements	✓	✓
Adobe Repoussé technology		✓
Shadow catcher		✓
3D materials library and picker		✓
Overlays for materials and mesh boundaries		✓
Depth of Field for 3D		✓
Enhanced ray tracer with progressive rendering		✓
Image-based light option		✓
Context-sensitive widget for easy control of objects, cameras, meshes and lights		✓
3D merging and scene compositing improvements		✓
3D workflow improvements		✓
Preferences that allow for the customization of 3D features		✓

Better 3D more easily

Previous releases of Photoshop Extended have concentrated on providing easier ways to work in allied areas such as video, animation, medical and technical imaging and architectural illustration. In CS5 we see the Adobe team put a lot of effort into creating new tools and features to help photographers better explore the creative opportunities available in the world of 3D. Taking much of the confusion out of building simple 3D models, Adobe Repoussé lets you take your work to the next level by adding 3D elements to 2D designs. The feature gives photographers the ability to easily create 3D extrusions from text and shapes. In addition, you can enhance the realism of your 3D artwork with one-click shadow creation, a rich library of easy-to-apply 3D materials and the option to use image-based-lighting.

Over the next few pages we'll take a closer look at the key new features in this release, highlighting specifically as we go, how you can take advantage of them in your own individual workflow.

Producing realistic composites of two or more images relies heavily on creating high quality selections/masks which are then used to blend the image content. The adaptive, edge detection technology located in the Refine Edge dialog box provides powerful, easy-to-use tools to help with this task.

Faster, more accurate, selections of complex subjects

The editing Holy Grail for many Photoshop users is the ability to quickly, accurately and seamlessly create a composite of two images. This task often involves the creation of complex masks or selections in order to hide parts of one layer while revealing sections of another. It is not that the process, in its simplest form, is a difficult one. After all, anyone can create a selection. Right? Well yes, but it is when we want to create complex, accurate, selections of difficult subjects to increase the appearance of a seamless transition between the two picture parts, that things start to get a little tricky.

No where is this more apparent than when trying to extract a portrait subject with fly-away hair from one background and layer it upon another. The wispy nature of the subject makes the task of accurate selection a difficult, tedious, and often, time-consuming one. Photoshop has a large range of selection tools that can be thrown at the job, but most of these options are 'dumb' in their approach to creating selections.

Experienced Photoshop users know that the best selections are created by constantly adapting the selection approach to variations in the qualities of the subject's edge. This process involves the user changing tools, approaches and techniques in order to customize the selection to better match the subject's edge. What is really needed is a selection technology that intelligently adapts to changes in edge characteristics of a subject. With Photoshop CS5 you have such technology at your fingertips in the form of the revamped Refine Edge dialog box. The tools and controls found here allow you to produce highly accurate masks and selections faster and simpler than before.

The revamped Refine Edge dialog now includes new View options (1), powerful Edge Detection features (2), selection refinement tools (3), Edge adjustment controls (4), and new Output settings (5).

The process starts with the creation of a rough selection of the key subject. This can be created with any of the Selection tools in Photoshop. Often the Quick Selection Tool is the fastest option to use. Next, the edge of the selection is modified with the set of new adaptive selection-edge modification controls located in the Refine Edge dialog box.

The Smart Radius setting and Radius slider automatically matches the best selection approach with the subject's changing edge characteristics — soft for hair and hard for the side of a building. The quality of the selection can be fine-tuned further with two refinement brushes. One for adding to the edge and one for subtracting from it. The new dialog box also includes two extra view modes, On Layers and Reveal Layer, as well as Show Radius and Show Original settings to assist you when previewing the quality of your selections. New output options control how your selections will be used when exiting the dialog box. You can choose from creating selections, masks, new masked layers or even a new document with the masked layer included.

The secret of creating great selections with the features in the updated Refine Edge dialog box is to adjust the Smart Radius so the selection around the hard edges of the subject are accurate and then brush in the softer edges using the Refine Radius Tool.

Finally the Decontaminate Color setting helps eliminate any residual background color from around the edges of your selections. This feature is particularly useful for creating seamless compositions as it increases the effectiveness of the blend between the masked layer and its new background.

Tests that we conducted during the Photoshop beta period have shown that the adjustment options in the new Refine Edge dialog box do provide a faster route for the creation of good selections. It is true that power users will still be able to create better selections through the use of tried-and-true masking methods, but in all cases, the creation of such superior selections took much longer for very little perceptible gain than when employing the new workflow.

When combining multiple overlapping photos together to form a panorama you are often left with areas of the frame that are missing details. Content-Aware Fill provides an efficient way to rebuild this missing detail and, although not perfect, the feature does the job faster than traditional methods.

Intelligent retouching

Photoshop has many tools that the image maker can use to repair problem areas of a photo. The Spot Healing brush is great for hiding sensor dust; its bigger brother, the Healing Brush works well with larger areas and for the traditionalists amongst us, the Clone Stamp tool also has its place. But as any retoucher knows, these tools, great as they may be, are not perfect. Most repair jobs require switching between tools to ensure a good result.

Well the good news is that Photoshop CS5 introduces a new tool to your editing arsenal. Actually, it is not so much a tool, as a new way of using existing tools such as the Fill command and Spot Healing Brush. To my mind, the Content-Aware Fill (CAF) option is one of the most exciting features in the new release as it has the remarkable ability to remove an image element and magically replace the missing pixels with details that match the lighting, tone, and noise of the surrounding area. In many instances the results are so good that it looks like the deleted content never existed.

Content-Aware Fill is perfectly placed for the removal of large objects in photo compositions or the creation of missing content in montaged images.

Two ways to use CAF

You can use Content-Aware Fill with the Spot Healing Brush or as an option of the Fill command to replace content in an active selection.

1. Selecting the Content-Aware setting from the Options bar of the Spot Healing brush changes the way the tool fills in the areas you paint. This retouching approach is designed to account more fully for the structure and detail of the image elements that surround the painted area, providing a near-invisible result when removing unwanted objects.

The feature can also be selected as an option when using the Spot Healing brush.

2. Alternatively, you can select the object to be removed, and then replace the area with synthesized details from the area surrounding the selection. Just create the selection and then choose the Content-Aware option in the Fill dialog box (Edit > Fill).

Compared to what was available in previous versions of Photoshop, the Merge To HDR Pro feature in CS5 dramatically changes a photographer's ability to control HDR merging and processing.

Getting creative with HDR Pro

The ability to build High Dynamic Range (HDR) photos in Photoshop first appeared a few revisions ago. At the time, I can still remember heralding the feature's arrival as an answer to shooters who are regularly faced with high-contrast dilemmas with their subjects.

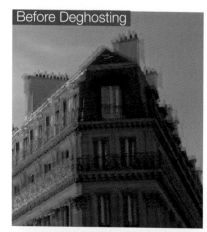

Before Deghosting

After Deghosting

Shooting moving subjects or without a tripod have traditionally been big no-nos when capturing the source files for HDR photos. Both these scenarios produce blurry results as the merging software is unable to align the source files. The deghosting feature in Merge To HDR Pro helps with this problem by giving priority to the content of one source image over the others. This can happen automatically or you can select the photo to use as the basis of the correction.

After all, the idea of going beyond the capture range of your camera by stitching together several differently-exposed photos does solve one of our fundamental problems, namely how to record the massive contrast range that typify many outdoor scenes. It is not unusual for an architectural photographer to be working with a scene that has a 15 f-stop range from darkest to lightest areas. With the average digital camera only capable of capturing 8–9 f-stops this means sacrificing detail (clipping) at either the highlight or shadow end of the tonal range.

The promise of HDR is with multiple source photos, the photographer can record detail of the darkest shadows, the brightest highlights and the midtones. Photoshop then magically combines the exposures to produce a single HDR file that preserves the full tonal range of the high contrast scene. The HDR photo is different from traditional Photoshop documents in that it is a 32-bit file capable of storing up to 15 f-stops in brightness range or a contrast ratio of 100,000:1.

That's the promise of the HDR system. In reality, Photoshop provided a fairly basic toolset for working with HDR images. It contained controls for the creation of precise merges of source files that produced objectively accurate 32-bit renditions of the file, but there was little in the way of creative tools for the HDR photographer. CS5 changes all this. The new version introduces a completely new take on HDR photo creation and processing.

More creativity and control

Renamed HDR Pro, Photoshop CS5's High Dynamic Range system now provides far more control over the HDR merging process, a greater degree of adjustment power when mapping tones and when styling the HDR output. You can still produce 'accurate', photo-realistic images using the system but it is now also possible to create highly stylized and dramatic renditions of the scene as well.

This is massive step forward as HDR Pro offers extended controls via a completely revamped and enhanced dialog box. New algorithms enable more accurate alignment of source files and an in-built deghosting system does its best to fix any problem areas caused by camera shake or moving subjects. New tone-mapping tools and adjustment controls give photographers the power to implement their own HDR styles, producing photos that range in style from fully textured images of high-contrast scenes to wildly hyper-realistic creations. The production of HDR monochromes is even possible.

HDR photos can be processed in a wide range of different styles. A good starting point for producing different looks is to select one of the many presets that ship with the feature and then fine-tune the settings to suit your image. (1) Photorealistic, (2) Monochromatic. (3) Surrealistic Low Contrast. (4) Surrealistic High Contrast.

Processing presets

Processing settings can be saved making styling of successive HDR images faster and more efficient. The settings presets can also be shared using the Save/Load options in the pop-up presets menu located in the top right of the dialog box.

Single image HDRish

And for times when you don't have multiple source files, you can create the look of an HDR-processed image from a single photo with the HDR Toning feature that allows you to mimic the tone-mapping results traditionally achieved in high dynamic range photos. Find this feature in the Image > Adjustments menu.

ACR Gets an Engine Change

Even though it has only been a few short years, it seems like the Adobe Camera Raw (ACR) plug-in has been with us forever. During its lifetime the raw editing and conversion utility has undergone some major changes, including the ground-breaking, non-destructive, local adjustments, tools of the last release. So the first time you run ACR 6 you may be left thinking that there are no big, game-changing features this time around. Well, you would be wrong! Drastically wrong!

Where are the changes?

It is true that at first glance the big song-and-dance changes seem few and far between. Okay we have the addition of a new FX tab which houses an add Grain type filter and revamped post-

The new noise removal system is all the more powerful when tied to the default image settings and in turn to specific cameras and ISO settings. This way of working automatically attributes a group of noise reduction settings to images based on their camera and capture ISO. (1) Noise Reduction settings. (2) Camera Raw Default. (3) Camera Raw Preferences.

crop vignetting controls, but apart from these features, what else has changed?

The answer is, the very way that Camera Raw functions has changed. The plug-in has received a complete revamp of its demosaicing algorithm. In layman's terms, this means that the very engine used for converting the semi-processed data of a raw file into a format that we can preview, edit, and enhance has been completely rebuilt. This is the first time since 2003 that such core changes have been made to the way that ACR works.

But wait there is more!

The new engine not only provides better processing (interpolation) of the raw file but also ties in with ACR's new sharpening and noise removal systems. Yes, you read right! Adobe has opted to call their method for decreasing the appearance of digital noise in high ISO photos Noise Removal, not Noise Reduction. At fist, I was a little sceptical, thinking that this change in terminology was more marketing spin, than reality. Boy how wrong was I. A few passes of old low-light photos through ACR6 was enough to convince me of the power of this new system. Shots that

The Noise Reduction system in ACR6 is a substantial improvement over the offering previous versions of the plug-in.

were initially rejected because of the presence of ugly grain and the inability of any of my existing software tools to render the pics usable, have now been reworked with great results.

It's your choice

The changes are so substantial that I am now in the process of reworking my catalog of raw files achieving better results than I thought possible. Now when you open a file that has been processed with a previous version of ACR an exclamation mark warning appears at the bottom right of the preview space. Clicking the icon switches the processing of the file to the 2010 algorithm. Don't panic, you can always switch back (if you really want to) by selecting the 2003 entry in the Process menu under the Camera Calibration tab.

Photoshop turns painterly

In the hands of a master skilled in illustration techniques Photoshop's Brush tool is capable of producing fantastically creative effects. And I think that most users would agree that the development in this area of the application over the last few revisions has been steady more than spectacular. The same can't be said of CS5!

It is now possible to produce extraordinary painting effects with the inclusion of three new technologies – the Mixer Brush, Bristle Tips, and a new mechanism for sampling and blending colors. Even if you are not a naturally gifted artist, CS5 will redefine the way that you interact with your pixels. More natural and realistic painting effects make it easy to produce illustrations from photo originals and to create sketches and paintings from scratch.

Introducing the Mixer Brush

The Mixer Brush lets you define multiple colors on a single tip, and then blend them with the underlying hues on your canvas. This ability helps achieve life-like control over the colors you use, and how those colors are blended. When starting with a photo original, a dry, empty brush can be used to blend the existing colors while, at the same time, adding a painterly effect to the image.

Color can be loaded into the reservoir well by selecting the color in the Foreground Color Swatch, or by loading a color from the canvas by holding down the Alt/Opt key while clicking the mouse button over the picture part to be sampled. The color in the pickup well is continuously loaded from the canvas as the brush moves over the image.

Starting with a photo original (left above) this example photo illustration was produced (right above) using the new Mixer Brush. The new brush tips feature a Bristle Brush Preview which displays a live 3D view of the brush tip in action. When used with a Wacom tablet the preview mimics the movements of the stylus in 3D space.

Lightness and Saturation selector   Hue selector

A key aspect of the new painting system is being able to quickly select the colors you paint with. To help with this process Adobe engineers created a new color picker HUD (Heads Up Display).
Right-click while pressing Shift+Option/Alt keys to display the HUD Color Picker.
There are two different styles of the HUD Color Picker—Hue Strip (above left) and Hue Wheel (above right). The new picker provides a quick way to select colors and alter their saturation and lightness. You can change display modes with the settings in the General pane of the Preferences dialog box.

Adjust the qualities of Bristle Tips using the controls in the Brush panel.

How the contents of these color wells interact is determined by the Wet, Load and Mix settings in the Mixer Brush options bar. The Wet setting controls the amount of paint picked up by the brush from the canvas, Load adjusts the amount of paint stored in the reservoir of the brush, and Mix determines the mixing rate between reservoir and pickup colors used for the stroke.

....and Bristle Tips

In conjunction with these new mixing features, Photoshop CS5 incorporates unprecedented control over stroke characteristics of its painting tools with Bristle Tips. The settings contained in the Bristle Qualities section of the Brush Presets panel enable you to define key bristle properties such as shape, length, stiffness, thickness, angle, and spacing, affecting how the color is laid on the image as you paint.

The Live Tip Preview provides a visual representation of these changes and, when used with a stylus, shows a 3D version of the brush in use. Options in the Brush panel Settings menu allow you to save the tip for future use, allowing you to build a customized collection of Bristle Tips to experiment with when creating photo illustrations.

The Mind-Bending Power of Puppet Warp

The Liquify Filter is one of those Photoshop features that you either love, and use a lot, or are pretty ambivalent about. There is no doubting the power of the feature in its ability to apply free-form transformations to photos, but it does have its limitations. Especially if you want to push and pull your pixels around in the main editing space rather than a dedicated dialog box.

Starting with a base image, and a text layer to act as a guide, a series of image parts were warped to fit the different letter shapes. The Puppet Warp tool provides the ability to manually distort a group of pixels to fit any shape.

The Puppet Warp feature in Photoshop CS5 gives you picture reshaping power right in the main workspace. The new feature allows the precise repositioning of any element within a Photoshop document by simply clicking and dragging. The feature works equally well with selections, layers, and whole photos (just as long as the content you are trying to transform is not a background layer).

The tool works by overlaying a mesh on your picture. You place a series of pins on the mesh and then click-drag any pin to deform the mesh, and in turn, the photo. The other pins anchor the rest of image but can be used at anytime to reshape the section of the image they are anchoring. Settings in the feature's options bar provide controls for:

- the Density of the mesh,
- the deformation approach or Mode – Rigid, Normal, Distort,
- how the mesh fits with the picture element – Extension,
- Pin Depth, used for layering one meshed element over another, and
- a setting for how the element Rotates when warped.

Warping effects

As a rough guide I have found that I am able to get more precision when warping picture elements by using the Rigid mode, the More Points density setting, and the Fixed rotation option. If I am looking for more creative, some may say wacky results, then I choose the Distort mode, Normal mesh density and the Auto rotate setting.

Photoshop gets into the lens building business

Well not quite, but almost! When I apply the new Lens Correction features found in Photoshop CS5 to my photos it certainly feels like I shot the images with a new lens. Designed to provide a quick and accurate way of correcting three of the most common lens-based errors (geometric distortion, chromatic aberration and vignetting), your processed images will take on a whole new lease of life when you pass them through the new Lens Correction dialog (Filter > Lens Correction).

The Lens Correction features in Photoshop CS5 automatically correct three typical lens based errors. Here the barrel distortion (1) is corrected removing the bent-line syndrome (2). The corrected image is then automatically scaled to fill the frame (3).

Lens- and camera-specific

Photoshop has had manual lens correction controls for several versions now, but the feature employed a hit and miss approach that produced good results, but took time and wasn't accurate enough for many purists. Third-party camera and lens manufacturers too provide a range of correction options, of which the most notable is Nikon's Capture NX2 software which offers rectilinear correction of fish-eye photos. But Photoshop CS5's new Lens Correction system beats both these approaches hands-down. It provides not only the mechanism for correcting images but also a utility for characterizing your own camera and lens combinations. The system corrects bulging photos suffering from barrel distortion, removes bands of color that are often seen on the edge of contrasting objects and applies a graded exposure adjustment across the whole photo to fix lens-based vignetting.

With the aid of the Adobe Lens Profile Creator (pictured above) which is available free from labs.adobe.com, you can produce custom profiles characterising the optical aberrations of your camera lenses. When installed and selected in the Lens Correction filter in Photoshop CS5, the resulting profile automatically removes or corrects the three types of distortion.

DIY profile creation

Yes, you read correctly. You download the free Adobe Lens Profile Creator application from labs.adobe.com and, with the aid of the included instructions and test charts, you set about profiling your own camera setup. The resultant Lens Correction Profiles are then used by Photoshop to correct your images. Adobe has tried to build depth to the system as well. Lenses can be tested using different focal lengths, and focus distances, ensuring that a variety of shooting scenarios are covered for any given lens.

If you don't have time to make your own profiles, the utility ships with some profiles pre-installed, plus a special Search Online button, that looks in Adobe's database for a suitable profile and then automatically fetches and installs the profile in the dialog.

For some lenses the changes are dramatic. Others less so. The utility works with all manner of glass including fish-eyes and extreme telephoto lenses.

Repoussé – Photoshop's Fast Track to 3D Modelling

In the last few years there has been a growing interest and involvement of photographers in the world of 3D imaging. You don't have to look too far before seeing some great examples of what is possible when you mix 2D photos with 3D models to create a convincing composite. I firmly believe that this is an area that will become more and more important for the commercial and editorial photographers as client's commission sales images of virtual products, but for the average image maker, it is pretty difficult to know where to start.

The Extended version of Photoshop has always had a few 3D bells and whistles and for those image makers who have experience with full-blown 3D modelling programs, the tools and features, and how to use them, were pretty self evident. But for the rest of us mere mortals, the workflow, language, range of settings and even the way that you interact with the model all seems pretty alien. Well, the changes in Photoshop CS5 go a long way to address these concerns.

Repoussé for creating and editing 3D models

In this release, Adobe has included a new feature called Repoussé, to help ease us all into the world of creating and working with 3D models. The name comes from a French term for a process where parts of an illustration on a sheet of metal were beaten to add depth and form a low relief sculpture. The feature performs a similar function in Photoshop allowing you to easily turn a two dimensional artwork into three dimensional object. It creates a sense of depth by extruding the artwork to form a 3D model.

Simple Creation Steps

The process for this is simple. Start by making a selection or choosing a text or layer mask from the Layers panel. Next, convert the content to three dimensions by selecting the entry that matches your content type from the 3D panel. After the conversion is complete, the Repoussé dialog box

Fast track the creation of new 3D objects with the settings in the Create New 3D Object section of the 3D panel.

will be displayed. Here you can alter the look of your 3D model by manipulating five of its key extrusion properties: depth, scale, bend, shear or twist.

In addition to these controls, you can also inflate the cap of the extrusion and apply a custom bevel to the front or back of your model. The Scene controls include tools for positioning your 3D model and for setting the mesh quality, view and render settings presets. And the toolbar on the left of the dialog box provide direct control over the mesh/model.

Rotate the Mesh

Roll the Mesh

Pan the Mesh

Slide the Mesh

Scale the Mesh

Return the Mesh
to its original position

Extrusion controls

Inflation controls

Internal controls

View options

Material selector

Shape presets

Bevel Controls

Scene settings

Repoussé

Repoussé Shape Presets

Materials

All   Front   Bevel1

Sides   Bevel2   Back

Bevel

Sides: Front and Back

Height: 0   Contour:

Width: 0

Extrude

Depth: 1   Scale: 1

Twist: 0   Texture: Scale

○ Shear   ● Bend

X Angle: 0   Y Angle: 0

Inflate

Sides: Front

Angle: 0   Strength: 0

Scene Settings

Lights: Custom

View: Default

Render Settings: Custom

Mesh Quality: Better

Internal Constraints

Type: Inactive   Angle: 1

Side: Both   Strength: 1

X: Y: Z: Add(Selection)   Add(Path)   Delete

OK   Cancel

✓ 3D Axis
✓ 3D Ground Plane
✓ 3D Light
✓ 3D Selection

Show All

Hide All

The Repoussé dialog box groups together the key controls for adjusting the look of your 3D object. The Shape Presets provide a fast way to get a specific look to your extrusion. Once applied these default settings can be fine-tuned to suit the specific design.

❶   ❷   ❸   ❹

The surface qualities of the model can be easily changed by altering the Materials settings. Select from the materials that ship with CS5 or even make your own. Here the same model is rendered with the following ray-traced materials: (1) Brushed Metal, (2) Chrome, (3) Frosted Glass and (4) Glossy Plastic. These materials ship with CS5 Extended but must be loaded separately into the Materials Selector.

With the ever-increasing power of Photoshop Extended in the area of 3D manipulation I believe that tasks such as combining 2D photos and 3D models will be undertaken more and more by photographers and not be relegated to CGI experts. In this simple example you can see how plausible such a scenario is.

Photoshop 3D continues to grow

Along with the Repoussé feature, Adobe has been busy revamping and increasing the power of the 3D features in the Extended version of Photoshop. It is true that the ability to play with 3D models in a Photoshop document has been around for a couple of versions now, but in CS5 it feels like Adobe is getting a better idea of where they want to be positioned in the world of 3D.

A modeller's best friend

Don't expect Photoshop CS5 Extended to be a replacement for your favorite 3D modelling tool. This is not its role. Instead, think of Photoshop more as a best friend to your modelling program. You can't create complex 3D models in Photoshop but you can certainly create complex compositions that include complex models.

Thankfully, this sophistication doesn't come at the cost of increasing complexity. On the contrary, Adobe is working hard to try to make sure that the interface is as simple as possible, and, even more important, easy to use. Now simple and easy are relative terms, and when you first look at the 3D feature you may think that I wasn't paying attention when I wrote those lines, but in 3D terms, the Photoshop approach is pretty simple. Believe me!

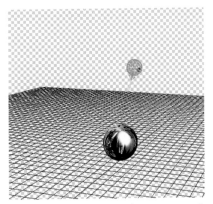

Use the Light Rotate tool to interactively position lights around your model so that you can quickly preview changes in texture, highlights and shadows.

Images can also be used as light sources to illuminate 3D models, making it easier to add realistic scene-based reflections to your images.

17

What's new in CS5 Ext. ?

Changes for Photoshop CS5 Extended include new overlay controls which provide instant feedback about where specific materials and meshes are located in your model and the updated 3D axis widget works more intuitively with lights, cameras and objects.

Also included is a new one-click Shadow Catcher feature that lets you easily generate a shadow on the ground plane of the scene, and then adjust how the shadow interacts with image content of other layers by altering its opacity and its softness. This will be a photographer's favorite for sure.

To further enhance realism you can create a light source from

Change the look of the model by selecting new materials from the entries listed in the Materials Preset Browser.

a photo making it possible to use any picture, Photomerge panorama, or even a 32 bit HDR image to light your model. It is also possible to recreate traditional depth of field effects in your rendered scene where you control the zone of sharpness with the new Distance and Blur controls in the Camera Zoom tool.

You can quickly change the look of your model using the range of materials such as chrome, glass, grass, and cork that ship with Photoshop CS5 Extended. You can select materials from the included presets, create your own, or even edit existing materials to customize them for your needs. Options in the 3D panel allow you to apply a single material to all surfaces as well as the ability to choose different treatments for individual sections and surfaces of your models.

The Material Selection tool can be used to select individual materials directly on the canvas and the Material Pick and Drop tools work like the traditional Eyedropper and Paint Bucket tools, allowing you to sample and apply materials interactively.

Dozens of customer-inspired improvements

Photoshop users have never been backward in offering an opinion about how best to improve their favorite imaging product. The very popular Beta programs for both Photoshop and Lightroom demonstrate just how vocal the 'faithful' can be when given the chance. And Adobe, to their credit, take on board as many of their comments and ideas as possible and use them to continuously improve their products. But with Photoshop CS5, the engineering team went one step further, taking a couple of weeks of the normal production cycle to work on refining existing tools and features. The result is dozens of small changes that may at first go unnoticed, but will in the end, help to boost productivity and creativity throughout the whole of your editing workflow.

Some of these user inspired changes include:

A new convert to Black and White action (needs to be loaded from the goodies folder on the install DVD) that uses the LAB mode to help preserve detail during the conversion mode and the Hue/Saturation control to tint the final result.

An option for reversing the clone source using the flip buttons in the Clone Source panel.

A neutral-density preset for the Gradient tool to facilitate darkening of skies and bright foreground details.

The ability to move a selection while the active layer is hidden

The ability to save 16-bit Photoshop documents in 8-bit JPEG format in a single step without the need to change bit-depth first.

A new layer command for deleting all empty layers located in the File > Scripts menu.

A Straighten button on the Ruler tool options bar...at last!!

A Close All Open Images Without Saving option accessed by first selecting the File > Close option and then Apply To All before clicking the No button.

New Paste Outside and Paste Into commands, along with the previously existing Paste In Place option, are included in a new Edit > Paste Special menu.

Layer groups can be nested more than five levels deep.

An overlay grid, with an option for two different grid layouts, can be displayed when using the Crop tool.

Customized print settings can be recorded as part of an Action providing an automated way to print with different settings.

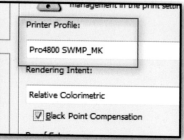

Printer-specific profiles are selected automatically when choosing a printer reducing searching for the right profile.

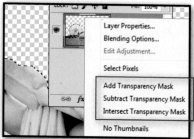

Selecting a printer automatically lists the profiles installed for that printer at the top of the profile list.

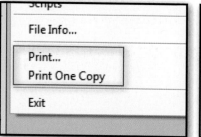

Print settings saved with the image file, allowing one-button printing with user-selected values

Pick and mix colors faster using the new on-screen color HUD displayed by right-clicking while pressing shift and Alt/Opt.

The ability to create a selection from the transparent areas of a layer with the right-click menu options of the layer thumbnail.

An option for changing the opacity of multiple selected layers with one action.

New 3D shapes added to the list of meshes that can be created from a layer.

New creative resources, including actions, tools, presets, brushes, swatches, shapes, gradients, styles and tool presets.

Default value for Shadows/Highlights changed from 50% to 35% which represents a more realistic starting setting.

A Save As option for always defaulting to the folder to which you last saved an image.

Multiple improvements in Lens Correction filter options, including:
- Move to the Filter menu from the Filter > Distort menu.
- Grid Display is off by default
- Show Grid, Grid Size and Grid Color settings are now sticky
- Default grid size is increased from 16 to 64 pixels
- Decimal point adjustments are allowed as values for the Chromatic Aberration sliders
- A third Chromatic Aberration slider enables the correction of green/magenta fringing
- The Background Color Edge setting is replaced with the Black Color entry
- A White Color option is available in the Edge menu
- Reset options are changed so that only the calibration settings are reset, not the Grid options

The ability to drag and drop a file onto an open Photoshop document to create a new layer.

Zoom in and out with the new scrubby zoom tool activated via a setting in the Zoom tool's options bar.

The ability to use keystrokes to set values in the Adjustments panel text fields.

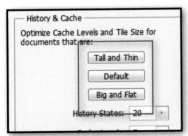

A new Cache Tile Size control in the Performance section of the Preferences dialog box.

Sample colors faster using the new on-screen color ring built into the eyedropper tool.

Customizable default values for Layer styles.

Ed Purnomc

bridge

essential skills

- Gain a working knowledge of Bridge.
- Understand how to change the contents and appearance of the workspace.
- Learn how to use Mini Bridge to access assets inside Photoshop.
- Download, sort, add keywords and process files from Bridge.

Introduction

For most photographers the world of digital has heralded a new era in picture taking. The apparent lack of cost (no film or processing charges) involved in the recording of each frame means that most of us are shooting more freely and more often than ever before. More pictures not only means more time processing, enhancing and printing them but also more time sorting, searching, naming, tagging and storing. In fact, recent studies of how photographers spend their time have shown that many spend 10–15% of their working day involved in just these types of management activities. For this reason many use specialized Digital Asset Management (DAM) systems or software to aid with this work. Though, for many image workers, asset management is the least stimulating part of their job, it is a key area where building skills will free up more time for those parts of the process that you enjoy the most – taking and processing pictures.

Bridge – the center for asset management

Over the last few revisions of Photoshop, Adobe has become increasingly more involved with including image management tools for the working photographer as part of the editing program. Initially this meant the inclusion of a File Browser which could be opened from inside Photoshop, but more recently a totally separate program called Bridge has replaced the standard file browser option. The application can be opened by itself via the program menu, or from within Photoshop with the File > Browse command or button on the Applications bar. In CS5 yet another option has become available with the release of Mini Bridge, a panelized version of Bridge that sits inside Photoshop.

Bridge is a 'super browser' tool that can be used for managing your image assets.

The fastest way to open a file from your picture library is to search for, and select, the file from within Bridge and then press Ctrl/Cmd + O or, if Photoshop is not the default program used for opening the file, select File > Open With > Photoshop. If you are opening a photo captured in a Raw file format, then the file will be displayed in Adobe Camera Raw (ACR) first and then transferred into Photoshop. If you select the File > Open With Camera Raw option then the picture will be displayed in the ACR workspace only and will be transferred to Photoshop only if you decide that this is the next step in your processing. Multi-selected files in the browser can also be opened in this way.

Keep in mind that Bridge is a separate stand-alone application from Photoshop, has its own memory management system and can be opened and used to organize and manage your photo files without needing to have Photoshop running at the same time.

Bridge can be opened in a variety of different ways: individually via the Start menu (1), from inside Photoshop using the dedicated button on the Application bar (2) or the File > Browse command (3). Mini Bridge can also be opened with the dedicated button on the Application Bar (4) or with the Browse In Bridge entry (5) in the File menu.

Panel tabs   Content panel   Selected image   Preview panel

Collections panel   Capture details ('metadata panel')   Thumbnail size slider   Mini Bridge

Bridge retains the interface introduced in CS4, three panel areas, side-by-side preview options, but introduces a new Output panel and a version of the program that sits inside Photoshop – Mini Bridge (right). The view shown above is a customized version of the 'Essentials' workspace options. Many different variations are possible, and can be saved, and selected from the Workspace Switcher in the options bar.

The CS5 version of Bridge

Bridge was first introduced a couple of versions ago; it has quickly become an important part of most photographers' daily workflow. Rather than just being a file browser, Bridge also enables photographers to organize, navigate image assets, add metadata and labels, process Raw files and, in the version that ships with CS5, output your photos directly to web galleries and PDF-based presentations with saved user-templates, quickly change the name of multiple files with batch renaming and access your photos inside Photoshop with Mini Bridge, a panelized version of Bridge.

The interface has remained relatively the same as the previous release of the program. Bridge CS5 still retains the customizable layout options, most of which revolve around a three-panel setup (see above). The interface design, and its many variants, make the most of the wide-screen displays that many image makers are now using. A variety of panels can be displayed in any of the areas and the new Live Workspaces feature auto-save any changes you make to a task-specific workspace, so that if you switch to a different workspace and then back again during an editing session, your panels remain exactly where you left them.

Displayable panels in Bridge include:

- **Folders panel** – displays a folder-based view of your computer.
- **Favorites panel** – provides quick access to regularly used folders you select.
- **Metadata panel** – shows metadata information for the selected file.
- **Keywords panel** – use for adding new or existing keywords to single or multiple photos.
- **Filter panel** – provides sorting options for the files displayed in the Content panel.
- **Preview panel** – shows a preview of selected files or file. Includes the loupe option.
- **Inspector panel** – displays a variety of custom details controlled by options in the preferences.
- **Collections panel** – this panel was new for CS4 and displays all available saved and Smart collections.
- **Export panel** – houses different export modules that provide a fast track method of either saving your photos to another format or transferring them to a social networking or gallery website.

The layout and design of the Bridge interface is customizable by the user. You get to decide what information panels (1) are displayed and where they are placed. The final layout design can be saved and reused and is called a workspace. Several presaved workspaces (2) are supplied with Bridge so that you can quickly flick between screen layouts that suit different image management and editing tasks.

Setting up Bridge

Viewing options

As you can see, one of the real bonuses of Bridge is the multitude of ways that the interface can be displayed. So let's look a little closer at the two different controls that alter the way that Bridge appears – Workspace and View.

Workspace controls the overall look of the Bridge window and is centered around the Window > Workspace menu. Panels can be opened, resized, swap positions, be grouped together and pushed and pulled around so that you create a work environment that really suits your needs and specific screen arrangements. It is even possible to stretch Bridge over two screens so that you can use one screen for previewing and the other for displaying metadata, favorites or content. You also have the option to run a synchronized second version of Bridge that displays an alternate view of the photos currently selected. This means that you can display thumbnails and metadata on one screen and a larger preview on another. To activate a second Bridge view go to Window > New Synchronized Window.

Once you are happy with the layout of the workspace use the Window > Workspace > New Workspace option to store your design. Alternatively you can select from a number of preset workspace designs located in the Window > Workspace menu.

Bridge contains a range of preset workspace options:

1. **Essentials** – displays all panels.
2. **Filmstrip** – Folders, Favorites, Filters, Preview and Collections panels.
3. **Metadata** – Favorites, Metadata and Filters panels.
4. **Output** – Folders, Favorites and Preview panels.

5. **Keywords** – Favorites, Keywords and Filters panels.
6. **Preview** – Folders, Favorites, Filter, Keywords and Collections panels.
7. **Light Table** – Just the content area is displayed.
8. **Folders** – Folders and Favorites panels.

The Workspace Switcher located on the options bar, stores the preset workspaces and any custom entries you have saved. You can change the position of any entry by dragging it to a new location on the bar.

Bridge CS5 introduces the concept of **Live Workspaces** which auto-save any changes you make to the workspace layout as you make them. This allows switching between workspaces and having them appear just as you left them. You can return a workspace to its original layout by selecting the Rest option from the Window > Workspace menu. Also for CS5 the number of entries displayed in the collapsible **Workspace Switcher** (located in the Options Bar) can be altered, and the position of each workspace can be rearranged. Just click-drag the entry to a new position.

Most **View** options are grouped under the View menu and essentially alter the way that Content area data or thumbnails are presented. Here you can choose to show the thumbnails by themselves with no other data (View > Show Thumbnail only) or with metadata details included (View > As Details).

The Slideshow feature provides the option for users to display their images in an automated presentation. After selecting the photos to include it is a simple matter of choosing View > Slideshow to start the presentation. Options for customizing the style of presentation can be found in the Slideshow Options dialog displayed by selecting the entry in the View menu (1).

Other ways to display your photos in Bridge

Slideshow – There is also an option to display the content thumbnails as an impromptu slideshow. With no images selected choose View > Slideshow to include all pictures in the content panel in the show. To display a few photos, multi-select the pictures first (hold down the Cmd/Ctrl key as you click on thumbnails), and then pick the Slideshow command. The overall slideshow options such as duration, transitions and caption content can be altered via the option settings (View > Slideshow Options).

In a variation of this type of slideshow display, CS5 also contains the ability to switch to a full screen view of the current selected image. By selecting View > Full Screen Preview or hitting the Spacebar, the Bridge workspace is replaced with a large preview of the selected image. While in the Full Screen Preview mode, a single click of the mouse will display a 100% view of the file. Click-dragging will move the magnified view around the picture. Pressing the Spacebar a second time reverts the display back to the Bridge workspace.

Multi-selecting images in the content space displays the photos in the Preview pane. Clicking onto the preview image displays a loupe designed to magnify a portion of the photo. Holding down the Ctrl/Cmd key allows the user to synchronize the loupe views of multiple photos as the device is dragged around the images.

Multi-image preview – In addition, Bridge also contains a couple of other view options. The first is the ability to display multiple pictures in the preview panel in a side-by-side manner. Simply multi-select several items in the content area to display them in the preview panel in this compare mode.

Loupe Tool – The second feature is the Loupe Tool, which acts like an interactive magnifier. The loupe size changes with the size of the displayed preview image and works best with a large preview image. To use, click the cursor on an area in the preview picture. By default a 100% preview of this picture part is then displayed, but you can change the degree of magnification of the loupe by clicking the + and – keys. Click and drag the cursor to move the loupe around the photo. When multiple photos are displayed in the Preview pane you can display extra loupe views by clicking onto each photo in turn. The loupes can then be dragged around each photo to check sharpness and subject details like 'someone blinking' in portrait images. Holding down the Ctrl/Cmd key while dragging a loupe will synchronize its movement with other display loupes. This technique is great for checking the same area of similar photos when trying to choose which images to keep and which to discard.

Bridge also contains a Review mode that displays images selected in the content panel in a 3D circle. Left and right arrow keys are used for navigating through the group.

Close and revert to Bridge

Forward and back buttons

Drop image from review group button

File name and current rating

Loupe

Create new Collection from images

Review Mode – The Review Mode (View > Review Mode) displays a set of images in a rotating web gallery-like display. The user can move from one image to another by clicking sideways arrow keys or by clicking the mouse on the forward and back arrows; unwanted pictures can be dropped from the display set using the down arrow key and the photos left after reviewing are automatically added to a new collection when returning to Bridge. Dropping images does not delete the photo, it does not remove it from content view; it does remove it from the multi-photo view that shows up in preview after you 'Esc' out of the review mode While in Review Mode you can add or change photo Labels and/or Ratings, and examine pictures closer using the Loupe Tool. This option was added to Bridge to help photographers quickly review their images, make choices about suitable photos that deserve more attention and then save these candidate images in the easily retrievable form of a Collection. When used in combination with the Collections pane, this workflow should make accessing key photos quicker than in previous version of Bridge.

The content of some panels and the way that this information is displayed can be adjusted using either the fly-out menus at the top right of the panels, right-click menu options for panel items or Bridge preference settings. Fly-out menu for the Metadata panel (left) and right-click menu for Favorite panel entries (right) are shown.

Custom panel display

Some panels also contain custom options that govern the type of information displayed and the way that it is presented in the panel. For both the Keyword and Metadata panels, these options are located in the fly-out menu accessed at the top right of the panel. You can add folders to the Favorites panel by right-clicking on them in the Folder panel and then choosing the Add

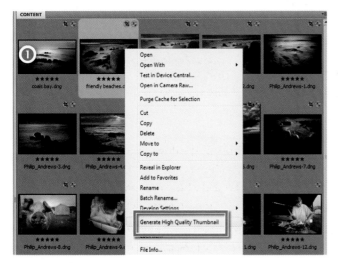

to Favorites entry from the menu that appears. To remove listed folders right-click the entry and choose the Remove from Favorites option.

The Inspector panel display and the types of data shown with thumbnails in the Content panel are controlled by settings in Preferences (Edit > Preferences).

Images with low quality, but fast to display, thumbnails are displayed with a black border (1). Create a higher quality thumbnail by selecting the option from the right-click menu.

Speedy thumbnail and preview generation

The images that you see in the Content and Preview panels are both based on thumbnails generated by Bridge. By default Bridge initially uses the thumbnails generated by your camera at the time of capture and then creates higher resolution images that will be used in the preview pane. Via the settings in Preferences the user has control over whether the thumbnails are built to a standard size or optimized specifically for your screen or monitor. Choose the Generate Monitor-Size previews option in the Advanced section of Bridge's Preferences (Edit > Preferences). You can force the generation of high quality thumbnails manually for an individual image or groups of multi-selected photos by selecting the pictures in the Content pane and then choosing the Generate High Quality Thumbnail entry from the right-click menu. Images with low quality thumbnails are displayed in the content area with a black line border.

You can speed up the display of images by pre-caching the folders they are saved in using the Build and Export Cache option in the Edit > Preference > Cache menu. After selecting the entry you can then choose to build 100% previews for faster display and to export the cache, which helps with display on other machines.

Caching decisions

The cache is an allocated space on your hard drive that is used to store thumbnail and metadata information (Labels and Ratings) for the images displayed in the Content panel. Bridge uses this cache to speed up the display of thumbnails. The information in the cache is generally built the first time the contents of a specific folder are displayed. This process can take some time, especially if the folder contains many pictures. For this reason, there is also an option to build the cache of a selected folder in the background while you continue other work. Select the directory to be cached in the Folder panel and then choose Tools > Cache > Build and Export Cache. If for any reason you want to remove a previously created cache from a specific directory, then select the folder and choose the Tools > Cache > Purge Cache for Folder option.

The location of centralized cache files as well as the ability to store the cache in the same folder as the images is controlled by settings in the Cache section of the Preferences dialog.

The location of the cache impacts indirectly on performance for two reasons:

1. Cache files can become quite large and it is important to ensure that the drive selected to house the cache has enough space to be able to adequately store the file.
2. When image files are copied to another drive or location, a new cache has to be constructed when the folder is first viewed unless the cache is copied along with the picture files.

The settings contained in the Cache section of the Preferences dialog provide the option to select the place where the central cache is stored. Use this setting to ensure that the cache file is located on a drive with sufficient space. Also included here is an option for exporting cache files to folders whenever possible. Use this setting to employ a distributed cache system (rather than a centralized one), which enables image and cache files to be stored together in the same folder. If this folder is then moved, copied or written to a new location the cache will not have to be rebuilt for the photos to be displayed in Bridge. The cache should also be copied to CD, DVD or other locations that are locked. New changes will be written to the central location but, overall, browsing will be speeded up by the cache.

The preferences also contain additional controls for the number of items stored in the cache. More items means faster display but more disk space is required for cache storage. The dialog also includes a button for compacting the cache, which helps improve performance, and another for purging or deleting all cached thumbnails and previews. This option is useful if you are having problems with the consistency of quality of thumbnail and preview images.

Using Bridge

It is important to view Bridge as a key component in the photographer's workflow. From the time that the photos are downloaded from the camera, through the selection, editing and processing stages and then onto archiving and, later, locating specific pictures, the application plays a pivotal role in all image management activities. Let's look a little closer at each of these areas.

Bridge ships with the Adobe Photo Downloader utility designed to simplify the transfer of image files from camera or card reader to computer. When working with the Downloader you have a choice of two modes – Standard (1) and Advanced (2).

Transferring with the Adobe Photo Downloader

Step 1: Select the Get Photos from Camera option from the File menu inside Bridge or click the new Get Photos button in the Applications bar. Next you will see the new Adobe Photo Downloader dialog. The utility contains the option of either Standard or Advanced modes. The Advanced option not only provides thumbnail previews of the images stored on the camera or card, but the dialog also contains several features for sorting and managing files as they are downloaded. But let's start simply, with the options in the Standard dialog.

Step 2 Standard mode: To start you need to select the source of the pictures (the location of the card reader or camera). In the Standard mode all pictures on the card will be selected ready for downloading. Next set the Import Settings. Browse for the folder where you want the photographs to be stored and if you want to use a subfolder select the way that this folder will be named from the Create Subfolder drop-down menu. To help with finding your pictures later it may be helpful to add a meaningful name, not the labels that are attached by the camera, to the beginning of each of the images. You can do this by selecting an option from the Rename File drop-down menu and adding any custom text needed. At the same time selecting the Preserve Current Filename in XMP option will ensure the image can be found at a later date using the original file name. There are also options to open Bridge after the transfer is complete and convert to DNG or save copies of the photos on the fly (great for backing up images). Clicking the Get Photos button will transfer your pictures to your hard drive – you can then organize the pictures in the Bridge workspace. For more choices during the download process you will need to switch to the Advanced mode.

Step 3 Advanced mode: Selecting the Advanced Dialog button at the bottom left of the Standard mode window will display a larger Photo Downloader dialog with more options and a preview area showing a complete set of thumbnails of the photos stored on the camera or memory card. If for some reason you do not want to download all the images, then you will need to deselect the files to remain, by unchecking the tick box at the bottom right-hand corner of the thumbnail. This version of the Photo Downloader has the same location for saving transferred files, rename, convert to DNG and copy files options that are in the Standard dialog. In addition, this mode also contains the ability to add metadata to the photos during the downloading process. You can also select a predefined metadata template (created with the File Info dialog in Bridge or Photoshop) from the drop-down menu or manually add in author and copyright details. Pressing the Get Photos button will start the download process.

Locating files

Files can be located by selecting the folder in which they are contained using either the Favorites or Folders panel or the Look In menu (top of the dialog). Alternatively, the Edit > Find command can be used to search for pictures based on filename, file size, keywords, date, rating, label, metadata or comment.

Locate specific pictures or create collections of photos using the sophisticated Find options in Bridge.

Filtering the files displayed

The options in the Filter panel provide an interactive way to find specific photos among the thousands of files that sit on photographers' hard drives. The feature is housed in a panel of its own which displays a list of attributes such as file type, orientation, date of creation or capture, rating, labels, keywords and even aspect ratio.

Clicking on a heading activates the filter and alters the Content display to show only those files that possess the selected attribute. Selecting a second Filter entry reduces the displayed content further. Using this approach, it is possible to reduce thousands of photos to a select few with several well-placed clicks in the Filter panel.

To remove all filters and view all items in a folder click the folder icon in the bottom right of the panel or Ctrl/Cmd Alt/Opt A. To continue using the filtration settings when navigating to other folders or directories press the Map Pin icon in the bottom left of the pane.

The Filter panel contains a selection of file attributes that can be selected as ready-made search criteria in order to quickly create a subset of photos. 1) Menu of Sort choices. 2) Remove or clear all filters. 3) Lock current filtration settings while browsing.

Stacking alike photos

One way to help organize pictures in your collection is to group photos of similar content together. Bridge contains a stacking option designed just for this purpose. After multi-selecting the pictures to include from those displayed in the content area, select Stacks > Group as Stack. All images will be collated under a single front photo like a stack of cards. The number of images included in the stack is indicated in the top left of the stack thumbnail. Stacks can be expanded or collapsed by clicking on this number (stacks expand downwards in workspaces where the thumbnails are arranged vertically).

Collapsed stack   Expanded stack

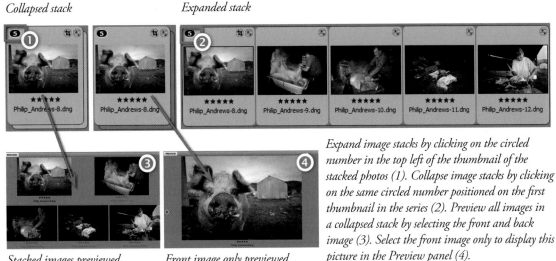

Stacked images previewed   Front image only previewed

Expand image stacks by clicking on the circled number in the top left of the thumbnail of the stacked photos (1). Collapse image stacks by clicking on the same circled number positioned on the first thumbnail in the series (2). Preview all images in a collapsed stack by selecting the front and back image (3). Select the front image only to display this picture in the Preview panel (4).

Selecting the top of the front image of a collapsed stack displays this picture only in the Preview panel. Clicking onto the frame of the bottom image in the collapsed stack (it will change color when selected) will display all stacked photos in the Preview panel. Options for ungrouping the photos in a stack or changing the picture used as the front image can be located in the Stacks menu.

Auto stacking options

Added to this manual stacking functionality is the ability for Bridge to automatically collect High Dynamic Range (HDR) sets and panoramas and collate the files as stacks and then process them in Photoshop. This functionality can be accessed in two ways, via an option in the Stacks menu (Stacks > Auto Stack Panorama/HDR) or by choosing Tools > Photoshop > Process Collections in Photoshop.

When building stacks Bridge uses the EXIF information stored with each picture to search groups of photos looking for images taken with less than an 18-second gap. Once located these images are grouped into those that have exposure differences of more than one stop; these are earmarked for processing as HDR source files, and those with similar exposure settings are marked as candidates for Photomerge processing. Next Bridge searches through the images a second time, but this time the program looks at the images themselves with Photoshop's Auto Align feature. Sequential images that are assessed to overlap by at least 80% are assumed to be HDR candidates. Photos that overlap by no more than 80% are considered to be panorama source images and are stacked as such. Finally the stacked photos are transferred to Photoshop and either processed using the Merge to HDR or Photomerge features.

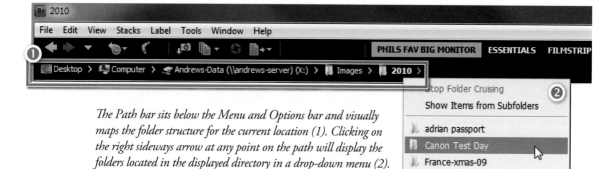

The Path bar sits below the Menu and Options bar and visually maps the folder structure for the current location (1). Clicking on the right sideways arrow at any point on the path will display the folders located in the displayed directory in a drop-down menu (2).

Always know where you are with the Path bar

Also new for the latest version of Bridge is the Path bar. Located just below the menu and shortcuts bar at the top of the Bridge workspace the bar provides a folder trail, working from parent directories on the left to child or subdirectories on the right. In its simplest form this bar visually displays the name and location of the folder currently selected, but this is not the end of the feature's functionality. By clicking the sideways arrow after a folder entry a drop-down menu of all the subfolders for this directory will be displayed. Navigating to a different directory option is then just a matter of selecting the folder from the menu. Just like the other interface components in Bridge, the Path bar can be displayed or hidden by selecting its entry on the Window menu.

Using Bridge's Collections

Collections are a way for photographers to group together images that relate to each other in some way. You might want to group all the photos of a particular subject, those taken for a single client or pictures captured with a specific camera and lens combination. Once created selecting the collection entry will then display all the photos contained within the group. The collections features in Bridge are now centered around the new Collections panel. Here you can view and manage existing collections and create new ones. If not displayed it can be selected from the Window menu.

Bridge uses two different collection types – **Smart Collections** and **Standard Collections**.

Collections

Standard Collections contain a selected group of images which represent a subset of all the photos in your collection and are related in some way – content, event, subject, photo, style, etc. The pictures contained in a collection are displayed when the collection entry is selected in the Collections panel. New collections can be created in several different ways:

- **From the Collections panel** – When the Collections panel is displayed, simply right-click on the panel area and choose the New Collection option from the pop-up menu. This will create a new entry in the panel that you can then name. To add images to the collection, select the photo or photos in the content area of Bridge and drag them over the collection entry in the panel.

- **From Review Mode** – A new collection can also be created from the results of selection editing using the new Review Mode. Start by selecting some images in the Content panel. Next choose the Review Mode option from the View menu or click Ctrl/Cmd + B. Flick between the images using the sideways arrows. When you come across a photo that you want to remove from the group press the down arrow key. Once you have only the images that you want in the group displayed, click the Create New Collection

button at the bottom right of the Review Mode screen. You will be returned to the Bridge interface and a new entry will have been added to the Collections panel.

Smart Collections

Smart Collections are created by establishing a set of search criteria. The photos that meet the criteria automatically are added to the collection. These collections are dynamic in that each time the collection entry is selected a new search is conducted and any photos that match the criteria are added to the collection. In this way the contents of Smart Collections are always kept up to date automatically. Smart Collection entries are colored blue.

- **From the Collections panel** – Smart Collections can also be created by right-clicking on the Collections panel and choosing the New Smart Collection entry. A Find dialog will then be displayed in which you can set your search criteria. Clicking the Find button will execute the search and create a new Smart Collection entry.

- **As the result of a search** – Another way to create a Smart Collection is to locate the images to include via a search. Select the Find option from the Edit menu. Using the

settings in the Find dialog, establish a set of search criteria to help locate the required files. Click the Find button to execute the search. All images that match the search criteria will be displayed in the Content panel. To add these photos to a new collection press the Save as a Smart Collection button at the top right of the panel.

- **Via a set of filters** – The same functionality is available when you use the settings in the Filter panel to display a selection of images in the Content panel. When filters are being applied the Save as a Smart Collection button is displayed in the top right of the Content panel. Clicking the button will create a Smart Collection based on the current filter settings.

Collections can also be added as an entry in the Favorites panel. Simply right-click on the collection entry in the Collections panel and choose the Add to Favorites option from the menu. Collection entries can be removed from the panel by right-clicking on the entry and choosing the Delete option from the menu. Existing collections can also be renamed in the same way. The search criteria used in a Smart Collection can be adjusted by selecting the entry and then either clicking on the Edit button at the bottom left of the panel or by selecting the Edit entry from the right-click menu.

The Collections panel displays both Smart Collection (1) and Standard Collection (2) entries. There are options for creating new collections, renaming, deleting and adding collections to the Favorites panel in the right-click menu (3). Edit button (4). New Collections buttons (5). Delete Collection button (6).

Downloading pictures

For the last couple of releases Bridge has included the Adobe Photo Downloader (APD) utility. The downloader manages the transfer of files from a camera or a card reader to your computer. In doing so the transfer utility can also change file names, convert to Adobe's Digital Negative format (DNG) on the fly, apply pre-saved metadata templates and even save copies of the files to a backup drive. This feature alone saves loads of time and effort for the working photographer over performing these tasks manually and for this reason should be your first point of call when downloading from your camera.

Labeling pictures

As you are probably realizing Bridge is more than just a file browser; it is also a utility that can be used for sorting and categorizing your photos. Using the options listed under the Label menu, individual or groups of photos can be rated (with a star rating) or labeled (with a colored label).

These tags can be used as a way to sort and display the best images from those taken at a large photo-shoot or grouped together in a folder. Labels and ratings are applied by selecting (or multi-selecting) the thumbnail in the Bridge workspace and then choosing the tag from the Label menu. Shortcut keys can also be used to quickly attach tags to individually selected files one at a time.

In addition to adding the star ratings and the colored labels you can also mark photos as a reject (Label > Reject) and then have these photos hidden from view (View > Show Reject Files).

Labels or ratings are often used as a way of indicating the best images in a group of pictures taken in a single session. The photos displayed in the Content panel can be sorted according to their label or rating using the settings in the Filter panel.

Keywords are words that summarize the content of the photo. They are used extensively by photo libraries for cataloging multiple photos. Keywords can be created and applied in Bridge using the Keywords panel (1). Also in Bridge CS5 the keywords and metadata associated with individual images can be displayed using the new Keywords workspace (2).

Adding keywords

Along with labeling and rating photos for easy editing and display options, it is also possible to assign specific keywords that help describe the content of your images. The keywords are stored in the metadata of the photo and are used extensively not only by Bridge as a way of locating specific photos but also by photo libraries worldwide for cataloging.

Most keyword activity is centered around the Keywords panel in Bridge. Here you can create and apply keywords to images or groups of images. To help manage an ever growing list keywords can also be grouped into keyword sets. To apply a keyword to a photo, select the image first and then click on the check box next to the keyword or keyword set to add. Click on the check box again to remove a keyword. Buttons for creating keywords and sub-keywords as well as for deleting existing keywords can be found at the bottom of the panel. A search pane is also located here making the task of finding specific keywords a simple job. Use the Find feature to locate images that have a specific associated keyword.

The settings menu for the Keywords panel (1) contains options for adding and removing keywords as well as the ability to import and export keyword sets. The bottom left of the panel contains a search field (2) and the three buttons on the right are for creating keywords, sub-keywords and deleting keywords (3).

A summary of all the Assigned Keywords for a specific photo is displayed at the top of the panel. New keywords or keyword sets are created, and existing ones deleted, using the buttons at the bottom right of the panel. Keep in mind that the CS4 version of Bridge also has a special Keywords workspace (Window > Workspace > Keywords), that can also be used to display metadata and associated keywords for individual files in the Content panel.

Keywords are often used as the primary method for locating appropriate images in stock libraries. For this reason accurate allocation of keywords is an important task for photographers wanting to ensure that their images feature prominently in search results. Some libraries should supply a list of pre-compiled keywords that are used by photographers to categorize their photos. Working this way helps ensure consistency in approach. To add saved keyword lists to Bridge select the Import option from the Settings menu (top right of the Keywords panel) and choose the file in the browser dialog that is displayed. Similarly the keywords lists that you create can be exported and reused using the Export option in the Settings menu.

Introducing Mini Bridge

New for CS5 is the inclusion of Mini Bridge, a panelized version of Bridge that you can access from inside Photoshop CS5. Mini Bridge makes use of the Flash-based interface which also underpins many of the third-party panels that are available to instal in Photoshop.

To launch Mini Bridge just click on the Mini Bridge button in the menu bar of Photoshop CS5. When the panel first opens you might see a warning that Bridge is disconnected, just click the OK button to connect the panel by opening the Bridge in the background. If you are shown the Home screen then click the Browse Files button to display your assets in the panel.

You can resize the Mini Bridge display by dragging the panel's edges and adjust the pods displayed, such as the Path bar, Navigation Pod, and Preview Pod, by choosing their entries from the menu accessed by clicking the Panel View button. Individual files can be located via the folder structure in the Path bar or with the entries in the Navigation pod. I prefer to create collections of working images in Bridge proper, which can then be accessed quickly and easily with Mini Bridge.

Images can be opened into Photoshop CS5 by double-clicking them in the Content Pod or dragging them from the Content Pod directly to the Photoshop CS5 window. Pressing the spacebar will display a selected image or video in Full Screen Preview mode. Other display options are available from the Preview menu at the bottom of the Content pod. The slider to the left of this menu adjusts the size of the Thumbnails and entries in the View menu, on the right, determine the type of content shown in the pod and how it is displayed.

You can also use Photoshop tools like Batch, Image Processor, Load files Into Photoshop Layers, Merge To HDR Pro, and Photomerge by first selecting the images in the Content Pod, then clicking the Tools button at the top of the Content Pod, and choosing the appropriate menu entry. Select which files are displayed and change their order with the Select, Filter, and Sort options, accessed in the title bar of the Content Pod.

Launch settings as well as options for controlling the appearance of Mini Bridge are housed in the Settings pane which can be displayed by clicking the Settings button on the Home pane.

The Mini Bridge Home pane (1) contains buttons to take you to the Settings pane (2) and to display your files (3).

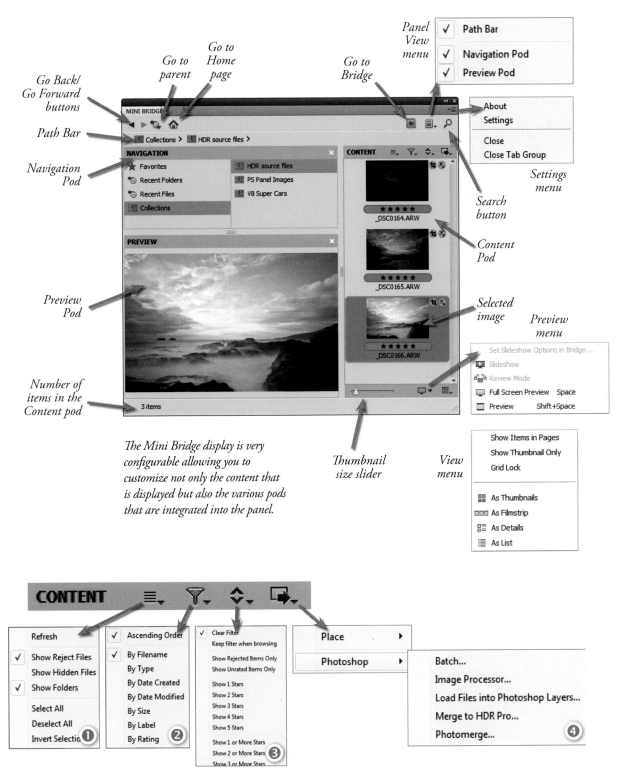

Go Back/
Go Forward
buttons

Go to
parent

Go to
Home
page

Go to
Bridge

Panel
View
menu

✓ Path Bar
✓ Navigation Pod
✓ Preview Pod

Path Bar

About
Settings
Close
Close Tab Group

Settings
menu

Navigation
Pod

MINI BRIDGE

Collections > HDR source files >

NAVIGATION

★ Favorites   HDR source files
Recent Folders   PS Panel Images
Recent Files   V8 Super Cars
Collections

CONTENT

_DSC0164.ARW
_DSC0165.ARW
_DSC0166.ARW

Search
button

Content
Pod

Preview
Pod

PREVIEW

Selected
image

Preview
menu

Set Slideshow Options in Bridge...
Slideshow
Review Mode
Full Screen Preview   Space
Preview   Shift+Space

Number of
items in the
Content pod

3 items

Thumbnail
size slider

View
menu

Show Items in Pages
Show Thumbnail Only
Grid Lock

As Thumbnails
As Filmstrip
As Details
As List

The Mini Bridge display is very configurable allowing you to customize not only the content that is displayed but also the various pods that are integrated into the panel.

CONTENT

Refresh
✓ Show Reject Files
  Show Hidden Files
✓ Show Folders
  Select All
  Deselect All
  Invert Selectio ❶

✓ Ascending Order
✓ By Filename
  By Type
  By Date Created
  By Date Modified
  By Size
  By Label
  By Rating ❷

✓ Clear Filter
  Keep filter when browsing
  Show Rejected Items Only
  Show Unrated Items Only
  Show 1 Stars
  Show 2 Stars
  Show 3 Stars
  Show 4 Stars
  Show 5 Stars
  Show 1 or More Stars
  Show 2 or More Stars
  Show 3 or More Stars ❸

Place
Photoshop

Batch...
Image Processor...
Load Files into Photoshop Layers...
Merge to HDR Pro...
Photomerge... ❹

The title bar of the Content Pod contains the Select (1), Filter (2), Sort (3), and Tools (4) menus.

Tools used in Bridge

Although no real editing or enhancement options are available in Bridge, it is possible to use the browser as a starting point for many of the operations normally carried out in Photoshop. For instance, photos selected in the workspace can be batch renamed, printed, used to create a Photomerge panorama, compiled into a contact sheet or combined into a PDF-based presentation, all via options under the Tools menu or the Output workspace. Some of these choices will open Photoshop before completing the requested task whereas others are completed without leaving the browser workspace. The Lens Correction entry is new for CS5 and

Bridge is a great starting place for many of the tools contained in the File > Automate menu in Photoshop as you can select the images to include before starting the editing feature from the Tools > Photoshop menu.

facilitates batch correction of images using the new correction technology in Photoshop and Merge to HDR has been replaced with Merge to HDR Pro which uses the new HDR system.

Processing Raw inside Bridge

One of the real bonuses of Bridge is the ability to open, edit and save Raw files from inside the browser workspace. There is now no need to open the files to process via Photoshop. All key enhancement steps can be handled directly from the browsing workspace by selecting (or multi-selecting) the files and then choosing File > Open in Camera Raw. All Raw processing is undertaken by the latest version of Adobe Camera Raw (ACR) which ships with Photoshop CS5 and both TIFF and JPEG files can also be processed with the feature as well.

Previous versions of Adobe Camera Raw were only able to enhance globally. That is, the changes they made to the picture were made to the whole of the image. Enhancing specific picture parts was strictly a task for Photoshop. Now ACR is capable of local correction or applying changes to just some of the picture, so more of the image enhancement tasks can occur in ACR and via Bridge. More details on localized correction can be found in the Raw Processing chapter.

Raw, TIFF and JPEG files can be processed with Adobe Camera Raw from inside Bridge without having to open Photoshop first.

To open a file directly into Photoshop you can right-click the thumbnail and choose Open With > Photoshop or, as long as the file type is associated with Photoshop, you can also double-click the photo inside the Content panel.

Processing in Photoshop

It is a simple matter to transfer photos from the Bridge workspace into Photoshop. You can either double-click a thumbnail or select the image and then choose Open With > Photoshop CS5 from the right-click menu. By default double-clicking Raw images will open them into the Adobe Camera Raw utility inside Photoshop, but this behavior can be changed to process the file inside Bridge by selecting the Automatically Open option in the JPEG and TIFF Handling section of the Camera Raw Settings (Edit > Camera Raw Settings) in Bridge.

First introduced in CS4 and improved for this release is the ability for Bridge to output selected files to a Flash-based Web Gallery or a PDF-based presentation. The style and type of output is controlled by the settings in the Output panel (1) and the presentation or website is previewed in the Output Preview panel (2).

Output to web or PDF presentation from Bridge

One of the big changes for Bridge in the last couple of revisions is the ability to output to web and PDF from inside the Browser. First introduced in CS4 the Output workspace (Workspace > Output) has been updated in this release. It now includes precise adjustment of the size and quality of images, ability to display filenames, and to save templates within the Web Gallery feature and text- and image-based watermark options when exporting PDF documents in this release.

Once this workspace is selected, the right-hand panel is used to display the output options and settings in a format that will be familiar to many Lightroom or Photoshop Elements users. You can choose between creating a PDF document (presentation or print document) or a web gallery (mostly Flash-based) via the buttons at the top of the Output panel. Next the settings for the design and the information to be included are added via the various controls and text fields and the final design is previewed in the special Output Preview panel by clicking the Refresh Preview button.

PDF

The PDF output option allows the user to create either screen-based presentations or PDF documents that are designed for printing. The feature ships with a range of predesigned output options listed in the Template drop-down menu (at the top of the output panel). Here you will find designs for documents as diverse as greeting cards, contact sheets, triptychs (three images to a page) and full page images. Selecting a template is a good starting point for designing your PDF document and the options in the next sections of the Output panel will help fine-tune or customize the design. The Document and Layout sections adjust the page size and the number and position of images upon it. The Overlay and Watermark sections contain options for the inclusion of text with the photos and now include the ability to use image-based watermarks. The Playback controls are used when the PDF will be used in a screen presentation format. With all the settings adjusted the selected images can be previewed in the design by clicking the Refresh Preview button at the top of the panel. Finally use the Save button to store the PDF document.

Web galleries

Also included as a Output option is the ability to produce a web gallery from the selected images in the Bridge Content panel. Yes it was possible to create a gallery inside Photoshop in previous versions of the software but in this panel allows the production to occur inside Bridge, the website can be previewed before creation and, once produced, the whole site can be uploaded via FTP directly to the web.

To start the process click the Web Gallery button at the top of the Output panel. Next pick the Template and then Style of gallery to create, add in the Site Info, adjust the Color Panel used and the Appearance settings before setting up the Create Gallery options. Finally, click the Save button to output the gallery to your own computer or press the Upload button to transfer the completed site to the web. There are better sizing controls and the ability to save gallery templates in CS5.

The Output panel contains a range of options to control the creation of the final PDF document.

Similar controls are present in the Output panel for the production of web galleries.

Using Bridge to access the project resources

Use Bridge to access the project resources that are available on the supporting DVD. Access the DVD from the Favorites panel in Bridge. Double-click the Photoshop_CS5 DVD icon to access the chapter folders. Images can be opened directly from Bridge or alternatively a folder of images can be dragged from the Content panel in Bridge to a location on your hard drive if required.

Inside each chapter folder the resources are divided into the different file formats. The same images can be accessed as JPEG, TIFF or Raw files (.dng). The JPEG images are compressed versions (lower quality) but take up little hard drive space. The TIFF files are uncompressed and may contain saved selections that can be used to speed up the editing process in some projects.

Most of the images are available as Raw files. These are required for many projects in the Advanced Retouching and Montage chapters, where some of the editing process is performed in the Adobe Camera Raw workspace (see Adobe Camera Raw). Each project in the 'Imaging Projects' module (last four chapters) is also supported by a movie. Movies can be watched in Bridge or can be opened directly in the QuickTime player (when installed) by double-clicking the movie file icon in the Content panel.

Seok-Jin Lee

workflow

Sam Everton

essential skills

- Examine different professional workflows.
- Capture high-quality digital images for image editing.
- Gain control over the color, tonality and sharpness of a digital image.
- Duplicate, optimize and save image files for print, presentation and for web.

Introduction

Over the last few years the way that photographers manage, edit and present their images has changed. Now we have more choices about the workflow that we use when optimizing our images for specific outcomes. In recognition of these changes this chapter will look at current professional workflow practice and the capture, editing and enhancing steps it involves.

Options for capture

When it comes to decisions about capture, if camera equipment considerations are put to one side, it boils down to a choice of shooting format. Do we shoot in JPEG or Raw?

This decision not only impacts on issues such as how many shots will fit on a memory card, but more importantly, it determines the nature of the photographer's workflow as well as the degree of control that he or she has over the adjustments made to the image.

In this book we unashamedly promote a Smart Raw Workflow which is based firmly on the idea that there is a direct relationship with the quality of the final image produced, and being able to perform as much editing/enhancing as possible on the virgin pixels that exited the camera as a Raw file.

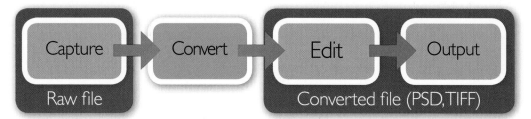

*The **'Convert then Edit'** approach is the most popular workflow currently used by Raw shooting photographers. The Raw file is downloaded from the camera and the first task in the process is to convert the file to a type that is more readily supported by Photoshop, such as TIFF or PSD.*

Processing your photos

Photos captured in JPEG do not require any intermediate processing before the images can be edited in programs like Photoshop. Raw images, on the other hand, need to be processed using a special Raw enabled utility such as Adobe Camera Raw (ACR) initially before further Photoshop based editing is possible. In the process often the file is converted from its Raw state to a file format that can be easily edited and enhanced in Photoshop. Despite the fact that programs designed specifically for working with Raw files such as ACR are becoming more and more sophisticated and feature rich most photographers still convert their Raw photos and move them to Photoshop for further processing.

Gradually this approach of 'convert and then edit' for Raw files is changing. With the increasing abilities of ACR, along with the Smart Object technology found in Photoshop, Raw shooters can put off the file conversion process while still taking advantage of the majority of the feature set of Photoshop. Keeping your photos in a Raw state maintains the flexibility of the format and is the basis of many non-destructive editing techniques designed for high-quality production. See Chapter 4 for more specific details on Raw processing.

*In contrast to the previous way of working, a **'Full Raw Workflow'** approach maintains the Raw file throughout the whole digital imaging process. This completely non-destructive workflow is the way of the future for Raw shooters and it is growing in support, with special editing and enhancement techniques for Photoshop and Bridge users now being promoted.*

Editing and enhancing

Once the captured image is in a usable form the next step is to edit or enhance the photo. Digital shooters have much more control over their images in this editing and enhancement phase than was ever possible when working with historical darkroom methods. This is largely thanks to the host of tools, features and commands available in programs such as Photoshop, Bridge and Adobe Camera Raw.

In this phase of the workflow the digital photograph can be enhanced and edited in many ways, including changes to color, brightness, contrast and sharpness (see Foundation Project 1). In addition it is also possible to make more substantial changes such as retouching marks and dust spots, montaging several photos together, and adding text and special effects to the photo.

Producing your pictures

Even these days, many precious pictures end up as prints. Sometimes the prints are kept in an album, on other occasions they are hung on a wall, or they may just be simply passed from friend to friend or photographer to client, but gradually other production outcomes are becoming easier to use and therefore more popular.

Now you can just as easily produce a web gallery, photo book or multimedia slideshow as output a bunch of 6 × 4 inch prints. On the whole, the same software that is used for editing and enhancing digital photos also contains the ability to output pictures in a range of different forms. The latest version of Bridge, for instance, is able to produce high-quality PDF slideshows as well as polished Flash-based websites directly from inside the program.

Sharing your imagery

For many photographers having their images seen is one of the key reasons they capture pictures in the first place. With so many ways of producing your photos there are now a host of different ways of sharing your images. Modern image makers are no longer limited by distance or geographic borders. With the ability to easily produce web galleries, attach photos to e-mails or create High Definition slideshows, the whole world is truly a smaller place.

A few key concepts before we start...

Raw – the ultimate 'capture' and 'processing' format

Until recently, Raw files were viewed as a capture-only format with the first step in any workflow being the conversion of the picture to another file type so that editing, enhancing and output tasks could be performed. I say recently because with the latest release of products such as Adobe Camera Raw, Photoshop and Bridge it is no longer necessary to change file formats to move your pictures further through the production workflow.

Photoshop and Bridge are now sufficiently Raw-aware to allow the user to edit, enhance, print and even produce contact sheets, PDF presentations and web galleries all from Raw originals. Yes, sometimes the files are converted as part of the production process for these outcomes, but I can live with the intermediary step of conversion if it means that my precious pictures stay in the Raw format for more of the production workflow. With a little trickery associated with Photoshop's Smart Object technology it is now even possible to edit individual pictures inside a standard Photoshop document without having to convert the file first, thus maintaining the untouched capture pixels throughout the editing process.

Differences between Raw and other formats

Raw files differ from other file types in that some of the options that are fixed during the processing of formats such as TIFF or JPEG can be adjusted and changed losslessly with a Raw format. In this way you can think of Raw files as having three distinct sections:

- **Camera Data**, usually called the EXIF or metadata, including things such as camera model, shutter speed and aperture details, most of which cannot be changed.

- **Image Data** which, though recorded by the camera, can be changed in a Raw editor and the settings chosen here directly affect how the picture will be processed. Changeable options include color space, white balance, saturation, distribution of image tones (contrast) and application of sharpness.

- **The Image itself**. This is the data drawn directly from the sensor sites in your camera in a non-interpolated form (Bayer pattern form). For most Raw cameras, this image data is captured in either 12- or 14-bit per pixel color depth. This color depth provides substantially more colors and tones to work with when editing and enhancing than the standard 8-bit JPEG or TIFF camera file.

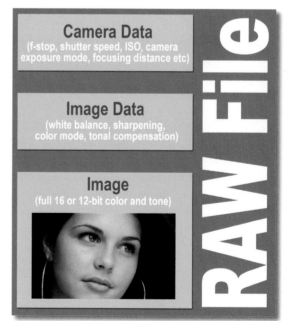

Camera Data
(f-stop, shutter speed, ISO, camera exposure mode, focusing distance etc)

Image Data
(white balance, sharpening, color mode, tonal compensation)

Image
(full 16 or 12-bit color and tone)

RAW File

The importance of DNG

No discussion about Raw files is complete without mentioning the importance of Adobe's Digital Negative format or DNG. As we have mentioned (and will see throughout the book) capturing in Raw has many advantages for photographers, offering them greater control over the tone and color in their files, but there is only one standard available for the Raw files. One problem is that each camera manufacturer has their own flavor of the file format.

Adobe developed the DNG or Digital Negative format to help promote a common Raw format that can be used for archival as well as editing and enhancement purposes. As well as including output DNG options in Photoshop, Lightroom and Photoshop Elements, Adobe provides a free DNG converter that can change proprietary Camera Raw formats to DNG. The converter can be downloaded from www.adobe.com. Also files imported into Bridge with the Adobe Photo Downloader can be automatically converted to DNG on the fly (during the transfer process).

Raw files can be converted to the DNG format either at time of import via the Photo Downloader, when saving from Adobe Camera Raw or batches of images converted via the free DNG converter utility.

In addition to providing a common Raw file format, the DNG specification also includes a lossless compression option which, when considering the size of some Raw files, helps to reduce the space taken up by the thousands of images that photographers accumulate. The specification includes the ability to embed the original proprietary capture file (e.g. .nef, .crw, .arw etc.) if required. Also all development settings applied to the photo are self-contained within the DNG file instead of being stored in an extra file (called a sidecar file) that is linked with the original Raw file.

Synchronizing development settings

Archiving is one reason to switch to using the DNG format but by far the most important reason to use DNG is that it makes the synchronizing of development settings between Raw enabled editing programs such as Adobe Camera Raw and Photoshop Lightroom easier.

Preparing your system to use Raw files

One of the difficulties when working with Raw files is that sometimes the computer's operating system is unable to display thumbnails of the images when viewing the contents of folders or directories. When using Windows XP it was necessary to install Microsoft's Raw Image Thumbnailer and Viewer utility before the operating system was able to recognize, and display, Raw files. The system was slow and most users reverted to employing Bridge as the main way they viewed their files.

Now Windows users are migrating to the Windows 7 or Vista operating system. Recognizing that Raw files are a key component of the photographer's workflow, Microsoft has taken a different approach to the problem in its latest operating system offering. In creating a more 'Raw aware' operating system, Microsoft has made use of a structure where the various camera manufacturers supply their own CODECs (Compression Decompression drivers) to be used with their particular type of Raw files inside Windows 7 or Vista.

In this approach the user has to install the CODEC for the camera that he or she uses before they are able to view their images in the system folders or directories. This process is also needed to view thumbnails of your DNG files as well. Though a little troublesome to start with, as you need to install CODECS for all the cameras you use or have used in the past, this approach will hopefully 'future proof' the operating system's support for Raw files. Supporting the latest camera, or Raw file type, is a simple upgrade installation of the latest CODEC from the manufacturer. Use the following steps as a guide for Raw enabling your own Windows 7 or Vista machine.

Locate the CODEC – Step A

Start by searching the internet, or your camera manufacturer's support site, for the specific Windows 7 or Vista CODEC that supports your Raw files. Once located, download, and in some cases extract or decompress, the files to your desktop ready for installation.

Follow the instructions – Step B

Next follow the install instructions. Here I am installing the Nikon Raw CODEC for Vista. As part of the process, the user is required to input location and language selections.

Reboot the computer – Step C

As the CODEC forms part of the file processing functions of the operating system it may be necessary to reboot (turn off and turn back on again) your computer after installing the software.

Test the install – Step D

After rebooting check to see that the CODEC is functioning correctly by displaying an Icon View of an image folder that you know contains Raw files. You should see a series of thumbnails representing your image files.

What about Mac machines?

The ability to display thumbnails of Raw files in the Macintosh operating system is driven mainly by the Preview and iPhoto utilities. Ensuring that these programs are always up to date will help guarantee that the latest camera formats are supported by the system and thumbnails and previews are displayed in the computer's browser windows.

The need for enhancement

Every digital capture or scanned image should be enhanced further so that it may be viewed in its optimum state for the intended output device. Whether images are destined to be viewed in print or via a monitor screen, the image usually needs to be resized, cropped, retouched, color-corrected, sharpened and saved in an appropriate file format. The original capture will usually possess pixel dimensions that do not exactly match the requirements of the output device. In order for this to be corrected the user must address the issues of 'Image Size', 'Resampling' and 'Cropping'.

To end up with high-quality output you must start with the optimum levels of information that the capture device is capable of providing. The factors that greatly enhance final quality are:

- A 'subject brightness range' that does not exceed the exposure latitude of the capture device (the contrast is not too high for the image sensor).
- Using a low ISO setting to capture the original subject.
- The availability of 16 bits per channel scanning or the camera Raw file format.

Optimizing image quality

In the next section of this chapter we will step our way through a typical digital capture workflow using Raw files. We will focus on the standard adjustments made to all images when optimum quality is required without using any advanced techniques. Standard image adjustments usually include the process of optimizing the color, tonality and sharpness of the image. With the exception of dust or blemish removal, these adjustments are applied globally (to all the pixels). Most of the adjustments in this chapter are 'objective' rather than 'subjective' adjustments and are tackled as a logical progression of tasks. Automated features are available for some of these tasks but these do not ensure optimum quality is achieved for all images. The chapter uses a 'hands-on' project to guide you through the steps required to achieve optimum quality.

Save, save and save

First, good working habits will prevent the frustration and the heartache that are often associated with the inevitable 'crash' (all computers crash or 'freeze' periodically). As you work on an image file you should get into the habit of saving the work in progress and not wait until the image editing is complete. It is recommended that you use the 'Save As' command and continually rename the file as an updated version. The Photoshop (PSD) file format should be used for all work in progress. Before the computer is shut down, the files should be saved to a removable storage device or burnt to a CD/DVD. In short, save often, save different versions and save backups. Also when working with programs that make use of Library or Catalog structure such as the system used in Lightroom, be sure to back-up this database as well.

Stepping back

Digital image editing allows the user to make mistakes. There are several ways of undoing a mistake before resorting to the 'Revert' command from the File menu or opening a previously saved version. Photoshop allows the user to jump to the previous state via the Edit > Undo command (Command/ Ctrl + Z). The user can 'Step Backward' through several changes by using the keyboard shortcut Ctrl + Alt + Z (PC) or Command + Option + Z (Mac). Alternatively, 'Histories' allows access to any previous state in the History palette without going through a linear sequence of undos.

Advantages and disadvantages of 16-bit editing

When the highest quality images are required there are major advantages to be gained by starting off the editing process in '16 Bits/Channel' mode. In 16 bits per channel there are trillions, instead of millions, of possible values for each pixel. Spikes or comb lines, that are quick to occur while editing in 8 bits per channel, rarely occur when editing in 16 bits per channel mode. Thankfully, cameras capable of Raw capture record their images in either 12 or 14 bits per channel (which are then saved in a 16 bits per channel file) which means that Raw shooters get the advantages of high-bit capture inherently.

The disadvantages of editing in 16 bits per channel are:

- Not all digital cameras are capable of saving in the Raw format.
- The size of file is doubled when compared to an 8 bits per channel image of the same output size and resolution.
- Some editing features (including many filters) do not work in 16 bits per channel mode.
- Only a small selection of file formats support the use of 16 bits per channel.

Comb lines that appear in the histogram will usually disappear if editing in a 16 bits per channel file.

Choosing your bit depth

It is preferable to make all major changes in tonality or color to the Raw file in Adobe Camera Raw (ACR). This ensures that the enhancement steps are performed on high-bit data. Using a Smart workflow involving embedded Raw files the decisions about depth and space can be further delayed as we have the option of re-opening the file in ACR and adjusting the color and tone at 12 or 14 bits and changing the gamut to accommodate a larger or small gamut output device. Non-Raw images can be converted from 8-bit (Image > Mode > 16 Bits/Channel) or captured in 16-bit (the preferred choice). Most scanners now support 16 bits per channel image capture with many referring to the mode as 48-bit RGB scanning. Some offer 14 bits per channel scanning but deliver a 48-bit image to Photoshop. Remember, you need twice as many megabytes as the equivalent 8-bit image, e.g. if you typically capture 13.2 megabytes for an 8 × 10 @ 240 ppi you will require 26.4 megabytes when scanning in 16 bits per channel.

Note > Photoshop also supports 32 Bits/Channel editing which is primarily used for editing images with a high dynamic range (see Montage Projects – High Dynamic Range).

Foundation Project 1

Follow the eleven steps over the following pages in order to learn how to create one image optimized for print and one image optimized for web viewing from the same image file.

Image capture – Step 1

Capture a vertical portrait image using soft lighting (low-contrast diffused sunlight or window lighting would be ideal). The image selected should have detail in both the highlights and shadows and should have a range of colors and tones. An image with high contrast and missing detail in the highlights or shadows is not suitable for testing the effectiveness of the capture or output device. An example file for this project is located on the book's DVD.

Pro's Tips for Best Capture

To achieve optimum image quality ensure as many of the following steps as possible are carried out.

1. Set the camera's ISO setting to no more than double the base level ISO of the sensor (typically 100 or 200 ISO for most digital cameras). Alternatively use a low ISO film, e.g. 100 ISO.

2. Avoid using either the minimum or maximum apertures on the camera lens.

3. Mount the camera on a sturdy tripod and switch off any image stabilization, steady-shot or vibration reduction settings.

4. Use a remote shutter release or self-timer to release the shutter.

5. Ensure accurate exposure metering and setting of the camera's shutter speed and aperture.

6. Match the camera's white balance setting for the light source that is illuminating the subject. If need be, use a custom white balance setting in mixed lighting to ensure cast-free capture. For best results though, you should create a custom white balance setting for your location and lighting setup using a photographer's gray card, or a white balance reference card, such as WhiBal or X-rite's ColorChecker Passport. Consult the camera manual to see how you can create a custom white balance. Then capture a 'reference' image using this custom white balance setting (hold the photographers gray card or a white balance reference card just below the face and angled towards the dominant light source. **Important > Do not photograph in a location where vibrant or bright colors are close to your subject (this could result in a strong color cast).**

7. Check the lens aperture is stopped down (but not to f/22) and the ISO is low (no more than double the base ISO of the sensor – the base ISO of a DSLR camera is usually 100 or 200 ISO).

8. Check image is sharp and shutter speed is 1/60 second or faster (mount your camera on a tripod and use a remote release, timed release or 'tethered capture' – see below for details).

    Note > If your shutter speed is slower than 1/60 second, check your aperture is not stopped down excessively. Your aperture must, however, be stopped down at least one full stop from maximum aperture. Note that most cameras adjust aperture settings in half or one-third stop increments. One adjustment of the command/ control dial is therefore not one full stop. Choose a brighter location if required. Using shutter speeds slower than 1/60 second can result subject blur.

9. Check for overexposure (clipping) or underexposure on the camera's LCD panel (using the histogram). If shadows are pressed against the left hand wall of the histogram use a reflector, or diffuse the light source to reduce subject brightness range or choose an alternative location or time of day.

10. Create an additional portrait image that does not contain the gray card or white balance reference but uses the same custom white balance setting as the reference image.

Digital capture via a digital camera

Images can be transferred directly to the computer from a digital camera or from a card reader if the card has been removed from the camera. Images are usually saved on the camera's storage media as JPEG or Raw files. If using the JPEG file format to capture images you should choose the high or maximum quality setting whenever possible to select low levels of image sharpening, saturation and contrast in the camera's settings to ensure optimum quality and editing flexibility in the image-editing software. If the camera has the option to choose Adobe RGB instead of sRGB as the color space this should also be selected if one of the final images is destined for print. For best results we suggest to always capture in Raw.

Tethered Image Capture

Many DSLR cameras now offer the option of capturing Raw photos while the camera is connected to a computer. Some photographers would never need, nor see the benefits of, shooting in this fashion; for their chosen area of speciality the added burden of dragging around a laptop computer as well as all their camera gear is a complication that they can well do without. However, for studio, product, architectural, commercial and even some landscape photography the ability to preview,

and even process, the photos captured almost immediately on a large screen ensures better results.

The utility software that comes bundled with most mid- to high-end DSLR cameras and medium format camera backs does an admirable job of providing the required software link between camera and computer. The physical connection is generally provided via a USB or Firewire connection, although some models can now connect wirelessly using a pretty standard setup. The 'remote capture' software supplied by the camera companies ranges from something as simple as a dialog containing a shutter release button right up to a full control panel that allows focus, metering, drive and exposure control right from your desktop. Once on the desktop the files can be imported into Bridge and even displayed in Adobe Camera Raw.

Lightroom 3 provides a tethered solution

Lightroom 3 also provides a tethered shooting solution and at the time of release provided support for recent Canon and Nikon models. So if you are using a combined workflow that brings together the management, processing and presentation abilities with the editing power of Photoshop then you can take advantage of this new feature.

Tethered shooting advantages

There are several advantages for viewing pictures in this type of setup:

- You can review images on a larger, higher resolution camera LCD screen at the time of shooting either via the remote capture software or after downloading into Bridge,
- Critical exposures can be checked closely using histograms derived from the full high-bit Raw image data rather than a processed JPEG, as is the case with most back of camera histograms, and
- It is possible to quickly apply some post-capture processing to the images when in Bridge to display the style of the treatment that will be applied to the final photos. This is a great way to show a client how the images will look seconds after they are shot.

Use the following steps to set up for tethered shooting:

Install camera drivers – Step A

Before connecting the camera ensure that you have installed any camera drivers that were supplied with the unit. These small pieces of software ensure clear communication between the camera and computer and are usually installed along with other utility programs such as a dedicated browser (e.g. Nikon View, Canon's ZoomBrowser/ImageBrowser or Sony's Image Data Suite) and camera-based Raw conversion software (e.g. Nikon Capture, Canon's Digital Photo Professional or Sony's Remote Camera Control). Follow any on-screen installation instructions and, if necessary, reboot the computer to initialize the new drivers.

Connect the camera – Step B

The next step is to connect the camera to the computer via the USB/Firewire cable or wireless network. Make sure that your camera is switched off, and the computer is on, when plugging in the cables. For the best connection and the least chance of trouble it is a good idea to connect the camera directly to a computer USB/Firewire port rather than a hub.

Check the connection – Step C

With the cables securely fastened, switch the camera on and, if needed, change to the PC connection mode. Most cameras have two connection modes – one that uses the camera as a card reader (often called 'Mass Storage' mode) and another that connects the device as a camera (generally referred to as 'PTP' mode but sometimes also called Remote PC mode). The remote capture software or tethering utility will work with one of these modes only.

Most cameras no longer require a change from whatever mode is selected by default, but check with your camera manual just in case. If the drivers are installed correctly the computer should report that the camera has been found and the connection is now active and a connection symbol (such as PC) will be displayed on the camera. If the computer can't find the camera try reinstalling the drivers and, if all else fails, consult the troubleshooting section in the manual. To ensure a continuous connection use fully charged batteries or an AC adaptor.

Start the remote shooting software – Step D

FOR CAMERA-BASED SOFTWARE: With the connection established you can now start the remote capture software (e.g. Nikon Capture Camera Control, Canon's Digital Photo Professional or Sony's Remote Camera Control). With some models the action of connecting the camera will automatically activate the software. In other cases it will be necessary to start the software and wait for the program to locate the attached camera. Most versions of these utilities provide more than just a means of releasing the shutter from the computer and instantly (well nearly, it does take a couple of seconds to transfer big capture files) viewing captured photos. The utilities contain options to set most camera functions including items such as shutter speed, ISO, aperture, capture format, contrast, saturation and white balance controls.

FOR LIGHTROOM 3 USERS: With the connection between camera and computer established, Lightroom users need to adjust some basic settings before starting to shoot. To do this you need to launch Lightroom 3 and choose File > Tethered Capture > Start Tethered Capture. This will display the Tethered Capture Settings dialog box. Add a name for the shooting session and then choose a naming scheme for individual photos from the options in the drop-down list. Next click the Choose button in the Destination section to navigate to the folder that you want to use to save the captured files. Select the metadata to be recorded with each photo from the entries in the drop-down menu. You can easily create a custom entry by clicking the New option and adding the required details before saving this set of values as a new preset. Finally, type any keywords that you want added to the photos (separated by a comma) in the box at the bottom of the dialog. Click OK to save the settings and display the Tethered Capture widget.

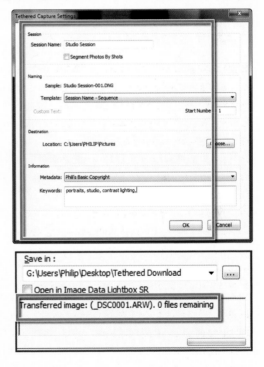

Guidelines for setting download options

With all these settings to play with, where do you start? Start by adjusting the download options found in the remote capture software. The four big settings are:

- Where the files are to be transferred to,
- How they are to be labeled,
- What metadata is to be added to the files during this process, and
- What happens to the file once it is transferred.

It is a good idea to create a new folder or directory for each shooting session and to select this folder as the place to download the captured files. Now choose a naming scheme that provides enough information to allow easy searching later. This may mean a title that includes date and name of shoot, a shooting session, or subject as well as a sequence number. In terms of additional metadata at the very least you should always attach a copyright statement as well as any pertinent keywords that describe the subject. If these last options aren't available with your software then keywords can be added, and filenames changed, using the features in Bridge. Finally, you need to choose what happens to the captured files. Most users will want to transfer the pictures directly to a preview utility such as one of the browser programs, or alternatively, if you want to process the photo on the spot, you could pass the file directly to a Raw converter. One way of achieving this automatically is to set the download folder you have nominated to the Hot or Watched folder for Lightroom's Auto Import function.

Note > This part of the process is handled automatically for Lightroom 3 users who are employing the tethered shooting option in the program.

Compose, focus and release the shutter – Step E

Now to the nuts and bolts of the capture. Most remote capture systems don't offer a live preview feature so composing and framing is still a through the viewfinder and lens event. Some photographers adopt a shoot and review policy, preferring to capture a couple of test images and review these full size on their computer screens to check composition, focus and even exposure. Once you are happy with all your settings, release the shutter and automatically the file is captured and transferred from camera to computer.

Disconnecting the camera – Step F

Before turning the camera off or disconnecting the cable make sure that any transfer of information or images is complete. Interrupting the transfer at this point will mean that you lose files. Mac users can drag the camera volume from the desktop to the trash. It may be necessary to choose a menu option in the remote capture software to stop the tethering process. In Lightroom 3, you simply close Tethered Capture widget or choose the Stop Tethered Capture option from the File > Tethered menu. Next, Windows users should click the Safely Remove Hardware icon in the system tray (bottom right of the screen) and select Safely Remove Mass Storage Device from the pop-up menu that appears.

Downloading files – Step 2

For all photographers apart from those using a tethered shooting setup the very next step after capture is transferring the photos to your desktop machine. For this workflow we will assume that Bridge will be the center of all image management and that the Adobe Photo Downloader (APD) will be used for transferring files. You could just as easily use a system-based 'copy' or 'move' function, but APD contains inbuilt features that make the process easier and relieve you of some tasks such as renaming that you would normally have to undertake manually.

In the last chapter we looked at the basic steps involved in using APD to transfer your images so we won't repeat them here, but instead we'll concentrate on the other options that you may want to use to fine-tune your downloads. Most are accessed by clicking on the Advanced Dialog button in the APD dialog (see opposite for details).

Note > For Lightroom 3 users many of these options are covered when initially setting up the Tethered Capture session.

Storage location – *A good workflow starts with the transfer of images to your computer. Choosing an appropriate storage location and folder hierarchy for saving your pictures is a key decision. Some photographers use data-based storage, others create a folder structure based on client or job type. Once you have decided on a system, stick to it as this will help with locating your images later.*

Rename photos – *The renaming options revolve around three key pieces of data – the current date, the shot date, a custom name and a sub-folder name. Each menu entry uses a different combination or sequence of these details. There are 21 different naming formats and when dates are part of the renaming process both US- and UK-based date formats are included.*

Convert to DNG – *Adobe's Digital Negative format or DNG is an open source Raw file format designed to be used as the primary file type for archiving. To help reduce the steps involved in managing the thousands of photos that are transferred each year, the Adobe team has included an automatic conversion option in APD. When selected, the picture files are converted from their native Raw format (i.e. .NEF, .CRW) to the DNG automatically. From this point onwards they can still be processed as standard Raw files.*

Preserved filename – *It is handy to have the option to include the original filename stored in the XMP data associated with the photo as XMP data is searchable via the Find option in Bridge's Edit menu.*

Open Adobe Bridge – *When APD starts automatically because you have attached a camera or card reader to the computer you then have the option of opening Bridge and displaying the transferred files in a new window.*

Save Options

Location:
G:\Users\Philip\Pictures\20080730   [Browse...]

Create Subfolder(s):
Today's Date (yyyymmdd) ▾

Rename Files:
Custom Name + Shot Date (yyyymmdd) ▾
PHILIPANDREWS   + 1
Example: PHILIPANDREWS_20070427_0001.inf
☑ Preserve Current Filename in XMP

▽ Advanced Options
☑ Open Adobe Bridge
☑ Convert To DNG   [Settings...]
☑ Delete Original Files
☑ Save Copies to:
G:\Users\Philip\Pictures   [Browse...]

▽ Apply Metadata
Template to Use:
Basic Metadata ▾
Creator:
Philip Andrews
Copyright:

Delete Original Files – *Deletes the photos from the camera card after transferring is complete.*

Apply Metadata – *The Apply Metadata section contains an option for inserting author and copyright information quickly and easily. To display these input fields you will need to select the Basic Metadata option in the Template to Use drop-down menu. Also listed on this menu are any other metadata templates you have created and saved, either in Bridge (via the Metadata panel) or in Photoshop (with the File Info dialog).*

Automated backup – *The 'Save Copies to' option provides the ability to automatically store a separate copy of each downloaded file as a primary backup. This saves having to manually back up photos at a later date or transfer the files twice from the camera or memory card – once to the drive used for processing and a second time to the backup device. It is important to note that even when the Convert to DNG setting is selected the file type of the photos copied as a backup is in the original capture format and not DNG.*

Image management – Step 3

Now I know that you are eager to get editing but a largely overlooked step in any good professional workflow is image management, sometimes called DAM (Digital Asset Management). Directly after downloading is a good time to start to manage your files. A little discipline shown at this point will save time later. As we saw in the last chapter Bridge is not just a tool for viewing your photos, it is a key technology in the managing, sorting and enhancing of those files. And this pivotal role is never more evident than when one is managing Raw files. So the next step is to add keywords to your images and then select the best photos from the group and label these with ratings.

Add keywords

Keywords are single-word descriptions of the content of image files. Most photo libraries use keywords as part of the way they locate images with specific content. The words are stored in the metadata associated with the picture. Users can allocate, edit and create new keywords (and keyword categories) using the Keywords panel in the Bridge browser and File Info dialog box in Photoshop.

New keywords (categories or sets of keywords) and sub-keywords can be added to the Keywords panel by clicking the New Sub-Keyword and New Keyword buttons at the bottom of the panel. Unwanted sets or keywords can be removed by selecting first and then clicking the Delete button. Unknown keywords imported with newly downloaded or edited pictures are stored in the panel under the Other Keywords set.

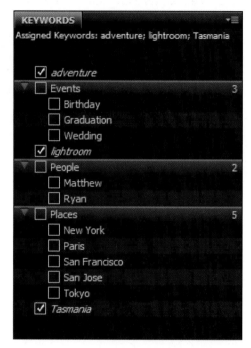

Rate and label files

One of the many ways you can organize the Raw files displayed in the Bridge workspace is by attributing a label to the picture. In CS5 the labels option is supplied in two forms – a color tag, called a Label, or star rating, called a Rating. Either or both label types can be applied to any picture. The Label tag can then be used to sort or locate individual pictures from groups of photos.

Image processing steps

The next steps are concerned with basic processing and optimizing of your photos. With the growing use of Raw files as the basis of professional capture these changes will be made to several Raw files using Adobe Camera Raw (ACR). Make sure that the ACR plug-in is the latest available by selecting Help > Updates in Bridge. In previous editions of this book we have used Photoshop for these steps; this is still possible, but would generally require the Raw file to be converted to a non-Raw format before any enhancements could be applied. The example files foundations project 1.dng, foundations project 2.dng and foundations project 3.dng located on the book's DVD can be used to practice these steps in the absence of your own images.

Note > For readers using non-Raw formats (Jpeg and Tiff) we suggest that you still use Adobe Camera Raw as there are very real advantages to adjusting your files with the utility and it is possible to display the images in ACR by selecting the Open in Camera Raw option from the right-click menu when selecting thumbnails in the Content panel in Bridge.

Rotating and cropping an image – Step 4

The easiest way to open a file, or files, into ACR is by selecting the image(s), right-clicking (Mac:-Ctrl Clicking) on one of the thumbnails in Bridge and then selecting Open in Camera Raw. Working with ACR in Bridge allows for faster Raw processing as the conversions take place without the need to share computer resources with Photoshop at the same time. The selected images will be displayed on the left of the dialog as thumbnails. Click onto the thumbnail containing the reference card to select the photo for editing and display it in the main workspace.

Next, if you need to you can rotate the image using either of the two Rotate buttons at the top of the workspace. If you are the lucky owner of a recent camera model then chances are the picture will automatically rotate to its correct orientation. This is thanks to a small piece of metadata supplied by the camera and stored in the picture file that indicates which way is up.

Pro's tip: The preferences for Bridge can be adjusted so that double-clicking a thumbnail of a Raw picture will automatically open the file in Camera Raw in the Bridge workspace. If this option is not selected, then double-clicking will open the file in ACR in the Photoshop workspace.

You can fine-tune the rotation of the picture with the Straighten Tool. After selecting the tool click and drag a straight line along an edge in the photo that is meant to be horizontal or vertical. Upon releasing the mouse button ACR automatically creates a crop marquee around the photo. You will notice that the marquee is rotated so that the edges are parallel to the line that was drawn with the Straighten Tool. When you exit ACR by saving or opening (into Photoshop) the picture, the rotated crop is applied.

The crop tool in ACR can be used for basic cropping tasks as well as for cropping to a specific format. The feature works just like the regular Crop Tool in Photoshop proper, just select and then click and drag to draw a marquee around the picture parts that you want to retain. The side and corner handles on the marquee can be used to adjust the size and shape of the selected area. The crop is applied upon exiting the ACR dialog.

Custom Crop

Predefined crop formats are available from the menu accessed by clicking and holding the Crop Tool button. Also included is a Custom option where you can design your own crops to suit specific print or other outcome requirements.

In this instance, we will crop the picture to fit a standard 6:4 format, so select choose the Custom option from the Crop menu, input the 6 to 4 ratio, choose inches from the drop-down menu and then drag a vertical crop marquee around the image. Select any other tool from the ACR toolbar to apply the crop.

Note > Keep in mind that any crops you make with ACR are reversible. Just open the file back into ACR and select the Crop Tool and then hit the Esc key to remove the current crop.

Perfecting the crop

Once you have a cropping marquee located on your image you can resize the marquee with the corner handles. The marquee can be click-dragged to reposition and if the image is still a little crooked you can rotate the cropping marquee by moving the mouse cursor to a position just outside a corner handle of the cropping marquee. A curved arrow should appear, allowing you to drag the image straight. In ACR you just need to move the cursor outside the crop marquee to see the curved arrow.

Before completing the crop, you should check the entire image edge to see if there are any remaining border pixels that are not part of the image. Press Ctrl/Cmd + 0 to see all the image in the workspace and Ctrl/Cmd + to zoom in, or Ctrl/Cmd – to zoom out. Holding down the Spacebar activates the Hand Tool so that you can quickly move the window if the image is larger than the workspace. Press the 'Return/Enter' key on the keyboard or select another tool to complete the cropping action. Alternatively press the 'Esc' key on the keyboard to cancel the crop.

Color adjustments – Step 5

Unlike other capture formats (TIFF, JPEG) the white balance settings are not fixed in a Raw file. This fact provides much greater control over the colors in the photo than when such settings are fixed. ACR contains three different ways to balance the hues in your photo:

Preset changes

You can opt to stay with the settings used at the time of shooting ('As Shot') or select from a range of light source-specific values in the White Balance drop-down menu of ACR. For best results, try to match the setting used with the type of lighting that was present in the scene at the time of capture. Or choose the Auto option to get ACR to determine a setting based on the individual image currently displayed.

Manual adjustments

If none of the preset White Balance options perfectly matches the lighting in your photo then you will need to fine-tune your results with the Temperature and Tint sliders (located just below the Presets drop-down menu). The Temperature slider settings equate to the color of light in degrees kelvin – so daylight will be 5500 and tungsten light 2800. It is a blue to yellow scale, so moving the slider to the left will make the image cooler (more blue) and to the right warmer (more yellow). In contrast the Tint slider is a green to magenta scale. Moving the slider left will add more green to the image and to the right more magenta.

The White Balance Tool

Another quick way to balance the light in your picture is to choose the White Balance Tool and then click onto a part of the picture that is supposed to be neutral gray or white. This approach is perfect in our situation as we have included a reference card in the image. When you click on the gray card (or other neutrals that are in the photo) ACR will automatically set the Temperature and Tint sliders so that the selected picture part becomes a neutral gray and in the process the rest of the image will be balanced. So in the example photo use the White Balance Tool to create a custom white balance setting in ACR by clicking on the gray card or white balance reference. If your custom white balance created in camera was accurate you should not see a big change. If the color temperature changes more than 200° kelvin then your custom white balance in camera is not accurate. This may require a re-shoot.

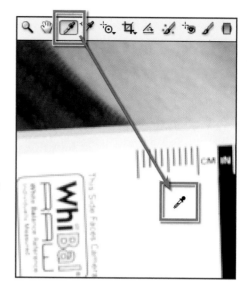

Note > For best results when not working with a reference card select lighter tones with the tool, ensure that the area contains detail, and is not a blown or a specular highlight (reflected light source with no details).

Both the Vibrance and Saturation sliders control the strength of the colors in your photos.

Other ACR color controls

As well as options for adjusting the white balance in a photo, Adobe Camera Raw also contains two sliders that are concerned with controlling the strength of the hues in your pictures – Vibrance and Saturation.

Vibrance

The Vibrance slider, like the Saturation control, increases the vividness of the colors in photos but applies the changes selectively to only those hues that are desaturated in the first place.

This means that the slider targets the more pastel tones and doesn't boost those colors that are already rich and vibrant. In addition, the Vibrance slider tends to safeguard Caucasian skin tones when it is applied.

Saturation

In contrast the Saturation slider increases the saturation, or vividness, of all the colors in a photo irrespective of their original value. These factors make the Vibrance slider perfect when working with portraits or photos where selective adjustment is needed. The Saturation slider, on the other hand, is very useful for bumping the color of the whole photo up a few notches. Moving the slider all the way to the left creates a grayscale image devoid of color, but don't be tempted to create monochromes in this way as ACR contains more appropriate controls for this process. See the Raw Processing chapter for more details about ACR-based grayscale conversions.

Note > Adobe Camera Raw contains a variety of other color controls that are capable of adjusting specific color ranges. These and other more sophisticated ACR features are discussed in the next chapter – Raw Processing.

Tonal adjustments – Step 6

The starting point to adjust the tonal qualities of EVERY image is the six slider controls (Exposure, Recovery, Fill Light, Blacks, Brightness and Contrast) in the Basic pane of ACR (or the 'Levels' dialog box in Photoshop).

It is important to perform tonal adjustments with reference to some objective feedback about the nature of the changes you are making. For this reason the Histograms located at the top right of the ACR workspace (or inside the Levels dialog) should always be consulted when enhancing your photos. Features like Brightness/Contrast, that don't include this objective feedback, should never be used.

Histograms

Essentially the histogram is a graph of the pixels in your photo. The horizontal axis of the histogram displays the brightness values from left (darkest) to right (lightest). The vertical axis of the histogram shows how much of the image is found at any particular brightness

(1) Shadows. (2) Midtones. (3) Highlights. (4) Clipped Highlight Areas.

level. If the subject contrast or 'brightness range' exceeds the latitude of the capture device or the exposure is either too high or too low, then tonality will be 'clipped' (shadow or highlight detail will be lost and no amount of adjustment will recover it). ACR's histogram also displays the information of each channel (red, green, blue) that make-up the photos as colored parts of the graph and include clipping warning features in the top corners of the dialog.

During the capture stage it is often possible to check how the capture device is handling or interpreting the tonality and color of the subject. This useful information can often be displayed as a 'histogram' on the LCD screen of high-quality digital cameras, on the screen of a tethered computer, or in the scanning software during the scanning process. The histogram displayed shows the brightness range of the subject in relation to the latitude or 'dynamic range' of your capture device's image sensor. Most digital camera sensors have a dynamic range similar to color transparency film (around five stops) when capturing in JPEG or TIFF. This may be expanded beyond seven stops when the Raw data is processed manually.

When capturing using a tethered workflow, the accuracy of the histogram is increased in that you are able to view, and base your exposure decisions on, a graph of the captured Raw file (displayed in ACR) rather than a processed JPEG as is the case for many back of camera LCD histograms.

Note > You should attempt to modify the brightness, contrast and color balance at the capture stage to obtain the best possible histogram before editing begins in the software.

Optimizing tonality

In a good histogram, one where a broad tonal range with full detail in the shadows and highlights is present, the information will extend all the way from the left to the right side of the histogram. The histogram on the left (below) indicates missing information in the highlights (right side of histogram) indicating overexposure. The histogram on the right indicates a small amount of 'clipping' or loss of information in the shadows (left side of histogram) or underexposure.

ACR histograms indicating image is either too light (left) or too dark (right).

Brightness

If the digital file is too light a tall peak will be seen to rise on the right side (level 255) of the histogram. If the digital file is too dark a tall peak will be seen to rise on the left side (level 0) of the histogram.

Solution: Decrease or increase the exposure/brightness in the capture device.

Levels histograms indicating image either has too much contrast or not enough.

Contrast

If the contrast is too low the histogram will not extend to meet the sliders at either end. If the contrast is too high a tall peak will be evident at both extremes of the histogram.

Solution: Increase or decrease the contrast of the light source used to light the subject or the contrast setting of the capture device. Using diffused lighting rather than direct sunlight or using fill flash and/or reflectors will ensure that you start with an image with full detail.

Previewing clipping

One of the critical areas of image adjustment is ensuring that any changes to tone or color don't clip captured details in either the shadow or highlight areas of the photo. In ACR the preview image in conjunction with the histogram form a key partnership in providing this clipping feedback to the user when they are making changes to the photo. By activating the highlight and shadow clipping warnings in the histogram (click on the upwards-facing arrows in the top left, for shadows, or top right, for highlights of the histogram), areas being clipped are displayed in the preview image. Clipped shadow details are displayed in blue and clipped highlights in red. As well as the warning in the preview image, the actual clip warning arrows in the histogram area reflect the color of the channels (red, green, blue or combinations thereof) being clipped. If details for more than one channel are being clipped then the arrow turns white. If no details are being clipped then the arrow is black.

Optimizing a histogram after capture

The final histogram should show that pixels have been allocated to most, if not all, of the 256 levels. If the histogram indicates large gaps between the ends of the histogram and the sliders (indicating either a low-contrast scan or low-contrast subject photographed in flat lighting) the subject or original image should usually be recaptured a second time. In situations when this is not possible use the following ACR controls to adjust the look of the histogram and therefore the tones in the photo.

Setting the white point

To start, adjust the white point with the Exposure slider. Moving the slider to the right lightens the photo and to the left darkens it. The settings for the slider are in f-stop increments (or EVs), with a +1.00 setting being equivalent to increasing exposure by 1 f-stop. Use this slider to place or set the white tones. Your aim is to lighten the highlights in the photo without clipping (converting the pixels to pure white) them. To do this interactively, hold down Alt/Option while moving the slider. This action previews the photo with the pixels being clipped against a black background. Move

the slider back and forth until highlights with detail start to clip; the aim is to lighten the highlights where you want to preserve detail without clipping and losing that detail.

Note > An alternative to holding down the Alt/Opt key is to keep an eye on the clipping warning triangles at the top of the histogram. When they are black no clipping is occurring, when colored the channel containing these pixels is being clipped and when white multiple channels are being clipped. Clicking the warning triangles (so that they are surrounded by a white rectangle) activates the clipping warning in the preview without the need to hold down the Alt/Opt key.

Adjusting the blacks (shadows)

The Blacks slider (previously Shadows) performs a similar function with the shadow areas of the image. Again the aim is to darken these tones but not to convert (or clip) delicate details to pure black. Just as with the Exposure slider, the Alt/Option key can be pressed or the clipping warning triangles consulted, while making Blacks adjustments to preview the pixels being clipped.

The Recovery slider is designed as a fine control for the highlight tones in your photo.

Tweaking problem areas

When a photograph is overexposed, one of the consequences can be that the lighter tones in the image lose detail and are converted to pure white. As we have seen, this process is called clipping. Digital images are created with details from three color channels (red, green, blue). In situations of slight overexposure, when only one channel is clipped, it is possible to recreate the lost detail with the highlight information from the other two (non-clipped) channels. The Recovery slider attempts to recreate lost highlight details in such cases. Moving the slider to the right progressively increases the degree of highlight recovery. The Fill Light slider is used to lighten the darker tones in a picture without affecting the middle to highlight values. Use this control to brighten backlit subjects or boost shadow details. The beauty of this control is that the changes it makes do not generally impact on mid to highlight values.

Brightness changes

The next control, moving from top to bottom of the ACR dialog, is the Brightness slider. At first glance the changes you make with this feature may appear to be very similar to those produced with the Exposure slider but there is an important difference. Yes it is true that moving the slider to the right lightens the whole image, but rather than adjusting all pixels the same amount the feature makes major changes in the midtone areas and smaller jumps in the highlights. In so doing the Brightness slider is less likely to clip the highlights (or shadows)

as the feature compresses the highlights as it lightens the photo. This is why it is important to set white and black points first with the Exposure and Blacks sliders before fine-tuning the image with the Brightness control. That said, always make sure that your clipping warnings are activated when making tonal changes as this will mean that any clipping that occurs as a result of your adjustments will be clearly displayed in the preview.

Increasing/decreasing contrast

The last tonal control in the dialog, and the last to be applied to the photo, is the Contrast slider. The feature concentrates on the midtones in the photo, with movements of the slider to the right increasing the midtone contrast and to the left producing a lower contrast image. Like the Brightness slider, Contrast changes are best applied after setting the white and black points of the image with the Exposure and Blacks sliders.

More sophisticated tonal control

When the overall tonality has been optimized using either the sliders in ACR, or the Levels feature in Photoshop, the midtone contrast and appearance of the details in the shadow and highlight areas may require further work. One of the limitations of Photoshop's Levels adjustment feature is that it cannot focus its attention on only the shadows or the highlights, e.g. when the slider is moved to the left both the highlights and the shadows are made brighter. More control is available with the four key tonal sliders in ACR (Exposure, Recovery, Fill Light and Blacks) where specific attention can be paid to these areas.

The Curves feature in ACR has two different modes for adjusting how the tones in your images are spread between black and white. The Point mode (immediate right) works in a similar way to the curves feature in Photoshop whereas the Parametric mode (far right) provides four sliders that can be used to tweak specific tonal ranges.

More targeted adjustments can be achieved using the Curves adjustment features found in both ACR (Tone Curve tab) and Photoshop (Image > Adjustments > Curves). Curves allows the user to target tones within the image and move them independently of other tones within the image, e.g. the user can decide to make only the darker tones lighter while preserving the value of both the midtones and the highlights. It is also possible with a powerful editing feature such as Curves to move the shadows in one direction and the highlights in another. In this way the contrast of the image could be increased without losing valuable detail in either the shadows or the highlights. Slightly different approaches are taken with the feature in ACR and Photoshop. See 'Advanced Retouching – Projects 1 and 2' for more information on using Curves in Photoshop. Adobe Camera Raw provides two different Curve modes – Parametric and Point.

Parametric: This version of the ACR Curves feature provides four slider controls (Highlights, Lights, Darks and Shadows) as the means to adjust the shape of the curve. The slider controls tend to offer a fast way to manipulate different parts of the curve.

Point: The Point mode works in a similar way to Curves in Photoshop. Control points can be added to the different parts of the curve. These points can then be pushed and pulled to change the curve shape. Points can also be used to anchor specific tonal values so that they don't change while altering other parts of the curve. Holding down the Ctrl/Cmd key allows the user to place a control point on the curve by clicking on a specific part of the preview image. Using the Color Sample Tool it is also possible to add a sample entry by clicking on a part of the photo. This displays RGB values of the selected point at the top of the ACR dialog.

The shape of the curve determines how the tones are distributed within the photo. To produce the following standard enhancements replicate the curve shapes you see here by click-dragging points on the curve or using the sliders in Parametric mode.
(1) Lighten midtones.
(2) Darken midtones.
(3) Lighten highlights but watch out for possible clipping as seen here.
(4) Darken highlights.
(5) Lighten shadows.
(6) Darken shadows but again be careful not to clip as is the case in this example.
(7) Decrease contrast.
(8) Increase contrast.
(9) Default or Linear curve.
Note > In practice it is not a good idea to move the white and black points in Curves after they have been accurately established using the Blacks and Exposure sliders.

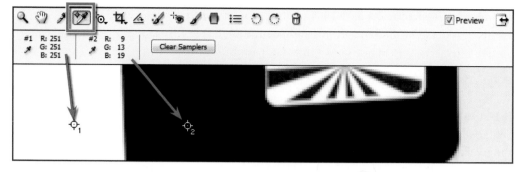

Targeting key values

To ensure highlights do not 'blow out' and the shadows do not print too dark it is possible to target, or set specific tonal values, for the highlight and shadow tones within the image using the Color Sample Tool in ACR or the eyedroppers (found in Photoshop's Levels and Curves dialog boxes). The tones that should be targeted are the lightest and darkest areas in the image with detail. The default settings of these eyedroppers are set to 0 (black) and 255 (white). These settings are only useful for targeting the white paper or black film edge. After establishing the darkest and lightest tones that will print using a step wedge (see 'Digital Printing') these target levels can be used as a guide with the Color Sample Tool display or assigned to the Photoshop eyedroppers.

Here we will use some generic values. When using ACR look for maximum RGB values around 250 for highlights and close to 5 for shadows. Make sure that you ignore specular highlights when adjusting highlight areas. These areas are generally reflections of light sources and can have a value of 255 as they typically contain no texture. Now unless you are targeting a neutral tone, the three color values will be different; make sure that the highest, for highlights, and lowest, for shadows, are close to these targets (in Photoshop we use a Brightness setting, taken from the HSB readout, of between 4 and 8 for shadows and 92 and 99 for highlights).

Setting target values in Adobe Camera Raw

To help with keeping an eye on how changes are affecting key parts of the picture, ACR has a special Color Sample Tool which can be used to display the RGB values of these picture parts. Use the following steps to use the Color Sample Tool:

1. Start by selecting the tool from the toolbar at the top of the workspace. Now move the tool around the image until you find the darkest part of the photo. To help with this process, turn on the clipping warnings and temporarily drag the Black slider to the right until you start to see clipping occur in the preview. The parts of the picture where the clipping is first noticeable will be the darkest part of the image.

2. Click the Color Sample Tool on this picture part. Notice that a small crosshairs icon has been placed on the picture and an entry area is now displayed below the toolbar and a new RGB entry is present. Now adjust the Black and/or Fill Light sliders until the RGB display shows 5 as the lowest of the values.

3. With the highlight clipping warning selected, drag the Exposure slider to the right until the preview shows a part of the photo that is being clipped. Place a second Color Sample Tool on this part of the photo. Using the Exposure and Recovery sliders adjust the picture part until the highest of the three values is around 250.

Note > Because the ACR Color Sample Tool displays RGB values, the targeted clipping areas might not necessarily be the blackest or whitest parts of the picture.

Cleaning an image – Step 7

The primary tools for removing blemishes, dust and scratches are the Spot Removal brush in Adobe Camera Raw and the 'Clone Stamp Tool', the 'Healing Brush Tool' and the 'Spot Healing Brush Tool' in Photoshop. The process for using ACR's Spot Removal tool borrows from both the Clone Stamp and Spot Healing Brush Tools in Photoshop.

The tool contains two components: a circle that indicates the target of the retouching, which is generally placed over the mark to remove, and a circle to select the source area that will be used as a reference for the color, tone and texture that will be painted over the mark. Sound familiar? It should – this is how the Clone Stamp Tool works. The difference is that with ACR's Spot Removal tool, the target area is selected first by click-dragging the cursor to the size of the mark. ACR then automatically searches for a suitable source point in the nearby pixels.

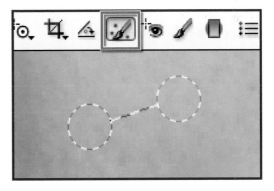

For ease of recognition the target circle is colored red and the source circle is a green hue. Both circles are linked with a straight line to indicate which source belongs to which target. For the majority of the time ACR does a pretty good job of selecting a source point, but there will be occasions when you may want to choose your own. This is a simple matter of click-dragging the source circle to a new location. The same technique can be used for moving the target circle. To change the target size use the Radius slider in the side bar at the right of the dialog. Holding down the Alt/Option key while clicking on the target circle deletes or cuts the retouching entry.

To Heal or Clone

The tool works in two modes – Heal and Clone. The Heal mode uses the technology found in the Spot Healing Brush to help match texture and tone of the source area to the target surrounds.

The Clone option gives more weighting to the specific qualities of the source area when over-painting the mark.

1. Start the process by ensuring that the preview window is enlarged to at least 100%. Select the magnification level from the pop-up menu on the bottom left of the dialog. Viewing the image zoomed in helps guarantee accuracy when specifying both target and source areas and presents a more precise preview of the results. Switch to the Hand Tool using the H keyboard shortcut, to click-drag the preview area around the photo. You can switch back to the Retouch Tool by pressing the letter B key.

2. Now drag the preview until you locate an area to be retouched. Select the Spot Removal tool from the ACR toolbar at the top of the dialog. By default the tool draws from the center, so move the pointer over the middle of the mark and click-drag the circle until it encompasses the blemish. This action sets the red target circle or the area to be retouched.

3. Unlike the situation with the Clone Stamp or Healing Brush Tools there is no need to select the sample area separately. Adobe Camera Raw automatically searches the surrounds of the target area for a likely source and draws a corresponding circle attached with a single straight line. The source circle is colored green to distinguish it from the red target circle. If the source circle has been positioned incorrectly or is providing less than acceptable results in the target area then simply click-drag the circle to a new location.

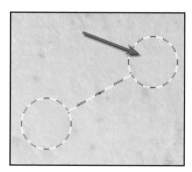

4. Once the target and source have been positioned, the retouching entry can be modified in a couple of different ways. The size of the target circle can be adjusted by clicking onto the circle and then changing the Radius setting in the tool's options contained in the right panel of the dialog (use the up and down arrows for 1 pixel changes). The mode used for retouching can be switched between Heal (the technology used by the Spot Healing Brush) and Clone (which simulates the way that the Clone Stamp Tool functions) using the drop-down menu also contained here. The Opacity option can be used to let more of the spot details below show through the correction.

5. Individual retouching entries can be removed or deleted altogether by cutting the entry. With the Spot Removal tool selected, hold down the Alt/Opt key while positioning the cursor over either the source or target circles of the retouching entry. The cursor will switch shapes to a pair of scissors (see aside). Clicking the mouse button will then delete the entry.

6. Once you have positioned and adjusted all retouching entries for a given image you can preview the results,

without the target and source circles, by deselecting the Show Overlay setting in the tool's options. To re-display the circles, reselect the option.

7. As all retouching entries created in Adobe Camera Raw are non-destructive they can be removed at any time, even if the file has been saved and reopened. To remove all retouching entries for the current image, select the Clear All button in the Retouch Tool options bar.

Sharpening an image – Step 8

Sharpening the image is the last step of the editing process. Many images benefit from some sharpening even if they were captured with sharp focus. The sliders in Adobe Camera Raw's Detail pane and Photoshop's 'Unsharp Mask' and the 'Smart Sharpen' filters from the 'Sharpen' group of filters are the most sophisticated and controllable of the sharpening filters. They are used to sharpen the edges by increasing the contrast where different tones meet. The pixels along the edge on the lighter side are made lighter and the pixels along the edge on the darker side are made darker.

BEFORE SHARPENING

AFTER SHARPENING

In the latest versions of ACR the sharpening controls have been increased to four from a single slider a couple of versions ago. Where originally users were only able to control the Amount of sharpening, now it is possible to manipulate how the effect is applied. Sharpening effects are controlled via the following sliders – Amount, Radius, Detail and Masking.

The **Amount** slider controls the strength of the sharpening effect. Move the slider to the right for stronger sharpening, to the left for more subtle effects. The **Radius** slider determines the number of pixels from an edge that will be changed in the sharpening process. The **Detail** slider is used to increase the local contrast around edge parts of the picture. An increase makes the picture's details appear sharper. The **Masking** control channels the sharpening effect through an edge locating mask.

Detail	≡
Sharpening	
Amount	121
Radius	1.5
Detail	13
Masking	22

Both the Detail and Masking sliders are used to target the sharpening more precisely in the image. Increasing the Detail value will raise the local contrast around smaller picture parts.

Reducing the value will decrease the appearance of haloes around these areas. Moving the Masking slider to the right gradually isolates the edges until the sharpening is only being applied through the most contrasty sections of the photograph.

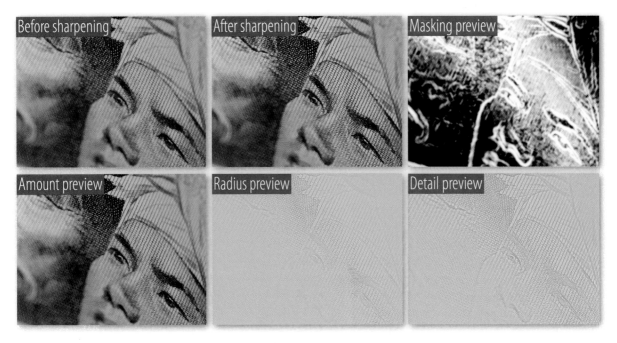

Previewing sharpening effects

With the preview at 100% magnification, holding down the Alt/Opt key will display different previews for each of the Sharpening sliders. The preview for the Amount slider shows the sharpening applied to the luminosity of the image. Both Radius and Detail sliders preview the value of the slider and the Masking option displays the mask being used for restricting where the sharpening is being applied. Remember the black areas of the mask restrict the sharpening and the light areas allow the sharpening to be applied.

Setting Workflow Options – Step 9

The section below the main preview window in ACR contains the Workflow Options settings. Here you can adjust the color depth (8 or 16 bits per channel), the color space (ICC profile), the image size (maintain capture dimensions for the picture or size up or down) and the image resolution (pixels per inch or pixels per centimeter). It is here that you adapt image characteristics to suit different outcomes. You can resize images to suit screen dimensions and also adjust the resolution of the file to match the dpi of the monitor or upsize a photo, select an appropriate ICC profile and depth for a poster print. With these options set you can then move onto deciding how to output the file.

For the project images, set the space to Adobe RGB, Depth 16 Bits/Channel, Resolution 240 ppi and Matte Paper Standard in the 'Sharpen For' section of the Workflow Options dialog.

Multiple photos can be selected in Bridge and passed to ACR for speedier processing.

Applying changes to multiple files – Step 10

We now have an idea about the types of changes that are regularly applied to images in order to optimize them. Although there are not many steps, applying them to a number of images could be a time-consuming task. This is especially true when shooting Raw as there are extra processing options available with this format than if you capture in TIFF or JPEG. For this reason there are several 'batch' processing features available in Bridge and ACR that can help speed up the enhancement of groups of photos.

Quality versus quantity

Now some of you might already be thinking to yourselves that any type of processing applied to a series of images rather than individual pictures will have to be less than optimal for each picture, and you would be right. But because of the nature of non-destructive editing and enhancing techniques that we are advocating here it is possible to apply some generic enhancement settings to groups of images quickly and then 'drill down' to each individual photo to apply the fine-tuning. This way of working is often used by photographers who take multiple images under the same lighting conditions or in the same environment.

General, overall adjustments are made to all the photos before working through each photo to fine-tune the results. And while we are talking of speeding up our photo workflow don't forget that other parts of the process such as adding metadata and outputting photos to a specific format, size and ICC profile can also be handled by batch processing. Let's see how we can apply the changes made to the first image to the others photographed at the same time.

Multi-select and Open In Camera Raw

As well as being able to process files one at a time, Adobe Camera Raw is capable of queueing multiple Raw files and working on this either in sequence or in sets of pictures. After several Raw photos are selected inside Bridge and then opened into ACR (File > Open in Camera Raw), you will notice the pictures are listed on the left side of the dialog. The same scenario occurs when selecting multiple pictures in the File > Open dialog from inside Photoshop. Once loaded into ACR, the files can be worked on individually by selecting each thumbnail in turn, making the necessary changes, and then moving to the next picture in the list.

Synchronized processing

But there is a more efficient way to process multiple files. Start with a group of images either taken under the same conditions with similar subject matter, or that you are wanting to process in a similar way (e.g. convert to grayscale and then sepia tone) open in Adobe Camera Raw. Now pick one of the photos that best represents the characteristics of the group (in the project files we used the image with the reference card) and proceed to make the corrections to color, tone and sharpness.

When complete, pick the Select All button at the top of the queue section of the dialog to pick all queued photos, or multi-select a subset of photos and then push the Synchronize button. The Synchronize dialog will be displayed, listing all the ACR controls that can be copied from the initial photo to the rest of the group. Select, or deselect, the controls as desired, and then click OK. Automatically the settings are synchronized across all the selected photos.

For the project images, this technique allows us to apply the enhancement changes made to the reference photo (the one containing the white balance card) across the other photos taken in that same studio session.

But don't forget to fine tune

The synchronization of development settings provides a good starting point for the enhancement process; all that now remains is to flick through each individual image and double-check that the settings are working for that specific photo. If need be, the settings can be fine-tuned to better suit any image.

In the case of the example images, the crop should be applied manually for each photo and slight changes made to highlight areas to account for small changes in lighting.

Note > Another way to select a subset of images from those displayed on the left of the workspace in ACR is to rate the pictures you want to apply common settings to and then select these photos with the Select Rated button (hold down the Alt/Opt key). With the Alt/Opt key still depressed, clicking the Synchronize button will synchronize using the last settings without displaying the Synchronize dialog.

Outputting processed files – Step 11

Now to the business end of the optimization task – outputting the file. When working with Raw files in Adobe Camera Raw you have more options at this point than if you were enhancing the photos in Photoshop. There is no longer a need to convert the picture from its Raw state in order to save the changes you have made. These alterations can be either

- stored with the Raw file,
- applied to the file and the photo then saved as a non-Raw format such as TIF or PSD,
- applied to the photo which is then passed to Photoshop, or
- the Raw file can be embedded as a Smart Object in a new Photoshop document.

Opening into Photoshop

The most basic option is to process the Raw file according to the settings and adjustments selected and then open the picture into the editing workspace of Photoshop. To do this click the Open Image button at the bottom right of the dialog. Select this route if you intend to edit or enhance the image beyond the changes made during the conversion.

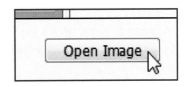

This option will maintain the Raw file in Bridge and create a new Photoshop document of the converted (no longer Raw-based) photo.

Saving the processed Raw file

There is also the ability to save converted Raw files from inside the ACR dialog via the Save button. This action opens the Save Options dialog which contains settings for inputting

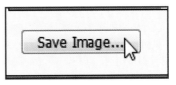

file names, choosing file types and extensions as well as file type-specific characteristics such as compression. Opt for this approach for fast processing of multiple files without the need to open them in Photoshop.

Applying the Raw conversion settings

ACR also allows the user to apply the current settings to the Raw photo without opening the picture into Photoshop. Just click the Done button. The great thing about working this way is that the settings are applied to the file losslessly. The photo remains in the Raw format. No changes are made to

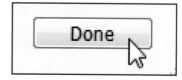

the underlying pixels, only to the instructions that are used to process the Raw file. When next the file is opened, the applied settings will show up in the ACR dialog ready for fine-tuning, or even changing completely.

When the ACR dialog is closed the thumbnail for the photo is updated in Bridge to reflect the changes. If adjustment settings have been applied to the photo, then a small settings icon is placed in the top right-hand corner of the thumbnail. When a picture has been cropped, a crop icon is displayed as well.

Creating a Smart Object

If you are wanting to continue working with your unconverted Raw file inside Photoshop then you will need to embed the file in a Smart Object layer within a Photoshop document. Unlike the earlier versions of ACR where this process had to be accomplished manually, it is now possible to embed the file using a single button inside ACR. While holding down the Shift key, press the Open Object button. This action automatically creates a new Photoshop document and embeds the Raw file in a Smart Object layer. Alternatively you can set this as a default option in the workflow options dialog box.

For the purposes of the project, select the portrait file without the reference card and open the file into Photoshop as a Smart Object.

Outputting more than one enhanced file

The same output options apply when working with multiple photos in ACR. Once all the settings have been applied, the images can be saved, opened, copied or opened as objects just like any other files. When more than one picture is selected from the queue grouping, the output button titles automatically change to plural to account for the fact that multiple photos will be saved, opened, copied, etc.

Saving, duplicating and resizing for web – Step 12

With the newly created Photoshop document open, go to the 'File' menu and select 'Save As'. Name the file, select 'Photoshop' as the file format and select the destination 'Where' the file is being saved. Check the 'Embed Color Profile' box and click 'Save'.

Keep the file name short using only the standard characters from the alphabet. Use a dash or underscore to separate words rather than leaving a space and always add or 'append' your file name after a full stop with the appropriate three- or four-letter file extension (.psd). This will ensure your files can be read by all and can be safely uploaded to web servers if required. Always keep a backup of your work on a remote storage device if possible.

Resize for web page viewing

Duplicate your file by going to 'Image > Duplicate'. Rename the file and select OK. Go to 'Image > Image Size'. Check the 'Constrain Proportions' and 'Resample Image' boxes. Type in 600 pixels in the 'Height' box (anything larger may not fully display in a browser window of a monitor set to 1024 × 768 pixels without the viewer having to use the scroll or navigation bars). Use the Bicubic Sharper option when reducing the file size for optimum quality.

Note > Internet browsers do not respect the resolution and document size assigned to the image by image-editing software – image size is dictated by the resolution of the individual viewer's monitor. Two images that have the same pixel dimensions but different resolutions will appear the same size when displayed in a web browser. A typical screen resolution is often stated as being 72 ppi but actual monitor resolutions vary enormously.

JPEG format options

After resizing you should set the image size on screen to 100% or 'Actual Pixels' from the View menu (this is the size of the image as it will appear in a web browser on a monitor of the same resolution).

Go to 'File' menu and select 'Save As'. Select JPEG from the Format menu. Label the file with a short name with no gaps or punctuation marks (use an underscore if you have to separate two words) and finally ensure the file carries the extension .jpg (e.g. portrait_one.jpg). Click 'OK' and select a compression/quality setting from the 'JPEG Options' dialog box. With the Preview box checked you can check to see if there is excessive or minimal loss of quality at different compression/quality settings in the main image window.

Choose a compression setting that will balance quality with file size (download time). High compression (low quality) leads to image artifacts, lowering the overall quality of the image. There is usually no need to zoom in to see the image artifacts as most browsers and screen presentation software do not allow this option.

Note > Double-clicking the Zoom Tool in the Tools palette will set the image to actual pixels or 100% magnification.

Image Options: The quality difference on screen at 100% between the High and Maximum quality settings may not be easily discernible. The savings in file size can, however, be enormous, thereby enabling much faster uploading and downloading via the Internet.

Format Options: Selecting the 'Progressive' option from the Format Options enables the image to be displayed in increasing degrees of sharpness as it is downloading to a web page, rather than waiting to be fully downloaded before being displayed by the web browser.

Size: The open file size is not changed by saving the file in the JPEG file format as this is dictated by the total number of pixels in the file. The closed file size is of interest when using the JPEG Options dialog box as it is this size that dictates the speed at which the file can be uploaded and downloaded via the Internet. The quality and size of the file is a balancing act if speed is an issue due to slow modem speeds.

Save for Web & Devices

The Save for Web & Devices command from the File menu offers the user an alternative, all-in-one, option for resizing, optimizing and previewing the image prior to saving the file in the JPEG format. Access the Save for Web & Devices feature from the File menu. Click on the 2-up tab to see a before and after version of your image. Click on the second image and, from the 'Preview Menu', choose Internet Standard sRGB from the listed options: Monitor Color, Legacy Macintosh (No Color Management), Internet Standard sRGB (No Color Management) or Use Document Profile. This will enable you to anticipate how your image may be viewed in software that cannot read the ICC profile that Photoshop normally embeds as part of the color management process, e.g. most web browsers.

To adjust the color or tone prior to saving as a JPEG exit the Save for Web feature and go to View > Proof Setup and then choose Internet Standard sRGB option. With the Proof Setup switched on, adjustments may be required to both image brightness and saturation in order to return the appearance of the image to 'normal'. Brightness should be controlled via the 'Gamma' slider in the 'Levels' adjustment feature and color saturation via the 'Hue/Saturation' adjustment feature.

Capture and enhance workflow overview

1. Capture an image with sufficient pixels for the intended output device.
2. Download or transfer files.
3. Rate and add keywords to files.
4. Resize and crop the image.
5. Adjust the color.
6. Tweak the tonality.
7. Clean the image.
8. Sharpen the photo.
9. Apply the processing and output the picture.

Paul Allister

raw processing

Coals Bay, Tasmania by Philip Andrews

essential skills

- Take Raw processing beyond the basics outlined in the last chapter.
- Apply localized corrections to images inside Adobe Camera Raw.
- Convert Raw files to digital negatives for archival storage.

Introduction

One of the big topics of conversation over the last few years has been the subject of 'Raw' files and 'digital negatives'. During this time the capture format has gone from being an option for high-end work only to a key part of most professionals' workflows. For this reason we have reworked much of the content of the book to take into account Raw enabled workflows. In the last chapter we looked at the first few steps involved in optimizing a digital capture, be it raw based or TIFF or JPEG. And you will have noticed that we suggest that these basic steps should be undertaken in Adobe Camera Raw irrespective of if you shoot in Jpeg, Tiff or Raw. Here we will delve further into Raw processing and pay particular attention to the other editing and enhancement options that are possible when altering your photos directly in Adobe Camera Raw or as an embedded Raw file within Photoshop CS5.

Camera Raw

Note > Keep in mind that for many of the techniques there is no longer the need to convert your file from its native raw format in order to continue editing the picture in Photoshop. This way of working ensures that not only are your images always derived from the primary capture data and not a second generation derivative, but that you maintain the flexibility of the Raw format for altering characteristics such as white balance, tonality, color space and sharpness non-destructively.

All digital cameras capture in Raw but only Digital SLRs and the medium- to high-end 'Prosumer' cameras offer the user the option of saving the images in this Raw format. Selecting the Raw format in the camera instead of JPEG or TIFF stops the camera from processing the color data collected from the sensor. Digital cameras typically process the data collected by the sensor by applying the white balance, sharpening and contrast settings set by the user in the camera's menus. The camera then compresses the bit depth of the color data from 12 to 8 bits per channel before saving the file as a JPEG or TIFF file. Selecting the Raw format prevents this image processing taking place. The Raw data is what the sensor 'saw' before the camera processed the image, and many photographers have started to refer to this file as the 'digital negative'. The term 'digital negative' is also used by Adobe for their archival format (.dng) for Raw files.

Processing Raw data

In the last chapter we saw that unprocessed Raw data is edited and enhanced in Adobe Camera Raw (ACR) and the resultant file can be opened in Photoshop or Bridge. Variables such as bit depth, white balance, exposure, brightness, contrast, saturation, sharpness, noise reduction and even the crop can all be assigned as part of this process. There are also tools for performing localized corrections. Think 'dodge and burn' but with the power to paint on changes of saturation, contrast, exposure, clarity and sharpness in portions of the photo. In the version of Adobe Camera Raw that ships with Photoshop CS5, the raw processing engine has been rewritten to provide better sharpness and noise control. There is also a sophisticated lens correction system (available in the ACR 6.1 update) and creative options for adding stylized grain and improved handling of post-crop vignetting (especially for images where highlights appear in the vignette area). When these improvements are added to the existing spread of tools in the utility you can see why more and more key editing activities should be undertaken in ACR before moving to Photoshop.

In addition, performing these image-editing tasks on the full high-bit Raw data (rather than making the changes after the file has been processed by the camera) enables the user to achieve a higher quality end-result. Double-clicking a Raw file, or selecting 'Open in Camera Raw' in Bridge, opens the Adobe Camera Raw (ACR) dialog box, where the user can prepare and optimize the file which can then be passed to Photoshop for further processing. If the user selects 16 Bits/Channel in the Workflow Options, the 12 bits per channel data from the image sensor is rounded up – each channel is now capable of supporting 32,769 levels instead of the 256 levels we are used to working with in the 8 bits per channel option. Choosing the 16 Bits/Channel option enables even more manipulation in the main Photoshop editing space without the risk of degrading the image quality.

When the optimized raw file is passed to Photoshop from ACR we have the option of converting a copy of the photo from raw to a Photoshop document (.psd) or embedding the picture in a Smart Object, which in turn is stored in a new Photoshop document. The advantage of the second approach is that as an embedded Smart Object the Raw file format of the original capture is maintained (and protected). In both pathways any changes you make to the appearance of the image in the ACR will be applied to the image that is opened in Photoshop's main editing space but won't alter the original image data of the Raw file. The adjustments you make in the ACR dialog box are instead saved as either a sidecar file (.xmp) or in the computer's Camera Raw database.

Foundation Project 2

In the last chapter we looked at the basic adjustments that you would make to a Raw file in order to optimize the photo; here we will employ some of the additional features to take our ACR-based editing even further. If you don't have your own Raw files to work on, the example file, named Foundation_Project_02, is located on the book's accompanying DVD. The reader should not see this as a rigid step-by-step guide but instead use the project file to get a feel for the techniques discussed here.

One of the strengths of working with Raw files is their ability to capture and use large amounts of data. This project uses the power of the new local correction tools in ACR together with the extra detail contained in high-bit Raw capture to reveal hidden detail in the blown highlight area of this photojournalism photo.

Lens corrections – Step 1

In the 6.1 update of Adobe Camera Raw the features in the Lens Corrections pane have been dramatically improved to include both automatic (Profile tab) and manual (Manual tab) controls for the removal, or correction of the three most common lens-based errors: geometric distortion, chromatic aberration, and vignetting. The Automatic corrections are lens and camera specific and are applied to the whole of the image making this a good first step for your processing.

Profile-Based Corrections

After selecting Enable Lens Profile Corrections under the Profile tab of the Lens Corrections panel, an installed profile that matches your camera and lens combination are used to apply precise distortion corrections to your photos. Suitable profiles can be automatically located based on the EXIF data recorded with the image, or selected by camera make, model and profile. Individual error types can be adjusted via the Correction Amount sliders in the lower section of the pane. When set to 100 the slider applies the profile correction fully. Values of less than 100 reduce the correction effect and amount over 100 multiply the effect.

Note > These Lens Correction features are also available as a filter in Photoshop CS5 and can be used in Bridge CS5 to batch process multiple files in a single step. For more details about these applications, plus a guide for creating your own compatible lens profiles go to the Filters chapter later in the book.

Manual Corrections

Brand new for ACR6 is the inclusion of five new transformation sliders. Previously these controls have only been available in Lens Correction filter in Photoshop. Their inclusion here provides an extra level of manual adjustment for tweaking your photos. It is important to note that these controls work in addition to the profile-based corrections and so can be used to fine-tune those enhancements.

Transform: The Distortion slider controls barrel and pincushion adjustments and the Vertical option is used to reduce the appearance of converging verticals which are often present in images taken with wide angle lenses when the camera is tilted upwards. The Horizontal slider pivots the image towards or away from the viewer correcting horizontal perspective issues and Rotate is used to straighten a titled photo. The final slider, Scale, can be used to adjust the magnification of the picture after the corrections have been made.

The new Transform controls provide the ability to manually adjust key distortion characteristics of the photo. The examples here show the changes produced with the following settings (1) Distortion –65, (2) Vertical –47, (3) Horizontal –35, (4) Rotate 10, and (5) Scale 50.

Chromatic Aberration: Two sliders are available to help with Chromatic Aberration, or the situation where edges recorded towards the outer parts of the frame contain slight misalignment of colors. This is caused by a lens not focusing all the visible wavelengths together on a sensor. The sliders are designed to realign the problem areas and, in so doing, remove the colored edges.

Fringing: Also included is the ability to lessen the sensor 'flooding' caused by overexposure in picture areas such as specular highlights. The Defringe drop-down menu contains three options – Off, Highlight Edges and All Edges. Selecting the Highlight Edges option decreases the purple-colored areas that often surround brightly lit metallic surfaces or sparkly water reflections. These errant colors are not caused by lens aberrations but rather result from a small selection of sensor sites being overexposed. Switching to the All Edges setting applies the effect to all the fringe areas in the image.

The Defringe option helps remove the purple color that can surround very bright highlights.

Lens Vignetting: Vignetting is the slight darkening or lightening of the corners of a photo due to the inability of the lens to provide even illumination across the whole surface of the sensor. This is most prevalent in lower quality ultra-wide-angle lenses when coupled with cameras with full frame sensors. Two sliders are included in the Lens Vignetting section of the Lens Corrections pane to deal with this problem. When the Amount slider is moved to the right it lightens the corners. Dragging the control to the left has the opposite effect. The Midpoint control alters the amount of the frame affected by the vignetting correction. Higher settings concentrate the corrections to the corners of the frame.

Note > Post-crop vignetting controls have been moved to the new Fx pane. Instructions for applying this adjustment along with adding grain to your photo can be found in later in the chapter.

Project application: To apply lens correction in the example image, click on the Profile tab in the Lens Corrections pane in Adobe Camera Raw. Select the Enable Lens Corrections setting and choose Sony, DT 18–200mm f3.5–6.3, Sony A-700 from the Make, Model and Profile menus.

Straighten, crop and size – Step 2

Start the process by straightening and cropping the photo. Select the Straighten Tool on the top left-hand side of the ACR dialog box. Click on one end of a part of the framing in the roof structure that is meant to be horizontal, and drag the cursor to the other end and then let go of the mouse button to automatically straighten the image. Cropping in ACR does not delete pixels but merely hides them and these pixels can be recovered if necessary.

Crop the image to the correct aspect ratio or shape using the Crop Tool. Select one of the existing aspect ratios or create your own using the 'Custom' command found in the Crop menu. The aspect ratio of the bounding box will change when a new format is selected. Click and drag on any corner handle to alter the composition or framing of the image. Use the keyboard shortcut Command/Ctrl + Z to undo any action that you are not happy with.

Note > The Crop Tool setting affects the Straighten Tool so make sure Crop is set to normal.

The Crop Size (pixel dimensions) and Resolution can also be set in ACR. If your target output is specified in inches or cms you will need to perform some calculations to ascertain the optimum crop size (divide the dimensions of the document needed by the optimum image resolution required by the output device). As crop sizes are only approximate in ACR you should choose a size that is slightly larger than the actual dimensions required.

Color space – Step 3

There are four choices of color space in the ACR dialog box and it is important to select the most appropriate one for your workflow before you start to assign color values to the image in ACR (using the controls located in the Workflow Options dialog displayed by clicking the highlighted blue text at the bottom of the screen). ColorMatch RGB is rarely used these days (it was a space commonly used before color management came of age back at the end of the last decade) so the choice is now limited to just three.

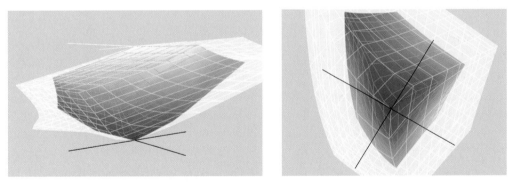

The wide gamut ProPhoto space (white) compared to the Adobe RGB (1998) space (color).

The main difference between the three major spaces is the size of the color gamut (the range of colors that each space supports). There is not much point in working with a color space larger than necessary as the colors outside of the monitor space will not be visible and they cannot be reproduced by an output device with a limited gamut range. The three color spaces are as follows:

sRGB – This is the smallest of the three common color spaces (with a range of colors similar to a typical monitor) and should be selected if your images are destined for screen viewing or are destined to be printed by a print service provider using the sRGB color space.

Adobe RGB (1998) – This space is larger than the sRGB space and is the most common color space used in the commercial industry, where the final image is to appear in print. It is a good compromise between the gamut of a color monitor and the gamut of an average CMYK printing press. It is also a space that is suitable for some Print Service Providers and standard quality inkjet prints, e.g. a budget inkjet printer using matte or semi-gloss paper.

ProPhoto RGB – This is the largest color space and can be selected if you have access to a print output device with a broad color gamut (larger than most CMYK devices are capable of offering). When working in ProPhoto the user must stay in 16 Bits/Channel for the entire editing process. Converting to smaller color spaces in Photoshop's main editing space usually results in loss of data in the channels regardless of the rendering intent selected in the conversion process. This loss of data may not be immediately obvious if you do not check the histogram after the conversion process. The data loss is most apparent in bright saturated colors where texture and fine detail may be missing as the color information in the individual channels has become clipped in the conversion process.

Choosing a bit depth – Step 4

Select the 'Depth' in the Workflow Options (click on the blue text at the base of the ACR dialog box). If the user selects the 16 Bits/Channel option, the 12 bits per channel data from the image sensor is rounded up – each channel is now capable of supporting 32,769 levels. In order to produce the best quality digital image, it is essential to preserve as much information about the tonality and color of the subject as possible.

If the digital image has been corrected sufficiently in ACR for the requirements of the output device, the file can be opened in Photoshop's main editing space in 8 bits per channel mode. However, if the digital image has further corrections applied in the 8 bits per channel mode, the final quality will be compromised. Sixteen-bit editing is invaluable if maximum quality is required from an original image file that requires further editing of tonality and color in Photoshop after leaving the Camera Raw dialog box. If you have assigned the ProPhoto RGB color space in ACR you must use the 16 Bits/Channel color space in Photoshop to avoid color banding or posterization.

Final histograms after editing the same image in 8 and 16 bits per channel modes.

The problem with 8-bit editing

As an image file is edited extensively in 8 Bits/Channel mode (24-bit RGB) the histogram starts to 'break up', or become weaker. 'Spikes' or 'comb lines' may become evident in the resulting histogram after the file has been flattened. This is due to the fact that there are only 256 levels or tones per channel to describe the full color range of the image. This is usually sufficient if the color space is not huge (as is the case with ProPhoto RGB) and the amount of editing required is limited. If many gaps start to appear in the histogram as a result of extensive adjustment of pixel values this can result in 'banding'. The smooth change between dark and light, or one color and another, may no longer be possible with the data supplied from a weak histogram. The result is a transition between color or tone that is visible as a series of steps in the final image.

A 'Smart' solution

By opening a Raw file as a Smart Object (Open Object – hold down the Shift key if this option is not visible or better yet set as the default opening action in the Workflow Options dialog) the user can open a Raw file in 8 Bits/Channel but keep the integrity of the histogram by returning to the ACR dialog box to make any large changes to hue, saturation or brightness (luminosity) values. Though working with 16 bits per channel is always preferable, with some filters there is only the option to apply the changes to an 8 bits per channel file.

White balance – Step 5

As we saw in the last chapter, the first step in optimizing the color and tonal values for the color space we have chosen to work in is to set the white balance by choosing one of the presets from the drop-down menu. Remember that there are three approaches to setting white balance:

- Select a preset White Balance option based on specific lighting sources – Daylight, Cloudy, Shade, Tungsten, etc.
- Manually adjust the 'Temperature' and 'Tint' sliders to remove any color cast present in the image, or
- Alternatively you can simply click on the 'White Balance' eyedropper in the small tools palette (top left-hand corner of the dialog box) and then click on any neutral tone you can find in the image.

For more details on using these features with your image, revisit the White Balance section in the previous chapter.

Control the White Balance in your image using either the drop-down presets, the Temperature and Tint sliders or the White Balance tool.

Note > Although it is a 'White Balance' you actually need to click on a tone that is not too bright. Clicking on a light or mid gray is preferable. A photographer looking to save time may introduce a 'gray card' in the first frame of a shoot to simplify the task.

Advanced WB fine-tuning

If precise white balance is extremely critical the photographer can shoot a xRite ColorChecker Chart that uses a range of color and gray patches. The user can then target the Red, Green and Blue patches and fine-tune the white balance using the Camera Calibration controls in ACR. The settings grouped here enabled photographers to alter the way the colors captured by their cameras, and recorded in the raw file, are interpreted by the software. Essentially this is a process that edits the default profile that Adobe had developed for the camera. These Adobe based camera profiles are not strictly ICC profiles but they are the core technology used in Lightroom and ACR for interpreting the colors and tones captured by the camera.

Though daunting to start with, the options found under the Calibrate tab do provide an amazing amount of control and are used by many professional photographers to 'profile' the way that the color from their cameras is interpreted by the Raw converter. This is particularly useful for building a profile for neutralizing the casts that are present in images photographed under mixed artificial lighting conditions.

Camera Calibration section in Camera Raw.

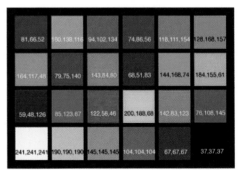

An xRite ColorChecker Chart.

Given the level of complexity involved in this process, most photographers simply do not bother, preferring to use the general profiles supplied by Adobe for their specific camera.

Custom Profile Creation

Now for those of you who really like to 'tinker under the hood', you can create your own custom profiles, which in turn, leads to better color capture. The process involves photographing a reference board like the xRite ColorChecker Passport under the lighting conditions that are typical for the scene. The Raw file is then opened into Adobe Camera Raw and the color and tones of the captured file are adjusted with the sliders in the Camera Calibration section of ACR to match the 'true' values of the patches. Performing this process manually is tedious and takes a lot of time; a better approach is to employ the help of the software that accompanies the ColorChecker Passport.

With pretty much drag and drop simplicity, the program uses the reference image to create a new profile. The original capture is converted to DNG, Adobe's Digital Negative format, before being imported into the ColorChecker Passport software where the swatches are analyzed and a custom profile produced. The resulting file is then saved and made available as one of the Profile options in the drop-down menu of the Camera Calibration pane/tab in Adobe Camera Raw.

Automating Profile Settings

To automate the process of applying the profile simply change profiles for an example image and then select the Save Settings option from the Settings button (the button icon looks like a list) at the top right of the Presets pane. Deselect all Settings except Calibration and save the preset. To use this preset, simply select the Preset tab on the far right and select the preset of your choice from the list. It will automatically be applied to the image open in ACR.

The ColorChecker Passport reference target.

Custom profile creation in the ColorChecker Passsport software.

Custom Camera profiles loaded into the drop-down menu in Adobe Camera Raw.

Note > Using a custom profile with your photo won't permanently change your picture. To revert the image back to its original settings all you need to do is select one of the Adobe created profiles from the Camera Profile menu in the Camera Calibration section of ACR.

Reprocessing older Raw files

As we have already mentioned one of the biggest changes for Adobe Camera Raw is the reworking of the engine that builds the images we see from the raw data captured by the camera. It is largely this engine swap that underpins much of the improved sharpness and noise reduction results produces in ACR 6, but how does it fit in with images that have been processed in previous versions of the utility?

When opening the file, Adobe Camera Raw 6.0 respects the processing I have already made to the photo and dutifully displays the picture using these settings. I do, however, have the addition of a warning button displayed in the bottom right of the display. This indicates that the photo is being processed using the 2003 demosaicing engine and that it is possible for me to reprocess the file with the 2010 version. When you click this button, ACR does its thing, the warning button disappears and new life is breathed into the old picture.

The warning button is displayed in the bottom right of the workspace when a raw file that has been processed with the 2003 engine is opened in ACR 6. Clicking the button will rework the photo with the new 2010 engine.

FULL IMAGE

2010 PROCESSING @ 300%

2003 PROCESSING @ 300%

The details in the examples clearly show the difference between the two different demosaicing methods. The 2010 option displays more detail and at the same time smoother transitions than its 2003 counterpart.

What's the difference?

At first glance you mightn't see much difference between the two versions of the file but if you do a side-by-side comparison at 300% you will start to notice some distinct differences. The first thing you should see is that the somewhat plastic-looking flat areas of tone that appear with some images has disappeared. Instead, in its place is a more textured rendering of the photo.

There is more detail present in the 2010 processed file and the detail is more refined. The graduation between contrasting areas is smoother and the middle values of the picture, in particular, feel sharper and cleaner. In fact, the differences are so pronounced that many photographers are now revisiting their older images and reworking them with the new version of Adobe Camera Raw (or Lightroom 3 – which has the same engine) to take advantage of the image improvements the new engine offers.

Global tonal adjustments – Step 6

In the last chapter we looked at how careful adjustment of the tonal controls listed directly beneath the White Balance sliders will allow you to get the best out of the dynamic range of your imaging sensor, thereby creating a tonally rich image with full detail. For more details on using these controls revisit the appropriate section in the last chapter.

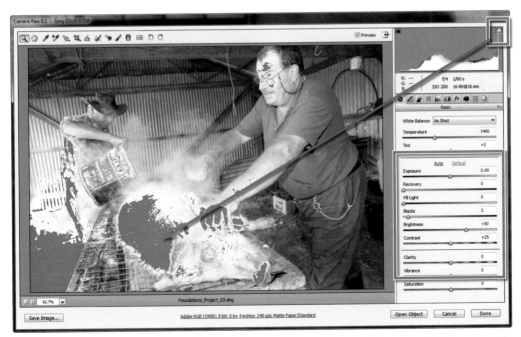

The example image has some real problems with overexposure and therefore potential clipping in the highlight areas of the photo. Careful adjustment of the Exposure and Recovery sliders will help with this problem but not totally remove it.

In this example we will start by adjusting the tones and color 'globally'. That is, making changes to the whole of the image. Next, unlike in the previous chapter, we will fine-tune the results by using the new Adjustment Brush to alter specific sections of the photo. These types of changes are brand new to ACR and are called 'local' corrections.

But we're getting ahead of ourselves. To start with the global changes you will need to set the brightest points within the image using the 'Exposure' slider and darkest points using the 'Blacks' slider. Make sure that the clipping warnings for both highlights and shadows are active when making these changes. Immediately you will notice how much of the highlight detail is displayed with the red highlight warning. Dragging the Exposure slider to the left will help reduce this problem, but don't go so far as to render the face of the subjects too dark. Some clipping will still be apparent at this point. Use the 'Recovery' slider to help rescue these highlight tones, which may otherwise clip, and also employ the 'Fill Light' slider to lighten the very dark shadow tones that may not print with any texture or detail (think of Recovery and Fill Light as non-destructive variants of the shadow/highlight adjustment feature). The 'Brightness' and 'Contrast' sliders can be used to fine-tune the midtone values. If the image becomes too dark because you are dragging the Exposure slider to the left in order to protect highlight detail, instead use the Recovery slider to darken the highlight detail without darkening the midtone values.

Advanced clipping information

Remember that holding down the 'Alt/ Option' key when adjusting either the 'Exposure' or 'Blacks' slider will also provide an indication in the image window of the channel, or channels, where clipping is occurring. Excessive color saturation for the color space selected, as well as overly dark shadows and overly bright highlights, will also influence the amount of clipping that occurs. Clipping in a single channel (indicated by the red, green or blue warning

The channel, or mix of channels, being clipped are also displayed as a change of color of the arrow in the clipping warning buttons at the top left and right of the histogram.

colors in the arrows) will not always lead to a loss of detail in the final image. However, when the secondary colors appear (cyan, magenta and yellow), you will need to take note, as loss of information in two channels starts to get a little more serious. Loss of information in all three channels (indicated by black when adjusting the shadows and white when adjusting the exposure) should be avoided.

Note > Large adjustments to the 'Brightness', 'Contrast' or 'Saturation' sliders may necessitate further 'tweaking' of the Exposure, Recovery, Fill Light or Blacks sliders.

Controlling saturation and vibrance – Step 7

Increasing saturation in ACR can lead to clipping in the color channels. Clipping saturated colors can lead to a loss of fine detail and texture. Saturation clipping is especially noticeable when you have selected the smaller sRGB color space and have captured an image with highly saturated colors. As this image will end up being a split-toned monochrome we'll step away

High levels of saturation clipping present in this file were corrected with the help of the Saturation controls in the HSL tab – saturation could then be increased reasonably non-destructively using the Vibrance slider.
Image of Melissa Zappa by Victoria Verdon Roe

from the example photo for a moment in order to illustrate saturation and vibrance. Instead we will use the more colorful image to illustrate these issues. The Vibrance slider applies a non-linear increase in saturation (targeting pixels of lower saturation). It is also designed to protect skin tones in order to prevent faces from getting too red. It should create less clipping problems when compared to the Saturation control.

In images where some colors readily clip due to their natural vibrance (especially when using a smaller gamut such as sRGB), lowering the global saturation in order to protect the clipping of a single color can result in a lifeless image. In these instances the user can turn to the HSL tab to edit the saturation of colors independently.

Note > Choosing a larger color space such as ProPhoto RGB, where the colors rarely clip, is only a short-term solution. The color gamut must eventually be reduced to fit the gamut of the output device. ACR is currently the best place in CS4 to massage these colors into the destination space.

Localized correction – Step 8

In previous versions of ACR, with the exception of the Spot Removal tool, which corrected dust marks on small portions of the image, all alterations were applied to all of the image. This meant that for those of us who wanted to perform a seemingly simple operation, such as a little dodging or burning, we needed to transfer the file from ACR to Photoshop where the editing changes could be made. 'Okay this is only a small inconvenience' you may say, but it was the changes made to the file during this transfer that had Raw devotees frustrated. In moving the picture from ACR to Photoshop, the file needed to be converted from its Raw origins to a standard file format such as PSD (Photoshop), TIFF, or JPEG. All the advantages of non-destructive editing changes that constitute the very basis of enhancement steps in ACR are lost in the conversion process. There is no getting around the fact that after conversion any alterations applied to the dodged and burnt file were being made to processed pixels, not the virgin captured pixels of the original file.

The red areas indicate some of the masking involved in the application of local correction to this image. You can preview the adjustment areas by holding the mouse cursor over the pin icon used to indicate the starting point for the adjustment or selecting the Show Mask option in the Adjustment Brush pane.

In the last couple of releases it is possible to perform localized corrections (as opposed to global ones) directly inside the program. More important is the fact that these corrections are applied in the same non-destructive manner as all other alterations in the program. In other words, the changes are made via a series of parameter settings which are stored in an associated file and are used to create a preview of how the Raw file would look with the settings applied. It is this processed preview that we see in the ACR preview and Bridge Content and Preview panes. The primary Raw file is never converted to a non-Raw format (except when exporting or opening in Photoshop) and as the enhancements are simply a series of stored settings, the file can be restored to its original appearance at any time.

Two new local correction features are contained in the ACR toolbar – the Adjustment Brush (shortcut key – K) and the Graduated Filter (shortcut key – G).

But how do local corrections work?

Most localized corrections are based around a new tool called the Adjustment Brush (shortcut key – K). The tool uses a brush type icon and is grouped together with the other tools in the toolbar that sits at the top of the workspace. Here you will also find a new Graduated Filter Tool as well, but more on this later.

Applying a localized correction is essentially a two-step process. First you mark out the adjustment area (similar to making a correction) and then you fine-tune the degree and type of adjustments made to this area. It is important to understand that unlike an action such as dodging and burning, performed in Photoshop, working with local adjustments in ACR means that you can manipulate the degree of adjustment and, if need be, you can also switch the image parameter you are adjusting as well after the changes have been made. For example, after painting on the adjustment area using an Exposure value of –2.80 EV so that the effects can be clearly seen on the image, you can then change to the Edit mode for the tool and drag the Exposure value back to 0 and input a value for Saturation instead. If that isn't powerful enough you can also create a custom adjustment mix that includes settings for multiple image characteristics all applied to the same adjustment area.

Adjustment Brush workflow:

A. Select the Adjustment Brush – The first step in the process of using localized corrections in Adobe Camera Raw involves selecting the new Adjustment Brush Tool situated in the toolbar at the top of the workspace. This will open up a new pane containing a range of image characteristics that you can adjust within your image. Select the primary effect that you wish to change from the pane. Here I used Exposure with a setting of – 2.74 EV.

B. Set Brush tip characteristics – Next you need to set the brush tip characteristics. You essentially have four controls here – Size, Feather, Flow (similar to airbrush where multiple strokes build up the effect) and Density or level of effect. The brush tip is displayed with two concentric circles. The outer one represents the edge of the brush, the inner circle outlines where the brush is solid and the space between is the width of the feather.

C. Paint in the adjustment mask – With the effect and the brush tip now set, move the cursor over the image and paint in the area to be adjusted. Notice that the adjustment is made in real time on your image. I purposely used a strong 'underexposure' setting so that I could clearly see the extent of the painted area. Don't be concerned if the effect is too strong or not the style required as these can be tweaked later. Continue to build up the mask by painting in the areas to be adjusted. Alternatively you can click the Show Mask option to display the selected areas.

D. On-the-fly masking – At the bottom of the Adjustment Brush pane is an Auto Mask option. Use this setting to get ACR to only apply the adjustment up to the edge of a painted area. When painting with this option selected make sure to keep the inner circle within the area to be adjusted.

E. Fine-tune the adjustment – Notice that once you start to paint, the mode at the top of the pane switches from New to Add. While in the Add mode you can proceed to fine-tune the changes made to the various image characteristics using the sliders. Despite the fact that I initially selected the Exposure slider, I can now include other characteristics in the mix.

Adding to, subtracting from and creating new localized corrections

Adding to – Once an adjustment area or mask has been created it is possible to extend the area by selecting the Pin icon for the area. This activates the Add mode for an existing painted area. Now continue to paint with the brush tip. The enhancement changes for the newly painted area will be exactly the same style and degree as those already existing in the previously painted section. While in the Add mode it is possible to change the image's characteristics (e.g. Exposure, Brightness, Contrast, etc.) that are being changed by the adjustment. The tool is automatically placed in this mode after creating a new mask. You must select another mode (New or Erase) or choose another tool from the ACR toolbar to cease the Add function.

Subtracting from – As well as being able to add to an existing adjustment area you can also remove parts from this mask. To do so either hold down the Alt/Opt key and paint away the areas to remove or click on the Erase entry in the Adjustment Brush pane. While in this mode you can refine the areas of the picture that are being affected by the localized adjustment.

Creating new – When first selecting the Adjustment Brush the feature is placed in the New mode in anticipation of creating a fresh or initial localized adjustment. The Adjustment Brush automatically changes from New to Add modes when you apply the first stroke of a new mask. From that time forward additional painting strokes will continue to build the mask until a new mode is selected or you select another tool.

Note > To jump out of the Adjustment Brush mode, just click on another tool.

Project application: Using the example image and the Adjustment brush, make two separate localized corrections to the photo. First, burn in extra detail to the lower left part of the picture and the back of the pig by painting in negative Exposure. Next, use the Auto Mask to isolate the blue shirt area on the subject on the right and reduce the saturation of the shirt. Try switching between Add and Erase modes to fine-tune the areas being adjusted.

Raw versus JPEG corrections

Being able to perform localized corrections in ACR is a real improvement in tricky situations such as the example image used here. This is because the corrections are performed on the Raw file. Stated like that, this fact may seem a little underwhelming but have a look at the example images on the next page and you will see why this is a key issue.

By capturing and enhancing in Raw it is possible to make use of all the information contained in the high-bit file to burn in some of the seemingly lost details using the new local correction options (the Adjustment Brush) in Adobe Camera Raw 5.0. In contrast, trying to burn in lost detail using a JPEG version of the image with Photoshop tools only results in muddy textureless areas.

The original was shot in an open barn on one of the back roads of Tasmania. The lighting was always going to be tricky so to help even out the foreground some fill flash was added to the foreground. This worked fine in that portion of the image, but further back and to the left, the extra light coming into the barn blew out the highlights.

It is easy to lose detail in highlight and shadow areas with incorrect exposure settings. When a camera is set to JPEG as the capture format, often subtle details that would be held in the high-bit Raw file are lost during the conversion to the lower-bit JPEG format. If we take the process one step further and try to burn the lost detail back into the photo using the Burn Tool in Photoshop you will start to see the problem. Rather than ending up with extra visual information we end up with a muddy mess.

If, instead, the image was captured and stored in Raw and then processed in Adobe Camera Raw 5.0 using the new localized correction tools then the outcome would be drastically different (see above for the comparisons). Because of the extra bit depth of the Raw file, more of the original details are retained in the highlight areas of the image. When ACR is put to work on these details a substantial amount of seemingly lost information can be revealed. If you have been wavering about whether to switch from JPEG capture to Raw then this example should help you with the decision.

Grayscale conversion and toning – Step 9

At this point the example image has been adjusted both globally and locally and, if we wanted a color outcome, we would apply some sharpening and noise reduction (see Step 11) and then output the file (see Step 12), but in this instance the end result is a split-toned monochrome. So the next part of the process is to convert to gray and then we'll tint the photo with separate colors for highlights and shadows.

HSL/Grayscale

Drawing inspiration from the type of features located in Lightroom, the options in the HSL/Grayscale pane provide control of the Hue, Saturation and Luminance of each color group (red, orange, yellow, green, aqua, blue, purple and magenta) independently.

This is a great improvement over what was available previously, when color changes were limited to red, green and blue channel-based divisions and saturation control. There are also three tabs across the top of the pane that allow color range adjustments to be made to the Hue (color), Saturation (color strength) and Luminance (brightness) independently. Clicking the Grayscale tickbox switches the pane to a monochrome conversion mode where the color range sliders adjust the type of gray that the hue is being mapped to. Let's look at each section in turn.

The HSL/Grayscale pane provides color range-based controls for altering the hue, saturation and luminance of the colors in your photo. In the Grayscale mode you can adjust how specific colors are mapped to gray.

Hue – The Hue tab in the HSL control provides the ability to tweak the flavor of a specific color range. Unlike the drastic changes brought about by the Hue control in Photoshop's Hue/ Saturation feature, the sliders here manipulate the color of a selected color within a given range. The Reds slider, for instance, moves from a magenta red through to a pure red to an orange red. Moving this slider would enable the fine-tuning of just the reds in a photo between these limits.

Saturation – The Saturation control provides the ability to customize the saturation of not the whole image as is provided with the Saturation slider in the Basic pane, but a specific range of colors. Try adjusting the Blues slider with the example image and notice the change in the strength of the color of the shirt worn by the subject on the right.

Luminance – The third tab in the HSL control deals strictly with the luminance of specific colors. With the sliders grouped here it is possible to change the brightness of a color grouping, which can translate into altering the color contrast in a photo by selectively increasing and decreasing the brightness of opposite hues.

Grayscale – By clicking the Convert to Grayscale option the feature changes to provide a method for creating custom mapping of the same color groupings to gray. Using this control it is possible to restore contrast to a grayscale conversion when the different colors in the photo have translated to similar tones of gray, producing a low-contrast monochrome.

Project application: In the example image you may need to flip back to the controls in the Basic pane and make some adjustments to Contrast, Exposure and Blacks sliders alongside the changes made with the HSL sliders in order to ensure sufficient contrast results in the conversion.

Targeted Adjustments in ACR

The majority of the image changes made with the editing features in ACR are done so via a set of controls in a panel. These generally come in the form of sliders which are dragged to alter the appearance of the image. But there is a way to adjust your photos which is much more direct. The Targeted Adjustment Tool (TAT) is accessed via a button located on the utilities toolbar at the top of the workspace.

✓ Parametric Curve	Ctrl+Shft+Alt+T
Hue	Ctrl+Shft+Alt+H
Saturation	Ctrl+Shft+Alt+S
Luminance	Ctrl+Shft+Alt+L
Grayscale Mix	Ctrl+Shft+Alt+G

First introduced in ACR 5.2 the Targeted Adjustment Tool, or TAT, as it is unfortunately referred to, provides direct control over the tones and colors in your image.

The unique characteristic of the TAT is that it is used to make changes by click-dragging on the image itself. After selecting the tool, move the cursor over the picture until it sits on an image part that you want to change. If you have the Tone Curve option selected then this would translate into either darkening or lightening the tones

that you select. Next, click-drag the cursor upwards to lighten the area, or downwards to darken it. This is a very interactive way of adjusting you pictures and all changes made with this tool are reflected in changes to the shape of the curve and the settings of the sliders below it.

Like Lightroom, the TAT in ACR can be used to alter the values of four different image characteristics. Simply select the type of changes that you want to adjust from the drop-down menu beneath the tool's button and click-drag to make the change. The choices are revealed by holding down the mouse button on the small downwards-facing arrow located at the bottom right of the tool's icon. Alternatively, you can switch between options by taking advantage of the shortcut keys associated with each image adjustment type.

Using TAT makes image adjustment a lot more intuitive and as long as you have the Highlight and Shadow Clipping Warnings active (in the top corners of the Histogram) you can edit freely knowing that any clipping that occurs as a result of the adjustments will be displayed on the preview image.

*Aside: In this example the model's skin was lightened by dragging the cursor upwards with the Parametric Tone Curve selected. **Below:** With several quick mouse click-drags the (1) Hue, (2) Saturation or (3) Luminance of the background can be altered. The TAT can also be used to adjust the mapping of particular colors to gray using the Grayscale Mix (4).*

Florian Groehn (photographer), Lea Lazarescu (Dallys Models), Lily Fontana (make-up), Lucia Martinez (styling) and Tim Ashton (photographic assistant).

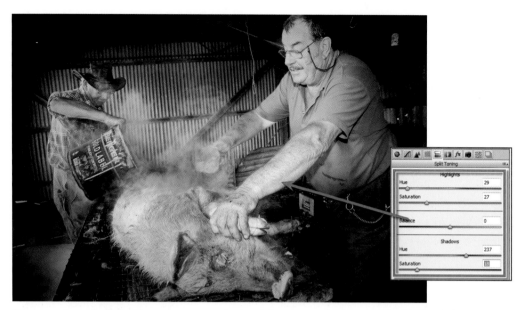

The controls in the Split Toning pane provide the ability to tint shadows and highlights slightly different colors. The Balance slider also allows for the adjustment of the split point between the tint used for highlights and the one used for shadows.

Split toning

When first introduced to ACR, monochrome workers rejoiced at the inclusion of the dedicated Split Toning pane as the controls it contains provide the ability to use the included Hue and Saturation sliders to tint highlights and shadows independently. Hue controls the color of the tint, and Saturation controls its strength. Holding down the Alt/Opt key while moving either of the Hue sliders will preview the tint at 100% saturation (full strength), allowing for easier selection of the correct color. After selecting the color you need to adjust the saturation. To understand how the Hue slider works imagine the control moving progressively through the colors of the rainbow from red, through yellow, green and blue to purple and magenta.

Also included is the Balance slider, which provides the ability to change the point at which the color changes. Movements to the right push the split point towards the highlights, whereas dragging the slider to the left means that more mid to shadow areas will be colored the selected highlight hue.

Remember to use split toning with a monochrome image you must make the conversion to grayscale first. Do this by selecting the Convert to Grayscale option in the HSL/Grayscale pane first. Then move back to the Split Toning pane and adjust Highlight and Shadow Hue and Saturation and then the Balance point to suit.

Note > Don't restrict your split toning activities solely to the realms of monochromes. The feature can also be applied to color images as well, providing some rather unusual but striking results.

Project application: Split tone the project image so that the highlights are tinted traditional sepia brown and the shadows contain a slightly blue tinge.

Adding special effects – Step 10

The post-crop vignetting features that sat with the lens vignetting options in the Camera Calibration pane in the previous releases has been moved to a new tabbed pane in ACR6 called the Fx pane. You will also find a new Grain feature included in the pane as well.

Remember that because both these artistic image adjustments are applied in Adobe Camera Raw they are added non-destructively to the photo. This means that not only can you return to the settings used and make changes when needed, but it is also possible to remove the effect totally without any residual changes being left in the original photo.

Grain: New for ACR6 is the ability to apply a grain effect to you photos. The feature contains three slider controls for adjusting the strength (Amount), Size and smoothness (Roughness) of the grain. You can use this feature to mimic old world photos or provide a film-like feel to your images.

The new Fx pane contains both the updated Post-Crop Vignetting controls and the new grain setting.

For the first time, you can add grain-like texture to photos as part of your non-destructive editing workflow. (1) Before adding grain. (2) After adding grain.

Post Crop Vignetting: The ability to apply vignetting adjustments to a cropped photo was first introduced in ACR 5.0, but has been updated for ACR6. This feature differs from the vignetting option found in the Lens Corrections pane where the vignetting changes are applied to the original full frame image, rather than the cropped picture. That approach is fine when used for correcting lens-based vignetting, but is not appropriate when photographers desire an artistic outcome rather than a lens correction solution. This second set of vignetting tools provides the ability to apply such artistic vignetting to the cropped image and to automatically adapt to a new format if the cropping is removed or changed.

With the inclusion of different vignetting styles and a dedicated slider for highlight adjustments, the updated version of the feature proves more greater control over the look of the vignette and how it interacts with the photo. Paint Overlay is the style found in the previous version of the feature and Highlight and Color Priority options give more weighting to either of these characteristic when darkening or lightening photo edges. The Amount slider controls the

The Post-Crop Vignetting settings in ACR6 have been updated and moved to the new Fx pane. There are now three different styles of vignetting and five slider controls providing a variety of adjustment options for the darkening or lightening of the edges of your photo.

strength of the correction effect and the Midpoint alters how much of the image is included in the enhancement. The Roundness slider controls the shape of the vignetted area and Feather is used to adjust the softness of the edge of the vignette. The highlights slider controls the way that the vignette blends with the lighter tones in the photo and is only available in the Highlight and Color Priority styles and when the Amount is set to darken edges (negative values).

Updated Post Crop Vignetting (PCV) options offer more creative control over the corner darkening and lightening process with the inclusion of a new Highlight Contrast slider and a choice of vignette styles. (1) PCV without highlight control. (2) PCV with highlight control.

Project application: To get you up to speed on the post-crop vignette tools, darken the edge of the project image using a vignette that has full Feather and a negative roundness value. This will add a soft-edged darkening of the picture edges. The Grain feature will be used in the next project.

The Noise Removal system has also been updated for ACR6. Now it is possible to produce substantially smoother images from noisy originals and still maintain fine details. (1) ISO 800 image before noise reduction. (2) After noise reduction.

Noise reduction and sharpening – Step 11

To access the sharpness and noise reduction controls click on the Detail tab. Set the image view to 200%. The Luminance and Color sliders (designed to tackle the camera noise that occurs when the image sensors' ISO is high) should only be raised from 0 if you notice image artifacts such as noise appearing in the image window.

Note > Zoom image to 200% to determine levels of noise present in the image.

Noise control

In the example image above, the sensor was set to 800 ISO on a budget DSLR. Both luminance noise (left)

Detail	
Sharpening	
Amount	111
Radius	1.3
Detail	34
Masking	0
Noise Reduction	
Luminance	20
Luminance Detail	50
Luminance Contrast	0
Color	25
Color Detail	50

and color noise (right) are evident when the image is set to 200%. When using more expensive DSLR cameras that are set to 100 ISO, it may be possible to leave the Luminance and Color noise sliders set to 0. In the revamp of the Noise Removal system for ACR6, not only were the algorithms used for reducing the appearance of noise re-engineered but three new sliders have also been added to the pane. Luminance Deatail and Color Detail sliders reintroduce a measure of texture into areas that have been overly smoothed by the Luminance and Color sliders and the Luminance Contrast slider increases the contrast areas which have been rendered flat by the system. Used in combination these five sliders have the ability to transform very noisy images into usable photos.

> **Warning > Though much improved for ACR6 the Luminance and Color sliders can remove subtle detail and color information that may go unnoticed if the photographer is not careful to pay attention to the effects of these sliders. Use the Luminance Detail and Color Detail sliders to bring back lost texture. Zoom in to take a closer look, and unless you can see either the little white speckles or the color artifacts keep these sliders set at 0.**

All digital photos can benefit from cleverly applied sharpening as it adds clarity to images, if left unsharpened, appear blurry. (1) No sharpening applied. (2) After global and localized sharpening in ACR.

The Three-Pass sharpening workflow

Sharpening is an enhancement technique that is easily overdone and this is true even when applying the changes at the time of Raw file editing. The best approach is to remember that sharpening is applied at three points in the process – capture, locally and output.

The settings applied in Adobe Camera Raw with settings in the Detail pane are used for overall capture sharpening, local or paint-on sharpening is applied with the Adjustment Brush set to Sharpness, and the output side of things is handled as the last step of the editing process. In Adobe Camera Raw this last sharpening step is applied via the Workflow Options settings and takes into account, output media, sharpening strength, size and resolution. In practice this means that all images should be sharpened to some extent in ACR first, specific areas sharpening more with the Adjustment Brush, and then specific sharpening, determined by output size and media surface, applied later in the process.

Capture sharpening: Adobe Camera Raw contains four sliders in the Detail pane that are designed to aid in overall or capture sharpening. The Amount slider determines the strength of the effect. The Radius slider is used to adjust the range of pixels used in the sharpness calculation. Detail and Masking both control where the sharpening effect is applied. Increasing the Detail value raises the local contrast around small picture parts, making these appear sharper. Moving the Masking slider to the right gradually restricts the sharpening to just the most contrasty edges of the picture (for visual examples of masking in action see the last chapter).

Localized sharpening:

Localized sharpening is added using the Adjustment Brush. Take a look at the example images on the opposite page. The detail on the left has no sharpening applied and represents the look of a file as it appears 'straight from the camera'. The detail on the right has had global sharpening (via the controls in the Detail pane)

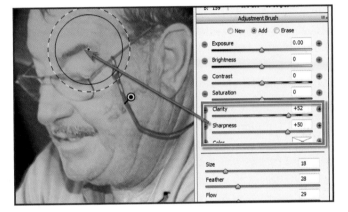

and local sharpening (via the Adjustment Brush) applied. In this instance, the adjustment brush was used to paint-on more clarity around the glasses and stubble area on the man's face.

Output sharpening:

Different output types require different degrees and styles of sharpening. The settings you would use when printing on matte paper for instance, will be very different to the sharpening values employed for the same photo being printed on glossy paper. The Sharpen For setting in the Workflow Options dialog gives you the choice of gloss paper, matte paper or screen and the Amount value determines the strength of the effect. You can opt for low, standard, high sharpening. The sharpening settings are applied to the image when opening or saving the file.

Note > Always make sure that the preview is zoomed to a value of 100% before manipulating these controls so that you can preview the effects. Holding down the Alt/Opt key when adjusting the sharpening sliders in the Detail pane provides a preview of the settings for each slider as the effect is applied. For more details on these Sharpening controls refer to the Sharpening and Image section in the previous chapter.

Output options – Step 12

Apart from the Open Image button Adobe Camera Raw provides several other options that will govern how the file is handled once all the enhancement options have been set. To this end, the lower part of the dialog contains four buttons, Save Image, Open Image, Cancel and Done, and a further four, Save Image (without the options dialog), Reset and Open Copy when the Alt/ Option button is pushed, and Open Object when the Shift key is pushed.

Cancel: This option closes the ACR dialog, not saving any of the settings to the file that was open.

Save Image: The normal Save Image button, which includes several dots (...) after the label, displays the Save Options dialog. Here you can save the raw file, with your settings applied, in Adobe's own DNG format as well as TIFF, JPEG and PSD formats. The dialog includes options for choosing the location where the file will be saved, the ability to add in a new name as well as format-specific settings such as compression, conversion to linear image and/or embed the original Raw file for the DNG option.

It is a good idea to select Save in Different Location in the Destination drop-down at the top to keep processed files separate from archived originals. Clearly the benefits of a compressed DNG file are going to help out with storage issues and compression is a big advantage with DNG. Embedding the original Raw file in the saved DNG file begs the question of how much room you have in the designated storage device and whether you really want to have the original Raw file here.

Save (without save options): Holding down the Alt/Option key when clicking the Save button skips the Save Options dialog and saves the file in DNG format using the default save settings, which are the same as those last set.

Open Image: If you click on the Open Image button ACR applies the conversion options and opens the file inside the Photoshop workspace. At this point, the file is no longer in a Raw format so when it comes to

Standard button display.

Alternative ACR button layout displayed when Alt/Option key is pressed.

Alternative ACR button layout displayed when Shift key is pressed.

Once you have adjusted all the controls in the Adobe Camera Raw workspace the last step is to choose how to handle the results of the conversion. To this end the utility contains four default buttons, Save Image (with options) Cancel, Open Image and Done, plus an extra four when the Alt/Option or Shift keys are pressed.

saving the photo from the Editor workspace Photoshop automatically selects the Photoshop PSD format for saving.

Reset: The Reset option resets the ACR dialog's settings back to their defaults. This feature is useful if you want to ensure that all settings and enhancement changes made in the current session have been removed. To access the Reset button click the Cancel button while holding down the Alt/Option key. This action cannot be undone.

Done: Clicking the Done button will update the Raw conversion settings for the open image or images. Essentially this means that the current settings are applied to the photo and the dialog is then closed. The thumbnail preview in the Bridge workspace will also be updated to reflect the changes. In effect this is also a save button.

Open Copy: Holding down the Alt key while clicking the Open button will apply the currently selected changes to a copy of the file which is opened inside the Photoshop workspace.

Open Object: The most exciting new addition to the list of ACR output options is the Open Object entry, which is displayed when the Shift key is held down. Choosing Open Object will create a new document in Photoshop and embed the Raw file in the document as a Smart Object. This route for transferring your files to Photoshop is the only one that continues to work with the picture in a lossless manner and is the core of many of the non-destructive editing techniques discussed in the next chapters.

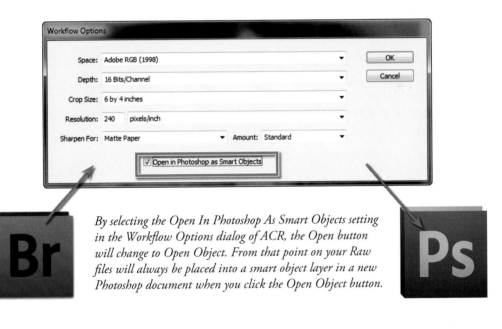

By selecting the Open In Photoshop As Smart Objects setting in the Workflow Options dialog of ACR, the Open button will change to Open Object. From that point on your Raw files will always be placed into a smart object layer in a new Photoshop document when you click the Open Object button.

Project application: Click the Save button (bottom left), pick DNG as the file format and input the following title – *foundations-proj-02-after*. This way you will be able to compare the before and after versions of the project files in the Bridge preview pane.

Before

The Graduated Filter Tool is another form of localized adjustment. This feature can be used to apply custom gradients across the full height or width of the photo. Once created, the size, position and rotation of the gradient remains editable along with the image characteristics that can be altered via the gradient.

After

Foundation Project 3

As an extension of the ability to apply localized corrections in Adobe Camera Raw, the engineering team at Adobe also added a Graduated Filter Tool to the utility. Working like a combination of the Photoshop's Gradient Tool and ACR's Adjustment Brush, the feature provides the user with the ability to add graduated enhancement changes to their images. This is useful for picture-wide changes such as darkening skies and can be used in conjunction with the Adjustment Brush in an 'add filtration and paint out the areas where it is not wanted' fashion. Again, application is a two-step process, just as it was with the Adjustment Brush. First, you define the size, position and direction of the gradient, then you fine-tune the filter effects using the same image parameter slider controls found in the Adjustment Brush.

In this project we'll apply the Graduated Filter Tool to a landscape image and then fine-tune its placement with the Adjustment Brush before adding some film-like grain with the new Grain feature.

Preliminary enhancements – Step 1

When opening the project file you will notice that no changes have been made to the image. This is the Raw file straight from the camera. Before commencing the application of the Graduated Filter work your way through the steps laid out in the previous project to enhance the image. Once you are happy with the results then move onto the next step.

In the project image the upper and lower portions of the photo have been adjusted with two separate Graduated Filters. The lower filter just altered exposure whereas the upper one also changed the Color characteristic as well.

Add Graduated Filter effect – Step 2

Start by selecting the Graduated Filter Tool from the toolbar at the top left of the ACR workspace. Next select, and adjust the primary enhancement change that you wish to make from those listed in the Graduated Filter pane that is displayed on the right of the workspace. Here I have chosen Exposure. Locate a starting point on the photo and then click-drag a gradient effect on the image. The starting point (displayed as a green pin) is where the effect is the strongest, gradually lessening until you release the mouse button (marked by a red pin). The longer the drag the more gradual the gradient change. Hold down the Shift key to add gradients either horizontally or vertically. A second Graduated Filter is added to the bottom of the image, dragging the effect up through the rocks.

Adjust the Graduated Filter effect – Step 3

Once you have added a Graduated Filter to the photo you can adjust the gradient to change the enhancement characteristics. Click onto either Pin icon that represents the filter and then adjust the slider controls in the pane. When a pin is selected the feature is switched to the Edit mode. To create a different Graduated Filter click-drag in another part of the image. In addition to these changes you can also rotate, move and adjust the size of the gradient by click-dragging either pin or, once the filter is selected, by moving any of the three lines displayed on screen. Gradients may be adjusted individually using this technique. Adjust the upper graduated filter is adjusted to –100 Saturation, –3.00 Exposure and then a Color is added to reflect the hue of the sea below. The lower Graduated Filter should be set to –2.50 Exposure only.

Graduated Filter	
○ New ◉ Edit	
Exposure	-2.25
Brightness	0
Contrast	+1
Saturation	-100
Clarity	+100
Sharpness	-100
Color	

Reclaim some of the filtered detail – Step 4

Dragging the lower filter over the foreground rocks causes them to be darkened with an effect that tends to blend into the background. Restore their original visual dominance by selecting the Adjustment Brush, setting it to Auto Mask to keep the corrections to just the rocks and painting on a change to Exposure and Contrast.

Examples of different grain types created with the new Grain feature in Adobe Camera Raw 6.
(1) No grain applied. (2) Grain settings -60, 5, 70 (Amount, Size, Roughness).
(3) 45, 20, 100. (4) 100, 20, 10. (5) 100, 100, 100. (6) 100, 100, 50.

Add a film-like grain effect – Step 5

The last step in this stylized enhancement is to add some texture to the image. Unlike the situation in the last project where our aim was to minimize noise and maintain sharpness and detail, here we will use the Grain feature to add a film-like quality to the photo. The feature contains three sliders – Amount for the density of grains in a given area, Size which controls the dimensions of the grain particles, and Roughness of how uniform the shape of the grain is. In our example I add small, tight grain to give the sense of texture to the image by using the settings – Amount 60, Size 5 and Roughness 70.

Digital exposure

Most digital imaging sensors capture images using 12 bits of memory dedicated to each of the three RGB color channels, resulting in 4096 tones between black and white. Most of the imaging sensors in digital cameras record a subject brightness range of approximately five to eight stops (five to eight f-stops between the brightest highlights with detail and the deepest shadow tones with detail).

Tonal distribution in 12-bit capture

Darkest Shadows	- 4 stops	- 3 stops	- 2 stops	-1 stop	Brightest Highlights

← ——————— 25% of all levels ——————— → ← ——— 75% of all levels ——— →

Distribution of levels.

One would think that with all of this extra data the problem of banding or image posterization due to insufficient levels of data (a common problem with 8-bit image editing) would be consigned to history. Although this is the case with midtones and highlights, shadows can still be subject to this problem. The reason for this is that the distribution of levels assigned to recording the range of tones in the image is far from equitable. The brightest tones of the image (the highlights) use the lion's share of the 4096 levels available while the shadows are comparatively starved of information.

An example of posterization or banding.

Shadow management

CCD and CMOS chips are, however, linear devices. This linear process means that when the amount of light is halved, the electrical stimulation to each photoreceptor on the sensor is also halved. Each f-stop reduction in light intensity halves the amount of light that falls onto the receptors compared to the previous f-stop. Fewer levels are allocated by this linear process to recording the darker tones. Shadows are 'level starved' in comparison to the highlights that have a wealth of information dedicated to the brighter end of the tonal spectrum. So rather than an equal amount of tonal values distributed evenly across the dynamic range, we actually have the effect as shown above. The deepest shadows rendered within the scene often have fewer than 128 allocated levels, and when these tones are manipulated in post-production Photoshop editing there is still the possibility of banding or posterization.

Adjusting exposure in ACR

For those digital photographers interested in the dark side, an old SLR loaded with a fine-grain black and white film is a hard act to follow. The liquid smooth transitions and black velvet-like quality of dark low-key prints of yesteryear is something that digital capture is hard pressed to match. The sad reality of digital capture is that underexposure in low light produces an abundance of noise and banding (steps rather than smooth transitions of tone). The answer, however, is surprisingly simple for those who have access to a DSLR camera and have selected the Raw format from the Quality menu settings in their camera. Simply be generous with your exposure to the point of clipping or overexposing your highlights and only attempt to lower the exposure of the shadows in Adobe Camera Raw.

Foundation Project 4

1. **In-camera:** The first step is the most difficult to master for those who are used to using Auto or Program camera exposure modes. Although the final outcome may require deep shadow tones, the aim in digital low-key camera exposure is to first get the shadow tones away from the left-hand wall of the histogram by increasing and NOT decreasing the exposure. It is vitally important, however, not to increase the exposure so far that you lose or clip highlight detail. The original camera exposure of the image used in this project reveals that the shadow tones (visible as the highest peaks in the histogram) have had a generous exposure in-camera so that noise and banding have been avoided (the tones have moved well to the right in the histogram). The highlights, however, look as though they have become clipped or overexposed. The feedback from the histogram on the camera's LCD should have confirmed the clipping at the time of exposure (the tall peak on the extreme right-hand side of the histogram) and if you had your camera set to warn you of overexposure, the highlights would have been merrily flashing at you to ridicule you of your sad attempts to expose this image. The typical DSLR camera is, however, misleading when it comes to clipped highlights and ignorant of what is possible in Adobe Camera Raw. Adobe Camera Raw can recover at least one stop of extra highlight information when the Exposure slider is dragged to the left (so long as the photographer has used a DSLR camera that has a broader dynamic range than your typical fixed-lens compact digicam).

Adobe Camera Raw rescues the highlights – sometimes automatically.

'Exposing right'

In ACR when the Auto checkbox in the Exposure slider is selected, Adobe Camera Raw often attempts to rescue overexposed highlights automatically. With a little knowledge and some attention to the camera's histogram during the capture stage, you can master the art of pushing your highlights to the edge. So if your model is not in a hurry (mine is watching a half-hour TV show) you can take an initial exposure on Auto and then check your camera for overexposure. Increase the exposure using the exposure compensation dial on the camera until you see the flashing highlights. When the flashing highlights start to appear you can still add around one extra stop to the exposure before the highlights can no longer be recovered in Adobe Camera Raw. The popular term for this peculiar behavior is called 'exposing right'.

PERFORMANCE TIP

If the highlights are merrily flashing and the shadows are still banked up against the left-hand wall of the histogram, the solution is to increase the amount of fill light, i.e. reduce the difference in brightness between the main light source and the fill light. If you are using flash as the source of your fill light, it would be important to drop the power of the flash by at least two stops and choose the 'Slow-Sync' setting (a camera flash setting that balances both the ambient light exposure and flash exposure) so that the flash light does not overpower the main light source positioned behind your subject. The harsh light from the on-camera flash can also be diffused using a diffusion device.

2. Before we adjust the tones to create our low-key image we must first check that our tones are smooth and free from color and luminance noise. Zoom in to 100% magnification for an accurate preview and look for any problems in the smooth dark-toned areas. Setting both the Luminance and Color reduction sliders to 25 (found in the Detail tab) removes the noise in this image. For this example, I would also recommend that the Sharpness slider be set to 0 at this point. Rather than committing to global sharpening using the Adobe Camera Raw dialog box, we can apply selective sharpening either in ACR using the Adjustment Brush or in the main Photoshop editing space. This may help to keep the tones as smooth as possible.

Tip: Click in the Exposure slider text box so it is selected (cursor line appears), then move the White Balance Tool in place over the deeper shadows. You can now use the up/down keys on the keyboard to move the slider and monitor the actual pixel value change on the screen during adjustment.

3. Create the low-key look by moving the Exposure and/or the Brightness sliders to the left in the Basic tab. You can continue to drop these sliders until the highlights start to move away from the right-hand wall of the histogram. Select the 'White Balance Tool' and move your mouse cursor over the deeper shadows – this will give you an idea of the RGB values you are likely to get when this image is opened into the editing space. Once you approach an average of 15 to 20 in all three channels the low-key look should have been achieved.

Expose right and adjust left.

'Expose right' and multiple exposures

This inequitable distribution of levels has given rise to the idea of 'exposing right'. This work practice encourages the user seeking maximum quality to increase the camera exposure of the shadows (without clipping the highlights) so that more levels are afforded to the shadow tones. This approach to making the shadows 'information rich' involves increasing the amount of fill light (actual light rather than the ACR's fill light) or lighting with less contrast in a studio environment. If the camera file is then opened in the Adobe Camera Raw dialog box the shadow values can then be reassigned their darker values to expand the contrast before opening it as a 16 Bits/Channel file. When the resulting shadow tones are edited and printed, the risk of visible banding in the shadow tones is greatly reduced.

Separate exposures can be combined during the image-editing process.

This approach is not possible when working with a subject with a fixed subject brightness range, e.g. a landscape, but in these instances there is often the option of bracketing the exposure and merging the highlights of one digital file with the shadows of a second. Choose 'Merge to HDR Pro' (high dynamic range) from the File > Automate menu or use the manual approach outlined in 'Advanced Retouching'. The example above shows the use of a layer mask to hide the darker shadows in order to access the bit-rich shadows of the underlying layer and regain the full tonal range of the scene.

Dust on the sensor – batch removal

As we saw in the last chapter a significant problem arises for many digital cameras when dust is allowed to accumulate on the sensor. This becomes most noticeable in smooth areas of light tone such as sky or white studio backdrops as dark spots. Use the Retouch Tool and click on a spot in the image. Photoshop will automatically choose an area of the image to heal this spot. The Radius can be changed by raising the Radius slider or dragging the red circle bigger. The source for the heal area (the green circle) can be dragged to an alternate location if required. Fortunately the dust is in the same place in each and every image and so after spotting one image you can choose 'Select All' and 'Synchronize' to remove the dust from all images you have open in the ACR dialog box. Be sure to check the Spot Removal option in the Synchronize dialog box before selecting OK.

In areas of continuous tone the heal area that is selected automatically by Photoshop is usually OK. In areas of fine detail the healing area may need to be relocated to ensure lines do not appear disjointed.

Archiving Raw files as digital negatives

Working with camera Raw files is going to create some extra strain on the storage capacity found on a typical computer's hard drive. What to do with all of the extra gigabytes of Raw data is a subject that people are divided about. You can burn them to CD or DVD disks – but are the disks truly archival? You can back them up to a remote Firewire drive – but what if the hard drive fails? Some believe that digital tape offers the best track record

for longevity and security. Why archive at all you may ask? Who can really tell what the image-editing software of the future will be capable of – who can say what information is locked up in the Raw data that future editions of the Raw editors will be able to access. Adobe has now created a universal Raw file format called DNG (Digital Negative) in an attempt to ensure that all camera Raw files (whichever camera they originate from) will be accessible in the future. The Digital Negative format also includes lossless compression to reduce the size of the Raw files. The Adobe DNG converter is available from the Adobe website or from the supporting DVD. The converter will ensure that your files are archived in a format that will be understood in the future. Expect to see future models of many digital cameras using this DNG format as standard. One thing *is* for sure – Raw files are a valuable source of the rich visual data that many of us value and so the format will be around for many years to come.

Melissa Zappa by Victoria Verdon Roe

Highly saturated colors carefully massaged into the Adobe RGB (1998) profile in Adobe Camera Raw.

digital printing

Ed Purnomo

essential skills

- Control the color accuracy between monitor preview and print.
- Understand the procedures involved with producing a digital print.
- Print a color-managed digital image using a desktop inkjet printer.
- Compensate for visual differences between the monitor preview and print.

Introduction

The secret to successful printing is to adopt a professional print workflow that takes the frustration out of seeing the colors shift as your image moves from camera to monitor, and from monitor to print. Color consistency has never been more easy and affordable to implement for the keen amateur and professional photographer. This project guides you along the path to ultimate print satisfaction, so that you will never say those often heard words ever again – 'why do the colors of my print look different to my monitor?'

The reward for your effort (a small capital outlay and a little button pushing) is perfect pixels – color consistency from camera to screen to print. Once the initial work has been carried out predictable color is a real 'no-brainer', as all of the settings can be saved as presets. As soon as you start printing using your new color-managed workflow you will not only enjoy superior and predictable prints, but you will also quickly recover the money you outlaid to implement this workflow (no more second and third attempts).

The range or 'gamut' of colors that each output device is capable of displaying can vary enormously. The illustration shows two different views of the same gamut comparison. The Adobe RGB monitor space (shown in white) is able to contain the gamut of a typical inkjet printer (shown in color) and so offers a better alternative than editing in sRGB, which is primarily a monitor space.

The problem and the solution

Have you ever walked into a TV shop or the cabin of an aircraft and noticed that all the TVs are all showing exactly the same TV program but no two pictures are the same color? All of the TVs are receiving exactly the same signal but each TV has its own unique way of displaying color (its own unique 'color characteristics'). Different settings on each TV for brightness, contrast and color only make the problem worse.

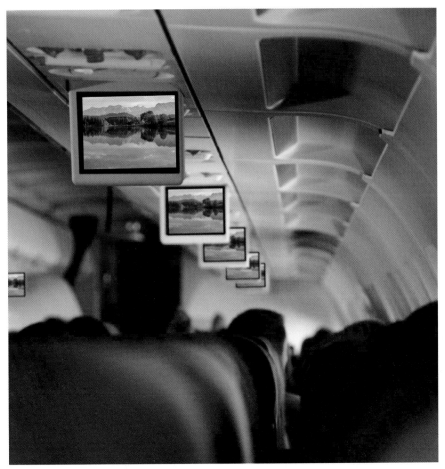

One signal – different pictures (image courtesy of iStockphoto.com).

In the perfect world there would be a way of making sure that all of the TVs could synchronize their settings for brightness, contrast and color, and the unique color characteristics of each TV could be measured and taken into account when displaying a picture. If this could be achieved we could then send 10 different TVs the same picture so that the image appeared nearly identical on all TVs, irrespective of make, model or age. In the world of digital photography, Adobe has made the elusive goal of color consistency possible by implementing a concept and workflow called Color Management. Color Management, at first glance, can seem like an incredibly complex science to get your head around, but if just a few simple steps are observed and implemented then color consistency can be yours.

*Don't position your monitor so that it faces a window and lower the room lighting so that your monitor
is the brightest thing in your field of vision (image courtesy of iStockphoto.com).*

Prepare your print workshop

1.   The first step is to optimize the room where your monitor lives. Ideally, the monitor should
be brighter than the light source used to illuminate the room and positioned so the monitor does
not reflect any windows or lights in the room (the biggest problems from light will all be behind
you and over your shoulders as you sit at the monitor). Professionals often build hoods around their
monitors to prevent stray light falling on the surface of the monitor but if you carefully position
the monitor in the room you should be able to avoid this slightly 'geeky' step. Stray light that falls
on your monitor will lower the apparent contrast of the image being displayed and could lead you
to add more contrast when it is not required. The color of light in the room (warm or cool) is also
a critical factor in your judgement of color on the screen. It is advisable to light the room using
daylight but this should not be allowed to reflect off brightly colored surfaces in the room, e.g.
brightly painted walls or even the brightly colored top you may be wearing when you are sitting
in front of your monitor. If the room is your own personal space, or your partner supports your
passion/obsession/addiction for digital imaging, then you could go that bit further and paint your
walls a neutral gray. The lighting in the room should be entirely daylight – without the possibility
of warm sunlight streaming into the room at certain times of the day. The brightness of the daylight
in the room can be controlled with blinds or you can introduce artificial daylight by purchasing
color-corrected lights, e.g. Solux halogen globes or daylight fluorescent lights. If the above
recommendations are difficult to achieve – lower the level of the room lighting significantly.

Overview of Step 1 > Position your computer monitor so that it does not reflect any windows,
lights or brightly colored walls in the room (when you sit at the monitor a neutral colored wall,
without a window, should be behind you). Use daylight or daylight globes to light the room
and make sure the room lighting is not as bright as the monitor (the monitor should be the
brightest thing in your field of view).

Prepare your monitor

2. Purchase a monitor calibration device (available for as little as US$100 from X-Rite or Data Color) and follow the step-by-step instructions. The calibration process only takes a few minutes once you have read through the instructions and adjusted a few settings on your monitor. It is now widely accepted that photographers should choose a D65 whitepoint (how cool or warm tones appear on your monitor) and a Gamma of 2.2 (this controls how bright your midtones are on your monitor). The next time you use your calibrated and profiled monitor, Photoshop will pick up the new profile to ensure you are seeing the real color of the image file rather than a version that has been distorted by the monitor's idiosyncrasies and inappropriate default settings.

MONITOR CALIBRATOR RECOMMENDATIONS

If you are on a budget I recommend the DataColor Spyder 2 Express or the Pantone Huey. If you have a little more money and are looking for a really professional tool, then the Eye One Display 2 is my personal favorite, although it costs a little more. If you decide on the Spyder 2 Express I found the only hiccup in an otherwise easy-to-follow guide was the instruction on how to decide whether your LCD monitor had a 'brightness' or 'backlight' control. As the vast majority of LCD monitors use a 'backlight' to control brightness I think this information is a possible source of confusion. The tiny Pantone Huey is really easy to use, completes the process in just a few minutes, and has an option to measure the brightness of the room and then adjust the brightness of the monitor accordingly. I would recommend that you lower the brightness of the LCD monitor to a setting of between 50% and 75% before calibrating an LCD screen with the Huey. The automatic brightness adjustment of the monitor is only useful if you can't maintain a standard level of illumination in your room. If you think small is cute, then the Huey will do an admirable job and you can put it in your shirt pocket when you're done.

Prepare your inkjet printer

3. Just as the color characteristics of the monitor had to be measured and profiled in order to achieve accurate color between camera and monitor, a profile also has to be created that describes the color characteristics of the printer. This ensures color accuracy is maintained between the monitor and the final print. When an accurate profile of the printer has been created, Photoshop (rather than the printer) can then be instructed to manage the colors to maintain color consistency. Photoshop can only achieve this remarkable task because it knows (courtesy of the custom profile) how the printer reproduces the color information it is handed.

Adobe RGB (1998)   Epson R2400

If you want to achieve optimum print quality at home it is recommended that you use a photo-quality printer (one with six or more inks), and that lets Photoshop manage the colors for the best results. A custom profile is only accurate so long as you continue to use the same ink and paper. Additional profiles will need to be created for every paper surface you would like to use. Printers come shipped with profiles, but these are of the 'one size fits all' variety, otherwise known as 'canned profiles'. For optimum quality, custom printer profiles need to be made for the unique characteristics of every printer (even if they are of the same brand and model number).

Note > Canned profiles for different paper stocks are also available on the web so check that you have the latest versions if you intend to proceed without making a custom profile.

PERFORMANCE TIP

In an attempt to make the first time not too memorable, for all the wrong reasons, check that your ink cartridges are not about to run out of ink and that you have a plentiful supply of good quality paper (same surface and same make). Refilling your ink cartridges with a no-name brand and using cheap paper is not recommended if you want to achieve absolute quality and consistency. I would recommend that you stick with the same brand of inks that came shipped with your printer and use the same manufacturer's paper until you have achieved your first successful workflow.

Important Note > Before proceeding to create a custom profile for your printer, check that all the ink nozzles are clean. Open your printer utility software and run a Nozzle check. This will print out a pattern on plain paper so that you can check all of the inks are running cleanly. If one or more of the inks are not printing or some of the pattern is missing then proceed to select the option to clean the heads in the Utility software.

Select appropriate color setting

4. Select a 'working space' for Photoshop that is compatible with the range of colors that can be achieved with your inkjet printer using good quality 'photo paper'. The most suitable working space currently available is called 'Adobe RGB (1998)'. To implement this working space choose 'Color Settings' in Photoshop and set the workspace to 'Adobe RGB (1998)' from the RGB pull-down menu. In the 'Color Management Policies' section, select 'Convert to Working RGB' from the 'RGB' pull-down menu and check the 'Ask When Opening' boxes.

Note > Selecting North America Prepress 2 from the Settings menu in the Color Settings dialog will automatically adjust the RGB working space to Adobe RGB (1998).

Obtain a profile target

5. You can profile your printer, but the equipment that is required for this step is a little expensive. You can, however, print out a test chart and mail it to a custom printer profile company that has the equipment and will make the profile for you. If this is the workflow you choose to follow download a profile target from the website of the company who will create your custom printer profile. The target print can be mailed back to the company and your profile can be emailed back to you once it has been created by analyzing the test print you created.

Open the profile target file in Photoshop

6. Open the target print and select 'Leave as is' in the 'Missing Profile' dialog box. If the file opens and no dialog box appears then close the file and check that you have changed the Color Settings as outlined in Step 4. The color swatches on the target print must remain unchanged by the color management mechanisms for this process to be effective.

Note > Do not attempt to print a profile target file or test chart using Photoshop Lightroom as Lightroom cannot leave a file 'as is', i.e. switch off the color management. Lightroom can use custom profiles but it cannot be used to make them.

Assign a profile to the target file

7. Go to Edit > Assign Profile. Click the Profile radio button and from the drop-down menu choose Adobe RGB (1998).

Note > This workflow is different to the workflow used in previous versions of Photoshop. This step is now required to prevent current operating systems from assigning an inappropriate profile to an untagged file.

Adjust the print settings in Photoshop

8. When the target image is open in Photoshop proceed to 'File > Print'. In order to measure the unique characteristics of the printer the colors on the test chart Photoshop must NOT change the RGB numbers. Assigning Adobe RGB as the document profile and the Printer profile will ensure the color numbers remain unchanged when they are sent to the printer driver.

1. Select your printer from the 'Printer' menu.
2. Rotate the paper orientation if required by clicking on the appropriate icon next to the Print Settings button.
3. Make sure that the Scale is set to 100%. The patches **MUST** be output at 100%.
4. In the 'Color Management' section of the dialog box choose 'Photoshop Manages Color' for the Color Handling option. The Source Space should read 'Adobe RGB (1998)' and there will be a reminder to switch off the color management in the Printer Preferences dialog.
5. Select Adobe RGB (1998) as the Printer Profile and Relative Colorimetric as the Rendering Intent.
6. Click the Printer Settings button to open the Printer Driver dialog.

The printer driver of an Epson R800 – the layout and naming of the various options will vary between different makes and models of printers.

Adjust the printer settings

9. Click on the 'Print Settings' button to open the printer driver dialog. Choose the size of your printing paper (large enough to print the target image at 100%). In the printer driver dialog box choose the paper or media type, the print quality and switch off the color management. Also switch off any Auto settings and the 'Gloss' option if available. For owners of Canon printers, make sure the 'Print Type' is set to 'NONE'. The precise wording for switching off the color management in the printer driver will vary depending on the make of the printer and the operating system you are using (you may need to select an 'Advanced' option in your printer driver to alter some or all of these settings). When using an Epson or Canon printer you may see that color management is referred to as ICM or ICC. Other manufacturers may refer to letting the software (Photoshop) manage the color, which is another way of saying that the color management in the printer driver will be switched off. When you print this target print, the colors are effectively printed in their raw state. In this way the lab that creates your profile can measure how the colors vary from one printer to another and they can then create a unique profile that best describes what your printer does with standard 'unmanaged' color. Click Save to return to Photoshop's Print dialog and then select the Print button in the bottom right-hand corner of the dialog.

Note > If in doubt consult your profile service provider for the precise settings you should use for your printer.

Create and install custom profile

10. Examine the target print to ensure that it is free from streaking (this may occur due to clogged printing heads) and if clean send this target print to the profiling company so that it can be measured using the more sophisticated and expensive profiling hardware that is required to complete this process. They will be able to send you the profile as an attachment to an email. If you are using a PC right-click the profile and choose Install, and Windows will install it in the correct location. If using a Mac you will need to locate the ColorSync folder on your hard drive (Library > ColorSync > Profiles) and copy the ICC profile to this location.

Tag images with the Adobe RGB profile

11. When you have installed your custom printer profile make sure that your images destined for print are tagged with the Adobe RGB profile. Select the Adobe RGB profile in the camera if possible when shooting in the JPEG file format (digital SLR cameras and many prosumer fixed-lens digicams allow the photographer to choose this setting). If capturing in the Raw file format you must click on the blue writing at the base of the ACR dialog box that will open the Workflow Options. Select Adobe RGB (1998) from the Space menu.

Test your color managed workflow

12. It is recommended that the first print you make using your custom profile is a test image – one that has a broad range of colors and tones (such as the one on the supporting DVD). A test image with skin tones can be very useful for testing the accuracy of your new print workflow. When you next open the 'Print' dialog box make sure you set the Color Handling to **'Photoshop Manages Colors'**. Select your new custom profile from the Printer Profile menu and in the Rendering Intent options choose either 'Perceptual' or 'Relative Colorimetric'. Select the Black Point compensation option and then select 'Print'.

Note > All of the printer driver settings that were used to print your target print must be duplicated with every other image to be printed using your custom profile.

Make printer presets

13. From the Printer Preferences menu select the same settings that were used to print the profile target (don't forget to ensure the color management is turned 'OFF'). Save a 'Preset' or 'Setting' for all of the printing options so that you only choose this one setting each time you revisit this dialog box. View your first print using bright daylight and you will discover, if you have followed these directions to the letter, that you have almost certainly found a solution to one of the mysteries of digital color photography – the search for predictable color.

normal	- saturation +	- brightness +	- red +	- green +	- blue +

Step Wedge																
Levels	0	3	5	8	10	13	15	18	20	23	26	28	31	245 247 250 252 255
Brightness	0	1	2	3	4	5	6	7	8	9	10	11	12	96 97 98 99 100

Use the test file on the supporting website to help you target the perfect color balance quickly and efficiently.

Assessing the test print for accuracy

14. View the print using daylight (not direct sunlight) when the print is dry, and look for differences between the print and the screen image in terms of hue (color), saturation and brightness.

1. Check that the colors are saturated and printing without tracking marks or banding. If there is a problem with missing colors, tracking lines or saturation, clean the printer heads using the available option in the printer driver.
2. View any skin tones to assess the appropriate level of saturation.
3. View any gray tones to determine if there is a color cast present in the image. If these print as gray then no further color correction is required.

PERFORMANCE TIP

Any differences between the monitor and the print will usually now be restricted to the differences in color gamuts between RGB monitors and CMYK printers. The vast majority of colors are shared by both output devices but some of the very saturated primary colors on your monitor (red, green and blue) may appear slightly less saturated in print. Choose a printer with an inkset that uses additional primary inks if you want to achieve the maximum gamut from a printer.

Step Wedge								
Levels	0	3	5	8	10	13	15	18	20
Brightness	0	1	2	3	4	5	6	7	8

Preserving shadow detail

15. If the dark shadow detail that is visible on screen is printing as black without detail then you could try switching from the 'Relative Colorimetric' rendering intent to the 'Perceptual' rendering intent. If this does not resolve the problem then establish a Levels adjustment layer to resolve the problem in Photoshop. The bottom left-hand slider in the Levels dialog box should be moved to the right to reduce the amount of black ink being printed in the shadows (raise it to a value of no higher than 10 otherwise the darkest tones will start to appear gray). This should allow dark shadow detail to be visible in subsequent prints. This adjustment layer can be switched on for printing and switched off for viewing the image on screen.

Note > It is important to apply these Output level adjustments to an adjustment layer only as these specific adjustments apply only to the output device and media you are currently testing. You may need to create another adjustment layer for a different output device.

PERFORMANCE TIPS

Materials
Start by using the printer manufacturer's recommended ink and paper.
Use premium grade 'photo paper' for maximum quality.

Monitor
Position your monitor so that it is clear of reflections.
If you are using an old CRT monitor let it warm up for a while before judging image quality.
Calibrate your monitor using a calibration device.

Adobe
Set the Color Settings of the Adobe software to allow you to use the Adobe RGB profile.
Select 'Photoshop Manages Color'.
Use a six-ink (or more) inkjet printer or better for maximum quality.
Select the 'Media Type' in the Printer Software dialog box.
Select a high dpi setting (1440 dpi or greater) or 'Photo' quality setting.
Use a custom printer profile.

Proofing
Allow print to dry and use daylight to assess color accuracy of print.

Soft proofing

Although the image that appears on your monitor has been standardized (after the calibration process and the implementation of the Adobe RGB working space), the printed image from this standardized view would appear different if printed through a variety of different inkjet printers onto different paper surfaces or 'media types'. In Photoshop it is possible to further alter the visual appearance of the image on your monitor so that it more closely resembles how it will actually appear when printed by your specific make and model of inkjet printer on a particular paper surface. This process is called 'soft proofing'.

To set up the soft proof view go to View > Proof Setup > Custom. From the Profile menu select the profile of your printer and paper or 'media type'. Choose 'Perceptual' from the 'Intent' menu. Check the 'Use Black Point Compensation' and 'Paper White' boxes if you intend to remove all other white and black tones from your display when you view your image (this would include Photoshop's panels, menu and the desktop colors). The image colors will look gray or washed out if you don't take this step.

Save the soft proof settings so they can be accessed quickly the next time you need to soft proof to the same printer and media type. When you view your image with the soft proof preview the color and tonality will be modified to more closely resemble the output characteristics of your printer and choice of media. The image can now be edited with the soft proof preview on, to achieve the desired tonality and color that you would like to see in print. It is recommended that you edit in 'Full Screen Mode' to remove distracting colors on your desktop and use adjustment layers to modify and fine-tune the image on screen.

Printing using a professional laboratory

Professional photographic laboratory services are now expanding into the production of large and very large prints using the latest inkjet and piezo technology. Many are also capable of printing your digital files directly onto color photographic paper. In fact, outputting to color print paper via machines like the Durst Lambda and Fuji Frontier has quickly become the 'norm' for a lot of professional photographers. Adjustment of image files that print well on desktop inkjets so that they cater for the idiosyncrasies of these RA4 and large inkjet machines is an additional output skill that is really worth learning.

With improved quality, speed and competition in the area, the big players like Epson, Kodak, Durst, Fuji and Hewlett Packard are manufacturing units that are capable of producing images that are not only visually stunning, but also very, very big. Pictures up to 54 inches wide can be made on some of the latest machines, with larger images possible by splicing two or more panels together. A photographer can now walk into a bureau with a CD containing a favorite image and walk out the same day with a spliced polyester poster printed with fade-resistant, all-weather inks the size of a billboard. In addition to these dedicated bureau services, some professionals, whose day-to-day business revolves around the production of large prints, are actually investing in their own wide-format piezojet or inkjet machines. The increased quality of pigment-based dye systems together with the choice of different media, or substrates as they are referred to in the business, provides them with more imaging and texture choices than are available via the RA4 route.

Before you start

Getting the setup right is even more critical with large-format printing than when you are outputting to a desktop machine. A small mistake here can cause serious problems to both your 48 × 36 inch masterpiece as well as your wallet, so before you even turn on your computer, talk to a few professionals. Most output bureaus are happy to help prospective customers with advice and usually supply a series of guidelines that will help you set up your images to suit their printers. These instructions may be contained in a pack available with a calibration swatch over the counter, or might be downloadable from the company's website.

Some of the directions will be general and might seem a little obvious, others can be very specific and might require you to change the CMYK settings of your image-editing program so that your final files will match the ink and media response of the printer. Some companies will check that your image meets their requirements before printing, others will dump the unopened file directly to the printer's RIP assuming that all is well. So make sure that you are aware of the way the bureau works before making your first print.

New

Name: Big Print

Preset: Custom

Size:

Width: 32   inches

Height: 20   inches

Resolution: 240   pixels/cm

Color Mode: RGB Color   8 bit

Background Contents: White

▲ Advanced

Color Profile: sRGB IEC61966-2.1

Pixel Aspect Ratio: Square Pixels

Convert to Profile

Source Space
Profile: Adobe RGB (1998)

Destination Space
Profile: FujiFlex TC918 SuperSat2_GAMUT

Conversion Options
Engine: Adobe (ACE)

Intent: Perceptual

☑ Use Black Point Compensation
☑ Use Dither
☐ Flatten Image to Preserve Appearance

General guidelines for professional labs

The following guidelines have been compiled from the suggestions of several output bureaus. They constitute a good overview but cannot be seen as a substitute for talking to your own lab directly.

1. Ensure that the image is orientated correctly. Some printers are set up to work with a portrait or vertical image by default; trying to print a landscape picture on these devices will result in areas of white space above and below the picture and the edges being cropped.

2. Make sure the image is the same proportion as the paper stock. This is best achieved by making an image with the canvas the exact size required and then pasting your picture into this space.

3. Don't use crop marks. Most printers will automatically mark where the print is to be cropped. Some bureaus will charge to remove your marks before printing.

4. Convert text to line or raster before submission. Some imaging and layout programs need the font files to be supplied together with the image at the time of printing. If the font is missing then the printer will automatically substitute a default typeface, which in most cases will not be a close match for the original. To avoid failing to supply a font needed, convert the type to line or raster before sending the image to the bureau.

5. Use the resolution suggested by the lab. Most output devices work best with an optimal resolution; large-format inkjet printers are no different. The lab technician will be able to give you details of the best resolution to supply your images in. Using a higher or lower setting than this will alter the size that your file prints so stick to what is recommended.

6. Keep file sizes under the RIP maximum. The bigger the file the longer it takes to print. Most bureaus base their costings on a maximum file size. You will need to pay extra if your image is bigger than this value.

7. Use the color management system recommended by the lab. In setting up you should ensure that you use the same color settings as the bureau. This may mean that you need to manually input set values for CMYK or use an ICC profile downloaded from the company's website.

Mark Galer

layers and channels

Serap Osman

essential skills

- Learn the creative potential of layers, adjustment layers, channels and layer masks.
- Develop skills and experience in the control and construction of digital montages.

Introduction

The traditional photograph contains all the picture elements in a single plane. Digital images captured by a camera or sourced from a scanner are similar in that they are also flat files. And for a lot of new digital photographers this is how their files remain – flat. All editing and enhancing work is conducted on the original picture but advanced techniques require things to be a little different.

Digital pictures are not always flat

Photoshop contains the ability to use layers with your pictures. This feature releases your images from having to keep all their information in a flat file. Different image parts, added text and certain enhancement tasks can all be kept on separate layers. The layers are kept in a stack and the image you see on screen in the work area is a composite of all the layers.

Sound confusing? Well try imagining, for example, that each of the image parts of a simple portrait photograph are stored on separate plastic sheets. These are your layers. The background sits at the bottom. The portrait is laid on top of the background and the text is placed on top. When viewed from above the solid part of each layer obscures the picture beneath. Whilst the picture parts are based on separate layers they can be moved, edited or enhanced independently of each other. If they are saved using a file format like Photoshop's PSD file (which is layer friendly) all the layers will be preserved and present next time the file is opened.

Layers and channels confusion

Another picture file feature that new users often confuse with layers is channels. The difference is best described as follows:

- Layers separate the image into picture, text, shapes and enhancement parts.
- Channels, on the other hand, separate the image into its primary base colors.

The Layers palette will display the layer stack with each part assembled on top of each other, whereas the Channels palette will show the photograph broken into its red, green and blue components (if it is an RGB image – but more on this later).

text layer
layer effects
adjustment layer
image layer
background layer

Example image showing the layer components.

all channels
red channel
green channel
blue channel

Example image showing the channels.

Layers overview

Being able to separate different components of a picture means that these pieces can be moved and edited independently. This is a big advantage compared to flat file editing, where the changes are permanently made part of the picture and can't be edited at a later date. A special file type is needed if these edit features are to be maintained after a layered image is saved and reopened. In Photoshop, the PSD (Photoshop document), Photoshop PDF and PSB (Large Document Format) formats support all layer types and maintain their editability. It is important to note that other common file formats such as standard JPEG and TIFF do not generally support these features (although JPEG2000 and TIFF saved via recent versions of Photoshop can support all layer types). They flatten the image layers while saving the file, making it impossible to edit individual image parts later.

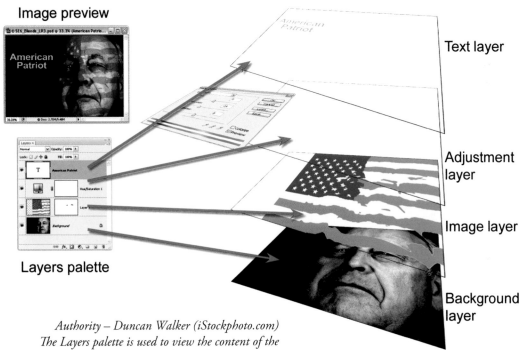

Image preview

Layers palette

Text layer

Adjustment layer

Image layer

Background layer

Authority – Duncan Walker (iStockphoto.com)
The Layers palette is used to view the content of the different layers that make up a picture.

Adding layers

When a picture is first downloaded from your digital camera or imported into Photoshop or Bridge it usually contains a single layer. It is a 'flat file'. By default the program classifies the picture as a background layer. You can add extra 'empty' layers to your picture by clicking the Create New Layer button at the bottom of the Layers dialog or choosing the Layer option from the New menu in the Layer heading (Layer > New > Layer). The new layer is positioned above the currently selected layer (highlighted in the Layers palette).

Some actions such as adding text with the Type Tool automatically or drawing a shape create a new layer for the content. This is also true when adding adjustment and fill layers to your image and when selecting, copying and pasting image parts.

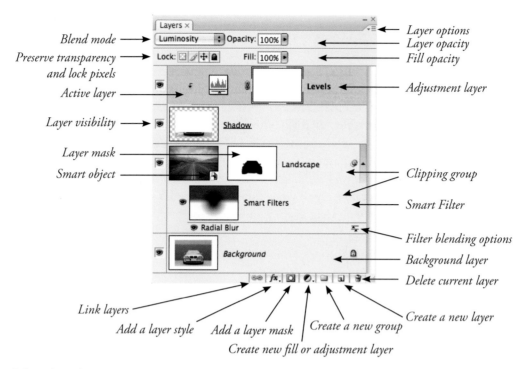

Blend mode → Luminosity | Opacity: 100%

Layer options
Layer opacity

Preserve transparency and lock pixels → Lock: [ ] / + 🔒   Fill: 100%

Fill opacity

Active layer →

Levels ←

Adjustment layer

Layer visibility →

Shadow

Layer mask →

Landscape ←

Clipping group

Smart object →

Smart Filters ←

Smart Filter

Radial Blur

Filter blending options

Background ←

Background layer

Delete current layer

Link layers

Add a layer style | Add a layer mask

Create a new group

Create a new layer

Create new fill or adjustment layer

Viewing layers

Photoshop's Layers palette displays all your layers and their settings in the one dialog box. If the palette isn't already on screen when opening the program, choose the option from the Window menu (Window > Layers). The individual layers are displayed, one on top of each other, in a 'layer stack'. The image is viewed from the top down through the layers. When looking at the picture on screen we see a preview of how the image looks when all the layers are combined. Each layer is represented by a thumbnail on the left and a name on the right. The size of the thumbnail can be changed, as can the name of the layer. By default each new layer is named sequentially (layer 1, layer 2, layer 3). This is fine when your image contains a few different picture parts, but for more complex illustrations it is helpful to rename the layers with titles that help to remind you of their content (portrait, sky, tree). This is especially true when working with 3D layers as the layer name is incorporated in other characteristics of the 3D environment. Layers can be turned off by clicking the eye symbol on the far left of the layer so that it is no longer showing. This action removes the layer from view but not from the stack. You can turn the layer back on again by clicking the eye space.

Working with layers

To select the layer that you want to change you need to click on the layer. At this point the layer will change to a different color from the rest in the stack. This layer is now the 'selected layer' or 'active layer' and can be edited in isolation from the others that make up the picture. It is common for new users to experience the problem of trying to edit pixels on a layer that has not been selected. Always check the correct layer has been selected prior to editing a multi-layered image. Each layer in the same image must have the same resolution and image mode (a selection from one image that is imported into another image will take on the host image's resolution and image mode). Increasing the size of any selection will lead to 'interpolation', which will degrade its quality unless the layer is converted into a 'Smart Object' first.

Manipulating layers

Layers can be moved up and down the layer stack by click-hold-dragging. Moving a layer upwards will mean that its picture content may obscure more of the details in the layers below. Moving downwards progressively positions the layer's details further behind the picture parts of the layers above. In this way you can reposition the content of any layers (except background layers).

Two or more layers can be linked together so that when the content of one layer is moved the other details follow precisely. Simply multi-select the layers to link (hold down the Shift key and click onto each layer) and click the Link Layers button (chain icon) at the bottom of the palette. A chain symbol will appear on the right of the thumbnail to indicate that these layers are now linked. To unlink selected layers click on the Link Layers button again.

Unwanted layers can be deleted by dragging them to the trash icon at the bottom of the Layers palette or by selecting the layer and clicking the trash icon.

Layer styles

Layer styles or effects can be applied to the contents of any layer. Users can add effects by clicking on the 'Add a Layer Style' button at the bottom of the Layers palette (the 'fx' icon), by choosing Layer Style from the Layer menu, by clicking on the desired effect in the Styles palette or by dragging existing effects from one layer to another. The effects added are listed below the layer in the palette. You can turn effects on and off using the eye symbol and even edit effect settings by double-clicking on them in the palette.

Opacity

As well as layer styles, or effects, the opacity (how transparent a layer is) of each layer can be altered by dragging the opacity slider down from 100% to the desired level of translucency. The lower the number, the more detail from the layers below will show through. The opacity slider is located at the top of the Layers palette and changes the selected layer only. In Photoshop CS5 you can adjust the opacity of multi-selected layers in one step.

Blending modes

On the left of the opacity control is a drop-down menu containing a range of blending modes. The default selection is 'normal', which means that the detail in upper layers obscures the layers beneath. Switching to a different blending mode will alter the way in which the layers interact.

Checking the 'preserve transparency' box confines any painting or editing to the areas containing pixels (transparent areas remain unaffected).

Layer shortcuts

1. To display Layers palette – Choose Window > Layers.
2. To access layers options – Click the settings icon in the upper right-hand corner of the Layers palette.
3. To change the size of thumbnails – Choose Panel Options from the Layers palette menu and select a thumbnail size.
4. To make a new layer – Choose Layer > New > Layer.
5. To create a new adjustment layer – Choose Layer > New Adjustment Layer and then select the layer type or click on the option in the Adjustment List in the Adjustment panel.
6. To create a new layer group – Choose Layer > New > Layer or Layer > New Group From Layers.
7. To add a style to a layer – Select the layer and click on the Layer Styles button at the bottom of the palette.

Individual layers　　　　　　　　　　**Layers in a group**

Layer groups

Layer groups are a collection of layers organized into a single 'folder'. Placing all the layers used to create a single picture part into a group makes these layers easier to manage and organize. Layers can be moved into the group by dragging them onto the group's heading. Layers in groups can have their stacking order (within the group) adjusted without ungrouping. To create a layer group click on the New Group button at the bottom of the palette or choose Layer > New > Group or multi-select the layers to include in the group and press Ctrl/Cmd + G. In previous versions of Photoshop this feature was referred to as Layer Sets. In Photoshop CS5 you can group layers beyond the five level limit of previous versions.

Layer masks

A '**layer mask**' is attached to a layer and controls which pixels are concealed or revealed on that layer. Masks provide a way of protecting areas of a picture from enhancement or editing changes. In this way masks are the opposite to selections, which restrict the changes to the area selected. Masks are standard grayscale images and because of this they can be painted, edited and erased just like other pictures. Masks are displayed as a separate thumbnail to the right of the main layer thumbnail in the Layers palette. The black portion of the mask thumbnail is the protected or transparent area and is opaque or shows the layer image without transparency. Grays, depending on the dark or lightness of the tone, will give varying amounts of transparency from partially transparent to almost opaque. Photoshop provides a variety of ways to create masks but one of the easiest is to use the special Quick Mask mode.

Layer types

Image layers: This is the most basic and common layer type containing any picture parts or image details. Background is a special type of image layer.

Text layers: Designed solely for text, these layers allow the user to edit and enhance the text after the layer has been made. It is possible to create '**editable text**' in Photoshop. If the text needs to be modified (font, style, spelling, color, etc.) the user can simply double-click the type layer. To apply filters to the contents of a text layer, it must be rasterized (Layer > Rasterize > Type or Layer > Rasterize > Layer) first. This converts the text layer to a standard image layer and in this process the ability to edit the text is lost.

Shape layers: Shape layers are designed to hold the shapes created with Photoshop's drawing tools (Rectangle, Ellipse, Polygon, Line and Custom Shape). Like text layers the content of these layers is 'vector' based and therefore can be scaled upwards or downwards without loss of quality.

Smart Object layers: Smart Object layers are special layers that encapsulate another picture (either vector or pixel based). As the original picture content is always maintained any editing action such as transforms or filtering that is applied to a Smart Object layer is non-destructive. Pixel-based editing (painting, erasing, etc.) can't be performed on Smart Objects without first converting them to a normal image layer (Layer > Smart Object > Rasterize). You create a Smart Object layer by either converting an existing image layer (Layer > Smart Objects > Convert to Smart Objects) or by opening the original file as a Smart Object (File > Open As Smart Object) when commencing initial editing. When a filter is applied to a Smart Object layer it is termed a Smart Filter and appears below the Smart Object layer. Because the effects of a Smart Filter can be altered or removed after application, this type of filtering is non-destructive.

Smart Object layers are used for some non-destructive editing techniques as they contain and protect the original picture.

3D Layers (Photoshop Extended only): The Extended edition of Photoshop also has the ability to open and work with three-dimensional architectural or design files. When Photoshop opens a 3D file it is placed on a separate layer where you can move, scale, change lighting and rendering of the 3D model. Apart from the extrusions possible with the new Repoussé feature creating complex 3D models is only possible in a 3D authoring program.

Selecting an Adjustment in the Adjustments pane automatically adds an adjustment layer to the layers stack.

Adjustment layers: These layers alter the layers that are arranged below them in the stack. Adjustment layers act as a glass filter through which the lower layers are viewed. They allow image adjustments to be made without permanently modifying the original pixels (if the adjustment layer is removed, or the visibility of the layer is turned off, the pixels revert to their original value). You can use adjustment layers to perform many of the enhancement tasks that you would normally apply directly to an image layer without changing the image itself. From CS4, adjustment layers are added automatically when clicking onto an Adjustment Type icon in the Adjustment panel. This is a big change in adjustment layer workflow from previous versions of Photoshop. Adjustment layers are always added to the stack with a linked layer mask.

Background layers: An image can only have one background layer. It is the bottom-most layer in the stack. No other layers can be moved beneath this layer. You cannot adjust this layer's opacity or its blending mode. You can convert background layers to standard image layers by double-clicking the layer in the Layers palette, setting your desired layer options in the dialog provided and then clicking OK.

Saving an image with layers

The file formats that support layers are Photoshop's native Photoshop document (PSD) format, Photoshop PDF, JPEG2000, PSB (Large Document Format) and Photoshop's version of TIFF. The layers in a picture must always be flattened if the file is to be saved as a standard JPEG. It is recommended that a PSD with its layers is always kept as an archived master copy – best practice would keep in progress archives as well as the final image. It is possible to quickly flatten a multi-layered image and save it as a JPEG or TIFF file by choosing File > Save As and then selecting the required file format from the pull-down menu.

Quick Masks, selections and alpha channels

Selections isolate parts of a picture. When first starting to use Photoshop it is easy to think of selections, masks and channels as all being completely separate program features, but in the reality of day-to-day image enhancement each of these tools is inextricably linked. As your skills develop most image-makers will develop their own preferred ways of working. Some use a workflow that is selection based, others switch between masking and selections and a third group concentrates all their efforts on creating masks only. No one way of working is right or wrong. In fact, many of the techniques advocated by the members of each group often provide a different approach to solving the same problem.

The masks created with the Quick Mask feature are stored as alpha channels which can be viewed and edited via the Channels palette. Switching from the Quick Mask mode changes the mask to a selection.

Switching between Mask and Selection modes

You can switch between Mask and Selection (also called 'Standard') modes by clicking on the mode button positioned at the bottom of the toolbox. Any 'marching ants' indicating active selections will be converted to red shaded areas when selecting the Mask mode. Similarly active masks will be outlined with 'marching ants' when switching back to Selection mode.

Selection mode   *Quick Mask mode*

Saving selections

Photoshop provides users with the option to save their carefully created selections using the Select > Save Selection option. In this way the selection can be reloaded at a later date in the same file via the Select > Load Selection feature, or even after the document has been closed and reopened. Though not immediately obvious to the new user, the selection is actually saved with the picture as a special alpha channel and this is where the primary link between selections and masks occurs. Masks too are stored as alpha channels in your picture documents.

Alpha channels are essentially grayscale pictures where the black section of the image indicates the area where changes can be made, the white portion represents protected areas and gray values allow proportional levels of change. Alpha channels can be viewed, selected and edited via the Channels palette.

When you save a selection you create a grayscale alpha channel. You can name the selection inside the Save Selection dialog.

Quick definitions

Selections – A selection is an area of a picture that is isolated so that it can be edited or enhanced independently of the rest of the image. Selections are made with a range of Photoshop tools including the Marquee, Lasso and Magic Wand tools.

Masks – Masks also provide a means of restricting image changes to a section of the picture. Masks are created using standard painting tools whilst in the Quick Mask mode.

Alpha channels – Alpha channels are a special channel type that are separate to those used to define the base color of a picture such as Red, Green and Blue. Selections and masks are stored as alpha channels and can be viewed in the Channels palette. You can edit a selected alpha channel using painting and editing tools as well as filters.

Channels

As we have already seen, channels represent the way in which the base color in an image is represented. Most images that are created by digital cameras are made up of Red, Green and Blue (RGB) channels. In contrast, pictures that are destined for printing are created with Cyan, Magenta, Yellow and Black (CMYK) channels to match the printing inks. Sometimes the channels in an image are also referred to as the picture's 'color mode'.

Viewing channels

Many image-editing programs contain features designed for managing and viewing the color channels in your image. Photoshop uses a separate Channels palette (Window > Channels). Looking a little like the Layers palette, hence the source of much confusion, this palette breaks the full color picture into its various base color parts.

Changing color mode

Though most editing and enhancement work can be performed on the RGB file, sometimes the digital photographer may need to change the color mode of his or her file. There are a range of conversion options located under the Mode menu (Image > Mode) in Photoshop. When one of these options is selected your picture's color will be translated into the new set of channels. Changing the number of channels in an image also impacts on the file size of the picture. Four-channel CMYK images are bigger than three-channel RGB pictures, which in turn are roughly three times larger than single-channel grayscale photographs.

The type and number of color channels used to create the color in your pictures can be changed via the Mode option in the Image menu.

When do I need to change channels?

For most image-editing and enhancement tasks RGB color mode is all you will ever need. Some high-quality and printing-specific techniques do require changing modes, but this is generally the field of the 'hardened' professional. A question often asked is 'Given that my inkjet printer uses CMYK inks, should I change my photograph to CMYK before printing?' Logic says yes, but practically speaking this type of conversion is best handled by your printer's driver software. Most modern desktop printers are optimized for RGB output even if their ink set is CMYK.

Channel types

RGB: This is the most common color mode. Consisting of Red, Green and Blue channels, most digital camera and scanner output is supplied in this mode.

CMYK: Designed to replicate the ink sets used to print magazines and newspapers, this mode is made from Cyan, Magenta, Yellow and Black (K) channels.

LAB: Consisting of Lightness, A color (green–red) and B color (blue–yellow) channels, this mode is used by professional photographers when they want to enhance the details of an image without altering the color. By selecting the L channel and then performing their changes only the image details are affected.

Grayscale: Consisting of a single black channel, this mode is used for monochrome pictures. Duo-, Tri- and Quad-tones are a special variation of grayscale images that include extra colors creating tinted monochromes.

Gray Mode

RGB Mode   *LAB Mode*

CMYK Mode

The most used color modes (channel types) are RGB, CMYK, LAB and Grayscale. Unless you are working in the publishing industry, or you want to use advanced image-editing techniques, you should keep your picture in RGB mode.

157

Adjustment and filter layers and editing quality

As introduced earlier, adjustment layers act as filters that modify the hue, saturation and brightness of the pixels on the layer or layers beneath. Using an adjustment layer instead of the 'Adjustments' from the 'Image' menu allows the user to make multiple and consecutive image adjustments without permanently modifying the original pixel values.

Non-destructive image editing

The manipulation of image quality using '**adjustment layers**' and '**layer masks**' is often termed 'non-destructive'. Using adjustment layers to manipulate images is preferable to working directly and repeatedly on the pixels themselves. Using the 'Adjustments' from the 'Image' menu, or the manipulation tools from the toolbox (Dodge, Burn and Sponge Tools), directly on pixel layers can eventually lead to a degradation of image quality. If adjustment layers are used together with '**layer masks**' to limit their effect, the pixel values are physically changed only once when the image is flattened or the layers are merged. Retaining the integrity of your original file is essential for high-quality output.

Note > For the last couple of versions of Photoshop it has been possible to scale or 'transform' a layer or group of layers non-destructively by turning the layer, or layers, into a 'Smart Object'. In CS3 it became possible to apply filters (called Smart Filters) non-destructively to these Smart Objects and since CS4 we can also Skew, Distort and add Perspective effects interactively to a Smart Object.

Retaining quality

The evidence of a file that has been degraded can be observed by viewing its histogram. If the resulting histogram displays excessive spikes or missing levels there is a high risk that a smooth transition between tones and color will not be possible in the resulting print. A tell-tale sign of poor scanning and image editing is the effect of '**banding**' that can be clearly observed in the final print. This is where the transition between colors or tones is no longer smooth, but can be observed as a series of steps, or bands, of tone and/or color. To avoid this it is essential that you start with a good scan (a broad histogram without gaps) and limit the number of changes to the original pixel values.

Layer masks and editing adjustments

The use of 'layer masks' is an essential skill for professional image retouching. Together with the Selection Tools and 'adjustment layers' they form the key to effective and sophisticated image editing. A 'layer mask' can control which pixels are concealed or revealed on any image layer except the background layer. If the layer mask that has been used to conceal pixels is then discarded or switched off (Shift-click the layer mask thumbnail) the original pixels reappear. This non-destructive approach to retouching and photographic montage allows the user to make frequent changes. To attach a layer mask to any layer (except the background layer) simply click on the layer and then click on the 'Add layer mask' icon at the base of the Layers palette.

Photoshop contains a special Masks pane with controls for adjusting the density and feather of a layer mask. Also included are buttons for refining the mask using Mask Edge, Color Range and Invert features. Remember that painting or adding gradients to a mask will reveal or conceal the adjustment when used with Adjustment layers.

A layer mask is automatically attached to every adjustment layer. The effects of an adjustment layer can be limited to a localized area of the image by simply clicking on the adjustment layer's associated mask thumbnail in the Layers palette and then painting out the adjustment selectively using any of the painting tools whilst working in the main image window. The opacity and tone of the foreground color in the toolbox will control whether the adjustment is reduced or eliminated in the localized area of the painting action. Painting with a darker tone will conceal more than when painting with a lighter tone or a dark tone with a reduced opacity.

A layer mask can be filled with black to conceal the effects of the adjustment layer. Painting with white in the layer mask will then reveal the adjustment in the localized area of the painting action. Alternatively the user can select the Gradient Tool and draw a gradient in the layer mask to selectively conceal a portion of the adjustment. To add additional gradients the user must select either the Multiply or Screen blend modes for the gradient in the Options bar.

Layer mask shortcuts

Disable/enable layer mask	Shift + click layer mask thumbnail
Preview contents of layer mask	Opt/Alt + click layer mask thumbnail
Preview layer mask and image	Opt/Alt + Shift + click layer mask thumbnail

Serap Osman

selections

Serap Osman

essential skills

- Develop skills in creating and modifying selections to isolate and mask image content.
- Develop skills using the following tools and features:
    - Selection Tools
    - Quick Mask, alpha channels and layer masks
    - Color Range and Extract filter
    - Pen Tool.

Introduction

One of the most skilled areas of digital retouching and manipulation is the ability to make accurate selections of pixels for repositioning, modifying or exporting to another image. This skill allows localized retouching and image enhancement. Photoshop provides several different tools that allow the user to select the area to be changed. Called the 'Selection' Tools, using these features will fast become a regular part of your editing and retouching process. Photoshop marks the boundaries of a selected area using a flashing dotted line sometimes called 'marching ants'. Obvious distortions of photographic originals are common in the media but so are images where the retouching and manipulations are subtle and not detectable. Nearly every image in the printed media is retouched to some extent. Selections are made for a number of reasons:

• Making an adjustment or modification to a localized area, e.g. color, contrast, etc.
• Defining a subject within the overall image to mask, move or replicate.
• Defining an area where an image or group of pixels will be inserted ('paste into').

Selection Tools overview

Photoshop groups the Selection Tools based on how they isolate picture parts. These categories are:

• The '**Marquee Tools**' are used to draw regular-shaped selections such as rectangles or ellipses around an area within the image.

• The '**Lasso Tools**' use a more freehand drawing approach and are used to draw a selection by defining the edge between a subject and its background.

• The '**Magic Wand**' and the '**Quick Selection**' Tools both create selections based on color and tone and are used to isolate groups of pixels by evaluating the similarity of the neighboring pixel values (hue, saturation and brightness) to the pixel that is selected.

Shape-based selections with the Marquee Tools

The Marquee Tools select by dragging with the mouse over the area required. Holding down the Shift key as you drag the selection will 'constrain' the selection to a square or circle rather than a rectangle or oval. Using the Alt (Windows) or Option (Mac) key will draw the selections from their centers. The Marquee Tools are great for isolating objects in your images that are regular in shape, but for less conventional shapes, you will need to use one of the Lasso Tools.

Selections based on shapes

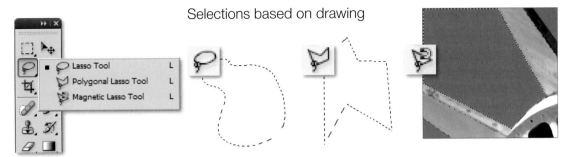

Selections based on drawing

Drawn selections using the Lasso Tools

Select by encircling or drawing around the area you wish to select. The standard Lasso Tool works like a pencil, allowing the user to draw freehand shapes for selections. A large screen and a mouse in good condition (or a graphics tablet) are required to use the Freehand Lasso Tool effectively. In contrast, the Polygonal Lasso Tool draws straight-edged lines between mouse-click points. Either of these features can be used to outline and select irregular-shaped image parts. A third tool, the Magnetic Lasso, helps with the drawing process by aligning the outline with the edge of objects automatically. It uses contrast in color and tone as a basis for determining the edge of an object. The accuracy of the 'magnetic' features of this tool is determined by three settings in the tool's Options bar. **Contrast** is the value that a pixel has to differ from its neighbor to be considered an edge, **Width** is the number of pixels either side of the pointer that are sampled in the edge determination process and **Frequency** is the distance between fastening points in the outline.

Double-clicking the Polygonal Lasso Tool or Magnetic Lasso Tool automatically completes the selection using a straight line between the last selected point and the first.

Note > Remember the Magnetic Lasso Tool requires a tonal or color difference between the object and its background in order to work effectively.

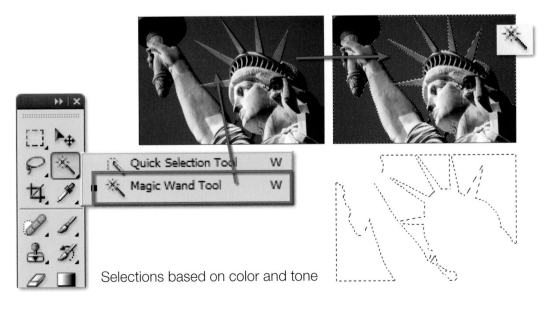

Selections based on color and tone

The Magic Wand

Unlike the Lasso and Marquee Tools the Magic Wand makes selections based on color and tone. It selects by relative pixel values. When the user clicks on an image with the Magic Wand Tool Photoshop searches the picture for pixels that have a similar color and tone. With large images this process can take a little time but the end result is a selection of all similar pixels across the whole picture.

Tolerance

How identical a pixel has to be to the original is determined by the **Tolerance** value in the Options bar. The higher the value, the less alike the two pixels need to be, whereas a lower setting will require a more exact match before a pixel is added to the selection. Turning on the **Contiguous** option will only include the pixels that are similar and adjacent to the original pixels in the selection.

The new Quick Selection Tool is grouped with the Magic Wand in the toolbar (1). The feature creates intelligent selections as you paint over the picture surface (2). The tool's options bar contains settings for adding to and subtracting from existing selections (3), using the tool over multiple layers (4) as well as a button to display the new Refine Edge feature (5).

Quicker selections

Right from the very early days of Photoshop most users quickly recognized that being able to apply changes to just a portion of their images via selections was a very powerful way to work. It followed that the quality of their selective editing and enhancement activities was directly related to the quality of the selections they created. This was the start of our love/hate relationship with selection creation.

Over the years Adobe has provided us with a range of tools designed to help in this quest. Some, like the Magic Wand, are based on selecting pixels that are similar in tone and color; others, such as the Lasso and Marquee Tools, require you to draw around the subject to create the selection.

The Quick Selection Tool was first introduced in Photoshop CS3. It is grouped with the Magic Wand in the toolbar. The tool is used by painting over the parts of the picture that you want to select. The selection outline will grow as you continue to paint. When you release the mouse button the tool will automatically refine the selection further.

Moving a selection

If the selection is not accurate it is possible to move the selection without moving any pixels. With the Selection Tool still active place the cursor inside your selection and drag the selection to reposition it. To move the pixels and the selection, use the Move Tool from the Tools palette. New for Photoshop CS5 is the ability to move selections even if the active layer is currently hidden.

To remove a selection

Go to Select > Deselect or use the shortcut 'Command/Ctrl + D' to deselect a selection.

Customizing your selections

Basic selections of standard, or regular-shaped, picture parts can be easily made with one simple step – just click and drag. But you will quickly realize that most selection scenarios are often a little more complex. For this reason the thoughtful people at Adobe have provided several ways of allowing you to modify your selections. The two most used methods provide the means to 'add to' or 'subtract from' existing selections. This, in conjunction with the range of Selection Tools offered by the program, gives the user the power to select even the most complex picture parts, often using more than one tool for the task. Skillful selecting takes practice and patience as well as the ability to choose which Selection Tool (or Tools) will work best for a given task. Photoshop provides two different methods to customize an existing selection.

Use the mode buttons located in a special portion of the tool's Options bar to start changing your selections. The default mode is 'New Selection', which means that each selection you make replaces the last. Once another option is selected the mode remains active for the duration of the selection session. This is true even when you switch Selection Tools.

The user can make a selection before creating the adjustment layer and then when the adjustment layer is created the selection is used to automatically create a mask.

New selection

Add to selection

Subtract from selection

Selection intersection

Add to a selection

To add to an existing selection hold down the Shift key while selecting a new area. Notice that when the Shift key is held down the Selection Tool's cursor changes to include a '+' to indicate that you are in the 'add' mode. This addition mode works for all tools and you can change Selection Tools as needed to make further refinements.

Keyboard shortcuts provide the fastest way to customize your selections.

Subtract from a selection

To remove sections from an existing selection hold down the Alt key (Option for Macintosh) while selecting the part of the picture you do not wish to include in the selection. When in the subtract mode the cursor will change to include a '−'.

Selection intersection

In Photoshop often the quickest route to selection perfection is not the most direct route. When you are trying to isolate picture parts with complex edges it is sometimes quicker and easier to make two separate selections and then form the final selection based on their intersection. The fourth mode available as a button on the Selection Tool's Options bar is the Intersect mode (Opt/Alt Shift). Though not used often, this mode provides you with the ability to define a selection based on the area in common between two different selections.

Inversing a selection

In a related technique, some users find it helpful to select what they don't want in a picture and then instruct Photoshop to select everything but this area. The Select > Inverse command (Ctrl/Cmd Shift I) inverts or reverses the current selection and is perfect for this approach. In this way foreground objects can be quickly selected in pictures with a smoothly graduated background of all one color (sky, snow or a wall space) by using the Magic Wand to select the background. Then the act of inversing the selection will isolate the foreground detail.

Professionals who know that the foreground will be extracted from the picture's surrounds often shoot their subjects against an evenly lit background of a consistent color to facilitate the application of this technique.

Sometimes it is quicker to select the area that you don't want and then inverse the selection to produce the required results.

Refining selections

As well as 'adding to' and 'subtracting from' existing selections, Photoshop contains several other options for refining the selections you make. Grouped under the Select menu, these features generally concentrate on adjusting the edge of the current selection. The options include:

Border – Choosing the Border option from the Modify menu displays a dialog where you can enter the width of the border in pixels (between 1 and 200). Clicking OK creates a border selection that frames the original selection.

Smooth – This option cleans up stray pixels that are left unselected after using the Magic Wand Tool. After choosing Modify enter a radius value to use for searching for stray pixels and then click OK.

Other options for modifying your selections can be found under the Select menu.

Expand – After selecting Expand, enter the number of pixels that you want to increase the selection by and click OK. The original selection is increased in size. You can enter a pixel value between 1 and 100.

Contract – Selecting this option will reduce the size of the selection by the number of pixels entered into the dialog. You can enter a pixel value between 1 and 100.

Feather – The Feather command softens the transition between selected and non-selected areas.

Grow – The Grow feature increases the size of an existing selection by incorporating pixels of similar color and tone to those already in the selection. For a pixel to be included in the 'grown' selection it must be adjacent to the existing selection and fall within the current tolerance settings located in the options bar.

Similar – For a pixel to be included in the 'similar' selection it does not have to be adjacent to the existing selection but must fall within the current tolerance settings located in the options bar.

Refine Edge – Adobe included a new Refine Edge feature in CS3 to coincide with the release of the Quick Selection Tool. In Photoshop CS5 the feature has been revamped and now provides a mechanism for intelligently adapting the qualities of the selection edge to the changing characteristics of the subject. Refine Edge is accessed either via the button now present in all the Options Bar of all Selection Tools, or via Select > Refine Edge. The dialog brings together a range of different controls for adjusting the edges of the selection with seven selection edge preview modes and the new Edge Detection ability (Smart Radius) and Output options. Smart Radius plus the Output and Preview modes edge refinement which used to be a pretty hit and miss affair, a lot easier to manage, with the ultimate result of the production of better selection edges for all.

Two other options are available only in Refine Edge:

Radius – Use this slider to increase the quality of the edge in areas of soft transition with background pixels or where the subject's edge is finely detailed.

Contrast – Increase the contrast settings to sharpen soft selection edges.

Shift Edge – Moves the selection edge effectively expanding or contracting the selection.

Smart Radius – Applies the edge detection technology to the selection. The Radius slider changes the width of the area around the selection edge being used in the detection.

Decontaminate – Removes the remnants of background color from the selection edge in order to produce a better blend when placing the subject on a new background. The Amount slider controls the strength of the effect.

The revamped Refine Edge dialog now includes new View options (1), powerful Edge Detection features (2), selection refinement tools (3), Edge adjustment controls (4), and new Output settings (5).

Previewing edge refinements – The View mode menu at the top of the Refine Edge dialog provides a range of different ways to view the selection on your picture. Press the F key to cycle through the view modes and the X key to temporarily display the full image view.

Output To – Also new for CS5 is the drop-down list of output options at the bottom of the Refine Edge dialog. There are options here to create layers, masks and even new documents from the refined selection.

Refine Edge in action

The power of the new edge detection and refinement features are best put to use when creating a seamless montage of a subject against a new background. Just as in the last release, using Refine Edge is a three step process. First you need to make a rough selection of the subject, next you use the feature's controls to adjust the selection edge before finally extracting the subject from its existing background and layering above the new background.

The first step is to create a selection around the subject. In the example above, the girl on the upper layer. I chose the Quick Selection Tool from the toolbar and painted a selection over the subject. The tool automatically selects the jumper, face, hat and hair as I drag the tool over the canvas.

If some of the background is included in your selection, remember you can adjust the selection further by holding down the Alt/Opt key to switch the tool to the Subtract From Select mode, and then painting over these parts to remove them.

With the newly created selection displayed, I chose Select > Refine Edge. This displays the Refine Edge dialog box. Next, I adjusted the settings so that the View was Black and White, Smart Radius was checked, Radius was 1 pixel, Decontaminate Colors was unchecked and all other settings were zero.

The Smart Radius feature automatically adapts the selection approach to the differences in edge between the subject's jumper, hat and hair. I moved the Radius slider to increase the width of the area either side of the selection's edge used by the Smart Radius. Pressing the J key displays the radius and adjusting the Shift Edge slider moves the position of the edge.

169

With some subjects a single Radius setting will not encompass all edge details. In these cases, you can customize the width and positioning of the edge with the Refine Radius and Erase Refinements tools. Here, I fine-tuned the mask around the subject's hair by painting with the Refine Radius Tool. I then pressed the F key to cycle through the preview modes to check the quality of the edge.

Next, I switched to the Erase Refinements Tool to remove any unwanted areas that had crept into the mask's edge. Here, I viewed the changes in the On Layer view so that it was possible to see the subject against the layer beneath.

If you intend to place the selected subject on a new background you can use the use the Decontaminate Colors setting and its associated Amount slider to remove any color remaining in the edge from the old background. These settings introduce a degree of transparency to the mask edge so that the subject is merged more seamlessly with the new background. The Output To menu contains a range of options that determine how the selected part of photo will be processed when exiting the Refine Edge dialog box. For this example I selected the New Layer With Layer Mask option.

Saving and loading selections

The selections you make remain active while the image is open and until a new selection is made, but what if you want to store all your hard work to use on another occasion? As we have already seen in the previous chapter Photoshop provides the option to save your selections/ masks as part of the picture file. Simply choose Select > Save Selection and the existing selection will be stored with the picture.

To display a selection saved with a picture, open the file and choose Load Selection from the Select menu. In the Load Selection dialog click on the Channel drop-down menu and choose the selection you wish to reinstate. Choose the mode with which the selection will be added to your picture from the Operation section of the dialog. Click OK to finish.

Save a selection.   *Load a selection.*

Feather and anti-alias

The ability to create a composite image or '**photomontage**' that looks subtle, realistic and believable rests with whether or not the viewer is able to detect where one image starts and the other finishes. The edges of each selection can be modified so that it appears as if it belongs, or is related, to the surrounding pixels.

Options are available in Photoshop to alter the appearance of the edges of a selection. Edges can appear sharp or soft (a gradual transition between the selection and the background). The options to effect these changes are:

- Feather
- Anti-aliasing.

Feather

When this option is chosen the pixels at the edges of the selection are blurred. The edges are softer and less harsh. This blurring may either create a more realistic montage or cause loss of detail at the edge of the selection.

You can choose feathering for the Marquee or Lasso Tools as you use them by entering a value in the tool options box, or you can add feathering to an existing selection (Select > Feather). The feathering effect only becomes apparent when you move or paste the selection to a new area.

Anti-aliasing

When this option is chosen the jagged edges of a selection are softened. A more gradual transition between the edge pixels and the background pixels is created. Only the edge pixels are changed so no detail is lost. Anti-aliasing must be chosen before the selection is made (it cannot be added afterwards). It is usual to have the anti-alias option selected for most selections. The anti-alias option also needs to be considered when using type in image-editing software. The anti-alias option may be deselected to improve the appearance of small type to avoid the appearance of blurred text.

Better with a tablet
Many professionals prefer to work with a stylus and tablet when creating complex selections. All models change a tool's characteristics using pressure sensitivity with some including options such as intuitive motion as well.

Defringe and Matting

When a selection has been made using the anti-alias option some of the pixels surrounding the selection are included. If these surrounding pixels are darker, lighter or a different color to the selection a fringe or halo may be seen.

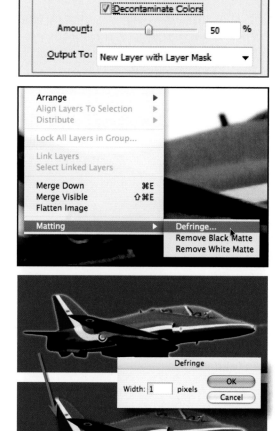

Your first point of call for fixing this problem should be the new Decontaminate Colors option in the Refine Edge dialog. For the best blending be sure to preview the subject against the new background as you adjust the Amount slider.

Alternatively, you can choose Matting > Defringe from the layers menu to replace the different fringe pixels with pixels of a similar hue, saturation or brightness found within the selection area.

The user may have to experiment with the most appropriate method of removing a fringe. The alternative options of Remove White Matte and Remove Black Matte may provide the user with a better result. If a noticeable fringe still persists it is possible to contract the selection prior to moving it using the Modify > Contract option from the Select menu.

Saving a selection as an alpha channel

Selections can be permanently stored as '**alpha channels**'. The saved selections can be reloaded and/or modified even after the image has been closed and reopened. To save a selection as an alpha channel simply click the '**Save selection as channel**' icon at the base of the Channels palette. To load a selection either drag the alpha channel to the '**Load channel as selection**' icon in the Channels palette or Command/Ctrl-click the alpha channel.

It is possible to edit an alpha channel (and the resulting selection) by using the painting and editing tools. Painting with black will add to the alpha channel whilst painting with white will remove information. Painting with shades of gray will lower or increase the opacity of the alpha channel. The user can selectively soften a channel and resulting selection by applying a Gaussian Blur filter. Choose Blur > Gaussian Blur from the Filters menu.

Note > An image with saved selections (alpha channels) cannot be saved in the standard JPEG format. Use the PSD, PDF or TIFF formats or JPEG2000 (optional plug-in) if storage space is tight.

Quick Mask or Refine Edge

The problem with feathering and modifying selections using the Modify commands in the 'Select' menu is that the ants give very poor feedback about what is actually going on at the edge. Viewing the selection against a Matte color in the Refine Edge dialog box or as a 'Mask' in 'Quick Mask mode' allows you to view the quality and accuracy of your selection. Quick Mask allows the user to modify localized areas of the edge whilst Refine Edge works on the entire edge. Zoom in on an edge to take a closer look. Double-click the Quick Mask icon to change the mask color, opacity and to switch between 'Masked Areas' and 'Selected Areas'. If the mask is still falling short of the edge you can expand the selection by going to Filter > Other > Maximum. Choose a 1-pixel radius, select OK and the mask will shrink (expanding the selection). A 'Levels' adjustment in Quick Mask mode provides a 'one-stop shop' for editing the mask, giving you the luxury of a preview as with Refine Edge, but also gives you the advantage of localized editing.

Using a 'Levels' adjustment (Image > Adjustments > Levels) in Quick Mask mode allows you to modify the edge quality if it is too soft and also reposition the edge so that it aligns closely with your subject. Make a selection of the edge using the Lasso Tool if you need to modify just a small portion of the Quick Mask. Dragging the shadow and highlight sliders in towards the center will reduce the softness of the mask whilst moving the midtone or 'Gamma' slider will move the edge itself. Unlike the Refine Edge dialog box you can paint in Quick Mask to refine localized areas of the selection.

Note > The selection must have been feathered prior to the application of the Levels adjustment for this to be effective.

Save the selection as an alpha channel. This will ensure that your work is stored permanently in the file. If the file is closed and reopened the selection can be reloaded. Finish off the job in hand by modifying or replacing the selected pixels. If the Quick Selection Tool or Magic Wand Tool is not working for you, try exploring the following alternatives.

'Color Range'

The Quick Selection Tool may be the obvious tool for making a selection of a subject with a good color or tonal contrast, but Color Range can be utilized for making selections of similar color that are not contiguous. 'Color Range', from the Select menu, is useful for selecting subjects that are defined by a limited color range (sufficiently different from those of the background colors). The feature contains Localized Color Clusters and Range options for better control over where the feature is put to work. Color Range is especially useful when the selection is to be used for a hue adjustment. Use a Marquee Tool (from the Tools palette) to limit the selection area before you start using the Color Range option.

Note > The Color Range option can misbehave sometimes. If the selection does not seem to be restricted to your sampled color press the Alt/Option key and click on the reset option or close the dialog box and re-enter.

Use the 'Add to sample' eyedropper and drag the eyedropper over the subject area you wish to select. In the later stages you can choose a matte color to help the task of selection. Adjust the Fuzziness slider to perfect the selection. Very dark or light pixels can be left out of the selection if it is to be used for a hue adjustment only. The dialog contains four options in the Selection Preview menu that will allow you to view the quality of the selection on the image to gain an idea of the selection's suitability for the job in hand.

The mask can be 'cleaned' using the Dust & Scratches filter and softened using a Gaussian Blur filter. A selection prepared by the 'Color Range' command is ideal for making a hue adjustment. It is also recommended to view the individual channels to see if the subject you are trying to isolate is separated from the surrounding information. If this is the case a duplicate channel can act as a starting point for a selection.

Channel masking

An extremely quick and effective method for selecting a subject with reasonable color contrast to the surrounding pixels is to use the information from one of the channels to create a mask and then to load this mask as a selection.

Click on each individual channel to see which channel offers the best contrast and then duplicate this channel by dragging it to the 'New Channel' icon.

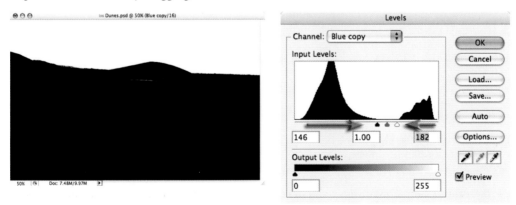

Apply a Levels adjustment to the duplicate channel to increase the contrast of the mask. Slide the shadow, midtone and highlight sliders until the required mask is achieved. The mask may still not be perfect but this can be modified using the painting tools.

Select the default settings for the foreground and background colors in the Tools palette, choose a paintbrush, set the opacity to 100% in the Options bar and then paint to perfect the mask. Zoom in to make sure there are no holes in the mask before moving on. To soften the edge of the mask, apply a small amount of Gaussian Blur.

Note > Switch on the master channel visibility or Shift-click the RGB master to view the channel copy as a mask together with the RGB image. This will give you a preview so that you can see how much blur to apply and if further modifications are required.

Click on the active duplicate channel or drag it to the 'Load channel as selection' icon. Click on the RGB master before returning to the Layers palette.

Channel masking may at first seem a little complex but it is surprisingly quick when the technique has been used a few times. This technique is very useful for photographers shooting products for catalogs and websites. A small amount of color contrast between the subject and background is all that is required to make a quick and effective mask.

176

Tone-based selections and masks

So as we can see masks and, their alter ego, selections, are very useful for controlling how layers are blended together and also how effects are applied to images, but they can also help us alter specific tones in a photo. Once created, a mask can be used in conjunction with a Curves or Levels Adjustment layer to restrict the changes made with these features to a specific tonal range.

Using the abilities of a luminosity mask it is possible to control adjustments so that they are applied proportionately to highlights, then midtones and shadows.

Luminosity masking

In this example, a Luminosity mask is used to alter the highlight details of the photo to provide more apparent detail. Because the mask was created with tones of the original image the adjustment is applied proportionately to the highlights most, then midtones, and finally, to the shadow areas. This is because of the basic nature of masks where white areas 'reveal' the effect and black areas 'conceal' the effect.

Start by displaying the Channels palette and then make a selection from the image. Drag the RGB channel to the Load Selection button at the bottom of the palette. Click the Save Selection button to create a new entry called Alpha 1. Rename the entry to Highlights.

The resulting luminosity mask is used in conjunction with the Adjustment layer to tweak the highlight tones in the image.

177

Click the RGB Channel entry at the top of the palette to make it active. This restores the color preview. Now, choose Select > Deselect to remove the marching ants from the preview.

Drag the channel to the Load Selection button at the bottom of the Channels palette. With the selection active you can now add a new Curves Adjustment layer. Make changes to the shape of the highlight end of the curve and click the OK button to apply the adjustments via the associated Highlights mask.

Before

After

Using a shadow mask, it is possible to alter the tones of the dark portions of the image while leaving much of the midtones and all of the highlights untouched. Here more detail was added to the dark curtains by boosting the brightness and contrast of these tones.

Shadow masking

Shadow luminosity masking, like the highlight masking we looked at in the previous technique, is a process by which the darker tones in an image are isolated with a mask. Once this has occurred, then it is possible to adjust just those values in the photo using an Adjustment layer. In this example the shadow areas have been changed using a Curves Adjustment Layer and in the process, the highlights in the image have been left unchanged.

The first step is to create a highlight mask. Do this by displaying the Channels palette and then dragging the RGB entry to the Load Channel as Selection button at the bottom of the palette. With the selection still active, click on the next button along to create a mask from the selection. Rename the new mask Highlights.

We will now use the Highlight mask to create the shadow mask. Start by deselecting any selections still active. Next, drag the Highlight mask entry to the Create New Channel button at the bottom of the palette. This will create a copy of the Highlight mask entry. Select the copied entry and click Ctrl/Cmd I to inverse the image. Rename the channel Shadows.

Inverting the Highlight mask effectively creates a mask that concentrates on the opposite end of the spectrum - the shadows. Now with the Shadow Channel selected click onto the Load Channel as Selection button at the bottom of the palette. Next deselect the Shadow channel and click onto the RGB channel entry. Then select Layer > New Adjustment Layer > Curves. Make your shadow adjustment via the Curves feature.

Middle values of a photo can also be altered via a midtone luminosity mask. This will largely restrict the changes from shadows and highlight areas.

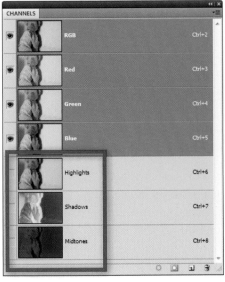

Mid-tone contrast boost

We have already looked at the how to adjust middle tones using controls such as Curves and Shadows/Highlights, but what if we want to use a masking approach for the task? In other words, apply the Curves control through a midtone mask which, by definition, restricts the changes from being applied to shadows or highlights. This technique is based on creating highlight and shadow masks first and then using these to generate a third mask that just isolates the middle values of the image.

Start by creating a luminosity Highlight mask. Do this by dragging the RGB entry in the Channels to the Load Channel as Selection button. Then click onto the Save Selection as Channel button. Rename the entry Highlights. Hit Ctrl/Cmd D to deselect the active selection.

Now to create the shadow luminosity mask. Start by dragging the Highlights mask to the Create New Channel button at the bottom of the Channels palette. Rename this entry Shadows. Select the new Shadows mask and inverse the tones of the mask by hitting the Ctrl/Cmd I keys.

To create the midtone mask, firstly click onto the RGB channel entry. Choose Select > All to create a selection of all the image. Now hold down the Ctrl/Cmd Alt/Opt keys while clicking both highlight and shadow mask channel thumbnails. This subtracts highlight and shadows from the whole image selection. During this process you may see a warning like the one above. Click OK to continue. Rename the new mask Midtones.

Now select the Midtones entry in the Channel palette. Click onto the Load Channel as Selection button at the bottom of the palette then select the RGB channel entry to reset the preview back to full color. You may not see the marching ants of the selection but it will be active. Now create a new Curves Adjustment layer. Automatically the midtone mask will be used in conjunction with the Curves feature. Now you can alter the curve's shape to adjust the middle values.

Selections from paths

The Pen Tool is often used in the creation of sophisticated smooth-edged selections, but strictly speaking it is not one of the selection tools. The Pen Tool creates vector paths instead of selections; these, however, can be converted into selections that in turn can be used to extract or mask groups of pixels. The Pen Tool has an unfortunate reputation – neglected by most, considered an awkward tool by those who have made just a passing acquaintance, and revered by just a select few who have taken a little time to get to know 'the one who sits next to Mr. Blobby' (custom shape icon) in the Tools palette. Who exactly is this little fellow with the 'ye olde' ink nib icon and the awkward working persona? The Pen Tool was drafted into Photoshop from Adobe Illustrator. Although graphic designers are quite adept at using this tool, many photographers the world over have been furiously waving magic wands and magnetic lassos at the megapixel army and putting graphics tablets on their shopping lists each year in an attempt to avoid recognizing the contribution that this unique tool has to offer.

Not everything you can see with your eye can be selected easily with a selection technique based on color or tonal values. The resulting ragged selections can be fixed in Quick Mask mode, but sometimes not without a great deal of effort. The question then comes down to 'how much effort am I prepared to apply, and for how long?' Its about this time that many image editors decide to better acquaint themselves with the Pen Tool. Mastering the Pen Tool in order to harness a selection prowess known to few mortals is not something you can do in a hurry – it falls into a certain skill acquisition category, along with such things as teaching a puppy not to pee in the house, called time-based reward, i.e. investing your time over a short period of time will pay you dividends over a longer period of time. The creation of silky smooth curvaceous lines (called paths) that can then be converted into staggeringly smooth curvaceous selections makes the effort of learning the Pen Tool all worthwhile.

Basic drawing skills

Vector lines and shapes are constructed from geographical markers (anchor points) connected by lines or curves. Many photographers have looked with curiosity at the vector tools in Photoshop's Tools palette for years but have dismissed them as 'not for me'. The reason for this is that drawing vector lines with the Pen Tool for the inexperienced image editor is like reversing with a trailer for the inexperienced driver. It takes practice, and the practice can be initially frustrating.

The pen can multi-task (just like most women and very few men that I know). The pen can draw a vector shape whilst filling it with a color and applying a layer style – all at the same time. Although tempting, this has nothing to do with selecting a bald man's head, so we must be sure to disarm this charming little function. We can also use the training wheels, otherwise known as the 'Rubber Band' option, by clicking on the menu options next to 'Mr Blobby'.

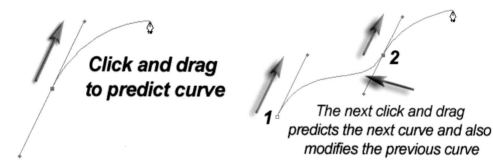

Click and drag to predict curve

1

2

The next click and drag predicts the next curve and also modifies the previous curve

Basics Step 1 – Go to 'File > New' and create a new blank document. Choose 'White' as the 'Background Contents'. Size is not really important (no really – in this instance anything that can be zoomed to fill the screen will serve your purpose). Click on the Pen Tool (double-check the 'Paths' option, rather than the 'Shape layers' option, is selected in the Options bar) and then click and drag (hold down the mouse clicker as you drag your mouse) in the direction illustrated above. The little black square in the center of the radiating lines is called an anchor point. The lines extending either side of this anchor point are called direction lines, with a direction point on either end, and that thing waving around (courtesy of the Rubber Band option) is about to become the path with your very next click of the mouse.

Basics Step 2 – Make a second click and drag in the same direction. Notice how the dragging action modifies the shape of the previous curved line. Go to the 'Edit' menu and select 'Undo'. Try clicking a second time and dragging in a different direction. Undo a third time and this time drag the direction point a different distance from the anchor point. The thing you must take with you from this second step is that a curve (sometimes referred to as a Bézier curve) is both a product of the relative position of the two anchor points either side of the curve, and the direction and length of the two direction lines (the distance and direction of the dragging action).

Basics Step 3 – Scenario 1: Let us imagine that the first click and drag action has resulted in a perfect curve; the second dragging action is not required to perfect the curve but instead upsets the shape of this perfect curve – so how do we stop this from happening? Answer: Hold down the Alt key (PC) or Option key (Mac) and then drag away from the second anchor point to predict the shape of the next curve. This use of the Alt/Option key cancels the first direction line that would otherwise influence the previous curve.

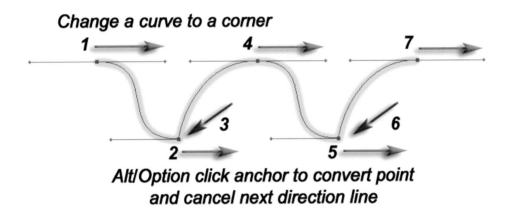

Scenario 2: Let us imagine that we have created the first perfect curve using two normal click and drag actions (no use of a modifier key). The direction lines that are perfecting the first curve are, however, unsuitable for the next curve – so how do we draw the next curve whilst preserving the appearance of the first curve? Answer: The last anchor point can be clicked whilst holding down the Alt/Option key. This action converts the smooth anchor point to a corner anchor point, deleting the second direction line. The next curved shape can then be created without the interference of an inappropriate direction line.

Note > The information that you need to take from this third step is that sometimes direction lines can upset adjacent curves. The technique of cancelling one of the direction lines using a modifier key makes a series of perfect curves possible. These two techniques are especially useful for converting smooth points into corner points on a path.

Basics Step 4 – Just a few more steps and we can go out to play. It is possible to change direction quickly on a path without cancelling a direction line. It is possible to alter the position of a direction line by moving the direction point (at the end of the line) independently of the direction line on the other side of the anchor point. To achieve this simply position the mouse cursor over the direction point and, again using the Alt/Option key, click and drag the direction point to a new position.

Basics Step 5 – If this path is going to be useful as a selection, it is important to return to the start point. Clicking on the start point will close the path. As you move the cursor over the start point the Pen Tool will be accompanied by a small circle to indicate that closure is about to occur. You will also notice that the final curve is influenced by the first direction line of the starting anchor point. Hold down the Alt/Option key when closing the path to cancel this first direction line. Alternatively, hold down the Alt/Option key and drag a new direction line to perfect the final curve.

Add, delete, convert or move anchor points

Alt/Option to convert   Ctrl/Command to select and move

Basics Step 6 – When a path has been closed it is possible to add, delete, convert or move any point. Although these additional tools are available in the Tools palette they can all be accessed without moving your mouse away from the path in progress. If the Auto Add/Delete box has been checked in the Options bar you simply have to move the Pen Tool to a section of the path and click to add an additional point (the pen cursor sprouts a plus symbol). If the Pen Tool is moved over an existing anchor point you can simply click to delete it. Holding down the Ctrl key (PC) or Command key (Mac) will enable you to access the Direct Selection Tool (this normally lives behind the Path Selection Tool). The Direct Selection Tool has a white arrow icon and can select and move a single anchor point (click and drag) or multiple points (by holding down the Shift key and clicking on subsequent points). The Path Selection Tool has to be selected from the Tools palette and is able to select the entire path.

Basics Step 7 – The final step in the creation of a Path is to save it. All Paths, even Work Paths, are saved with the image file (PSD, PDF, PSB, JPEG or TIFF). If, however, a Work Path is not active (such as when the file is closed and reopened) and then the Pen Tool is inadvertently used to draw a new Path, any previous Work Path that was not saved is deleted.

Click on the Paths palette tab and then double-click the Work Path. This will bring up the option to save and name the Work Path and ensure that it cannot be deleted accidentally. To start editing an existing Path click on the Path in the Paths palette and then choose either the Direct Selection Tool or the Pen Tool in the Tools palette. Click near the Path with the Direct Selection Tool to view the handles and the Path.

Magdalena Bors

filters

essential skills

- Apply filter effects to a picture.
- Use the Filter Gallery feature to apply several filters cumulatively.
- Use filters with text and shape layers.
- The 'Smart' way to apply filters.
- Filter a section of a picture.
- Paint with a filter effect.
- Install and use third party filters.

Filtering in Photoshop

Traditionally the term filter, when used in a photography context, referred to a small piece of plastic or glass that was screwed onto, or clipped in front of, the camera's lens. Placing the filter in the imaging path changed the way that the picture was recorded. During the height of their popularity there were literally hundreds of different filter types available for the creative photographer to use. The options ranged from those that simply changed the color of the scene, to graduated designs used for darkening skies to multi-faceted glass filters that split the image in many fragments. Even now when their popularity has waned most photographers still carry a polarizing filter, maybe a couple of color conversion filters and perhaps the odd graduated filter as well. But apart from these few examples, much of the creative work undertaken by in-front-of-camera filters is now handled by the digital filters that are shipped with your imaging program. These options, like the filters of old, are designed to change the way that your picture looks, but you will find that it is possible to create much more sophisticated effects with the digital versions than was ever possible before.

Statue of Liberty – Jeremy Edwards

Applying a filter is a simple process. After opening the image simply select the filter option from those listed under the Filter menu. This approach applies the effects of the filter to the whole of the photo, changing it forever. So be sure to keep a back-up copy of the original picture (or a copy of the background layer) just in case you change your mind later. Better still, use the Smart Filter option to apply your filter changes losslessly.

To get you started, I have included a variety of examples from the range that comes free with Photoshop that you will use most regularly. I have not shown Gaussian Blur or all the sharpening filters as these are covered in techniques elsewhere in the text, but I have tried to sample a variety that, to date, you might not have considered using. I have also included an overview of the updated Lens Correction filter which provides correction of three of the most common lens errors automatically. If you are unimpressed by the results of your first digital filter foray, try changing some of the variables or mixing a filtered layer (using the layer's Blending Mode or Opacity controls) with an unfiltered version of the image. An effect that might seem outlandish at first glance could become usable after some simple adjustments of the in-built sliders contained in most filter dialog boxes or with some multiple layer variations.

The 'Smart' way to filter

The concept of non-destructive editing is the future of editing for photographers and is ever growing in popularity and acceptance. Now many dedicated amateurs are working like professionals by embracing ways of enhancing and editing that don't destroy or change the original pixels in the end result. Masking techniques, Adjustment Layers and the use of Smart Objects are the foundation technologies of many of these techniques. But try as we may some changes have just not been possible to apply non-destructively.

Filtering is one area in particular where this is the case. For example, applying a sharpening filter to a picture irreversibly changes the pixels in the photo forever. For this reason, for many years, the smart photographer applied filters to copies of their photos in order to maintain the integrity of the original capture. Photoshop CS3 changed this way of working by including for the first time a new filtering option called Smart Filters and yes, you guessed it, this technology allowed users to apply a filter to an image non-destructively. Cool!

Based around the Smart Object technology, applying a Smart Filter is a two-step process. First the image layer needs to be converted to a Smart Object. This can be done via the new entry in the Filter menu, Convert for Smart Filters, or by selecting the image layer and then choosing Layer > Smart Object > Convert to Smart Object. Next pick the filter you want to apply and adjust the settings as you would normally before clicking OK.

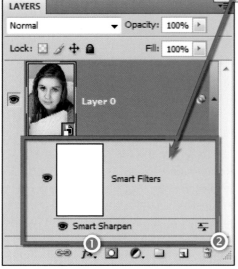

Applying Smart Filters

Applying a filter to a Smart Object layer will automatically create a Smart Filter entry in the Layers palette. Multiple filters with different settings can be added to a single Smart Object layer. The settings for any Smart Filter can be adjusted by double-clicking the filter's name (1) in the Layers palette. The blending mode of the Smart Filter can be changed by double-clicking the settings icon (2) at the right end of the entry. This changes the way that the filter is applied to the image. To apply a filter to several layers, convert the multi-selected layers to a Smart Object first and then filter.

189

Smart Filters are added as an extra entry beneath the Smart Object in the Layers palette. The entry contains both a mask as well as a separate section for the filter entry and its associated settings. Like Adjustment Layers, you can change the setting of a Smart Filter at any time by double-clicking the filter's name in the Layers palette. The blending mode of the filter is adjusted by double-clicking the settings icon at the right end of the filter entry.

The Smart Filter mask can be edited to alter where the filter effects are applied to the photo. In this release multiple Smart Filters can be added to a photo but they all must use the one, common mask.

Finally, with the Smart Filter technology we have a way to apply such things as sharpness or texture non-destructively.

Sharpness applied locally using a masked Smart Object.

Masking Smart Filters

You can easily localize the effects of a Smart Filter by painting directly onto the mask associated with the entry. Here the mask thumbnail was selected first and then inverted using the Image > Adjustments > Inverse option. Keep in mind that black sections of a mask do not apply the filter to the picture so inverting the thumbnail basically removes all filtering effects from the image. Next white was selected as the foreground color and the Brush Tool chosen. The opacity of the tool was reduced and with the mask thumbnail still selected, the areas to be sharpened are then painted in.

The Filter Gallery

Most Photoshop filters are applied using the Filter Gallery feature. Designed to allow the user to apply several different filters to a single image, it can also be used to apply the same filter several times. The dialog consists of a preview area, a collection of filters that can be used with the feature, a settings area with sliders to control the filter's effect and a list of filters that are currently being applied to the image. The gallery is faster and provides previews that are much larger than those contained in individual filter dialogs.

Filters are arranged in the sequence that they are applied. Filters can be moved to a different spot in the sequence by click-dragging up or down the stack. Click the 'eye' icon to hide the effect of the selected filter from preview. Filters can be deleted from the list by dragging them to the dustbin icon at the bottom of the dialog.

Filter settings

Filters applied to the picture

Delete selected filter entry

Preview area   *Gallery filters*   *New filter entry*

Filters that can't be used with the Filter Gallery feature are either applied directly to the picture with no user settings or make use of a filter preview and settings dialog specific to that particular filter, and they generally cannot be used on 16-bit images.

Fade Filter command

The opacity, or strength, of a standard filter effect can be controlled by selecting the Edit > Fade command when selected directly after the filter is applied. With a value of 0% the filter changes are not applied at all, whereas a setting of 100% will apply the changes fully. As well as controlling opacity the Fade dialog also provides the option to select a different blend mode for the filter changes. Note that the actual entry for the Fade command will change depending on the last filter applied and this option is not available when using Smart Filters.

Note > When using Smart Filters you can change the Blend Mode and filter amount (use the Opacity slider) via the Blending Options dialog. This is displayed by double-clicking the settings icon on the right of the filter entry in the Layers palette.

Improving filter performance

A lot of filters make changes to the majority of the pixels in a picture. This level of activity can take considerable time, especially when working with high-resolution pictures or underpowered computers. Use the following tips to increase the performance of applying such filters:

- Free up memory by using the Edit > Purge command before filtering.
- Allocate more memory to Photoshop via the Edit > Preferences > Performance (Windows) or Photoshop > Preferences > Performance (Mac) option before filtering.
- Try out the filter effect on a small selection before applying the filter to the whole picture.
- Apply the filter to individual channels separately rather than the composite image.

Installing and using third party filters

Ever since the early versions of Photoshop, Adobe provided the opportunity for third party developers to create small pieces of specialist software that could plug into Photoshop. The modular format of the software means that Adobe and other software manufacturers can easily create extra filters that can be added to the program at any time. In fact, some of the plug-ins that have been released over the years have became so popular that Adobe themselves incorporated their functions into successive versions of Photoshop. This is how the Drop Shadow layer effect came into being.

Most plug-ins register themselves as extra options in the Filter menu where they can be accessed just like any other Photoshop feature. The Digital SHO filter from Applied Science Fiction is an example of such plug-in technology. Designed to automatically balance the contrast and enhance the shadow detail in digital photographs, when installed it becomes part of a suite of filters supplied by the company that are attached to the Filter menu (see above). Other filters like those supplied by Pixel Genius Suite are automation filters and are therefore placed in the Automate folder.

Filtering a shape or text (vector) layer

Filters only work with bitmap or pixel-based layers and pictures. As text, vector masks and shape layers are all created with vector graphics (non-pixel graphics), these layers need to be converted to bitmap (pixel-based picture) before a filter effect can be applied to them. Photoshop uses a Rasterize function to make this conversion. Simply select the text or shape layer and then choose the Layer > Rasterize option. Alternatively, if you inadvertently try to filter a vector layer Photoshop will display a warning dialog that notifies you that the layer needs to be converted before filtering and offers to make the conversion before proceeding.

Note > Especially in the case of text, you may want to create a copy of the vector layer as a backup, to avoid the need to recreate the layer if the text layer needs to be edited again later.

The great filter round-up

The filter examples on the next few pages will give you an idea of how this type of technology can be used to enhance, change and alter your photos. Keep in mind that there are many more filters that ship with Photoshop or are available online. In fact, Photoshop also includes an option in the Filter menu (Filter > Browse Filters Online) that allows you to search for other Photoshop filters on the web.

Liquify filter

The Liquify filter is a very powerful tool for warping and transforming your pictures. The feature contains its own sophisticated dialog box complete with a preview area and no less than ten different tools (eight warp and two mask tools) that can be used to twist, warp, push, pull and reflect your pictures with such ease that it is almost as if they were made of silly putty. Since CS3 the filter has worked with 16-bit images but not Smart Objects. The effects obtained with this feature can be subtle or extreme depending on how the changes are applied. Stylus and tablet users have extra options and control based on pen pressure.

Liquify works by projecting the picture onto a grid or mesh. In an unaltered state, the grid is completely regular; when liquifying a photo the grid lines and spaces are intentionally distorted, which in turn causes the picture to distort. As the mesh used to liquify a photo can be saved and reloaded, the distortion effects created in one picture can also be applied to an entirely different image.

Regular mesh   *Before*   *Distorted mesh*   *After*

The tools contained in the filter's toolbox are used to manipulate the underlying mesh and therefore distort the picture. Areas of the picture can be isolated from changes by applying a Freeze Mask to the picture part with the Freeze Mask Tool. While working inside the filter dialog, it is possible to selectively reverse any changes made to the photo by applying the Reconstruct Tool. When applied to the surface of the image the distorted picture parts are gradually altered back to their original state (the mesh is returned to its regular form). Like the other tool options in the filter, the size of the area affected by the tool is based on the Brush Size setting and the strength of the change is determined by the Brush Pressure value.

Liquify Tools

Save/Load mesh

Tool options including brush size, density and pressure

Reconstruction options

Freeze Mask options

View options

Mask display options

Backdrop or underlying layer options

Usage summary

1. Open an example image and then the Liquify filter (Filter > Liquify). The dialog opens with a preview image in the center, tools to the left and tool options to the right. The Size, Pressure, Rate and Jitter options control the strength and look of the changes, whereas the individual tools alter the type of distortion applied. In order to create a caricature of the example picture we will exaggerate the perspective of the figure. Select the Pucker Tool and increase the size of the Brush to cover the entire bottom of the subject. Click to squeeze inwards the lower part of the subject.

2. Now select the Bloat Tool and place it over the head; click to expand this area. If you are unhappy with any changes you can use the keyboard shortcuts for Edit > Undo (Ctrl + Z) to remove the last changes. Use a smaller brush size to bloat the goggles.
3. To finish the caricature switch to the Forward Warp Tool and push in the cheek areas. You can also use this tool to drag down the chin and lift the cheekbones.
4. The picture can be selectively restored at any point by choosing the Reconstruct Tool and painting over the changed area. Click OK to apply the distortion changes.

Liquify tools

 Forward Warp Tool – used to push pixels in the direction you drag the cursor across the picture surface.

 Reconstruct Tool – restores the picture and mesh back to its original appearance before any distortion was applied.

 Twirl Clockwise Tool – used for rotating pixels in a clockwise direction. Use with the Alt key to twirl in an anticlockwise direction.

 Pucker Tool – designed to suck or pinch the pixels towards the center of the brush.

 Bloat Tool – balloons the pixels away from the center of the brush towards the outside edges.

 Push Left Tool – used to move the pixels to the left or to the right (Alt-drag) of the drag.

Mirror Tool – used to copy and reflect the pixels perpendicular to the direction of the stroke. Use Alt-drag to reflect the pixels in the opposite direction.

 Turbulence Tool – used for creating clouds, fire and waves by smoothly scrambling pixels.

Freeze Mask Tool – adds a mask that protects the masked area from liquify changes.

Thaw Mask Tool – acts as an eraser for the Freeze Mask Tool.

Before

After

The Vanishing Point filter edits and enhances using the perspective of the picture.

Vanishing Point

The Vanishing Point filter was first introduced in CS2 as an addition to the specialist filter line-up that includes Extract, Lens Blur and Liquify. Like the others, the feature has its own dialog complete with preview image, toolbox and options bar. The filter allows the user to copy and paste and even Clone Stamp portions of a picture whilst maintaining the perspective of the original scene. The filter evolved in CS3 so that it could be used in many more situations as that version allowed perspective plans to be linked at any angle (rather than just 90° as was the case in CS2). Vanishing Point cannot be used in conjunction with Smart Objects. Using the filter is a two-step process:

Step 1: Define perspective planes

To start, you must define the perspective planes in the photo. This is achieved by selecting the Create Plane Tool and marking each of the four corners of the rectangular-shaped feature that sits in perspective on the plane. A blue grid means that it is correct perspective, yellow that it is borderline, and red that it is mathematically impossible. In the example, the four corners of a window were used to define the plane of the building's front face. Next, a second plane that is linked to the first at an edge is dragged onto the surface of the left side wall.

Step 2: Copy and paste or stamp

With the planes established the Marquee Tool can be used to select image parts which can be copied, pasted and then dragged in perspective around an individual plane and even onto another linked plane. All the time the perspective of the copy will alter to suit the plane it is positioned on. The feature's Stamp Tool operates like a standard stamp tool except that the copied section is transformed to account for the perspective of the plane when it is applied to the base picture.

Edit Plane Tool ⟶
Create Plane Tool ⟶
Marquee Tool ⟶
Stamp Tool ⟶
Brush Tool ⟶
Transform Tool ⟶
Eyedropper Tool ⟶
Measure Tool
(Photoshop Extended only) ⟶
Hand Tool ⟶
Zoom Tool ⟶

Perspective plane grid 1
Perspective plane grid 2
Base image preview

Usage summary

1. Create a new layer above the image layer to be edited (Layer > New > Layer) and then choose the Vanishing Point filter from the Filter menu.

2. Select the Create Plane Tool and click on the top left corner of a rectangle that sits on the plane you wish to define. Locate and click on the top right, bottom right and bottom left corners. If the plane has been defined correctly the corner selection box will change to a perspective plane grid. In the example, the front face of the building was defined first.

3. To create a second, linked, plane, Ctrl/Cmd-click the middle handle of the plane and drag away from the edge. The left side of the building was defined using the second plane.

4. To copy the window from the building's front face, select the Marquee Tool first, set a small feather value to soften the edges and then outline the window to be copied. Choose Ctrl/Cmd + C (to copy) and then Ctrl/Cmd + V (to paste). This pastes a copy of the window in the same position as the original marquee selection.

5. Click-drag the copy from the front face around to the side plane. The window (copied selection) will automatically snap to the new perspective plane and will reduce in size as it is moved further back in the plane. Position the window on the wall surface and choose Heal > Luminance from the Marquee options bar.

6. Press 'T' to enter the Transform mode and select Flip from the option bar to reorientate the window so that the inside edge of the framework matches the other openings on the wall. Click OK to complete the process.

Vanishing Point tips

- Use the Edit Plane Tool to click and drag the corners of the grid if grid lines do not match up with the edges of the picture parts that are sitting on the perspective plane.
- In order to copy and paste in full perspective the source plane and destination plane must be joined by a series of linked perspective planes.
- Use the Heal option to help match tones of the copied parts and their new locations.
- Grids can be output as layers, are 16-bit capable, text can be pasted into a grid and are auto-saved as part of the PSD file format.

Vanishing Point goes askew

When the Vanishing Point filter first appeared in Photoshop CS2 there were many admirers of its power to manipulate objects in three-dimensional space but comparatively few people who could find a use for it in their day-to-day workflows. One reason for this lack of popularity was that the feature assumed that all adjoining perspective planes met at a 90° angle. This is fine for buildings and boxes but is limited when it comes to a good many other surfaces.

The version of Vanishing Point that appears in both CS3, CS4 and CS5 can create perspective-based planes at almost any angle, making the feature much more usable in a variety of everyday images.

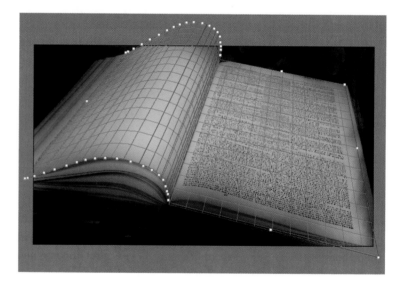

Vanishing Point 2.0 provides the ability to create perspective planes that join at angles other than 90°. In this example, the curve of the page was recreated with a series of small angled planes.

Usage summary

1. In the example image some text (or an image) needed to be added to the blank page on the left-hand side of the book. The text was photographed from another part of the book, the file opened in Photoshop and then copied to memory (Ctrl/Cmd + A, Ctrl/Cmd + C).
2. Next the book picture was opened into the Vanishing Point filter (Filter > Vanishing Point). To start, a new plane was created on the right side of the book using the edge of the text as a guide. The Create Plane Tool was selected and then the four corners of the plane dragged out to align with the edges of the text.

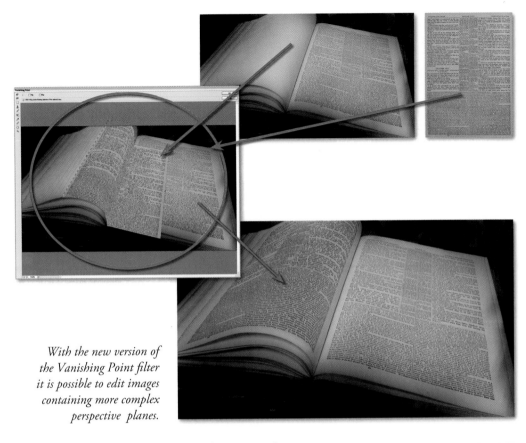

With the new version of the Vanishing Point filter it is possible to edit images containing more complex perspective planes.

3. Once the plane is created the tool reverts to the Edit Plane mode for fine-tuning. The corners of the plane were then adjusted so that it extended to the edges of the page and, more importantly, the spine of the book.

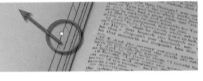

4. To create a linked plane for the other side of the book, the Create Plane Tool was chosen a second time (or you could hold down the Ctrl/Cmd key whilst in Edit Plane mode) and a new plane was dragged from the center handle on the edge of the existing plane.

5. Next the new Angle slider in the top of the dialog was used to rotate the plane so that it ran along the face of the curved page.

6. Using the page edge as a guide, add a series of small linked planes to the picture. Each need to be rotated and realigned to duplicate the perspective of the surface of the page.

7. Next the copied text was pasted (Ctrl/Cmd + V) into the Vanishing Point workspace and dragged to the first perspective plane.

8. The size of the text was then adjusted in the Transform mode (press T to enter) by click-dragging the corners of the marquee around the text before dragging into position on the curved page.

Blur filters

The Blur filters are designed to add a degree of softness to the photo. The most basic filters in this group are the Blur and Blur More options. These apply a set level of blur to your picture quickly and easily. For a more sophisticated and controllable Blur filter try Gaussian Blur or the Box, Shape, Smart and Surface Blur versions. They all contain controls that alter the style and strength of the effect.

Average
Blur
Blur More
Box Blur...
Gaussian Blur...
Lens Blur...
Motion Blur...
Radial Blur...
Shape Blur...
Smart Blur...
Surface Blur...

The Lens Blur filter

One popular application for the Blur filters is to recreate a shallow focus photo where the main subject is sharp and the rest of the picture is unsharp. By selecting the areas to blur and then applying a filter you can create a crude shallow focus result. This approach does create a simple in-focus and out-of-focus effect but it would be hard to say that the results are totally convincing. To achieve a depth of field (DOF) effect that is more realistic and believable, the basic idea of this technique needs to be coupled with the Lens Blur filter.

Spiral Staircase by Bart Broek
(www.iStockphoto.com)

Photoshop's Lens Blur filter is a dedicated feature designed to create realistic DOF effects in your pictures. Since CS2 the feature has been 16-bit enabled.

If realism is your goal then it is necessary to look a little closer at how camera-based DOF works and, more importantly, how it appears in our images. Imagine an image shot with a long lens using a large aperture. The main subject situated midway into the image is pin sharp. Upon examination it is possible to see that those picture elements closest to the main subject are not as 'unsharp' as those further away. In effect the greater the distance from the point of focus, the more blurry the picture elements become.

This fact, simple though it is, is the key to a more realistic digital DOF effect. The application of a simple one-step blurring process does not reflect what happens with traditional camera-based techniques. The Lens Blur filter (Filter > Blur > Lens Blur) is designed specifically to help replicate this gradual change in sharpness. The filter uses selections or masks created before entering the feature to determine which parts of the picture will be blurred and which areas will remain sharp. In addition, if you use a mask that contains areas of graduated gray (rather than just black and white) the filter will adjust the degree of sharpness according to the level of gray in the mask.

After masked Lens Blur

Mask

The Lens Blur filter uses a mask or selection to determine which parts of the picture will remain sharp and which areas will be blurred. In addition, the level of sharpness is directly related to the density of the mask. Graduated masks will produce graduated sharpness similar to that found in photographs with camera-based shallow DOF techniques.

Lens Blur filter options

Preview – Faster to generate quicker previews. More accurate to display the final version of the image.

Depth Map Source – Select the mask or selection that you will use for the filter from the drop-down list.

Invert – Select this option to inverse the alpha channel mask or selection.

Iris Shape – Determines the way the blur appears. Iris shapes are controlled by the number of blades they contain.

Gaussian or Uniform – Select one of these options to add noise to the picture to disguise the smoothing and loss of picture grain that is a by-product of applying the Lens Blur filter.

Before   After

The Lens Correction filter in Photoshop CS5 automatically corrects three typical lens based errors including the extreme barrel distortion seen here.

Correcting lens distortion with filters

We have already seen that the new version of Adobe Camera Raw contains a sophisticated lens correction system. The core technology used to correct raw files in ACR can also be employed inside Photoshop CS5 with the Lens Correction filter (Filter > Lens Correction). The feature is specifically designed to correct the three key imaging problems that can occur when shooting with different lenses. Apart from correcting barrel and pincushion distortion, the filter can also fix the color fringing (color outlines around subject edges) and vignetting (darkening of the corners) problems that can also occur as a result of poor lens construction.

As is the case in ACR, the corrections can be applied automatically by matching the lens used to take the picture, with a custom Lens Correction profile. This occurs in the Auto Correction section of the filter. The filter will try to locate such a profile automatically by matching the lens information recorded in the metadata of the photo with one of the profiles contained in the filter. For those times when an exact match can't be found, it is also possible to search for a suitable filter on the net using the Search Online button at the bottom of the dialog. You can choose to correct all three error types (Geometric Distortion, Chromatic Aberration and Vignette) or select only those options you wish to apply.

The controls located in the Custom section of the filter can be used to manually apply lens correction adjustments or to fine-tune those already applied with a correction profile. Extra controls located here can be used for changing the perspective of the picture (great for eliminating the issue of converging verticals) and manual handling of the vacant areas of the canvas that are created after distortion correction has been applied.

Lens Correction in action

To demonstrate the power of this feature I ran one of the images from a series of photos taken with a Nikkor DX 10.5mm f2.8 lens through the Lens Correction filter. With no manual adjustments at all the results were amazing. Yes the final image was cropped a fair bit but the photo was completely usable. A few more seconds fine-tuning the results with the controls in the Custom panel produced an even squarer result that still retained the feeling of exaggerated perspective but had lost the barrel distortion. Use these steps to correct your images.

Toolbar   Camera   Preview   Toggle   Show   Grid   Grid
          Information   Preview   grid   Divisions   Color

Lens Correction Dialog Box (Filter > Lens Correction): The Lens Correction dialog box has been revamped for Photoshop CS5 to include the new Auto Correction features. The manual slider controls found in the previous versions of the program are still available and are stored under the Custom tab. Photoshop attempts to locate the appropriate Lens Correction Profile based on the camera and lens metadata stored with the photo. In this case the Nikon DX 10.5mm f2.8 lens on a D90 body was the closest match for this image which was shot with a D100 and the 10.5mm lens.

Custom Tab Controls (these controls were available in Photoshop CS4 version of the Lens Correction filter)

Start by opening an example image in Photoshop CS5. Next, choose Filter > Lens Correction, and click onto the Auto Correction tab.

To ensure correction of all error types select Geometric Distortion, Chromatic Aberration, and Vignette in the Correction section of the panel on the right side of the dialog box.

To straighten the photo select the Straighten tool from the left of the dialog box and drag it along an image part that is meant to be horizontal or vertical.

Next, choose the Transparency mode from the Edge menu. This will produce the corrected image with transparent areas around the reshaped photo.

In this case the appropriate lens-correction profile was automatically matched with the example image, and the preview updated to display the corrected photo. If this doesn't happen with your photos you can select other profiles by Camera Make, Camera Model, and Lens Model, or locate them on the web by pressing the Search Online button at the bottom of the dialog box.

To fine tune the results switch over to the manual controls by clicking on the Custom tab. In this example a small change to the Geometric Distortion (-2) and Horizontal Perspective (+8) controls straightened the picture further.

Switching back to the Auto Correction panel make sure that the Auto Scale Image option is checked before clicking OK to process the corrected photo.

Batch Processing Your Lens Corrections

Correcting a single image at a time is all well and good when you only have a few files to process, but if your shooting session has amassed several hundred photos then any type of automated correction would be most welcome. Well the Adobe guys must have read my thoughts as there is a new Lens Correction batch tool in Bridge CS5.

The feature works like other Photoshop tools in Bridge, you multi-select the photos from the Content panel first and then choose the option from the Tools > Photoshop menu. This action opens a new Lens Correction dialog box in Photoshop and automatically adds the selected files.

The dialog contains sections to choose the destination folder for the corrected photos, settings to either automatically locate the best profile for the images or manually choose your own, and a series of check boxes to determine correction type and scaling. After working your way through the settings all you need to do is click the OK button to process the files.

Note > You can also display this batch processing dialog box by selecting File > Automate > Lens Correction from within Photoshop. It is then possible to add files that are already open in the program or to browse for the images you want to correct.

Photoshop CS5 and Bridge CS5 both include the ability to batch correct a group of images using the Lens Correction option in the Tools > Photoshop menu in Bridge and the File > Automate menu in Photoshop.

Start by locating the folder containing the photos inside Bridge CS5. In this example it is fastest to display the Filter panel (Window > Filter) and then select the 10.5 mm entry from the Focal Length section. This action displayed just the photos taken with this lens type in the Content panel.

Next multi-select several images by click-dragging a marquee around the thumbnails before selecting the Lens Correction entry from the Tools > Photoshop menu.

Photoshop opens and the files are listed in the batch-process Lens Correction dialog box. You can add or remove images using the buttons listed next to the file list. Now, select a destination folder and File Type. By default Photoshop stores the process photos in a folder titled Results.

Check the Match Best Profile option to instruct Photoshop to locate the best profile for each photo and finally choose the error type to be corrected. In this case, I chose all three of the available corrections.

With all the options set, click the OK button. The Lens Correction dialog box closes and one-by-one the photos are opened into Photoshop. Each image is then corrected and saved off to the folder in the format selected. And that's it! Job done!

Noise filters

The Noise filters group contains tools that are used for either adding noise (randomly colored pixels) to, or reducing the existing noise in, a photo. Dust & Scratches is designed to automatically hide picture faults such as hairs or scratches in scanned photos. Despeckle, Median and the Reduce Noise filter remove or hide the noise associated with high ISO pictures and the Add Noise filter is used to create and add noise to photos.

All the filters in this group, except Despeckle, are applied via their own filter dialog.

Note > With the substantial upgrading of the Noise Removal technology in Adobe Camera Raw 6 it is generally better practise to remove noise at the Raw processing stage than to wait until the image is opened in Photoshop.

The Reduce Noise filter

The feature includes a preview window, a Strength slider, a Preserve Details control and a Reduce Color Noise slider. As with the Dust & Scratches filter you need to be careful when using this filter to ensure that you balance removing noise while also retaining detail.

The best way to guarantee this is to set your Strength setting first, ensuring that you check the results in highlights, midtone and shadow areas. Next gradually increase the Preserve Details value until you reach the point where the level of noise that is being reintroduced into the picture is noticeable and then back off the control slightly (make the setting a lower number). For photographs with a high level of color noise (random speckles of color in an area that should be a smooth flat tone) you will need to adjust this slider at the same time as you are playing with the Strength control.

When the Advanced mode is selected the noise reduction effect can be applied to each channel (Red, Green, Blue) individually. This filter also works in 16-bit mode and contains saveable/loadable settings. There is also a special option for removal of JPEG artifacts. One of the side effects of saving space by compressing files using the JPEG format is the creation of box-like patterns in your pictures. These patterns or artifacts are particularly noticeable in images that have been saved with maximum compression settings. With the Remove JPEG Artifact option selected in the Reduce Noise dialog, Photoshop attempts to smooth out or camouflage the box-like pattern created by the overcompression. The feature does an admirable job but the results are never as good as if a lower compression rate was used initially.

Per Channel mode (Advanced section)

The Per Channel option provides the ability to adjust the noise reduction independently for each of the Red, Green and Blue channels. This allows the user to customize the filter for the channel(s) that have the most noise. The **Strength** setting controls the amount of Luminance or non-color noise reduction applied to each channel. The **Preserve Details** slider maintains the appearance of edge details at the cost of lowering the noise reduction effect. The best results balance both these options for each channel.

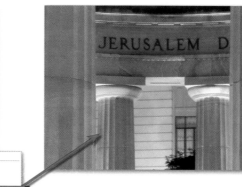

After creating an Image Stack Smart Object in the Extended Version of CS5 you can apply a rendering option such as Median to the stack. In this example this has the effect of reducing noise.

Reducing noise with Image Stacks

Another way to reduce noise is to take a series of images of the same scene in quick succession and then use the combined information from all the photos to produce a new, less noisy, composite picture. The process of achieving this outcome became possible in Photoshop CS3 Extended as Adobe introduced the concept of Image Stacks as well as the ability to apply functions, such as the Median command, to these stacks. The process involves layering the sequential source images in a single document, applying the Auto-Align option (to ensure registration) and then converting the layers into a Smart Object. Once in this Image Stack form it is possible to select one of a range of rendering options from those listed in the Layer > Smart Objects > Stack Mode menu. These options manage how the content of each of the layers will interact with each other.

In the noise reduction technique shown here the Median command creates the composite result by retaining only those image parts that appear (in the same spot) in more than 50% of the frames (layers). As noise tends to be pretty random, its position, color and tone change from one frame to the next and so are removed from the rendered photo, leaving just the good stuff – the picture itself.

Image Stacks are created by first layering separate photos in a single document, applying the Auto-Align command and then converting all layers to a single Smart Object.

In another example of how this technology can be used, in order to remove tourists from in front of your favorite statue there is no need to wait until they have all gone home, instead simply capture multiple pictures of the monument, group them together in an Image Stack and apply the Median function to the group. Hey presto, tourists be gone!

Using Image Stacks to remove noise in Photoshop Extended

1. Reducing noise using this technique is a multi-step affair that starts at the time of capture. If you are confronted with a scene where it is essential that you use either a long exposure or high ISO setting (or both) then you can be pretty sure that your resultant images will contain some noise. So in these circumstances shoot several photos of the same scene. For best results maintain the same camera settings and camera position throughout the whole sequence.

2. Next open all photos into Photoshop and drag each picture onto a single document, creating a multi-layer file containing all the photos in the sequence.

3. Multi-select all the layers and choose the Auto-Align option (Auto Projection) from the Edit menu. Photoshop will arrange all the layers so that the content is registered.

4. With the multiple layers still selected choose Layer > Smart Objects > Convert to Smart Object. This places all the layers in a single Smart Object.

5. The last step in the process is to select the Smart Object layer and then choose how you want to render the composite image. Do this by selecting one of the options from the Layer > Smart Objects > Stack Mode menu. To reduce noise we choose the Median entry.

Sharpen filters

Photoshop provides a variety of sharpening filters designed to increase the clarity of digital photographs. The options are listed in the Filter > Sharpen menu and include the Sharpen, Sharpen Edges, Sharpen More, Unsharp Mask filters as well as the Smart Sharpen option. Digital sharpening techniques are based on increasing the contrast between adjacent pixels in the image. When viewed from a distance, this change makes the picture appear sharper. The Sharpen and Sharpen More filters are designed to apply basic sharpening to the whole of the image and the only difference between the two is that Sharpen More increases the strength of the sharpening effect.

One of the problems with sharpening is that sometimes the effect is detrimental to the image, causing areas of subtle color or tonal change to become coarse and pixelated. These problems are most noticeable in image parts such as skin tones and smoothly graded skies. To help solve this issue, Adobe included the Sharpen Edges filter, which concentrates the sharpening effects on the edges of objects only. Use this filter when you want to stop the effect being applied to smooth image parts.

Customizing your sharpening

Out of all the sharpening options in Photoshop the Smart Sharpen and Unsharp Mask filters provide the greatest control over the sharpening process by giving the user a variety of slider controls that alter the way the effect is applied to their pictures. Both filters contain Amount and Radius controls. The Unsharp Mask filter includes a Threshold slider and the Smart filter contains controls for adjusting sharpness in Shadows and Highlights independently (in Advanced mode) as well as a Removal option for ridding images or specific blur types (Gaussian, Motion or Lens Blur).

Sharpening controls

The **Amount slider** controls the strength of the sharpening effect. Larger numbers will produce more pronounced results, whereas smaller values will create more subtle effects.

The **Radius slider** value determines the number of pixels around the edge that are affected by the sharpening. A low value only sharpens edge pixels. High settings can produce noticeable halo effects around your picture so start with a low value first.

The **Threshold slider** is used to determine how different the pixels must be before they are considered an edge and therefore sharpened.

The **Remove** setting locates and attempts to neutralize different blur types.

The **Shadow and Highlight** tabs contain options for adjusting the sharpening effects in these tonal areas.

Texture filters

The Texture filter group provides a range of ways of adding texture to your photos. Most of the filters apply a single texture type and include controls for varying the strength and style of the effect, but the Texturizer filter adds to these possibilities by allowing users to add textures they create themselves to a photo.

All filters in this group are applied via the Filter Gallery dialog.

The Texturizer filter

When applying the Texturizer filter the picture is changed to give the appearance that the photo has been printed onto the surface of the texture. The Scaling and Relief sliders control the strength and visual dominance of the texture, while the Light Direction menu alters the highlight and shadow areas. Different surface types are available from the Texture drop-down menu. The feature also contains the option to add your own files and have these used as the texture that is applied by the filter to the image.

Making your own textures

Any Photoshop file (.PSD) can be loaded as a new texture via the Load Texture option in the setting menu, top right of the Texturizer dialog. Simply shoot, scan or design a texture image and save as a Photoshop file (.PSD).

Other filters

The filters grouped together under the Other heading include the Custom filter, which is used for creating you own filter effects (see opposite page), the edge-finding High Pass filter, the Offset filter that shifts picture pixels by a set amount, and the Maximum and Minimum filters, which are most often used for modifying masks.

Filters in this group are not applied via the Filter Gallery dialog but rather have their own specific dialog containing both controls and preview.

Sharpening with the High Pass filter

The High Pass filter isolates the edges in a picture and then converts the rest of the picture to mid gray. The filter locates the edge areas by searching for areas of high contrast or color change. The filter can be used to add contrast and sharpening to a photo.

1. To start, make a copy of the picture layer that you want to sharpen, then filter the copied layer with the High Pass filter. Adjust the Radius so that you isolate the edges of the image only against the gray background and then click OK.
2. Next select the filtered layer and switch the blend mode to Hard Light.
3. Finally, adjust the opacity of this layer to govern the level of sharpening being applied to the picture layer.

The ten commandments for filter usage

1. *Subtlety is everything.* The effect should support your image not overpower it.

2. *Try one filter at a time.* Applying multiple filters to an image can be confusing.

3. *View at full size.* Make sure that you view the effect at full size (100%) when deciding on filter settings.

4. *Filter a channel.* For a change try applying a filter to one channel only – Red, Green or Blue.

5. *Print to check effect.* If the image is to be viewed as a print, double-check the effect when printed before making final decisions about filter variables.

6. *Fade strong effects.* If the effect is too strong try fading it. Use the 'Fade' selection under the 'Edit' menu.

7. *Experiment.* Try a range of settings before making your final selection.

8. *Mask then filter.* Apply a gradient mask to an image and then use the filter. In this way you can control what parts of the image are affected.

9. *Try different effects on different layers.* If you want to combine the effects of different filters try copying the base image to different layers and applying a different filter to each. Combine effects by adjusting the opacity of each layer.

10. *Did I say that subtlety is everything?*

Filter DIY

Can't find exactly what you are looking for in the hundreds of filters that are either supplied with Photoshop or are available for download from the Net? I could say that you're not really trying, but then again some people have a compulsion to 'do it for themselves'. Well, all is not lost. Photoshop provides you with the opportunity to create your own filtration effects by using its Filter > Other > Custom option.

By adding a sequence of positive/negative numbers into the 25 variable boxes provided you can construct your own filter effect. Add to this the options of playing with the 'Scale' and 'Offset' of the results and I can guarantee hours of fun. Best of all your labors can be saved to use again when your specialist customized touch is needed.

Chris Neylon

layer blends

essential skills

- Learn the practical applications of layer blend modes for image retouching and creative montage work.
- Develop skills using the following techniques:
    - blend modes
    - layers and channels
    - layer masks.

Introduction

When an image, or part of an image, is placed on a separate layer above the background, creative decisions can be made as to how these layers interact with each other. Reducing the opacity of the top layer allows the underlying information to show through, but Photoshop has many other ways of mixing, combining or 'blending' the pixel values on different layers to achieve different visual outcomes. The different methods used by Photoshop to compare and adjust the hue, saturation and brightness of the pixels on the different layers are called 'blend modes'. Blend modes can be assigned to the painting tools from the Options bar but they are more commonly assigned to an entire layer when editing a multi-layered document. The layer blend modes are accessed from the 'blending mode' pull-down menu in the top left-hand corner of the Layers panel.

The major groupings

The blend modes are arranged in family groups of related effects or variations on a theme. Many users simply sample all the different blend modes until they achieve the effect they are looking for. This, however, can be a time-consuming operation and a little more understanding of what is actually happening can ease the task of choosing an appropriate blend mode for the job in hand. A few of the blend modes are commonly used in the routine compositing tasks, while others have very limited or specialized uses only. The five main groups of blend modes after Normal and Dissolve that are more commonly used for image-editing and montage work start with:

- Darken
- Lighten
- Overlay
- Difference
- Hue

More blend modes than a photographer needs

There are 27 blend modes (counting 'Normal' as a mode) but photographers will usually only rely on less than half of these modes on a regular basis in their image retouching and montage projects. There are a few modes (such as Darker Color and Lighter Color) that offer the photographer with few if any practical uses. This chapter will focus on the 'essential' modes and skip over, or omit, the non-essential modes. The essential blend modes for photo-editing are:

- Normal
- Darken
- Multiply
- Lighten
- Screen
- Overlay
- Soft Light
- Difference
- Luminosity
- Color

Opacity and Dissolve

At 100% opacity the pixels on the top layer obscure the pixels on the layers underneath. As the opacity is reduced the pixels underneath become visible. The Dissolve blend mode only works when the opacity of the layer is reduced. Random pixels are made transparent on the layer rather than reducing the transparency of all the pixels. The effect is very different to the reduced opacity of the 'Normal' blend mode and has commercial applications as a transition for fading one image into another, but the effect has very limited commercial applications for compositing and photomontage of stills image work.

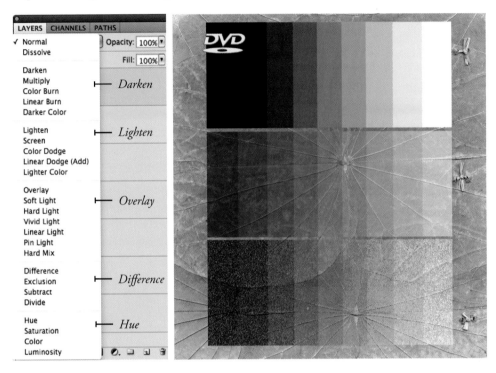

Image 02_Opacity. *The groups of blend modes are listed using the name of the dominant effect. The step wedge above shows 'Normal' at 100% and 50% opacity and the 'Dissolve' blend mode at 50% opacity.*

The 'Opacity' control for each layer, although not strictly considered as a blend mode, is an important element of any composite work. Some of the blend modes are quite 'aggressive' in their resulting effect if applied at 100% opacity. Experimenting with some blend modes at a reduced opacity will often provide the required result.

Shortcuts

The blend modes can be applied to layers using keyboard shortcuts (so long as a painting tool is not selected). Hold down the Shift key and press the '+' key to move down the list or the '−' key to move up the list. Alternatively, you can press the Alt/Option key and the Shift key and key in the letter code for a particular blend mode. If a tool in the painting group is selected (i.e. in use) the blend mode is applied to the tool rather than the layer. See Keyboard Shortcuts for more information.

The 'Darken' group

It's not too hard to figure out what this group of blend modes have in common. Although Darken leads the grouping, Multiply is perhaps the most used blend mode in the group.

Image 03_Darken. *The Darken mode can replace existing highlights while ignoring darker tones.*

Darken

When the top layer is set to Darken mode Photoshop displays the darker pixels, regardless of whether they are on the layer set to the Darken mode or on the underlying layers. Pixels on the layer with the blend mode applied that are lighter than the underlying pixels in the same location will no longer be visible. This mode is invaluable when retouching portraits or removing halos from around subjects due to masking errors (see Project 6 – Surface Blur in the Advanced Retouching chapter).

Multiply is a useful blend mode when overall darkening is required.

Multiply

The 'Multiply' blend mode belongs to the 'Darken' family grouping. The brightness values of the pixels on the blend layer and underlying layer are multiplied to create darker tones. Only values that are multiplied with white (level 255) stay the same, i.e. do not become darker.

Image 04_Multiply. *The Multiply mode is used to apply a dark edge to the image (white is neutral).*

Image 05_Multiply. *The Multiply blend mode is used to darken the sky in this landscape image.*

Image 06_Multiply. *The Multiply blend mode is used to darken the top half of the image. The layer is first duplicated and the Multiply mode set. A layer mask is added and a linear gradient in the layer mask shields the lower portion of the image from the effects of the blend mode.*

Image 07_Multiply. *The Multiply blend mode is the secret to success when masking hair that was first captured against a white background. The new background layer and layer mask are positioned above the portrait and the layer is then set to the multiply mode. Note the difference before and after the blend mode has been applied (see Montage Projects > Hair Extraction).*

Image courtesy of Shari Gleeson

Color Burn, Linear Burn and Darker Color

Color Burn increases the underlying contrast while Linear Burn decreases the underlying brightness. These are difficult blend modes to find a use for at 100% opacity. Saturation can become excessive and overall brightness, now heavily influenced by the underlying color, can 'fill in' (become black). Darker Color is very similar to the Darken mode in that only the darker pixels remain visible. The difference between the two 'darkening' modes is how Photoshop assesses the brightness value – channel by channel (Darken) or combined channels (Darken Color).

The 'Lighten' group

The name of this group of blend modes is self-explanatory. If one of the modes in this group is applied to the top layer it usually results in a lighter outcome in some areas of the image. Although Lighten leads the grouping, Screen is perhaps the most used blend mode in the group.

Image 08_Lighten. *Two exposures are combined to balance the bright ambient light and the comparatively dim interior lighting of a building. A second image is captured at night and placed on a layer above the daylight exposure. The layer is then set to the Lighten blend mode – original images by John Hay.*

Lighten

When the top layer is set to Lighten mode Photoshop displays the lighter pixels, regardless of whether they are on the layer set to the Lighten mode or on the underlying layers. Pixels on the layer with the blend mode applied that are darker than the underlying pixels in the same location will no longer be visible. This blend mode is particularly useful for introducing highlights into the underexposed areas of an image. This technique can also be useful for replacing dark colored dust and scratches from light areas of continuous tone.

Image 9_Screen. *Screen is useful when overall lightening is required.*

Screen

The 'Screen' blend mode belongs to the 'Lighten' family grouping. The 'inverse' brightness values of the pixels on the blend layer and underlying layers are multiplied to create lighter tones (a brightness value of 80% is multiplied as if it was a value of 20%). Only the underlying values that are screened with black (level 0) on the upper layer stay the same (see Project 5 in the Advanced Retouching chapter).

Image 10_Screen. *A background layer is duplicated and a Screen blend mode is applied to lighten all levels.*

Image 11_Screen. *The Screen mode can be used to apply a white border around an image.*

Blondee Goddess – Katja Govorushchenko (www.iStockphoto.com)

Image 12_Screen. *The Screen blend mode is useful when masking hair that was first captured against a black background (see Montage > Hair Extraction for more information about this technique).*

Girl by Shelly Perry (www.iStockphoto.com)

Image 13_Screen. *The Screen blend mode is particularly useful for quickly dropping in elements that were photographed against a black background such as smoke, bubbles, splashing or spurting water and fireworks. For transparent elements the lighting is usually positioned to one side or behind the subject matter to create the best effect.*

Color Dodge, Linear Dodge and Lighter Color

Color Dodge decreases the underlying contrast while Linear Dodge increases the underlying brightness. This again is a difficult blend mode to find a use for at 100% opacity. Saturation can become excessive and overall brightness, heavily influenced by the underlying color, can blow out (become white). Lighter Color is very similar to the Lighten mode in that only the lighter pixels remain visible. The difference between the two 'lightening' modes is how Photoshop assesses the brightness value – channel by channel (Lighten) or combined channels (Lighter Color).

The 'Overlay' group

This is perhaps the most useful group of blend modes for photomontage work.

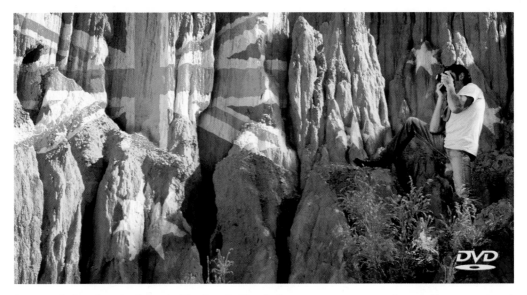

Image 14_Overlay. *Applying the blend mode 'Overlay' to a texture or pattern layer will create an image where the form appears to be modeling the texture. Both the highlights and shadows of the underlying form are respected.*

Image 15_Overlay. *The 'Overlay' blend mode is useful for overlaying textures over 3D form.*

Overlay

The Overlay blend mode uses a combination of the Multiply and Screen blend modes while preserving the highlight and shadow tones of the underlying image. The Overlay mode multiplies or screens the colors, depending on whether the base color is darker or lighter than a midtone. The effect is extremely useful when overlaying a texture or color over a form modeled by light and shade. Excessive increases in saturation may become evident when overlaying white and black. The 'Soft' and 'Hard Light' blend modes produce variations on this overlay theme.

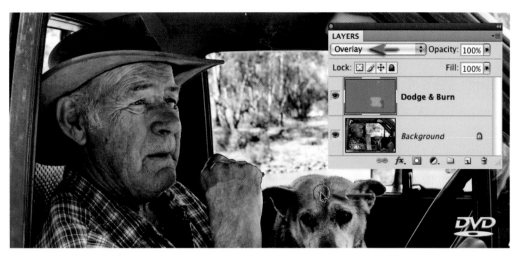

Image 16_Overlay. *A 50% Gray layer set to Overlay mode can be used to dodge and burn where increased localized contrast and saturation is required (such as dodging dark shadow tones).*

A layer filled with 50% Gray is invisible in Overlay and Soft Light mode and, as a result, is commonly used as a 'non-destructive' dodging and burning layer (see Project 3 in the Retouching chapter for a more in-depth look at this skill).

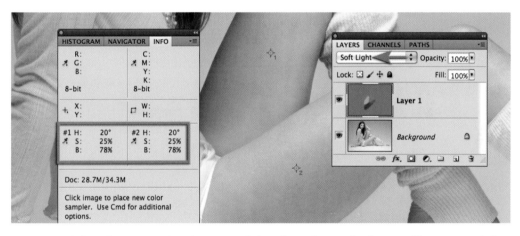

Image 17_Soft Light. *A 50% Gray layer set to Soft Light mode provides the most effective way to lighten or darken tones within an image. This is a more effective way than using Levels or Curves to change the luminance values. Using Levels or Curves to change localized luminance values always results in excessive shifts in Saturation and Hue values.*

Soft and Hard Light – variations on a theme

The Soft and Hard Light blend modes are variations on the 'Overlay' theme. Photoshop describes the difference in terms of lighting (diffused or harsh spotlight). If the Overlay blend mode is causing highlights or shadows to become overly bright or dark or the increase in saturation is excessive then the Soft Light blend mode will often resolve the problem. The Hard Light, on the other hand, increases the contrast – but care must be taken when choosing this option as blending dark or light tones can tip the underlying tones to black (level 0) or white (255).

Difference and Exclusion

The Difference blend mode subtracts either the underlying color from the blend color or vice versa depending on which has the highest brightness value. This blend mode used to be useful for registering layers with the same content but this has now largely been replaced with the Auto-Align Layers for layers that are not Smart Objects. The Exclusion blend mode works in the same way except where the blend color is white. In this instance the underlying color is inverted.

Image 18_Difference. *The Difference mode is used to align two layers.*

The Difference mode can also be used to create a 'solarized' or 'sabattier' effect. Duplicate the layer and go to Image > Adjustments > Invert and then apply the Difference blend mode to the copy layer.

Image 19_Difference. *Original image (Harmony) by Nicholas Monu (www.iStockphoto.com).*

Hue, Saturation and Color

The Hue and Color blend modes are predominantly used for toning or tinting images while the Saturation blend mode offers more limited applications. Saturation precedes Color in the Modes menu but is discussed after Hue and Saturation in this section due to their inherent similarities. See Project 1 in the Advanced Retouching chapter to see how the color mode is used to reintroduce some of the original color back into an image that has been converted to black and white.

Hue

The 'Hue' blend mode modifies the image by using the hue value of the blend layer and the saturation value of the underlying layer. As a result the blend layer is invisible if you apply this blend mode to a fully desaturated image. Opacity levels of the blend layer can be explored to achieve the desired outcome.

Color

The 'Color' blend mode is useful for toning desaturated or tinting colored images. The brightness value of the base color is blended with the hue and saturation of the blend color.

Image 20_Hue-Color. *Hue and Color blend modes.*

Image 21_Hue.

Note > Color fills can be used to tint or tone images by setting them to Hue or Color mode. Photoshop's Photo Filter layers perform a similar task but without the need to set the layer to the Hue or Color mode.

Saturation

The brightness or 'luminance' of the underlying pixels is retained but the saturation level is replaced with that of the blend layer's saturation level.

Note > This blend mode has limited uses for traditional toning effects but can be used to locally desaturate colored images. To work with this blend mode try creating a new empty layer. Then either fill a selection with any desaturated tone or paint with black or white at a reduced opacity to gradually remove the color from the underlying image.

Image 22_Saturation.

Image 23_Saturation. A Saturation layer is used to desaturate the underlying image.

226

Luminosity

Setting a layer to 'Luminosity' mode allows the Hue and Saturation values from the underlying layers to replace these on the Luminosity layer. The luminosity values within an RGB image have a number of very useful applications. The luminosity values can be extracted from an RGB image (from the Channels panel) and saved as an alpha channel, used as a layer mask or pasted as an independent layer above the background layer.

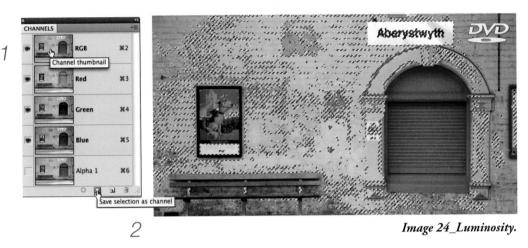

Image 24_Luminosity.

Creating a luminance channel

1. In the Channels palette Command/Ctrl-click the master RGB channel to select the luminance values.
2. Hold down the Option/Alt key and click on the 'Save selection as channel' icon to create an alpha channel. In the New Channel dialog select the Masked Areas option and select OK.
3. Go to Select > Deselect.

A Curves adjustment layer can be switched to Luminosity mode to eliminate shifts in saturation when contrast is increased. The example above illustrates what happens when contrast is increased using a Curves layer in Luminance and Normal blend modes. Open up the file and try it!

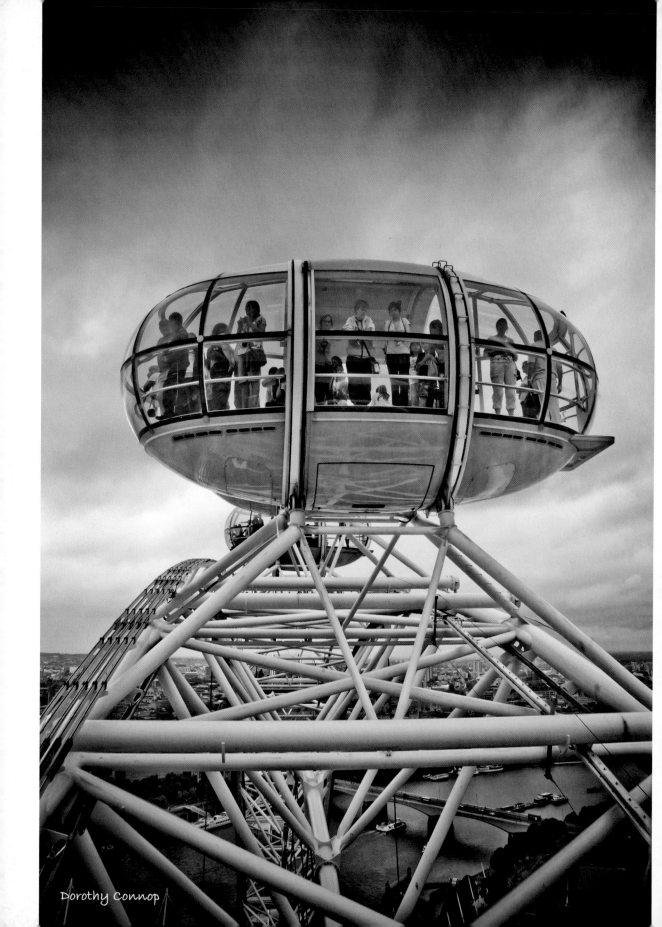

Dorothy Connop

retouching projects

Mark Galer

essential skills

- Develop skills using layers, adjustment layers, channels and layer masks.
- Retouch and enhance images using the following techniques and tools:
  - Adjustments in Adobe Camera Raw
  - Lens Correction Filter and Warp
  - Adjustment layers and layer masks
  - Target tones
  - Healing Brush, Clone Stamp Tool and Stamp Tool
  - Shadow/Highlight adjustment
  - High Pass, Unsharp Mask and Smart Sharpen.

Basic adjustments – Project 1

Most images that have come straight off the memory card of a camera benefit from some minor adjustments. These adjustments enable the images to be optimized for screen or print, or corrected for any in-camera auto settings that were not appropriate. Traditionally these adjustments were always carried out inside the main editing space of Photoshop. These included setting the white and black points, adjusting the brightness and contrast and optimizing the white balance of the image (ensuring the image does not have a color cast). These adjustments are now faster and easier to make in Adobe Camera Raw (ACR) even if the image is a JPEG file that has already been optimized in-camera.

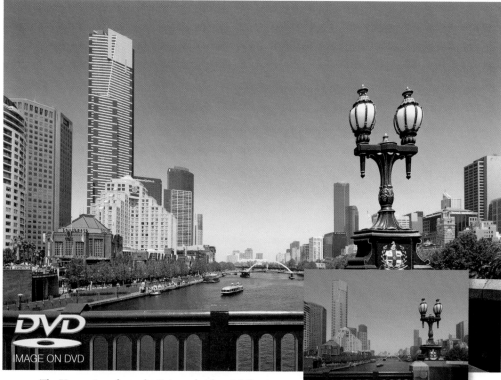

The Yarra river from the Princes bridge, Melbourne .

ACR has been around since Photoshop 7 and was created as a gateway for all Raw files so that they could be optimized before they were opened in the main editing space of Photoshop (Unlike JPEGs, Raw files are saved in the camera without any processing). The new revolutionary approach (or workflow) is to use ACR for Raw and JPEGs. ACR is non-destructive, simple and fast. The editing space of Photoshop is best used for specialized tasks. In this project we will perform the basic editing tasks to a JPEG image in ACR and complete the project with a single adjustment layer in the main editing space of Photoshop.

1. Raw images open automatically in Adobe Camera Raw (ACR) but JPEGs or TIFFs need to be coerced into opening into ACR. Go to File > Open (Mac) or File > Open As (PC), browse to the JPEG you want to open in ACR, and then from the Format menu in the Open dialog choose Camera Raw. If you are viewing the images in Adobe Bridge, right-click on the image and choose Open in Camera Raw.

Note > The R1 project image is a very low contrast image due to the hazy day and excessive amounts of UV light. If we look at the histogram in the top right-hand corner of the ACR dialog you can see the lack of shadow tones (on the extreme left) and highlight tones (on the extreme right of the histogram). Although this is how the camera has interpreted the scene it is very unlikely that this is the way the human vision would have remembered this scene. The adjustments that follow are designed to restore the image to how we remember it, rather than create something surreal.

2. Click the two clipping triangles above the histogram so that we can see if our attempts to increase contrast in this image will clip the luminance values (remove detail in the brightest and darkest tones). Luminance clipping is when shadows are pushed to black (level 0) and/or highlight tones are pushed to white (level 255). When this happens the shadows will appear with a blue overlay and the highlights with a red overlay. If you move the Exposure and Blacks sliders to the right you will see the overlay colors and you will also notice that the clipping triangles now appear white.

3. We need to return the Exposure slider all the way to 0.00 if we are to preserve the highlight tones in the lamp in the foreground (on the right side of the image). If you can still see some tiny spots of highlight clipping on the white glass on the lamp you will need to raise the Recovery slider to restore this detail. We can also raise the Blacks slider from its default position of 5 to a value of 10 before any shadow clipping occurs. Setting the black and white points is a basic adjustment that we tend to do to 99% of all images. The Exposure slider controls the white point while the Blacks slider controls the Black point. In the main editing space of Photoshop, the task of setting a black and white point in an image is most often performed using a Levels adjustment.

Localized levels with layer masks

Sometimes when the levels are optimized for the entire image a portion of the image still appears flat. A close examination of the image used in this illustration (also on the DVD) will reveal that the range of levels on the right of the histogram belong only to the sky. None of the highlights in the foreground have been rendered higher than level 200, even after the Highlight slider has been adjusted. Greater contrast can be achieved if the user ignores the sky when setting the Highlight levels slider and then masks the sky later by painting into the layer mask to restore the tonality to this area of the image (preventing the highlights in the sky from becoming clipped by the adjustment). In this example a black/white gradient has been applied to the upper portion of the layer mask. The mode of the Levels adjustment has been set to Luminosity to prevent the color saturation rising.

4. Although we now have a black and white point in this image, the contrast is still very low and the image appears a little too dark. This can be corrected by raising the Brightness and Contrast sliders. These sliders are usually non-destructive, i.e. they are slow to clip the shadow and highlight tones. If you do notice the clipping triangles above the histogram are no longer black, then you may need to fine-tune the Exposure and/or Blacks slider. If a clipping triangle appears as a color, then this indicates that one or more of the RGB channels are clipping. These colors may appear just prior to luminance clipping (all three channels are clipped) or because one or more of the colors in the image are very saturated or vibrant.

5. The image appears a little too blue or 'cold' for a sunny summers day. We can correct this by dragging the temperature slider to the right or by selecting the White Balance Tool in the top left-hand corner of the ACR dialog and then clicking on a neutral tone inside the image preview. I have clicked on the light gray tone in the glass of the lamp to correct the white balance automatically.

6. Just to the right of the White Balance Tool is the Targeted Adjustment Tool (TAT). If we click and hold on the TAT icon the drop-down menu will appear. Select the Luminance option and then move into the image preview and drag down on the sky to make all the blues in this image darker. Note how the HSL (Hue Saturation and Luminance) tab to the right is automatically selected.

Note > The Parametric Curve option is another great way of adjusting contrast in the image. Click up on a highlight tone and down on a shadow tone to increase contrast.

7. Return to the TAT menu and choose the Saturation option. Click on one of the warmer tones within the image (I have clicked on the brown wall in the foreground) and drag up to raise the saturation of all of the warmer tones within the image (yellows and oranges). This will retrieve the summer warmth to this image.

8. From the TAT menu choose the Hue option (color) and click and drag up on the sky to shift the hue of the blues to remove the cyan colorcast in the sky. With all of these HSL adjustments the user must take care not to 'overdo' the changes.

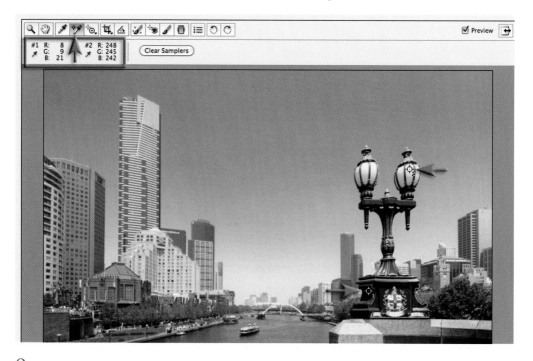

9. We can preview how dark and how bright the tones are within this image by selecting the Color Sampler Tool (next to the White Balance Tool) and clicking on the brightest and darkest tones within the image. A shadow sampler is especially useful if you intend to print an image as the printing process easily clips dark shadow tones if they are too dark. If the shadow tones are in the low single figures, they are too low. Raise the Fill Light slider slightly until one or more of the RGB figures in the high teens or low twenties.

10. Click on the blue writing at the bottom of the ACR dialog to open the Workflow Options dialog. We can use this dialog to set the appropriate color space for the file when it is opened in the main editing space (usually sRGB for screen and Adobe RGB for print). If the image requires no further editing in the main space select OK and then hit the Save button in the bottom right-hand corner of the ACR dialog. It is possible to apply output sharpening in the Workflow Options dialog if you are not going to edit the file further in the main editing space. To continue editing this file in Photoshop select OK in the workflow options dialog and then select the Open Image button or Open Object button (select this option in the Workflow Options dialog or hold down the Shift key and to access the Open Object button). Opening as an Object (Smart Object) allows the user to return to any of these settings in ACR to fine-tune the adjustments at a later date. This is a little like using an adjustment layer instead of applying the adjustment directly to the pixels. These are termed 'non-destructive' approaches to image editing. If you like the idea of always being able to return to ACR then select the Open in Photoshop as Smart Objects checkbox in the Workflow Options.

Note > All adjustments can be reset in ACR (go to the fly-out menu to the right of the Basic tab). No pixels in a JPEG, TIFF or Raw file are directly altered by these adjustments until we save a separate file from ACR (click the Save Image button in ACR). Another file is then processed from the master file with the adjustments 'baked in'.

11. Choosing the Open Object button in ACR will open a layer in the Layers panel. The layer in the Layers panel will appear with the name of the file and the thumbnail will have a Smart Object icon in the bottom right-hand corner. Double clicking the thumbnail will open the Raw file that has been embedded in the layer. From the Adjustments panel select a Curves adjustment layer so that we can fine-tune this image for print.

12. In the next two steps we will place color samplers in the image to target the darkest and lightest tones in the image. To help find these tones we will temporarily increase the contrast of the image using this Curves adjustment layer. In the Curves dialog move the black Input Levels slider under the bottom left-hand corner of the histogram to the right, and the white Input Levels slider under the bottom right-hand corner of the histogram to the left. This will clip both the highlights and shadows to help you locate the darkest and lightest tones within the image. Select the black eyedropper in the Curves dialog and then move your mouse cursor into the image preview and hold down both the Alt/Option key and the Shift key to see a threshold view of your image. An eyedropper icon will appear with a + icon and a target icon. When you click your mouse over one of the darkest shadows you will take a color sample.

13. Select the white eyedropper, hold down the Alt/Option and Shift keys, move into the image preview and take a color sample from one of the brightest highlights (you are probably getting a good idea where these tones in this image live now). In the bottom right-hand corner of the Curves dialog click on the Reset to adjustment defaults icon so that your shadows and highlights are no longer clipped. We are now ready to set appropriate output values to the tones we have targeted.

14. Open the Info panel and locate the two color samples '#1' and '#2'. Right-click on the tiny eyedropper icon underneath each of the # symbols and in the context menu change the RGB readout to HSB (Hue, Saturation and Brightness). It is easier to work out whether a shadow will print if we can see a brightness value rather than trying to average out three separate RGB values. To raise the Brightness value to 8% you may need to select the black point on the curve and raise the Output from 0 to something higher (highlight the Output field and use the up and down arrow keys on your keyboard to alter the Output value). Monitor the changing Brightness value in the Info panel to see when it reaches 8%.

Note > The value of 8% is an average figure for shadow tones that can be printed with detail on an average printer. This value will need to be adjusted for specific output devices.

Tina Lorien (www.iStockphoto.com)

Adjusting narrow ranges of color

The Hue/Saturation adjustment can target a very narrow range of color values and then adjust them to match other colors within the image. In the example above the sunburn is targeted and then matched with the surrounding skin colors. To achieve this level of control the user must first select the broad color range that the color belongs to from the Edit menu inside the Hue/Saturation panel, e.g. reds, yellows, greens, cyans, etc. By clicking and dragging the sliders that sit between the two color ramps (at the base of the dialog box) closer together, or by using the 'Add to Sample' or 'Subtract from Sample' eyedroppers, the precise colors can be targeted. Moving the Saturation slider temporarily to −100 or +100 can help determine when the target colors have been isolated from their neighboring colors of a similar hue. Be sure to return the Saturation slider to 0 before moving the Hue slider to achieve the required match. Some fine-tuning using the Saturation and Lightness sliders will usually be required before the match to the surrounding skin is perfect.

15. If you double-click the Smart Object thumbnail in the Layers panel (it is important to click the thumbnail and not the layer itself) then the Raw file embedded in the layer will open in ACR. This will allow us to sharpen the image when we have determined what the output device is (screen or print). In this image I have raised the Amount slider to 70% in the Sharpening section of the Detail tab so that this image has an appropriate amount of sharpening for print. The precise value for the Amount slider will vary depending on how much sharpening was applied to the JPEG image in camera. Raw images may require higher settings for the Amount slider as they have not previously been sharpened at all.

16. In the Basic panel I have raised the Clarity and Vibrance sliders to fine-tune the image. It is important to note that now we have optimized the image for print, any adjustment to the sliders above the Clarity slider could change the Color Sampler readouts in the main editing space. It is also important to note that if the Color Samplers are placed very close to an edge within the image, the process of sharpening could also change these output values (check the values in the Info dialog after applying these changes in ACR). Select OK in the bottom right-hand corner of the ACR dialog to update the preview in the main editing space.

17. Although the file has been optimized for print, it is easy to create a screen or web version by going to File > Save for Web & Devices. Select the file format (usually JPEG) and a compression setting (usually High). Check the Convert to sRGB checkbox and enter in the new size in the Image Size section. Set the Quality setting to Bicubic Sharper and preview the image in the Optimized tab (top right-hand corner of the dialog). Select Save to export a web version of your master file (the one you have been working on) and be sure to save this master file as a Photoshop (PSD) file.

Correcting perspective – Project 2

Many photographers prematurely jump to the conclusion that Photoshop is solely a tool for distorting reality or fabricating an alternative reality (the expression 'it's been photoshopped' still has negative connotations for some photographers). Although this may be the case in some instances, Photoshop can be used as a tool to correct the distortions introduced by the camera and lens. These corrections can return an image back to how we remember the original subject or location, rather than how the camera interpreted it.

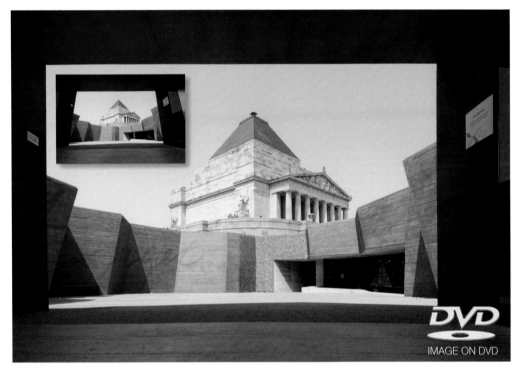

The Shrine of Remembrance, Melbourne – Nikon D200, Nikkor 12–24 mm 1:4 G ED @ 12 mm.

Wide-angle lenses are an essential tool for the commercial photographer but they can introduce an unnatural and unnerving sense of perspective. In the natural landscape this exaggerated perspective may go unnoticed but when the photographer is in the urban environment and the photographer has to tilt the camera up in order to frame the shot, the verticals will lean inwards – sometimes to an alarming extent. Architectural photographers may go into this environment equipped with specialized equipment such as shift lenses and large-format cameras (some even take their own ladders). This specialized equipment allows the photographer to frame the view they need without tilting the camera from the horizontal axis. There is, however, a post-production answer that allows the photographer to create a more natural sense of perspective. This first project focuses its attention on correcting rather than distorting images and will look at perspective correction and chromatic aberration (the misalignment of colors commonly found in the corners of an image). Photoshop CS5 is now capable of using specific lens profiles to correct lens distortions but sometimes we still need to perfect some images using the custom adjustments inside the Lens Correction dialog.

Auto Correction

The Lens Correction Filter now has a new Auto Correction tab. This filter can apply corrections to your image that are specific to the lens and lens settings you have been using. If a profile is not listed for your camera and lens combination you can hit the Search Online button to access additional online profiles. These in turn can be saved to your computer for future use.

In the example above the Geometric distortion has been removed but the chromatic aberration is actually made worse by the auto setting. When this occurs, use the settings in the custom tab. Moving the sliders in the Custom tab will override the auto settings.

Lens Correction in Adobe Camera Raw 6.1

Lens Correction is also available in Adobe Camera Raw if you update your camera Raw plug-in to version 6.1 or later. The Auto setting can only be used if Photoshop can locate a profile for the lens you are using. In the example above a small amount of distortion was still present in the image after the Auto setting was applied. Raising the Distortion slider in the Correction Amount section fixed the problem.

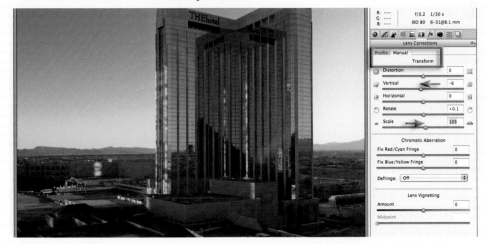

The vertical distortion, caused by the camera being tilted up, was corrected by going to the Manual tab and dragging the Vertical slider to the left. The image then had to be scaled up slightly (using the Scale slider) to ensure the final image fitted the frame.

1. Open the project image from the supporting DVD (R2_Correcting_Perspective.tif). Start the process by selecting an appropriate screen mode in the Options bar. Choosing the 'Full Screen Mode With Menu Bar' option will allow you to reposition the image anywhere on your screen by holding down the spacebar and dragging the image. This will be useful as we access the edges and corners of the image. Create a duplicate layer by dragging the Background layer in the Layers panel to the New Layer icon at the base of the panel (alternatively you can use the keyboard shortcut Ctrl + J (PC) or Command + J (Mac)). Select Filter > Lens Correction to open the Lens Correction dialog box.

2. At the time of writing this book there was no lens profile available for the Nikon 12-24mm DX f/4 lens that was used to capture the image used in this project. This project is designed to demonstrate how a manual lens correction can be made in the event that there is no profile available for the lens you are using. In the Auto Correction section of the Lens Correction dialog it is therefore important to deselect all of the Auto checkboxes including the Auto Scale Image. Then select the Custom tab. At the base of the Lens Correction dialog box make sure the Show Grid option is checked. Move your mouse cursor over the word 'Size' to the right of this checkbox. You should notice two arrows appear from the hand icon that indicate you can change the value in the field to the right (this tool for changing values in any numerical field is called a scrubby slider). If you now click and drag to the right the size of the grid will increase. Set the value to around 40.

3. To check for chromatic aberration (color fringing as a result of misalignment of color channels) we will need to zoom in to 100% or 200% and view the edge detail in the corners of the image. Click on the Zoom Tool in the upper left-hand corner of the dialog box or use the keyboard shortcut Ctrl + Spacebar (PC) or Command + Spacebar (Mac) to access the Zoom Tool and then click and drag to target a zoom area in the upper left-hand corner of the image (where the dominant vertical line meets the dominant horizontal line). Click on the tab to the right of the magnification size (underneath the image in the Lens Correction dialog box) and select 200% from the menu of sizes. This will ensure that we get an accurate view of any chromatic aberration that is present in this image.

4. The chromatic aberration, if present, can be seen as a fringe running alongside the edges of lines within the corners of the image. The amount of aberration visible depends on the camera and lens used to capture the image and also, to a large extent, on the size of the reproduction of the image. By slowly moving the Fix Green/Magenta Fringe and Fix Blue/Yellow Fringe sliders it should be possible to greatly reduce the width of the color fringing, if not eliminate it altogether.

Note > As well as chromatic aberration some lenses will produce noticeable darkening in the corners (especially at wide apertures). These overly dark corners can be removed using the Vignette slider. The Set Lens Default option is able to record these settings and apply them to subsequent images taken with the same lens. This feature is most useful where the chromatic aberration and vignetting do not vary as a result of zooming to a different focal length or by using a different aperture.

5. Now that the chromatic aberration is under control we can move on to the Transform section of the dialog box. Zoom out or select Fit in View. The sliders found in the Transform section are required to correct conversing verticals. Converging verticals are not corrected by the lens profile. In this image the Vertical Perspective slider is moved to the left (between −45 and −50) so that the verticals align with the grid lines that overlay this image. When a numerical field is highlighted you can use the up or down keyboard arrow keys to nudge a precise adjustment. Hold down the Shift key as you press an arrow key to increase or decrease the value in units of 10.

Note > There is a limit to the amount of correction that can be undertaken before some shapes within the subject become distorted. When the converging verticals are very pronounced it may be possible to reduce, but not eliminate, the distortion. It is worth remembering that verticals converge even when using standard focal length lenses.

6. For an accurate assessment of the degree of correction you should click the Move Grid Tool and click and drag the grid so that it aligns with edges within the image that are meant to be vertical and horizontal.

7. Use the Straighten Tool if the image appears slightly crooked when compared to the grid lines. Click on the tool located in the upper left-hand corner of the dialog box and then click and drag along either a vertical or horizontal line. Let go of the mouse button when you get to the other end of the straight line to automatically straighten the image.

Pincushion distortion and barrel distortion

If the vertical or horizontal lines with the image appear to be curved rather than straight this is an indication that either 'barrel distortion' or 'pincushion distortion' is present within the image as a result of the lens that has been used. The Geometric Distortion slider needed to correct this distortion appears at the top of the control panel but is sometimes best implemented after the image has first been straightened and the vertical perspective corrected. The image used in the illustration above is a typical example where the horizon line curves excessively. After first straightening the image a small amount of barrel distortion is corrected. Pincushion distortion can be found in some images where a long telephoto lens has been used to capture the image. The image used in this illustration can also be found on the supporting DVD.

8. As a result of being slightly off-center when photographed it will be impossible to align both the horizontals and verticals that frame the sky without one further adjustment. Moving the Horizontal Perspective slider slightly to the right will ensure everything aligns to the grid lines. You may need to revisit some of the sliders a second time to perfect the alignment.

9. Large transformations will soften image detail. If the scale of the image is reduced this will help retain image sharpness. High-resolution images may have sufficient pixels to allow a reduction in scale and yet still meet the final output requirements. Use the Scale slider in the bottom right-hand corner of the dialog box to reduce this image to 95%. Select OK to apply the changes and pass the corrected image back to the main Photoshop workspace.

10. After the Lens Correction filter has been applied it is still possible to fine-tune the correction in Photoshop's main workspace. Choose 'Rulers' from the View menu and then use the keyboard shortcut Ctrl + T (PC) or Command + T (Mac) to access the Free Transform command. Some images appear squashed after perspective correction so dragging the center handle of the transform bounding box either up or down can restore a more natural appearance to the image. The Transform command can correct lines that were not possible to correct using the Lens Correction filter.

Turn the rulers on (Ctrl/Command + R) and click and drag a guide from the vertical rule to each side of the entrance. Click on the top rule and drag in a guide to the top of the entrance and then drag a fourth guide to the lower portion of the image to align it with either end of the horizontal line on the concrete slab. You will notice how these lines in the lower portion of the image appear curved, even though the horizontal line in the top portion of the image appears comparatively straight. This is not something that the barrel distortion slider in the Lens Correction filter could compensate for (the uneven distortion is due to the fact that the horizontal lines near the base of the image are closer to the camera lens than the horizontal lines in the upper portion of the image, and have therefore been subject to a greater degree of barrel distortion). Click on the Warp icon in the Options bar and then move your mouse cursor over one of the curved lines in the central lower portion of the image. You can then click and drag gently upwards until the curved lines align with the guide you dragged into the image. To complete the process hit the Return/Enter key to accept the warp when everything is aligned. You can either hide or delete the guides by going to View > Show > Guides or View > Clear Guides.

11. Switch off the visibility of the background layer so that you can clearly see the part of the image that must be cropped. Select the Crop Tool and drag a cropping marquee around the picture area to be retained. If you are already know the final image requirements, you can enter the crop dimensions and resolution in the Options bar. Hit the Enter/Return key to apply the crop.

Move your cursor over the background layer and then right-click (PC) or Command-click (Mac) on the layer to open the context-sensitive menu. This menu will give you the option to flatten the image if you are now happy with the corrections. Select OK if you are presented with a warning dialog box asking you whether you want to discard the hidden layers.

12. To complete the project we need to sharpen this image as it has not been sharpened in-camera or in ACR (Adobe Camera Raw). Sharpening is a normal corrective process that must be performed either in-camera or in post-production to all images. The Smart Sharpen filter and the Unsharp Mask filter offer greater control than sharpening in either the camera or in ACR. Since CS3 we can apply filters non-destructively by first converting the layer for Smart Filters (Filter > Convert for Smart Filters). After converting the layer for Smart Filters (the layer is now known as a Smart Object) choose Filter > Sharpen > Smart Sharpen. We can use any filter on a Smart Object, not just the ones that have smart in their name.

Working spaces – Project 3

For Photographers shooting in the Raw format we can now optimize and enhance images either in Adobe Camera Raw (ACR) or in the main editing space of Photoshop. Increased flexibility and options brings increased confusion as to where is the best place to edit. Am I in the right space for the right job? What if I change my mind? Decisions, decisions.

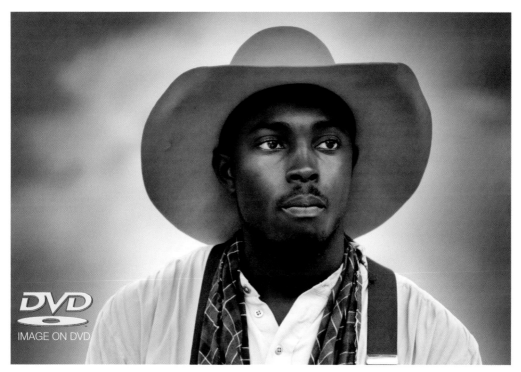

Cowboy - Fort Worth, Texas.

The un-edited Raw file leaves a little to be desired in terms of exposure and framing. This project corrects the exposure and explains how the decisions were made as to where to edit the file in order to achieve the best possible outcomes.

The project will also show how we can edit a single file in both spaces (ACR and the main editing space). The workflow outlined will give you the flexibility to return to ACR to tweak some of those initial settings – providing additional flexibility for those photographers (or art directors) who can never make up their mind.

Quick adjustments using Adobe Camera Raw

Adobe Camera Raw can offer fast and convenient control over tones that need adjustment, without the need for extended editing procedures in the main editing space. Using the Fill Light and Recovery sliders in Adobe Camera Raw the user can lighten the deep shadows and recover the bright highlight tones in this image. Localized contrast can be increased using the Clarity slider and finally the excessive saturation that results from these adjustments is put back in check by lowering the Saturation slider. The convenience and speed, however, come at a price – quality and control. Use the R3-Shadows.DNG file on the supporting DVD to try this technique.

The example on the left is a close-up view (the top of the dog's head) taken from the image edited in Adobe Camera Raw (ACR). Notice the dark line surrounding the window frame and the top of the fur – an artifact from the aggressive editing procedure in ACR. On the right is the same image edited in the main editing space using the Shadow/Highlight adjustment.

Note > Although the Recovery and Fill Light sliders in ACR are very powerful adjustment tools, when used aggressively together they can lead to image artifacts. When this is the case it is recommended to use the Shadows/Highlights adjustment feature in the main editing space.

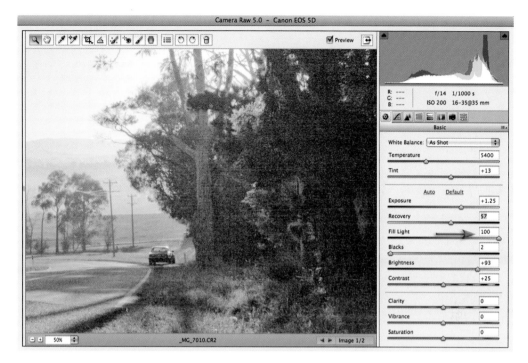

Underexposure – the Achilles heel of digital exposure

The illustration above shows the poor quality of underexposed shadow information captured on a full-frame 35 mm CMOS sensor at 200 ISO. Shadows in digital images contain low-quality data and the shadows of most digital images cannot always be rescued without compromising the quality. Shadow information will tend to be superior if the image is captured at low ISO on a large 14- or 16-bit image sensor.

In Adobe Camera Raw the noise can be reduced by raising the Color and Luminance Noise Reduction sliders. The effects of these sliders in ACR can only be viewed at magnifications of 100% and above. Ideally the photographer should raise the exposure at the time of capture to avoid underexposure (see Adobe Camera Raw) or capture multiple exposures (see HDR).

1. Open the project image into Adobe Camera Raw (ACR). Select the Crop Tool and create a tighter composition by dragging the tool over the head and shoulders of the cowboy. If required, move your cursor to a position just outside one of the corner handles to rotate the crop marquee. Select the Hand Tool or Zoom tool to apply this crop. It is important to remember that pixels are not discarded in the cropping process in ACR – just hidden from view. This is an advantage to using ACR rather than the main editing space for this task.

2. No fill flash reached the subject in any usable strength and the exposure compensation used in-camera was insufficient to lighten the dark shadows. Overall Luminance can be increased by raising the Exposure slider to +1.5, the Fill Light slider to +15 and the Brightness slider to +70. Contrast can also be increased by raising the Contrast slider to +50 and the Clarity slider to +20. As contrast increases so does saturation, so this needs to be controlled by reducing the Vibrance slider to –10. The Blacks slider also needs to be raised slightly to +7 so that the image still has a black point. Open the Image as a Smart Object (set this option in the Workflow Options, accessed from the base of the ACR dialog, or hold down the Shift key to access the Open Object button).

3. When the file opens in the main editing space of Photoshop go to the Layers panel and right-click on the Fill-Light Smart Object to access the context menu (be sure to right-click on the layer rather than the image thumbnail). Choose the New Smart Object via Copy command. This is not the same as dragging the Smart Object to the Create a layer icon in the Layers panel or using the duplicate layer shortcut. The New Smart Object via Copy command ensures that we can open the embedded Raw file back into Adobe Camera Raw (ACR) and adjust the settings without affecting the original smart object.

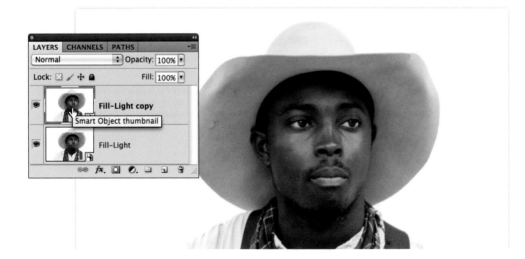

4. We can now use this copy layer to optimize the Raw file for the sky so that it does not appear clipped or 'blown out' in the final version. Double-click on the Fill-Light copy smart object thumbnail to open the embedded raw file in ACR. When the Raw file opens for the second time the Raw file will appear with all of the settings you used to optimize the shadow tones of this image.

5. Click on the Default button to reset all of the sliders except for Clarity and Vibrance and then lower the exposure slider to −2.00 stops and the Brightness slider to +25 to darken the sky. You will see that the sky is no longer clipped in the histogram in the top right-hand corner of the ACR dialog (an advantage of the extended dynamic range of the Raw format).

6. Go to the Effects panel and add a Post Crop Vignette to darken the edges of the sky even further. Select OK in the bottom right-hand corner of the ACR dialog to update the settings of the Fill-Light copy layer.

7. We now need to create a mask so that we can balance the two exposures. Select the Quick Selection Tool from the Tools panel and then click and drag over the sky to make a selection. If the selection invades the subject just hold down the Alt key (PC) or Option key (Mac) and drag over these areas to exclude them from the initial selection. Click on the Add layer mask icon from the base of the Layers panel.

8. The layer mask on the Fill-Light copy layer will now mask the dark cowboy on the top layer to reveal the lighter cowboy on the background layer. The extreme exposure variation between the two layers will, however, create an unsightly hard edge around the subject. By softening the layer mask we will create a more gradual transition between the two exposures. Check that the layer mask is the active component of the layer (you should see a dark line around the layer mask thumbnail). Click on the layer mask thumbnail to make it the active component if it is not already selected. Go to Filter > Other > Minimum and raise the Radius slider to 30 pixels and select OK. This will expand the mask. Don't worry about the white band, we will take care of that in the next step.

9. Go to Filter > Blur Gaussian Blur and apply a 250 pixel Gaussian Blur to the layer mask to soften the edge of the mask. Select OK to apply the adjustment to the layer mask.

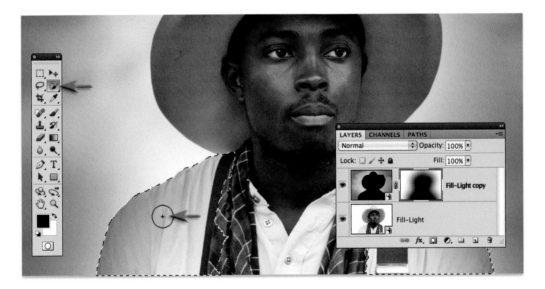

10. The blur will create a gradual transition between the two layers that is effective over much of the image. Some of the dark tones from the top layer are, however, bleeding over the shoulders of the cowboy so we need to clean this area. Select the Quick Selection Tool from the Tools panel and check the Auto-Enhance and the Sample All Layers checkboxes in the Options bar. Select the cowboy's white shirt and then from the Edit menu choose Fill. In the Fill dialog choose Black in the Contents section and then select OK.

11. The white shirt is now too light against the dark sky so we will now do some localized tonal control of just the highlights on this layer. Select the Fill-Light layer (the bottom layer) and then go to Image > Adjustments > Shadows/Highlights. Check the Show More Options checkbox. Set the Amount slider in the Shadows section to 0% and raise the Amount slider in the Highlights section to 25%. Reduce the Tonal Width slider in the Highlights section to 25% to limit the darkening effect to just the white shirt. Select OK to apply the adjustment.

12. Select the Smart Filters mask and then click the Invert button in the Masks panel or use the keyboard shortcut Ctrl + I (PC) or Command + I (Mac). The mask should now appear black instead of white and the effects of the smart filter will be removed. Select the Brush Tool from the Tools panel and set white as the foreground color. Use a soft-edged brush to paint in this adjustment over the shirt.

13. If some of the edges appear a little too hard select the Blur Tool from the Tools panel, set the strength to 100% in the Options bar and paint over any edges in the fill-light copy mask that require softening.

14. To increase contrast in just the midtones of the image (leaving the darkest shadow tones and brightest highlights unaffected), we can add a Levels adjustment layer. Set the mode of this adjustment layer to Soft Light (one of the contrast blend modes). Moving the Output Levels sliders to 80 and 180 will protect the shadows and highlights from contrast that results from the Soft Light blend mode.

15. If the Saturation climbs a little too high (a result of the increase in contrast) add a Hue/Saturation adjustment layer and drag the Saturation slider to the left slightly.

Smart Filter masks

The problem with the mask that accompanies a Smart Filter is that there is only one. If you wanted to apply a second smart filter it would have to share the same mask that has already been optimized for the Shadows/Highlights adjustment. It is possible, however, to obtain a clean mask that is dedicated a the new smart filter by embedding the Smart Object into another Smart Object. To try this out, select the Fill-Light layer and go to Layer > Smart Objects > Convert to Smart Object. This may sound a little strange as the layer is already a Smart Object but this action will give us the option to apply a new smart filter with a new layer mask. If we needed to edit the original Smart Filter at any time we would need to double-click the Smart Object thumbnail to reveal the original Smart Object and the original Smart Filter. Another option open to us is to Rasterize the smart object, which in turn applies the Shadows/ Highlights adjustment settings to the pixels and breaks the link with the Raw file and original data. This would, however, be a destructive edit as it would bake in the changes to the pixels.

16. With such an underexposed file the noise levels are starting to become a little aggressive. In ACR 6 we have some very sophisticated Noise Reduction controls that will be able to create much smoother tones. To access these controls double-click the Fill-Light Smart Object thumbnail (the base layer) to open the Raw file in ACR. Go to the Detail tab and raise the Luminance slider in the Noise Reduction section to 65. Raising the Luminance Detail slider to 75 will help restore some of the fine detail in this image. Click the OK button to update these changes in the composite file.

17. Click on the Create a new layer icon at the base of the Layers panel and set the mode of this layer to Overlay. Select the Brush Tool from the Tools panel and set white as the foreground color. Set the Opacity to 10% and set the Brush Hardness to 0 in the Options bar. Paint over the highlights on the face to 'dodge' these tones (make lighter). You can also 'burn' or make selected tones darker by switching the foreground color to black and then painting in localized areas.

18. The non-destructive workflow in this project allows us to make adjustments to any of the editing steps to fine-tune the visual outcome. Double-click the Shadows/Highlights smart filter instead to open the Shadows/Highlights adjustment dialog. Move the Amounts slider in the Highlights section to 60% and select OK to apply these changes.

19. If we double-click the layer thumbnail of the Fill-Light copy smart object the embedded Raw file opens in ACR. Lower the brightness slider to 0 to darken the sky even further. Select OK to apply the changes and update the visual appearance of the multilayered file open in the main editing space of Photoshop.

Although this workflow may seem unduly complex to basic Photoshop users it does offer the advanced user a completely non-destructive workflow that allows full control over every element of the editing workflow. No changes are baked into any of the pixels and therefore every element can either be deleted or modified.

The horizontal format image is transformed into a vertical format image with the careful relocation of the life-ring and the sign declaring that the water (or is it the paint) is indeed 'wet'.

Clone and stamp – Project 4

It has become a common retouching task in image editing to move, remove or replace details within an image to fine-tune the composition or clean the image area so everything is in its right place and there is no superfluous detail to detract from the composition or distract the viewer's attention. The Clone Stamp Tool is the Tool that is most often used for this task. With Photoshop CS3 a new panel called Clone Source appeared. This enabled a more controlled approach to copying pixels and painting them into a new location or into a new image. There is, however, a Stamp Tool that offers an additional performance feature that few photographers know about. The Vanishing Point dialog is a highly specialized editing space for working with perspective. The Stamp Tool that resides here has additional Heal feature that is not matched by the Clone Stamp Tool in the main editing space. Many photographers haven't known about the Stamp Tool in Vanishing Point because they may never have had the need to 'edit in perspective'.

1. A new feature for the Clone Stamp Tool in Photoshop CS4 was the ability to see a preview of what you are cloning to enable precise alignment without having to use the Clone Source panel that was introduced with CS3. Open the supporting image (R4_clone_stamp.tif) and click on the New Layer icon in the Layers panel to create an empty new layer. Click on the Clone Stamp Tool in the Tools panel. Choose a small soft-edged brush from the Options bar and set the Clone Stamp Tool Opacity to 100%. Choose All Layers from the 'Sample' options. Hold down the Option/Alt key and click on the top of the Wet sign where it meets the horizon. Move the mouse cursor over to the right side of the image and align the horizon line and side of the white pole before you click to paint or clone the sign into position. Although it is now easier to achieve precise alignment between the cloned pixel and the background layer the lack of a healing option makes it difficult to achieve a seamless result (the ocean and sky are slightly different tones).

2. Discard Layer 1 in the Layers panel by dragging it to the trash can icon at the base of the Layers panel. Create another new empty layer by clicking on the New Layer icon. All of the modifications will be stamped into this layer, leaving the background layer unaffected. Go to the Filter menu and choose 'Vanishing Point'. Be prepared for a short wait while Photoshop opens the image into the Vanishing Point dialog box.

Good advice for the astrophysicist

3. When the dialog box opens, Vanishing Point tries to be really helpful by giving you advice as to what to do next – sound advice that we will now ignore (unless of course you would like to 'tear off your perpendicular planes from the stretch nodes of existing planes'). What I would like you to do instead is to simply double-click the second icon from the top in the left-hand corner of the dialog box (the Create Plane Tool). This completely ignores Adobe's invitation to locate any planes of perspective (parallel lines that converge as they recede into the distance – a particularly rare animal in natural landscape and portrait photography) and instead just drops a nice blue grid over your entire image. This blue grid serves absolutely no purpose in this project – but is of course an essential step before Adobe will allow us to utilize the Stamp Tool.

4. Now select the Stamp Tool in the Vanishing Point dialog box. Set the Opacity of the tool to 100% and switch the Heal option to 'On'. Reduce the Hardness of the brush to around 60 and then increase the Diameter of the brush to around 150.

Note > If the complex process of creating the 'planes of perspective' on your first visit to Vanishing Point seemed more trouble than it is was worth then you probably missed the significant difference between the seemingly identical Stamp Tool in Vanishing Point and the our old friend that resides in the Tools panel of the main editing space. On closer inspection they are not the same animal at all. The luminosity or healing options in the Options bar within the dialog box enable the cloned pixels to achieve a seamless blend with the surrounding pixels. This is achieved when the tool draws in the hue and luminosity values of the surrounding pixels (or just the luminosity values as is the case with the Luminosity option) into the feathered edge of the brush you are using. The softer the brush the broader the area of healing that occurs, but this may also increase the risk of drawing in adjacent values of an inappropriate value. Care must be taken to adapt the brush size and hardness to the area you are cloning into.

5. Alt/Option-click on the horizon line where it meets the upright pole, just above the sign 'wet', to select a source point for the pixels you wish to clone. Now move over to the vertical pole on the right side of the image and click on the similar intersection point where the horizon line meets the pole. Hold down the mouse clicker as you paint; stamp or clone just enough pixels to reveal the sign and its shadow into its new location.

Note > Choosing a precise intersection of horizontal and vertical lines as your initial source point is critical when attempting to clone pixels into another area of the image that shares these strong geometric lines.

6. Turn your attention to cloning the life-ring when the sign has been relocated. To prevent the horizontal edge above the life-ring being cloned out of alignment it will be necessary to reduce the size of the brush and increase its hardness to 80%.

7. Increase the size of the brush and decrease the hardness once again before selecting a new source point from the foreground concrete to the left of the life-ring. Proceed to remove the original life-ring from the image. If the left side of the original life-ring starts to reappear when attempting to remove the life-ring try selecting a source point further over to the left side of the image. When the original life-ring has been successfully removed click OK to apply the changes made by the Stamp Tool. You will notice that all of your changes now appear in the new layer you created before using Vanishing Point and can be removed if you are not entirely happy by simply switching off the layer visibility.

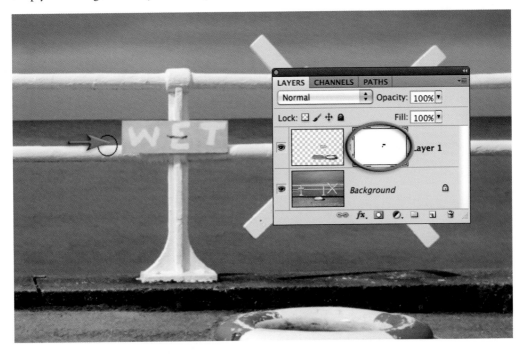

8. With the changes isolated to their own layer you have the option to erase or mask just a few of the changes that are not entirely convincing. In this image when the white pole and horizon line are aligned there is a small amount of alignment error just to the left of the sign. This can be masked by clicking on the 'Add layer mask' icon in the Layers panel and masking the error using the Brush Tool. Choose black as the foreground color and set the Opacity in the Options bar to 100%. Paint with a small brush to mask the alignment error.

9. It is possible to crop an image without discarding the pixels. This allows the user to recompose the composition, if required, even after cropping. To achieve this non-destructive crop in the main editing space, drag the lock on the background layer to the trash can in the Layers panel or hold down the Alt/Option key and double-click the background layer. Select the Crop Tool from the Tools panel and make a vertical composition from this horizontal image. In the Options bar select the Hide rather than the Delete radio button and then hit the commit icon in the Options bar or press the Return/Enter key. Hold down the Shift key and select both layers in the Layers panel. Select the Move Tool and drag to adjust the composition if required.

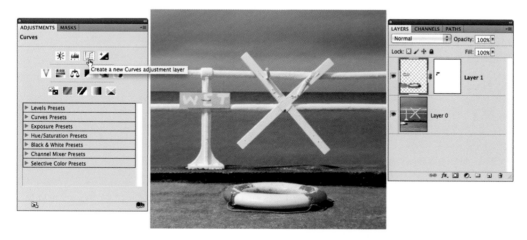

10. We will now complete this project by making the sky a little darker. From the Adjustments panel choose a Curves adjustment.

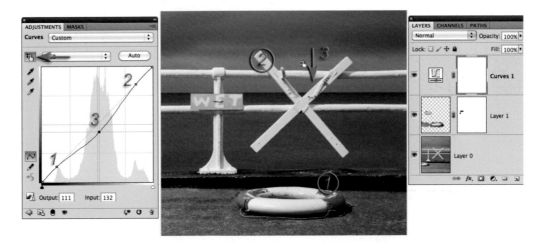

11. Select the On-Image Tool in the top left-hand corner of the Curves dialog. Click on a dark shadow and then a bright highlight in the image to set adjustment points on the curve. These will serve to anchor these tones when we adjust the midtones. Click on the sky in the image preview and drag down to make the sky a little darker.

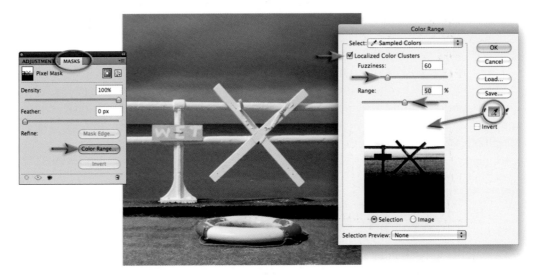

12. The adjustment to the sky can be further restricted by going to the Masks panel and selecting Color Range. In the Color Range dialog select the Add to Sample eyedropper underneath the Save button. Click in the sky in the image preview to sample a blue color. Return to the Color Range dialog and make sure the Localized Color Clusters option is checked and then lower the Range slider to 50%. Drag across the sky, either in the Image itself or in the preview in the Color Range dialog to clear the mask from this area of the image. Adjust the Fuzziness slider so that all of the sky is white and then select OK. The Color Range feature offers a quick and easy way to make a mask that will restrict the adjustment. The mask can be further refined by painting directly into the mask with either black or white as the foreground color.

IMAGE ON DVD

Clone or Heal

When cleaning an image of superfluous detail the question often arises as to which is the best tool for the job. When working in broad areas of texture to remove small blemishes the Spot Healing Brush Tool is hard to beat for speed and ease of use. As the areas requiring removal get larger, switching to the Healing Brush and selecting a source point avoids the errors that occur when using the Spot Healing Brush for this task. The limitations of the Healing Brush (and Spot Healing Brush) become apparent when working up against tones or colors that are markedly different to the area being cleaned. The Healing process draws luminance and color values from the surrounding area and when these colors are very different they contaminate the area to be healed. Problems can often be avoided in these instances by either using a harder brush or making a selection that excludes the neighboring tones that are different. When working up against a sharp edge even these actions may not be enough to avoid contamination – this is the time to switch to the Clone Stamp Tool. A selection will help to contain the repair while the Clone Source panel or Stamp Tool in Vanishing Point will help to align edges so that the repair is seamless.

Gradients and vignettes – Project 5

One of the top ten most powerful editing tools for Photoshop users, that's been around since the dawn of Photoshop time, is the mighty Gradient Tool. This project shows you how you can breathe drama into seemingly lifeless images using some of Mark Galer's super special tips and techniques, designed to extract the maximum performance from your images.

St Paul's Cathedral from Millennium Bridge, London.

This project explores how we can use a gradient in an Adjustment Layer Mask to merge the same Raw file processed in two different ways. The project will also utilize a colored gradient applied to two new layers that, in turn, have been set to two different blend modes. The idea is to extract every ounce of life from this underexposed image captured on a gray and wet day in London (nothing new here).

1. Open the Raw file in Adobe Camera Raw (ACR) and then optimize the image for the foreground content. Raise the Exposure Slider to +1.75, the Fill Light slider to +50, the Brightness slider to +25, the Contrast slider to +70, the Clarity and Vibrance sliders to +25. Then hit the Open Object button (hold down the Shift key if the button reads Open Image) to open this file into the main editing space of Photoshop (got to love ACR for fast editing!).

Graduated Filters

The Graduated Filter in ACR can be used to lower the exposure and increase the saturation and contrast of the sky. Although there is a lot of control over how the sky appears we are a few sliders short of a full load when compared to the sliders in the Basic panel. In this project we will open the file without applying a graduated filter here in ACR.

2. When we choose the Open Object button in ACR the Raw file is embedded in the layer. In the Layers panel right-click on the Millennium-Bridge smart object (not the layer thumbnail) and choose the command 'New Smart Object via Copy'. This allows us to open the Raw file embedded in the copy layer into ACR and change its settings without affecting the appearance of the original smart object. Now double-click on the Millennium-Bridge copy layer thumbnail to open the Raw image into ACR.

3. When the Raw file opens for the second time you will see all of the settings you used to optimize the image for the foreground. To clear all of these settings click the blue word 'Default'. This will clear all of the settings except for the Clarity, Vibrance and Saturation sliders. Optimize the image for the sky by reducing the Exposure slider to −1.75 stops and raising the blacks slider to +27, the Brightness and Contrast sliders to +100. Reset the Clarity and Vibrance sliders to 0 by double-clicking each slider control and then raise the Saturation slider to +100.

4. Select the Detail tab and reduce the Sharpening Amount to 0 and raise the Luminance slider in the Noise Reduction section to +50. This will ensure the sky is free from excessive noise. Now select the OK button to update the Millennium-Bridge copy smart object.

5. Add a layer mask to the Millennium-Bridge copy smart object by clicking the Add layer mask icon at the base of the Layers panel. Select the Gradient Tool from the Tools panel. In the Options bar click on the little triangle next to the Gradient ramp to open the gradient picker. Select the third gradient (the Black, White gradient). Select the Linear Gradient option, make sure the Opacity is set to 100% and make sure the Reverse option is NOT checked. Click on the layer mask to make this the active component of the copy layer and then click and drag a gradient from the people in the center of the image to a position just above the top of the spire on St Paul's cathedral. If you hold down the Shift key as you drag a gradient it will constrain it so that it is perfectly vertical. If the top of the cathedral still appears a little dark after dragging this gradient, drag a second one slightly higher in the sky.

6. We will now increase the intensity of the warm colors in the sky. Select the Eyedropper Tool from the Tools panel and in the Options bar select 5 by 5 Average from the Sample Size drop-down menu. This will ensure we can sample a color within the image when either the Gradient Tool or Brush Tool is selected. This setting is 'sticky' so you will not have to do this action again unless you choose Reset Tool or Reset All Tools. Click on the Create a new layer icon at the base of the Layers panel to add an empty new layer.

7. Set the mode of the new layer to Multiply (one of the darkening blend modes) in the Layers panel. Select the Gradient Tool and then hold down the Alt key (PC) or Option key (Mac) and click on the orange color in the sky to load this as the foreground color (otherwise known as 'sampling'). Make sure the Transparency option in the Options bar is checked.

8. Select the second gradient (the Foreground to Transparent gradient) from the gradient presets. While holding down the Shift key, drag a gradient from the top of the image window to a position just below the top of the spire on St Paul's cathedral. This will enhance the warm colors that are already an important aspect in this dramatic sky.

9. Add another new layer (click on the Create a new layer icon in the Layers panel) and set the mode to Overlay (one of the contrast blend modes). Hold down the Alt key (PC) or Option key (Mac) and take a sample of the darker orange color that has appeared in the sky after applying the first gradient. While holding down the Shift key drag a gradient from the base of the image window to a position just higher than the feet of the people in the center of the image. This will mirror the warm colors that are in the sky in the wet pavement.

10. It is possible to fine-tune the effects of a gradient using the Hue/Saturation adjustment feature. Use the keyboard shortcut Ctrl + U (PC) or Command + U (Mac) to open the Hue/ Saturation dialog. Adjust the Saturation and/or Lightness sliders to adjust the impact of this gradient on the composite view.

11. We can make the image more dramatic by adding a contrast vignette. Select the Rectangular Marquee Tool from the Tools panel and set a Feather value of 250 px in the Options bar. Click and drag 10% in from the top left-hand corner of the image to a position just short of 10% from the bottom right-hand corner of the image. This will create a selection with rounded corners.

12. From the Select menu choose 'Inverse'. We will now copy the visible pixels (rather than the pixels on a single layer) by going to Edit > Copy Merged. Again from the Edit menu choose Paste. This will paste the pixels from the clipboard onto a new layer. There will be no visible change in the image window at this point until we change the blend mode of the layer.

13. It is common to use either the Multiply or Screen blend modes when creating a vignette in this manner (to darken or lighten the edges of the image), but with this project we will use the Soft Light blend mode instead to increase contrast and color saturation at the edges of the image. If you find the effect is a little excessive, you have the choice to lower the opacity of the layer in the Layers panel. To increase the effect, change the blend mode from Soft Light to Overlay. To retain the increased levels of contrast but remove the changes in saturation, desaturate the layer using the keyboard shortcut Ctrl + Shift + U (PC) or Command + Shift + U (Mac).

14. To complete the project we will give the tonality a little bit of a lift, courtesy of a Brightness/Contrast adjustment layer. From the Adjustments panel choose Brightness/Contrast. Raise the Brightness to a value of +20 and the Contrast to a value of +10. Hold down the Alt key (PC) or Option key (Mac) and click on the visibility icon (the eye) on the bottom layer in the Layers panel so that you can see just how far we have come. Alt-click (PC) or Option-click (Mac) the visibility icon a second time to switch the visibility of all of the layers back on.

Advanced sharpening techniques – Project 6

Most, if not all, digital images require sharpening – even if shot on a state-of-the-art digital mega-resolution SLR with pin-sharp focusing. Most cameras or scanners can sharpen as the image is captured but the highest quality sharpening is to be found in the image-editing software. Sharpening in the image-editing software will allow you to select the precise amount of sharpening and the areas of the image that require sharpening most. When you are sharpening for the screen, it is very much a case of 'what you see is what you get'. For images destined for print, however, the monitor preview is just that – a preview. The actual amount of sharpening required for optimum image quality is usually a little more than looks comfortable on screen – especially when using an LCD monitor (TFT flat panel).

The basic concept of sharpening is to send the Unsharp Mask filter or Smart Sharpen filter on a 'seek and manipulate' mission. These filters make the pixels on the lighter side of the edge lighter still, and the pixels on the darker side of the edge darker. Think of it as a localized contrast control. Too much and people in your images start to look radioactive (they glow), not enough and the viewers of your images start reaching for the reading glasses they might not own. The best sharpening techniques to use with sharpening filters are those that prioritize the important areas for sharpening and leave the smoother areas of the image well alone, e.g. sharpening the eyes of a portrait but avoiding the skin texture. These advanced techniques are essential when sharpening images that have been scanned from film or have excessive noise, neither of which will benefit from a simple application of the Unsharp Mask filter. So let the project begin.

Note > If you have any sharpening options in your capture device it is important to switch them off or set them to minimum or low (if using Camera Raw set the sharpening amount to 0). The sharpening features found in most capture devices are often very crude when compared to the following technique. It is also not advisable to sharpen images that have been saved as JPEG files using high compression/low quality settings. The sharpening process that follows should also come at the end of the editing process, i.e. adjust the color and tonality of the image before starting this advanced sharpening technique. Reduce the levels of sharpening later if it proves too much.

Technique 1 – High Pass

1. Open the project image (R5_Sharpen-crop.tif). Duplicate the background layer and set the blend mode to Soft Light from the blend modes menu in the Layers panel. Change the name of this layer to High Pass. Go to Filter > Other > High Pass.

2. Choose a 5.0 pixels Radius for this project. A pixel Radius between 1.0 and 5.0 would be considered normal if you were not going to proceed beyond Step 4 in this project.

Note > Use lower Radius values when printing to Gloss paper and higher values if printing to Matte paper. To adjust the level of sharpening later you can either lower the opacity of the High Pass layer (to decrease the amount of sharpening) or set the blend mode of the 'High Pass' layer to 'Overlay' or 'Hard Light' (to increase the level of sharpening).

3. Click on the foreground color swatch in the Tools panel to open the Color Picker. To choose a midtone gray, enter 0 in the Hue and Saturation fields and 50% in the Brightness field. Select OK. Paint the High Pass layer to remove any sharpening that is not required, e.g. skin tones, skies, etc. Zoom in to 100 or 200% to obtain a clear view of the skin detail. This technique is especially useful for limiting the visual appearance of noise or film grain. Turn off the background layer momentarily to observe any areas you may have missed.

Detail from a portrait captured on a Nikon D1x. The Raw image was processed with 15% sharpening. First test has no subsequent sharpening. Second test uses a High Pass layer (3 pixel radius) in Soft Light mode. Third test has had the blend mode of the High Pass layer changed to Overlay mode. Fourth test has sharpening via a localized Unsharp Mask (100%) in Luminosity mode. The Opacity slider could be used to fine-tune the preferred sharpening routine.

4. Remember at this point the settings you have selected are being viewed on a monitor as a preview of the actual print. To complete the process it is important to print the image and then decide whether the image could stand additional sharpening or whether the amount used was excessive. If the settings are excessive you can choose to lower the opacity of the 'High Pass' layer.

Saturation and sharpening

Most techniques to increase the contrast of an image will also have a knock-on effect of increasing color saturation. As the High Pass and Unsharp Mask filters both increase local contrast there is an additional technique if this increased color saturation becomes problematic. You may not notice this in general image editing, but if you become aware of color fringing after applying the High Pass technique you should consider the following technique to limit its effects.

Technique 2 – Unsharp Mask/Smart Sharpen

The second technique is a continuation of the first technique. i.e complete the first four steps before commencing Step 5. This alternative technique is intended to address the issues of increased saturation leading to the effect of color fringing. This second technique looks at how the benefits of localized sharpening and Luminosity sharpening can be combined.

5. Change the blend mode of the High Pass layer back to Normal mode. Then apply a Threshold adjustment to the High Pass layer. Go to Image > Adjustments > Threshold.

6. Drag the slider just below the histogram to isolate the edges that require sharpening. The goal of moving these sliders is to render all of those areas you do not want to sharpen white. Select 'OK' when you are done. Paint out, with a white brush, any black pixel areas that you do not want sharpened, e.g. in the portrait used in this example any pixels remaining in the skin away from the eyes, mouth and nose were painted over using the Paintbrush Tool with white selected as the foreground color.

7. Go to the Channels panel and either Ctrl-click (PC) or Command-click (Mac) the RGB thumbnail or click on the 'Load channel as selection' icon from the base of the Channels panel to load the edge detail as a selection. Go to Select > Modify > Contract. Enter 1 pixel in the Contract dialog box and select OK. Click on the 'Save selection as channel' icon at the base of the Channels panel to save this modified selection as a channel. Go to Select > Deselect.

8. Switch off the visibility of the High Pass layer. Select the background layer in the Layers panel. Click on the 'Create a new layer' icon at the base of the Layers panel and then select the Spot Healing Brush Tool in the Tools panel. Select Sample All Layers in the Options bar and then spot any minor defects you can find in the image, e.g. there is a light spot in each eye that can be removed.

9. When your editing of the file is complete and you are ready for sharpening, stamp the visible elements to a new layer by holding down the Command, Option and Shift keys on a Mac or Ctrl, Alt and Shift keys on a PC and then pressing the letter E on the keyboard. This layer contains the combined elements from the layers below. Go to the Channels panel and load the Alpha channel you saved in Step 7 as a selection (drag the Alpha channel to the Load channel as selection icon or hold down the Command/Ctrl key and click on the Alpha channel. Make sure the Master RGB channel is the active component before returning to the Layers panel.

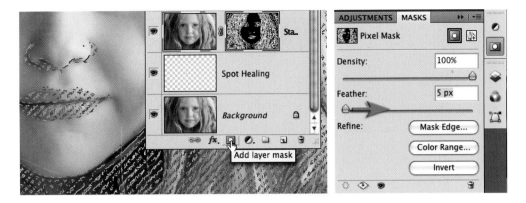

10. With the selection active hold down the Alt/Option key and click on the 'Add layer mask' icon. In the Masks panel increase the Feather of the mask to 5 pixels to soften the hard edges.

11. Now click on the image thumbnail rather than the layer mask in the Layers panel to make this the active component. Ensure the image is zoomed in to 100% for a small image or 50% for a larger print resolution image (200–300 ppi). Go to 'Filter > Sharpen > Smart Sharpen or Unsharp Mask'. Adjust the 'Amount' slider to between 100 and 300%. This controls how much darker or lighter the pixels at the edges are rendered. Choose an amount slightly more than looks comfortable on screen if the image is destined for print rather than screen. The Radius should be kept low, around 0.5 to 1.5 pixels. The mask protects the skin from the sharpening process but the Threshold can be raised to 3 or 4 to keep any noise in the image appearing soft.

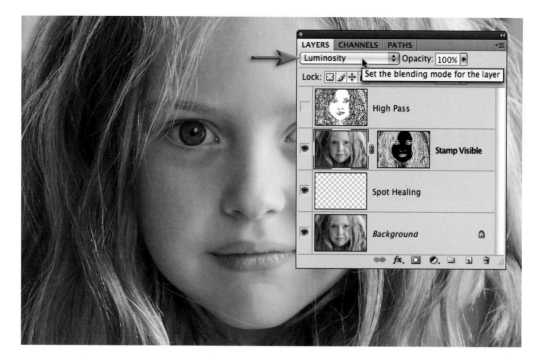

12. Change the blend mode of the sharpening layer (the Stamp Visible) to Luminosity mode. Luminosity mode will restrict the contrast changes to brightness only, and will remove any changes in saturation that have occurred due to the use of the Unsharp Mask. The changes are often very subtle but this technique is recommended for all images and is a fast alternative to a technique that advocates changing the mode of the image to Lab and then sharpening the L channel only (L for Luminosity).

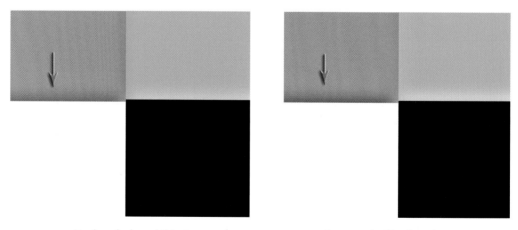

Darkened edge exhibits increased saturation prior to changing the blend mode to Luminosity.

The illustration above is a magnified view of the effects of changing the blend to Luminosity. These two cutting-edge sharpening techniques are capable of producing razor-sharp images that will really put the finishing touches to a folio-quality image.

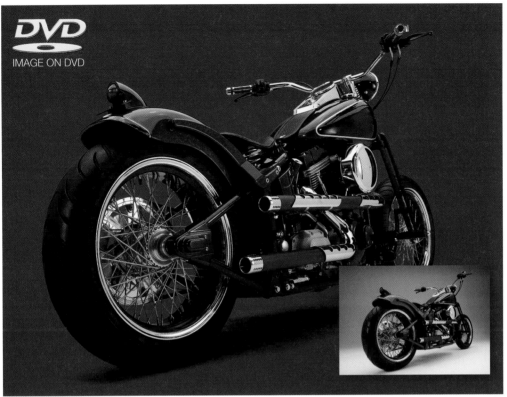

IMAGE ON DVD

Original photography by Scott Hirko

Replace color and tone – Project 7

This project will change the background color of a studio image and change target colors of the subject itself. The essential skill in this project is how to handle the shadows in the process. The preservation of the original shadows when the background color changes or the subject gets transported to a new location is one of the most essential ingredients for creating a realistic montage. The quickest way to destroy the dimensional illusion of the montage is to have conflicting light sources and shadows. Graphic designers all too often resort to recreating a shadow from scratch rather than preserving the original shadow, thereby creating a graphic, rather than a photographic, effect. When capturing a subject for a montage project try to capture all of the shadow on a smooth textured surface or on a surface with a similar texture to the new location. It is difficult to light a white backdrop so that it is white rather than gray but as shadows are always darker than the backdrop tone they can be separated quite easily if you know the technique to achieve this. The primary skills we will utilize in this tutorial are the controlled clipping of tones using Levels, the Hue/Saturation adjustment feature, duplicating and inverting layer masks, and a few blend modes thrown in.

Note > The studio backdrop does not have to be white in order to isolate the shadow from the surrounding background. Subjects are often photographed against a blue or green screen (chroma blue or chroma green) for video compositing but this can prove problematic when replacing backgrounds using Photoshop if the blue or background is not lit correctly.

1. Make a selection of the studio background surrounding the bike using the skills used in the Selections chapter. The selection can be created using a range of selection tools but if you are using the Pen Tool or Magic Wand as one of the selection tools you will need to use the other selection tools with a feather radius set to zero. When the selection is complete click on the 'Save selection as channel' icon at the base of the Channels panel. Alternatively use the saved selection that is available with the TIFF file on the DVD. The saved selection has had a 1-pixel feather applied to soften the edge of the mask.

2. With the selection still active (Ctrl- or Command-click the alpha channel in the Channels panel if the selection is **NOT** active) choose Levels from the Adjustments panel and set the mode of the resulting Adjustment layer in the Layers panel to Luminosity*. In the Layers dialog hold down the Alt key (PC) or Option key (Mac) and drag the white highlights slider underneath the histogram to clip the tones surrounding the shadow under the bike to white. As soon as the shadow becomes an island stop dragging the highlight slider. We can clip the rest of the tones behind the bike to white using the technique outlined in the next step.

*Note > The Luminosity mode will protect the existing saturation levels on the underlying layer when we make the following adjustment.

3. Hold down the Ctrl key (PC) or Command key (Mac) and click on the layer mask thumbnail to load the mask as a selection. Click on the 'Create new fill or adjustment layer' icon at the base of the Layers panel and choose 'Solid color'. Enter 255 in all three of the RGB fields in the Pick a Solid Color dialog (Color Picker) and select OK. Lower the opacity of the Color Fill adjustment layer to around 50% so that you can see the shadows on the underlying layer. Choose the Brush Tool and select black as the foreground color and then in the Color Fill layer mask paint over the faint shadows under the bike (including their soft edges). Be careful not to paint over any areas of the studio backdrop that were not rendered 255 by the Levels adjustment layer. When the painting is complete return the opacity of the layer back to 100%. The shadows should now appear natural with soft edges and the rest of the backdrop is white.

4. You can change the color of the paintwork quickly by selecting a Hue/Saturation adjustment layer from the Adjustments panel. Select Reds in the Edit menu and then move the Hue slider to –120 or just select the on-image tool, hold down the Ctrl key (PC) or Command key (Mac) and click on the paintwork and drag left. Lower the Saturation by dragging left without holding down the modifier key (Ctrl/Command key). As the center of the wheels are very close to red you may also notice these changing color along with the bright red paintwork. This will be corrected in the next step.

5. The observant among you will have noticed that we now have a blue tail-light and discolored wheels. This can be quickly restored to the original color by selecting the Brush Tool from the Tools palette, choosing black as the foreground color (press D on the keyboard) and then painting over the tail-light and the center of each wheel in the image preview to mask the adjustment in this area.

6. The following step shows how we can change the color of the background and yet still retain the original shadows. This is a useful technique that allows us to preview how the subject will appear if placed against a darker background in a montage or composite image (see the Montage Projects chapter). Load the Levels adjustment mask as a selection and then create another Color Fill (Solid Color) adjustment layer and this time choose a darker color from the Color Picker. In the illustration above the color is around 40% Brightness and Saturation. The mode of the adjustment layer has to be set to Multiply in order to preserve the original shadows.

7. A white line will appear around the motorcycle after applying this second Color Fill adjustment layer. If we shrink or choke the Color Fill mask this will allow the fill color to replace this white line. Click on the color fill 2 mask, go to Image > Adjustments > Levels and drag the center gamma slider beneath the histogram to the left. This adjustment can also be achieved using the Expand/Contract slider in the Refine Edge dialog (Select > Refine Edge).

8. Some parts of the bike will now appear too light as they were collecting some light reflected from the original white backdrop. We can create a layer to darken areas of the underlying image. Holding down the Alt key (PC) or Option key (Mac) click on the 'Create a new layer' icon at the base of the Layers panel. In the New Layer dialog box set the Mode to Overlay and check the 'Fill with Overlay-neutral color (50% gray)' option. Name the layer Burn and select OK to create this new layer.

9. Hold down the Alt key (PC) or Option key (Mac) and drag the layer mask from the Levels 2 layer to the 'Burn' layer to duplicate it. Use the keyboard shortcut (Ctrl + I for PC or Command + I for Mac) to invert the mask. Select the layer thumbnail rather than the Layer mask thumbnail (when selected it will have a second line running around the thumbnail icon). Select the Brush Tool from the Tools palette and Black as the foreground color (press the letter D key on the keyboard). Choose a large soft-edged brush and set the Opacity between 10 and 20% in the Options bar. Paint the underside of the tires and the bike darker so that the effect is consistent with the new background tone. If you should lighten the fill color or place the bike against a background with a lighter tone in a composite image the opacity of this burn layer can be adjusted.

10. The easiest way to transplant all of these layers into another image when we come to create a montage is to create a group from these layers. The first step is to double-click the background layer and select OK in the New Layer dialog (or drag the lock down to the trash). Now select Layer 0 and hold down the Shift key as you select the top layer (the Burn layer) so that all layers are selected. Use the keyboard shortcut Ctrl + G (PC) or Command + G (Mac) to load the layers into the group.

Dorothy Connop

Craig Banks

montage projects

Mark Galer

essential skills

- Use Quick Mask mode, alpha channels and layer masks to create a simple montage.
- Use the Pen Tool to create a smooth-edged mask.
- Create a simple montage using layer blend modes.
- Merge or blend a graphic with a three-dimensional form using a displacement map.
- Use Refine Edge, channel masking and a blend mode for a perfect hair transplant.
- Replace a sky and manipulate the tonality and color for a seamless result.
- Create a composite image while preserving the subject's original shadow.
- Replace the background behind a model while preserving the fine hair detail and the original shadow.

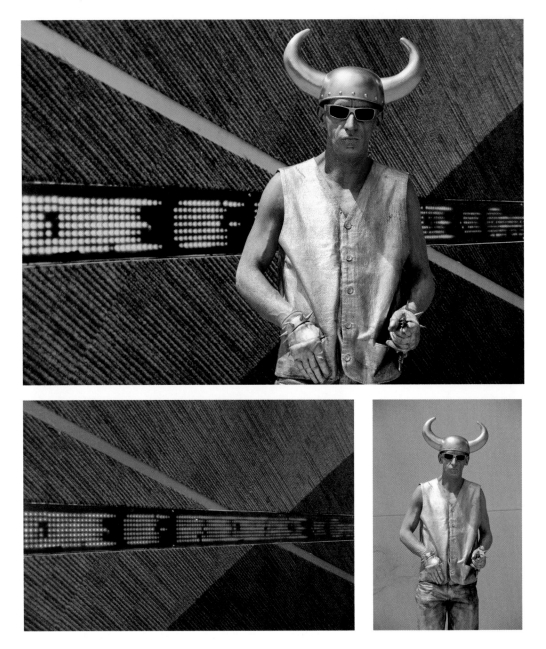

Layer masks – Project 1

A common task in professional digital image editing is to strip out the subject and place it against a new background – the simplest form of montage. The effectiveness of such a montage is often determined by whether the image looks authentic and not manipulated. In order to achieve this the digital photographer needs to modify the edge of any selection so that it is seamless against the new background. A crude or inappropriate selection technique will make the subject appear as if it has been cut out with garden shears and is floating above the new background. A few essential masking skills can turn the proverbial sow's ear into the silk purse.

Part 1 – Changing the background

1. In a non-destructive professional workflow it is preferable to hide or mask the background pixels rather than delete them. In this project we are going to learn how to make an accurate selection in order to create a layer mask. When we move the subject to a new background we may then need to modify and refine the edge of the mask. Open the M1 start image and then select the majority of the background behind the subject using the Magic Wand Tool. Select the background with the Magic Wand Tool with the Tolerance set to 20 in the Options bar. It is quicker to select the background rather than the subject because there are less differences in tone or color. Select the 'Contiguous' option in the Options bar and click on the 'Add to Selection' icon or hold down the Shift key as you add the isolated areas between the legs and under the arms. The Magic Wand tool does not have a 'Feather' option so the resulting selection will have a hard edge.

Quick Selection Tool alternative

Switch the 'Auto-Enhance' option in the Options bar off. Make an initial selection by dragging the tool over an area of the background. Then hold down the Option/Alt key and make a series of strokes around the inside edge of the subject to define the areas you don't want to be included in the selection. The effect of these subtractive strokes will not be immediately obvious at this stage, as you are only helping to educate the tool as to which pixels you intend to exclude from any further selections. These are pre-emptive strokes that will help prevent the selection made by the Quick Selection Tool from leaking outside of the area you wish to select. After making the subtractive stroke continue to add to the original selection until most of the background has been selected. Hold down the Option/Alt key and stroke any areas of the subject with a small brush to subtract any areas that have been included in the selection by mistake. Perfect the selection using the 'Quick Mask mode' (see next step) as no one tool can easily select the entire subject in this image.

2. We can perfect the selection using the Quick Mask feature. Set the foreground and background colors to their default setting in the Tools panel (press the D key). Next click on the 'Edit in Quick Mask Mode' icon in the Tools panel. Double-clicking the icon will open up the 'Quick Mask Options'. Click the color swatch to open the 'Color Picker' and select a color that contrasts with those found in the image you are working on. In this project it is appropriate to set the color to a saturated green with 50–70% Opacity.

3. The Quick Mask can be modified by painting directly into the mask or by making a selection and then filling the selection with either the foreground or background color. Editing the mask will change the resulting selection when we exit the Quick Mask feature. If the initial selection was made using the Magic Wand Tool it is important to paint into the Quick Mask with the brush set to maximum hardness and/or make selections with the feather radius set to 0 in the Options bar (this will ensure these modifications match the current edge quality created by using the Magic Wand or Quick Selection Tools). Painting or filling with black will add to the colored mask, while painting/filling with white will remove the mask color.

Useful shortcuts for masking work

1. Brush size and hardness

Using the square bracket keys to the right of the letter P on the keyboard will increase or decrease the size of the brush. Holding down the Shift key while depressing these keys will increase or decrease the hardness of the brush.

2. Foreground and background colors

Pressing the letter D on the keyboard will return the foreground and background colors to their default settings (black and white). Pressing the letter X will switch the foreground and background colors.

3. Fill with foreground or background color

Use the keyboard shortcut Command + Delete (Mac) or Ctrl + Backspace (PC) to fill a selection with the background color. Use the keyboard shortcut Option + Delete (Mac) or Alt + Backspace (PC) to fill a selection with the foreground color.

4. Zoom and Hand Tools

Use the keyboard shortcut Command + Spacebar (Mac) or Ctrl + Spacebar (PC) to access the Zoom Tool and the Spacebar by itself to drag the image around in its window.

5. Inverting the mask

Use the keyboard shortcut Command + I (Mac) or Ctrl + I (PC) to invert the mask if the mask is concealing the edge you are working on. The use of these shortcuts will make shorter work of creating accurate selections.

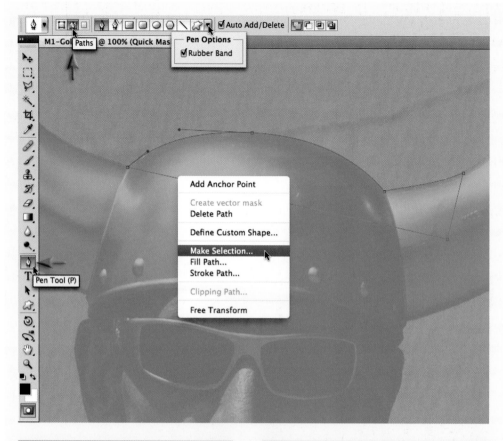

Modifying the mask using the Pen Tool

Making a path and then turning the path into a selection will create the smoothest edges and is often the easiest method for modifying the curved edges of a mask. Right-click after creating a path to access the 'Make Selection' option from the context menu. Choose a 'Feather Radius' of 0 pixels and then select OK. Fill the selection with Black to add to the mask or with White to remove a section of the mask (Edit > Fill).

Note > See 'Selections from paths' in the Selections chapter and Project 2 in this chapter to get more information on using the Pen Tool.

Edit mode button

4. Next we need to remove any parts of the mask that are not required (these were areas of the background that were left out of the initial selection). Select the Brush Tool from the Tools panel and an appropriate hard-edged brush from the Options bar and be sure the brush opacity is set to 100%. The foreground and background colors can be switched when painting to subtract or add to the mask. Zoom in on areas of fine detail and reduce the size of the brush when accuracy is called for. When the painted mask is complete press on the letter Q on the keyboard or click on the 'Edit in Standard Mode' icon in the Tools panel.

Note > Adding an adjustment layer to temporarily brighten or darken an image may help you to paint an accurate mask against some edges that may otherwise be difficult to work with. Delete the adjustment layer when the painted mask is complete.

5. Go to Select > Inverse so that the subject rather than the background is selected. Click on the 'Refine Edge' button in the Options bar. If the button is not visible (due to the fact that a painting tool rather than a selection tool is selected) go to the Select menu and choose 'Refine Edge'.

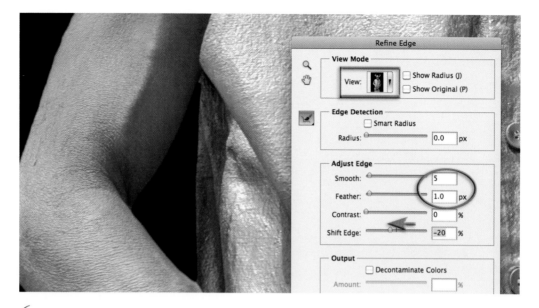

6. In the Refine Edge dialog box set the 'Radius' slider to zero (this slider does not need to be used as there are no soft edge transitions or fine detail around the edge of the subject that need to be modified or preserved). Choose the 'On Black' preview option from the View menu. Turn your attention to the Smooth slider and take the slider back to 0 and check the quality of the edges at 100% magnification (Command + Option + 0 on a Mac and Ctrl + Alt + 0 on a PC and then hold down the Spacebar to drag the image in the image window). Selections created using the Magic Wand or Quick Selection Tools can often be lumpy, and raising the Smooth slider will disguise this fault. Settings of **Smooth: 5, Feather: 1.0 px Contrast 0** and **Shift Edge** of –20% should soften the edge nicely and hide most of the background surrounding the edge. Click the OK button when you are satisfied with the settings. If the edge is too lumpy for your liking there are steps we can take later after this step has been completed. The Refine Edge dialog box works globally (on the entire edge) so a few compromises may be required at this stage.

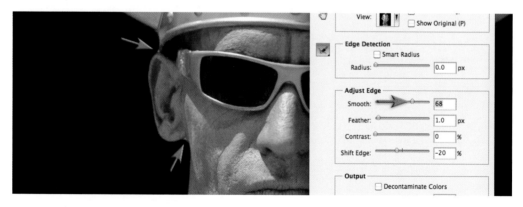

Note > Too much of a good thing results in webbed ears, i.e. if the Smooth slider is raised too high the corners of the selection will start to be 'rounded off', resulting in the old background showing through.

7. Save the selection as an 'Alpha' channel by going to the Channels panel and clicking on the 'Save selection as channel' icon. Now that the selection has been saved as an alpha channel save your work in progress (File > Save As). The selection can now be deselected (go to 'Select > Deselect') and reselected at any time during the editing procedure.

Note > Change the name of the original file and save as a Photoshop or TIFF file. Photoshop and TIFF files will save the record of your selection as an Alpha channel. JPEG files cannot contain Alpha channels. Alpha channels can be used to establish 'selection save points' and can be reloaded as a selection at any time – even if the file has been closed and reopened.

8. Click on the Alpha 1 channel to view the mask by itself or the 'visibility' or 'eye' icon to view the mask. Click on the RGB visibility icon to view the mask and image together. It is possible to continue working on the mask in this view as if you were in Quick Mask mode (the Alpha channel must be selected).

Quick Mask and Refine Edge

When edge contrast is poor the editing process usually requires a range of Photoshop's selection and painting tools. The best workspace for this may still be the Quick Mask mode. The Quick Mask mode allows the user to contract and expand localized portions of the mask by first making a selection (or by creating a path and then converting the path into a selection) and then using the Maximum/Minimum filters or Levels technique (see Step 13 in this project). The user can also paint directly into the mask using any painting tools. None of these localized or painting options are available in the Refine Edge dialog box.

The layer mask is selected and the Refine Edge dialog box opened (Select > Refine Edge). Feedback as to the most appropriate settings to use in the Refine Edge dialog box may be compromised when the mask is not on the subject layer (the saxophone player). Although we can view the subject as an Overlay in the Refine Edge dialog box we are unable to edit this mask using the painting tools.

Most professionals have traditionally preferred to refine masks rather than selections. Some may think that the new Refine Edge dialog box will change this working practice as Refine Edge can also be applied to masks (go to Select > Refine Edge). Although modifications to the selection edge in the Refine Edge dialog box are a vast improvement on the Feather and Modify commands found in previous versions of Photoshop, when the Refine Edge is applied to a mask attached to a new background layer (placed above the subject layer) the user may be unable to determine the appropriate settings to use in order to acquire the best possible edge. Unlike Quick Mask there are only limited options to adjust edges of the selection using the Refine Radius Tool in the Refine Edge dialog (not all edges of an object may appear equally sharp or soft and require the same global adjustment). If you make a selection of a portion of the mask and then use Refine Edge the dialog box defaults to working the edge of the selection rather than the edge of the mask. If quality of the visual outcome, rather than speed, is the primary objective when editing an image, then Quick Mask still offers many advantages over the new Refine Edge dialog box.

When using Refine Edge to work on a layer mask, the user may have to use a work-around in order to gain any useful feedback on the most appropriate settings to use. After the selection has been converted into a layer mask there may be no feedback when attempting to view the mask using the On White or On Black options. The user must either use the On Layers option from the View menu or Alt/Option click the Overlay view and set the mask color to 100% black or white to create a black or white matte. You will also need to switch the Quick Mask option from 'Masked Areas' to 'Selected Areas' so that the background instead of the subject is masked. When switching to Selected Areas in Quick Mask Options the Shift Edge slider then works in reverse.

Quick selections may not, by their very nature, be very accurate selections. Missing elements cannot be added from within the Refine Edge dialog box. In Quick Mask mode, however, a selection can be made and then filled with black or the missing elements can simply be painted in prior to using Refine Edge or editing the edge quality from within the Quick Mask mode itself.

9. Load the Alpha channel as a selection by holding down the Command key (Mac) or Ctrl key (PC) and clicking in the Alpha channel thumbnail. Before returning to the Layers panel, switch off the Alpha channel visibility and select the master RGB channels view at the top of the Channels panel.

Note > Leaving the Alpha channel as the active component in the Channels panel before returning to the Layers panel can create problems with some editing procedures, e.g. copying and pasting. If problems occur you may notice that the layer is grayed out in the Layers panel and the word 'Alpha' may appear in the title of the image window. If this occurs return to the Channels panel or use the keyboard shortcut listed on the RGB channel (Command/Ctrl + 2).

10. The pixels on a background layer cannot be masked until the layer has been converted to a normal (unlocked) layer. Double-click on the background layer to open the 'New Layer' dialog box. Just select OK if you do not want to rename it and then click on the 'Add layer mask' icon at the base of the Layers panel to add a mask that conceals the background pixels.

Note > It is important to note that although the background is no longer visible it has been masked and not removed permanently. The 'masked' and 'selected' areas are the reverse of each other. Areas that were not part of the original selection become the masked areas. Holding down the Alt/Option key as you select 'Add layer mask' reverses the layer mask so the selected areas become the masked areas.

11. Open the M1 background file and position the new background image alongside the image of the gold man. Click and drag the thumbnail of the gold man in the Layers panel into the image window of the new background. Let go of the mouse button to create an image file with two layers (holding down the Shift key as you let go of the mouse button will ensure the new layer is centered). A border will appear momentarily around the host image before you let go of the mouse button to indicate that it will accept the new layer.

12. The image now comprises two individual layers and the layer mask you created. Select the top layer (your subject) and then go to 'Edit > Free Transform' (Command/Ctrl + T). Use the keyboard shortcut Command/Ctrl + 0 to shrink or reduce the image so that you can fit the Transform bounding box on the screen. Hold down the Shift key and drag a top corner handle to resize the image. Holding down the Shift key as you drag will constrain the proportions of the image in the bounding box. Dragging inside the bounding box will move the image. Use the arrow keys for fine adjustments. Press the 'Commit' icon in the Options bar or press the Return/Enter key to apply the transformation.

13. There are a number of ways we can modify the edge of a mask in localized areas if required (remember the Refine Edge command can only work on the entire edge). Make a selection of a portion of the edge where a light halo (the old background) may be apparent. If the selection crosses an edge be sure to use a small amount of feather (in the Options bar) so the changes to the edge do not result in a ridge. We can expand the mask and hide more of the background pixels by applying a Levels adjustment to the mask. Make sure the mask is the active component of the layer (click on it so that a second dark line appears around the thumbnail in the Layers panel). Go to Image > Adjustments > Levels and then in the Levels dialog box move the central gamma slider to the right to expand the mask. The edge of the mask can be made harder by moving the white and black point sliders in from the edges of the histogram.

An alternative to using a Levels adjustment is to use the Minimum and Maximum filters to adjust the position of the edge of the mask. Go to 'Filter > Other > Minimum' to expand the mask (the Maximum filter contracts the edge of the mask by moving it in the opposite direction). Although not as controlled as having a gamma slider to move the edge, the advantage to this technique is that you can reapply the Minimum filter to other selected areas, after the initial application, very quickly by simply using the Command/Ctrl + F keyboard shortcut.

14. If you need to smooth out a section of the edge without smoothing the whole mask start by loading the layer mask as a selection (hold down the Command/Ctrl key and click on the layer mask thumbnail in the Layers panel). Select the Lasso Tool and select the 'Intersect' icon in the Options bar. Make a selection around the section you want to modify and then go to 'Select > Modify > Smooth'. Choose a generous 'Sample Radius' setting of 15 or 20 for the arm in this project. Check that the layer mask is selected, then fill the modified selection with white. When finished select the 'New Selection' icon in the Options bar and then go to Select > Deselect.

Note > You can use the Blur Tool from the Tools panel on any edge in the Layer mask that appears too hard.

15. The next few steps will balance the color and tonality between the two image layers. Click on the bottom layer in the Layers panel and then choose a Hue/Saturation adjustment layer from the Adjustments panel. Select the 'On-Image Tool' in the Adjustments dialog. Next, hold down the Command key (Mac) or Ctrl key (PC) and then click and drag right on a red hue in the image window to adjust the reds in the image to yellows (approximately +45 on the Hue slider). Let go of the Command/Ctrl key (this will allow you to target the saturation rather than the hues) and then click and drag left on the background to desaturate the cyans in the image.

16. Select the top layer in the Layers panel and then select another Hue/Saturation adjustment layer from the 'Create new fill or adjustment layer' menu. In the Hue/Saturation dialog select the 'Use Previous Layer to Create Clipping Mask' icon. Creating a Clipping Mask between the adjustment layer and the layer below will restrict any changes to just this layer and leave the bottom layer unadjusted. Increase the Saturation to match the yellow stripes on the bottom layer.

17. If you create an adjustment layer that is not part of the Clipping Mask it will affect all layers beneath it. In this project I have increased the Brightness and Contrast of both the image layers by creating a Brightness/Contrast adjustment layer at the top of the layers stack (the Brightness/Contrast adjustment feature is no longer destructive since CS3). Note how the Hue/ Saturation adjustment layer is indented and the layer name 'Layer 1' is underlined to show that the two layers form part of a Clipping Mask.

Part 2 – Finishing touches

18. The next few steps will paste an interesting reflection in those very dark sunglasses. Choose the Magic Wand Tool from the Tools panel and set the Tolerance to 32 in the Options bar (its default value). Click on the 'Add to selection' icon in the Options bar and then click on each black lens in the sunglasses to select them both. Click on the 'Refine Edge' button in the Options bar and then choose values of 'Smooth: 3, Feather: 1 and Contract/Expand: +10' in the Refine Edge dialog box. Select 'OK' to apply the changes.

19. Double-click on the background layer and in the New Layer dialog box that opens select OK to unlock the layer and convert it to Layer 0. Hold down the Alt key (PC) or Option key (Mac). Click and drag the bottom layer in the Layers panel (Layer 0) to the top of the layers stack. This will copy the layer and place the copy layer on top. Be careful not to drop the layer below the Hue/Saturation 2 layer otherwise it will enter the Clipping Mask. Go to Edit > Undo if this happens and then repeat the process until the Layer 0 copy appears at the top of the layer stack.

20. Add a layer mask to this copy layer and break the link between the two thumbnails in the Layers panel by clicking on it. This action will allow us to modify the position and size of the image layer but leave the layer mask pin-registered to the precise location of the glasses. Click on the image thumbnail (rather than the layer mask) to make this the active component of the layer. Select 'Free Transform' from the Edit menu and then scale and rotate the layer so that the red stripes appear in the lenses of the sunglasses (remember that Ctrl/Command + 0 fits the image and transform bounding box into the window). You have the option to lower the opacity of the layer in the Layers panel if required.

21. Hold down the Alt/Option key again and click and drag the Hue/Saturation 1 adjustment layer to the top of the layers stack. This action will copy the adjustment layer and change the red stripes to yellow but it will also affect the color of the golden Viking. To limit the changes to the reflections in the glasses, create a clipping group by holding down the Alt/ Option key and clicking on the dividing line between the adjustment layer (Hue/Saturation 1 copy) and Layer 0 copy in the Layers panel (alternatively you can choose the 'Create Clipping Mask' command from the Layer menu).

22. To give a sense of distance between the subject and new background you can add a drop shadow to darken the background selectively. Click on Layer 1, to make it the active layer, and then go to Layer > Layer Style > Drop Shadow (these layer styles are also available from the 'Add a layer style' menu in the Layers panel).

23. In the Layer Style dialog box increase the Distance and Size settings (around 200 px for each). Change the Angle so that the shadow is consistent with the direction of light that is falling on the golden Viking (around 150°). You can also click and drag in the image window to drag the shadow to the correct location. Lower the opacity of the shadow slightly and select OK to apply the changes.

The skills applied in this project are the professional techniques used to create the vast majority of high-quality montages where the viewer does not question the authenticity of the image.

Paths, masks and blend modes – Project 2

With the basic drawing skills covered in the Selections chapter we are ready to create a path that can be converted into a selection and then used as a layer mask. This project will see if you can create a path worthy of a Path Master (for the pen is sometimes mightier than the light sabre or magic wand). The resulting edge will be much smoother than an edge created with any of the selection tools. After an accurate path has been created we can use this to modify the subject and background separately.

Photograph of body builder by Abhijit Chattaraj

In the montage above the image of the body has been blended with an image of raindrops on a car body. The texture blended takes on the shadows and highlights of the underlying form but does not wrap itself around the contours or shape of the three-dimensional form.

1. Select the Pen Tool in the Tools panel and the Paths option (rather than the Shape layers option) and the 'Add to path area' option in the Options bar.

2. Zoom in using the keyboard shortcut Ctrl + Spacebar (PC) or Command + Spacebar (Mac) and work close. Drag the image around in the image window using the Spacebar key to access the Hand Tool. Make a path by clicking on the edge of the subject and dragging to modify the curves. If you encounter edges that are not well defined, work on the inside edge rather than the outer edge of the subject. Try to use as few anchor points as possible (see Selections, pages 181–185). Remember you can choose to cancel or move a direction line by holding down the Alt/Option key and clicking on either the last anchor point or its direction point before creating a new segment of the path.

3. You can backtrack at any time and Command + click (Mac) or Ctrl + click (PC) to select an anchor point to make it active again. Then hold down the Alt/Option key to adjust one of the direction lines or hold down the Control key (PC) or Command key (Mac) and click and drag an anchor point to reposition it. Moving the Pen Tool over a segment of the path already completed will give you the option to click and add an anchor point to the path. Moving the Pen Tool over a previous anchor point will enable you to click to delete the anchor points or drag out from the anchor point to add two new direction lines.

Note > Check that you have the 'Auto Add/Delete' option checked in the Options bar if the above is not happening for you. If you accidentally remove a direction line from an anchor point hold down the Alt/Option key and click and drag out from the anchor point to add new direction lines.

4. Where the blue jeans extend beyond the edge of the frame (at the bottom of the image window) place your anchor points outside of the image window rather than alongside the edge. Continue creating anchor points until you reach the point where you started drawing. When you click on the first anchor point you will close the path. Hold down the Alt/Option key as you click on the first point if the direction line on the first anchor points changes your last drawn curve.

5. In the Paths panel double-click the Work Path. This will bring up the option to save the Work Path and ensure that it cannot be deleted accidentally. Name the path 'Body' and click OK to save it. A saved path can be modified by first clicking on the path in the Paths panel, selecting the Pen Tool in the Tools panel and then selecting the 'Add to' or 'Subtract from path area' icon in the Options bar. Select the 'Subtract from path area' icon and proceed to remove the area of background under the man's arm using the same pen techniques as before.

6. Load the path as a selection by clicking on the icon in the Paths panel. Go to Select > Refine Edge and set the Radius, Contrast and Smooth sliders to zero. Apply a 0.5–1 pixel feather. To test the effectiveness of the path it is best to preview the selection over a white background (from the View menu in the Refine Edge dialog). In order to remove the old black background that may just be visible against the edge of the body you will need to move the Shift Edge slider to the left slightly. Select OK to apply the changes.

7. Click on the 'Create a new layer' icon in the Layers panel to create an empty new layer. Hold down the Alt/Option key and click on the 'Add layer mask' icon in the Layers panel. Then select the layer image and go to Edit > Fill and choose black as the contents. Select OK.

8. This step will create the effect of a backlight behind the subject that slowly fades to black in the corners of the image. Control-click (PC) or Command-click (Mac) on the layer mask to load the mask as a selection, click on the 'Create new fill or adjustment layer' icon in the Layers panel and choose a Curves adjustment layer. Select the Blue channel and click and drag the adjustment point sitting in the bottom left-hand corner of the diagonal line until the output value reads 90 or more. Repeat this process with the Red and Green channels but raise these only a little in order to desaturate the blue. In the master RGB channel raise the black point to raise the overall brightness of the color you have created.

9. Select the Gradient Tool in the Tools panel. Select the Foreground to Transparent and Radial Gradient options with black selected as the Foreground color, set the opacity to 100% and select the Reverse, Dither and Transparency options. Click and drag from a position in the center of the man's body out past the top right-hand edge of the image window to create the backlight effect.

Blending the texture

Blending two images in the computer is similar to creating a double exposure in the camera or sandwiching negatives in the darkroom. Photoshop, however, allows a greater degree of control over the final outcome. This is achieved by controlling the specific blend mode, position and opacity of each layer. The use of '**layer masks**' can shield any area of the image that needs to be protected from the blend mode. The blending technique enables the texture or pattern from one image to be merged with the form of a selected subject in another image.

10. Open the drops image from the supporting DVD. Click and drag the layer thumbnail of this image into the body image. Hold down the Shift key as you let go of the drops thumbnail to center the image in the new window. Use the Move Tool to reposition the texture if required. Use the Free Transform command (Edit > Free Transform) if required to resize the texture image so that it covers the figure in the image.

Selecting appropriate images to blend

Select or create one image where a three-dimensional subject is modeled by light. Try photographing a part of the human body using a large or diffused light source at right angles to the camera. The image should ideally contain bright highlights, midtones and dark shadows. Select or create another image where the subject has an interesting texture or pattern. Try using a bold texture with an irregular pattern. The texture should ideally have a full tonal range with good contrast. A subtle or low-contrast texture may not be obvious when blended. Alt/Option-click the document sizes in the bottom left-hand corner of each image window to check that the image pixel dimensions (width and height) are similar. It is possible to blend a colored texture with a grayscale image. If the color of the texture is to be retained when it is moved into the grayscale image containing the form, the grayscale image must first be converted to RGB by going to 'Image > Mode > RGB'.

11. Hold down the Alt/Option key and drag the layer mask from Layer 1 to Layer 2 to copy it. Invert the mask using the keyboard shortcut Command + I for a Mac or Ctrl + I for a PC. Set the blend mode of the drops layer (Layer 2) to Soft Light or Overlay. Experiment with adjusting the opacity of the layer using the Opacity control in the Layers panel.

12. After experimenting with the opacity and blend mode of the top layer you can adjust the tonality of the underlying background layer to suit the blend. Select the background layer and select a Curves adjustment from the Adjustments panel. Expand the contrast of the underlying layer by creating an S-curve and set the mode of the adjustment layer to Luminosity if you do not want to increase the saturation levels.

Photography by Abhijit Chattaraj

Creating a displacement map

The layer '**blend**' modes are an effective, but limited, way of merging or blending a pattern or graphic with a three-dimensional form. By using the blend modes the pattern or graphic can be modified to respect the color and tonality of the 3D form beneath it. The highlights and shadows that give the 3D form its shape can, however, be further utilized to wrap or bend the pattern or graphic so that it obeys the form's perspective and sense of volume. This can be achieved by using the 'Displace' filter in conjunction with a 'displacement map'. The 'map' defines the contours to which the graphic or pattern must conform. The final effect can be likened to 'shrink-wrapping' the graphic or pattern to the 3D form. Displacement requires the use of a PSD image file or 'displacement map' created from the layer containing the 3D form. This is used as the contour map to displace pixels of another layer (the pattern or graphic). The brightness level of each pixel in the map directs the filter to shift the corresponding pixel of the selected layer in a horizontal or vertical plane. The principle on which this technique works is that of 'mountains and valleys'. Dark pixels in the map shift the graphic pixels down into the shaded valleys of the 3D form while the light pixels of the map raise the graphic pixels onto the illuminated peaks of the 3D form. The alternative to using a displacement map is to use the Liquify filter.

The limitation of the displacement technique is that the filter reads dark pixels in the image as being shaded and light pixels as being illuminated. This of course is not always the case. With this in mind the range of images that lend themselves to this technique is limited. A zebra would be a poor choice on which to wrap a flag while a nude illuminated with soft directional lighting would be a good choice. The image chosen for this project lends itself to the displacement technique. Directional light models the face. Tonal differences due to hue are limited. Note how the straight lines of the flag are distorted after the Displace filter has been applied. The first image looks as though the flag has been projected onto the fabric, while the second image shows the effect of the displacement filter – it appears as though it has been woven or printed onto the surface of the fabric.

13. Switch off the visibility of the top two layers (the drops and the backlight effect). In order to apply the Displace filter you must first create a grayscale image to become the displacement map. In the Channels panel locate the channel with the best tonal contrast between the shadows and the highlights (in this case the Blue layer). Duplicate this channel by dragging it to the New Layer icon at the base of the panel. Increase the contrast of this channel using the Brightness/ Contrast adjustment (Image > Adjustments > Brightness/Contrast). You can further enhance the hills and valleys by selecting the Dodge or Burn Tools from the Tools panel. Set the Exposure to 20% or lower when using these tools and then proceed to either lighten the hills or darken the valleys as you see fit. Remember this is a displacement map not a photograph.

14. Export this channel to become the displacement map by choosing '**Duplicate Channel**' from the Channels menu and then '**Document > New**' from the Destination menu. When you select OK in the Duplicate Channel dialog box, a file with a single channel will open in Photoshop.

15. Apply 'Gaussian Blur' (Filter > Blur > Gaussian Blur) to the new file. Applying a higher Radius of Gaussian Blur (closer to a Radius of 10 pixels) will create a mask that produces a smooth-edged displacement (minor flaws in the skin will be ignored). Using a lower Radius of Gaussian Blur (1–4 pixels) will create a mask that produces a ragged-edge displacement (every minor flaw in the skin will lead to displaced pixels). Save this file as a Photoshop file (your 'displacement map') to the same location on your computer as the file you are working on. You will need to access this 'map' several times in order to optimize the displacement.

16. Open the flag image and drag the background layer thumbnail into the portrait image. Apply the 'Free Transform' from the Edit menu and drag the handles of the bounding box to achieve a 'good fit'. Hit the Return/Enter key to apply the transformation and then set the Opacity of the layer to 100% and the mode to either Soft Light, Overlay or Multiply.

17. Choose 'Filter > Distort > Displace' and enter 20–30 in the Horizontal and Vertical Scale fields of the Displace dialog box. Select OK and then browse to the displacement map you created earlier. The displacement is then applied to the layer. The Displace filter shifts the pixels on the selected layer using a pixel value from the displacement map. Grayscale levels 0 and 255 are the maximum negative and positive shifts while level 128 (middle gray) produces no displacement.

18. Apply 1.5 pixels Gaussian Blur to the flag layer and then hold down the Alt/Option key and drag the layer mask thumbnail from the drops layer (Layer 2) to the flag layer (Layer 3) to copy it. Lower the opacity of the flag layer to strike a good balance between the graphic and the tonality of the body.

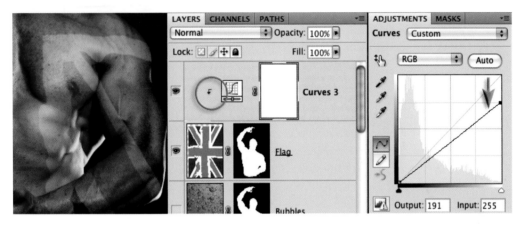

19. The tonality of the flag can be further optimized using adjustment layers that have been clipped to the flag layer. In this project a Curves adjustment was used to lower the brightness of the white tones in the flag and the saturation was reduced using a Hue/Saturation adjustment.

20. If you don't want the flag to appear on certain parts of the body you can paint with black into the layer mask. Use a soft brush at a reduced opacity if you want to fade the graphic in certain areas.

21. An alternative version of the composite image has been created by switching off the visibility of the Curves 1 layer that was creating the backlight effect. A new flag background (created using the same displacement technique) is pasted into the host image. A mask is copied from one of the underlying layers and inverted so that it only appears behind the subject. With so many alternative versions that are possible with just one layer mask (used many times) it is possible to keep track of them using the New Layer Comp panel.

Each time you create a version you like you can keep a record of the layers that were contributing to the overall effect. The New Layer Comp dialog will keep track of not only which layers are visible but also their opacity and position. If any layer styles are applied it will also keep track of these. After the comps have been created it is then easy to switch between the versions.

Alternative approach using the 'Liquify' filter

An alternative approach to distorting the flag using the Displacement filter in '**Project 2**' would be to use the '**Liquify**' filter. Instead of using the '**Blue copy**' channel to create a displacement map it can be used to '**freeze**' an area of the image prior to selectively displacing the unfrozen pixels using the '**Warp Tool**'. This alternative method of displacing pixels on one layer, to reflect the contours of another layer, is made possible in the Liquify filter due to the option to see the visibility of additional layers other than the one you are working on.

To try this alternative approach just proceed as normal until you reach Step 17, then, instead of using a displacement map, click on the flag layer and go to Filter > Liquify. Check the 'Show Backdrop' option in the dialog box and select 'background layer' from the menu. Adjust the opacity to create the optimum environment for displacing the pixels. To selectively freeze the darker pixels in the image load the 'Blue copy' channel in the 'Mask Options'. Select a brush size and pressure and then stroke the flag while observing the contours of the body to displace the lighter pixels. Select 'Invert All' in the 'Mask Options' so that you can displace the darker pixels.

Note > The Liquify filter cannot be applied to a Smart Object but the technique, although labor intensive, does offer the user a little more control over the displacement process. It is possible to save the distortions carried out in the Liquify filter as a 'Mesh'. This Mesh is like a topographic landscape and can be loaded to distort subsequent graphics to the same topography to create a similar distortion.

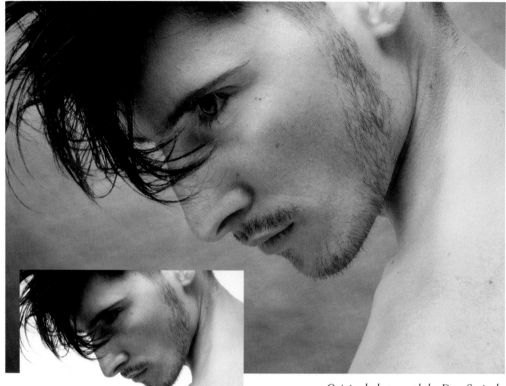

Original photograph by Dan Stainsby

Extracting hair – Project 3

One of the most challenging montage or masking jobs in the profession of post-production editing used to be the hair lift. When the model had long flowing hair and the subject needed to change location many post-production artists would call in sick. If you got it wrong, just like a bad wig, it showed. Extract filters, Magic Erasers and Tragic Wands didn't get us close but we now have a new Refine Edge feature in CS5 that has eased the burden of this task and made the task easier than ever before. The first step to ensure guaranteed success should be completed before you even press the shutter on the camera. Your number one essential step for success is to first shoot your model against a featureless background that is either very dark or very light. The background must be sufficiently illuminated so that it is captured as white rather than gray or the light must be shielded from a dark backdrop so that it records as black. This important aspect of the initial image capture ensures that the resulting hair transplant is seamless and undetectable. The post-production is now the easy bit – simply apply the correct sequence of editing steps for a perfect result. This is not brain surgery and there are no lengthy selection procedures required (the Refine Edge and Channels panel holds the secret to success).

Note > When masking hair that was captured against a black background the technique is basically the same as outlined in this project – just change the blend mode to Screen. See the Layer Blends chapter for additional information.

1. If you want to complete this step open the Raw file (M3_Hair.dng) instead of the JPEG or TIFF (the JPEG is ready to go). Select the White Balance Tool and click on the background in the image window to set the white balance. Raise the Exposure slider to +0.50 and then click on the Tone Curve tab. Raise the Highlights slider to +25 and make sure no tones are clipping (view the clipping warning in the histogram). These steps should render the background both neutral and bright.

2. To balance the exposure in this image (the shoulder is a little too bright) select the Graduated Filter and then adjust the Exposure slider to −0.50. Drag a diagonal gradient from the bottom right-hand corner of the image to a position just higher than the bottom of the chin.

3. Select the Adjustment Brush and adjust the Exposure slider to +0.75. Make sure the Auto Mask option is not checked and then brush over the dark shadow around the eye to brighten this area. Once the adjustment is complete you are now ready to open the image as a Smart Object. Set this option in the Workflows Panel or simply hold down the Shift key to access the Open Object button.

4. Open the Background image for this project and then drag the Smart Object layer thumbnail in the Layers panel into the Background preview to create a multi-layered file with the Smart Object sitting above the background layer.

5. Choose the Quick Selection Tool from the Tools panel and select the Auto-Enhance option in the Options bar. Drag the Tool across the subject to make a rough selection of the subject and his hair. If you accidentally select some of the white background just hold down the Alt/Option key and drag across this area to subtract it from the initial selection.

6. Go to Select > Refine Edge and from the View Mode drop-down menu choose the On Layers option. This will give you the most accurate view when you refine the edge of your mask. Don't worry about any areas of white background that may appear in the preview window at this stage.

7. In order to create a more effective edge we will increase the Radius in the Edge Detection section of the dialog to a value of 70 pixels. We could use the Shift Edge slider to try to remove the white halo that will sit around the edge of your subject but the most effective way to do this is to use the new Decontaminate Colors feature. Check the Decontaminate Colors checkbox and raise the Amount slider to 80%. You should now have an appropriate edge quality with all traces of the old white background removed from the face and shoulder. If you forgot to use the Auto-Enhance feature when you made the initial selection you may need to raise the Smooth and Feather sliders slightly in the Adjust Edge section of the dialog.

8. To remove all traces of the white background from around the hair, select the Refine Radius Tool and paint over any areas where there may be hair. There is an Options bar for controlling the brush size and switching to the Erase Refinements Tool. After a painting action there will be a short delay while Photoshop decontaminates the colors (replaces the white background pixels with pixels of a more appropriate color) and rebuilds the preview. In the Output To menu, select the New Layer with Mask option and then select OK.

9. If you hold down the Shift key and click on the Layer mask on the copy layer to switch the mask off you will be able to observe what Photoshop has been trying to do in order to decontaminate the white pixels that surround the subject. Colors from the subject itself have flooded the background to ensure a seamless composite view. Note also how the visibility of the original layer has been switched off.

10. Merge the visible elements of this project to a new layer by holding down the modifier keys Ctrl + Alt + Shift (PC) or Command + Option + Shift (Mac) and then press the E key. Double-click on the name of this composite layer and rename the layer Refine Selection. We will use this composite layer to compare edge quality with an alternative technique that has always been the preferred techniques by post-production professionals. Hold down the shift key and click on this new Refine Selection layer and the layer below (Hair Copy) to select both of them. Place the layers into a group using the keyboard shortcut Ctrl + G (PC) or Command + G (Mac).

11. Switch off the visibility of the group and then go to the Channels panel. In the Channels panel drag the Blue channel (the one with the most contrast between the background and the skin tones) to the 'Create new channel' icon to duplicate it. Go to Image > Adjustments > Brightness/Contrast and then increase the contrast of the channel and lower the brightness to a point just before the background starts to visibly darken.

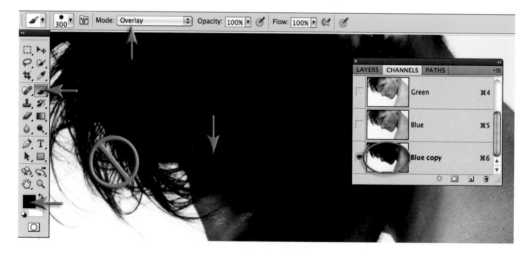

12. Select 'Black' as the foreground color and the 'Brush Tool' from the Tools panel. Choose a large hard-edged brush and 100% Opacity from the Options bar and set the mode to 'Overlay' (also in the Options bar). Painting in Overlay mode will preserve the white background and darken the rest of the pixels. Accuracy while painting in Overlay mode is not a concern when the background is white or is significantly lighter than the subject. Darken the body of the hair near the scalp but avoid the locks of hair that have white background showing through. Painting these individual strands of hair will thicken the hair and may lead to subsequent haloes appearing later in the montage process. Darken the skin on the chin, but not the stubble. The bright tones of the shoulders can be rendered black by repeatedly clicking the mouse in Overlay mode.

Note > If any of the white background has been darkened in the process of creating a black and white mask, switch the foreground color to 'White' and choose 'Overlay' in the Options bar. Paint to render any areas of gray background white.

13. Invert the Channel to make it easier to see any tones that are not quite black. Paint with white in Overlay mode if you are working on an inverted channel. Go to Image > Adjustments > Levels and clip the shadow tones and highlight tones by 10 Levels at each end. Invert the mask again when the process is complete.

14. Select the RGB view in the Channels panel and then hold down the Command key (Mac) or Ctrl key (PC) and click on the Blue copy channel thumbnail to load the channel as a selection. Return to the Layers panel when the selection is active.

15. In the Layers panel drag the Lock icon on the background layer to the trash can at the base of the panel to unlock the layer. Drag the background layer higher so that it sits above the original smart object layer, but below the group you created in the previous step. When the background is above the smart object layer click on the Add layer mask icon at the base of the Layers panel.

16. Set the blending mode for the layer to Multiply. Notice the difference in the quality of the strands of hair before and after you switch the blend mode to Multiply. Setting the blend mode of the adjustment layer to 'Multiply' will bring back all of the fine detail in the hair. The background will not be darkened by applying the 'Multiply' blend mode as white is a neutral color. The mask will, however require further refinement before the subtle detail in the fine strands of hair is preserved in all its glory.

17. Make sure the layer mask is the active component of the layer and then from the Select menu choose Refine Mask. Move the Shift Edge slider to the right to darken the fine strands of hair. Although the hair looks good, the harder edges of the body are not yet perfect. We will, however, not worry about these just at the moment as we will first compare the difference in hair quality between the two techniques outlined so far. The Output menu should read Layer Mask before you select OK.

18. Toggle the visibility of the Group on and off so that you can see the difference in quality between the two techniques. If you created a good channel mask you should notice that the manual technique, which uses the background layer above the subject, gives a slightly superior quality to the Refine Edge dialog technique where the background lies below the subject.

19. Although the hair quality is slightly superior in the manual technique the speed of the Refine Edge for masking hair is fast and reasonably effective. The quality of the other edges in the Refine Edge technique is also surprisingly good, e.g. the harder edges of the nose, lips and chest and also the softer edges of the chin and the back of the neck. Rather than struggle to compete with these edges using the manual technique click the Add layer mask icon at the base of the Layers panel to add a mask to the group. Select the Brush Tool from the Tools panel, set black as the foreground color and paint to mask the hair in the group approach to reveal the hair from the manual approach below.

20. Click on the Create a new layer icon in the Layers panel and set the mode of this layer to Darken. The Eyedropper Tool must be set to All Layers in the Options bar before you can sample a visible color rather than one from the active layer. Then, with the Brush Tool selected, hold down the Option/Alt key and click on an area of warm colored skin to sample the color.

Masking hair captured against a black background

When masking hair that was shot against a black background, setting the layer with the levels adjustment to the Screen Blend mode is the secret to success. Note the difference between Normal mode and Screen Blend mode in the illustrations above.

You will need to invert the layer mask when using a model shot against a black background (Filter > Adjustments > Invert) before painting in Overlay mode as in Steps 12 and 13 of the Extracting hair project.

image courtesy of www.iStockphoto.com

Original Venice image by Craig Shell (sky by Mark Galer)

Replacing a sky – Project 4

The sky is an essential ingredient of any memorable landscape image. Unfortunately it is not something the photographer can control unless we have limitless time and patience. The commercial photographer is often required to deliver the goods on a day that suits the client rather than the photographer and weather forecast. In these instances it is worth building a personal stock library of impressive skies that can be utilized to turn ordinary images with bland skies into impressive ones. A digital compact camera set to a low ISO is ideal for capturing these fleeting moments. The most useful skies to collect are the ones that include detail close to the horizon line, i.e. captured without interference from busy urban skylines, such as can be found at the beach or in the desert. A stock library of skies is included on the DVD to help you start, or add to, your own collection. In this project we explore how a sky can be adapted to fit the landscape so the montage is not immediately obvious.

1. In this step we will make a selection and then optimize it in Quick Mask mode. Open the file named M4_Venice.tif. Select the Magic Wand Tool from the Tools panel and set the Tolerance to 20 in the Options bar. Select the Add to Selection icon in the Options bar or hold down the Shift key as you click multiple times to select all of the sky. Zoom in to 100% or 'Actual Pixels' and select Quick Mask mode from the Tools panel. Invert the mask if necessary using the keyboard shortcut Command or Ctrl + I so that the buildings rather than the sky are masked. Make a selection using the Polygonal Lasso Tool to select any tops of the buildings that are not currently masked (due to the overzealous nature of the Magic Wand). Exclude the scaffolding and the TV aerials from the selection using the Brush Tool. Fill this selection with black (if black is the foreground color in the Tools panel you may use the keyboard shortcut Alt/Option + Backspace/Delete). Exit Quick Mask mode when this work is finished (keyboard shortcut is to press the letter Q). If the buildings rather than the sky is selected go to Select > Inverse.

2. In this step the selection will be converted into a layer mask. Open the Sky image used in this project and from the Select menu choose All. From the Edit menu choose Copy. Return to the Venice image (the selection should still be active) and from the Edit menu choose Paste Into to convert the selection into a layer mask. Don't be alarmed at how bad it looks at the moment, we have several more steps to go before things start to look OK. For the moment we must be content that the sky was captured at a similar time of day to the Venice image and the direction of light is also similar.

3. Make sure the image rather than the mask is the active component of the layer (the thumbnail will have a dark line around it if it is active) and then choose Free Transform from the Edit menu (Ctrl/Command + T). Click and drag inside the Transform bounding box to raise the sky into position. Click and drag on the top-center handle to further enhance the location and shape of the sky to fit the host image. Press the Enter/Return key to commit the transformation.

4. Click on the layer mask to make it active and then go to Select > Refine Edge. Choose a 1-pixel Feather and move the Shift Edge slider to the right until the light halo from around the majority of the buildings has disappeared. It is not possible to remove the halo around the buildings on the extreme left-hand side of the image without removing too much edge detail from the rest of the skyline. Use the levels adjustment technique (outlined in Project 1 of this chapter) in combination with lasso tools to correct the haloes around the buildings on the left.

5. Select a Curves adjustment from the Adjustments panel. Clip the layer to the sky layer below by clicking the icon next to the visibility icon in the Curves panel. Create a curve that renders both the highlights and midtones of the sky very bright so that they match the tones of the distant buildings. Use the on-image adjustment tool and click twice to create two adjustment points on the Curve. Drag these higher to lighten the sky. Skies that have been captured in less humid conditions will always require this adjustment if they are to look at home in a location where there is reduced contrast together with lighter tones in the distant subject matter.

6. Select the Gradient Tool from the Tools panel. In the Options bar choose the Black, White and Linear Gradient options and an Opacity setting of 100%. Click and drag a gradient from the top of the image to a position just above the horizon line. Hold down the Shift key to constrain the gradient. This will give the sky depth and ensure the sky retains its drama above the buildings in the foreground.

7. Create a second Curves adjustment and clip this to the layer below (as in Step 5). The purpose of this second adjustment layer is to increase the intensity of the light on the left side of the image. This will help establish the light source that is bathing the buildings on the right side of the image in a warm afternoon glow and help establish a realistic effect. Fill the layer mask on the second Curves adjustment with black by clicking on the 'Invert' button in the Masks panel (as the adjustments are non-modal there is no need to close the adjustment).

8. To punch a white hole in the mask select the Brush Tool from the Tools panel. Select a large soft-edged brush from the Options bar or hold down the keyboard shortcut keys to preview the size of the brush and hardness of the brush (OpenGL users only).

Note > If OpenGL is switched on in Preferences you can resize the brush by holding down the Alt key and right-clicking (PC) or hold down the Control + Option modifier keys (Mac) and then dragging to the left or right. To change the hardness of the brush, Shift + right-click + Alt (PC) or Control + Option + Command (Mac) and drag to the left or right.

9. Increase the warmth by raising the red curve and lowering the blue curve and then raise the overall brightness using the RGB channel. Observe the effect above the foreground buildings on the left side of the image. Getting the color and tone is easy now that the mask is in place. Working on a mask with an adjustment panel open in prior to CS4 was not possible.

10. Duplicate the adjustment layer but do not add it to the clipping group. Fill the layer mask with black (set the Foreground and Background colors to their default setting and then use the keyboard shortcut, Ctrl + Backspace for a PC or Command + Delete for a Mac). With the Foreground color set to white paint at 50% opacity to increase the warmth of the waters in the canal.

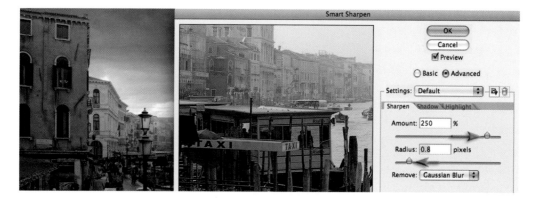

11. Click on the background layer and choose Convert Layer for Smart Filters. Go to Filter > Sharpen > Smart Sharpen. Sharpen the image and select OK. You can be generous with the sharpening as the opacity of the filter can be lowered or the settings modified at any point in the future in a completely non-destructive way.

12. Select the top layer (Curves 2) in the Layers panel and then click on the 'Create a new layer' icon in the Layers panel. Fill this layer with white and set the mode to Multiply. Go to Filter > Convert for Smart Filters. Go to Filter > Distort > Lens Correction. Go to the Vignette section of the dialog box and lower the Amount slider to −100 and raise the Midpoint slider to +60 so that the vignette does not encroach too heavily on the buildings on the extreme right-hand side of the image. Select OK to apply these changes. Adjust the opacity of the layer to make the vignette a little more subtle. The project is now complete and the scene carries all of the mood of an old Venetian painting courtesy of a dramatic sky.

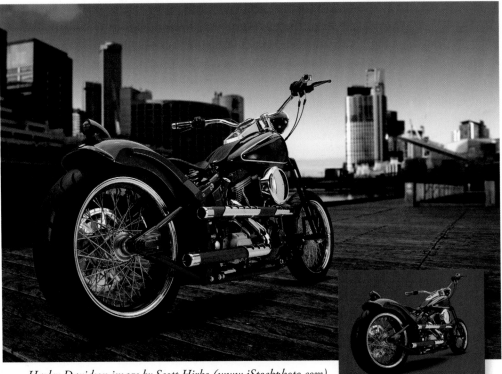

Harley Davidson image by Scott Hirko (www.iStockphoto.com)

Studio and location composite – Project 5

In the Retouching Projects chapter we learned how to prepare an image captured in the studio for a composite project. These techniques will enable the original shadow to be introduced into the new location rather than having to create an artificial one. When the subject is introduced into the new location there will be some additional work that needs to be carried out in order to create a realistic end-result. Sometimes a subject cannot be introduced into a particular location because of inconsistencies in the capture technique. To ensure a successful end-result it usually makes sense to capture the studio subject to match the location rather than having to scour the environment to find a location with the appropriate lighting to match your studio subject.

Critical factors in the creation of a realistic montage are as follows:

- Continuity of vantage point (the camera angle to the subject and the background should be the same).
- Continuity of depth of field (if in doubt shoot both the subject and the background at a small aperture and reduce depth of field in post-production).
- Continuity of perspective. Keep the same relative distance from your subjects (zoom in rather than moving close to small objects).
- Continuity of lighting. The angle of light source to the subject and background and the quality of lighting (harsh or diffuse) should be the same.

1. Open the M5 start image and your finished version of R6 image (or the finished R6 PSD image on the disk). Drag the Group that was created in Project 6 of the Retouching chapter into the host image. Double-click on the background layer and in the New Layer dialog rename the layer 'location' and select OK. In the Layers panel, drag the bike group so that it is below the location layer.

2. Lower the opacity of the location layer so that you can see the bike underneath. Select the Bike group and go to Edit > Free Transform. Hold down the Shift key and drag the corner handle of the Bike group to scale the bike proportionally and then click and drag inside the bounding box to reposition the bike in the bottom left-hand corner of the image (be careful not to double-click or you will commit the transformation before you are done). Press the Return/Enter key to commit the transformation if you are satisfied with the scaling amount.

3. Open the group so that you can see the layers of the bike image. Hold down the Alt/ Option key and drag the layer mask from the Color Fill 2 layer to the location layer to copy it. Switch off the visibility of the Color Fill 2 layer by clicking on the visibility icon. The bike should now be visible but without its shadow. Set the mode of the location layer to Multiply to reintroduce the shadow.

4. When a group of layers are scaled smaller the layer masks may acquire black edges that will need to be cleaned. In the illustration above this type of mask can create problems in the final image. To view the mask by itself hold down the Alt/Option key and click on the layer mask. To clean the mask select the Brush Tool and paint over the black edges as needed or make a selection using the Magic Wand Tool and fill with white.

5. Select the layer mask of the location layer (Layer 1) and refine the edge so that no halo is visible. You will need to zoom in to 100% (Actual Pixels) to obtain an accurate view of the edge, i.e. a halo that may be apparent at 25% may not be visible when the file is magnified further, printed or flattened. Go to Select Refine Edge and move the Contract/Expand slider if required. You will not need to add any additional feather as the edge of the mask has already been blurred. If you need to remove a halo in a localized area of the image make a selection with the Lasso Tool and go to Image > Adjustments > Levels and move the central gamma slider to the left (see Project 1 in this chapter for extended guidelines to optimize the edge).

6. The white balance between the studio image and location image is unlikely to be the same and one of the images will need to be adjusted to match the other. In this image it was decided to retain the warm light of the location and warm the bike to match. This can be achieved with a number of different adjustments from the Adjustments panel. In the illustration above a Warming Filter from the Photo Filter adjustment was applied above the Bike group.

Note > If the Group is closed the Photo Filter will be placed above the group rather than inside the Bike group. It does not really matter where the Photo Filter is placed so long as it is below the location layer (Layer 1).

7. The density of the shadow can be adjusted to suit the new location by selecting the Levels 1 adjustment layer in the Bike group (this is the adjustment layer that was used to clip the background tones to white). Move the central gamma slider in the Levels panel (underneath the histogram) to the left or right to adjust the shadow so that it is consistent with the host image.

8. If we need to reduce the depth of field of a photographic montage it is best done in post-production rather than in-camera. To create a depth map for the Lens Blur filter go to the Channels panel and create a new channel. Fill this channel with white (Edit > Fill). Switch on the visibility of the composite RGB channel so that you can see your image. Select the Gradient Tool from the Tools panel and select the Black, White and Linear options in the Options bar. Check that the Alpha 1 channel is selected and then drag a gradient from just in front of the wheel to the horizon line in the image. Select the composite RGB channel and switch off the visibility of this Alpha channel. More complex depth maps can be created by reviewing the Lens Blur project in the Advanced Retouching chapter.

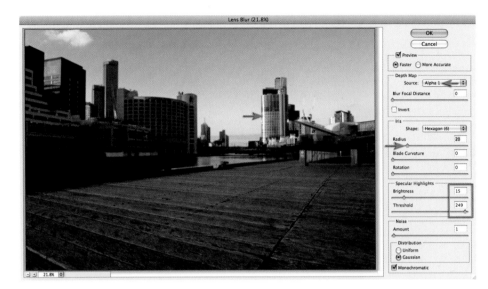

9.   Duplicate Layer 1 in the Layers panel and then go to Filter > Blur > Lens Blur. Select the Alpha 1 depth map from the Source menu and raise the Radius slider to increase the blur. If you have any specular highlights in the image that you want to flare reduce the Threshold slider slightly and increase the Brightness slider to create a realistic effect. Select OK to apply the filter.

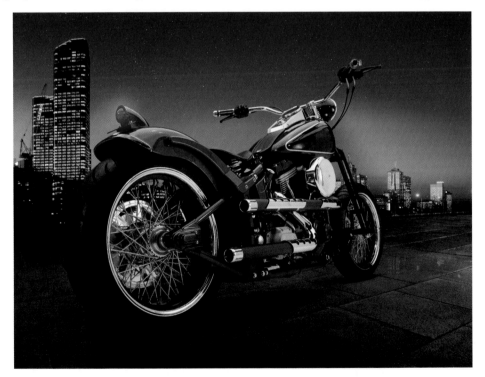

The bike can be moved to a variety of locations. In this alternative the bike has been moved to a location constructed from two images (foreground pavement and background nightscape). A cooling filter is applied and the lights are turned on to complete the picture.

The best technique for subtle shadows

The technique to preserve shadows provides those photographers burdened with a meticulous eye a useful way of retaining and transplanting subtle and complex shadows. Observe the subtle shadow cast by the leaf above that would be virtually impossible to recreate using any other technique. The primary reasons for not being able to use this technique are when the shadow falls over a surface with a different texture to the one in the new location, or the surface over which the shadow falls is particularly uneven or moves from a horizontal to a vertical plane over the length of the shadow.

Original images and concept by Jakub Kazmierczak

PERFORMANCE TIP

This technique for preserving shadows does not have to be restricted to objects sitting on a white background. The technique is just as effective when isolating the shadow of a much larger object captured in its natural surroundings. If, however, the subject has been captured on a textured or rough surface this surface quality will be transferred to the new background when using this technique. A surface quality mismatch can occur that can make the shadow look unnatural.

To ensure a shadow with a rough surface texture does not look out of place against the smooth surface of a new background you can apply a small amount of Gaussian Blur to soften the quality of the shadow. In the illustration on this page a colored Linear gradient in Overlay mode has also been used to warm up the cool colors evident in the panels of the car. The detail in the car windows has also been softened using a Gaussian Blur. These measures ensure the car is perfectly at home in its new surroundings – even if it is balancing on water!

Creating shadows

If it is not possible to preserve the original shadow, try to capture a second image of the subject from the direction of the light source. This second image will allow you to create a more accurate shadow than simply using the outline of the subject as seen from the camera angle. Start this technique by making a mask of your subject and place it on a layer above a new background you wish to use. Import the second image (captured from the direction of the light source) and position it between the subject layer and the background layer. Make a selection of the subject in this second image, create a new empty layer and then fill your selection with black. You can then hide or delete the layer that the selection was made from. Place your new shadow layer in Multiply mode. Lower the opacity of your shadow layer and apply the Gaussian Blur filter. Use the Free Transform command to distort and move the shadow into position.

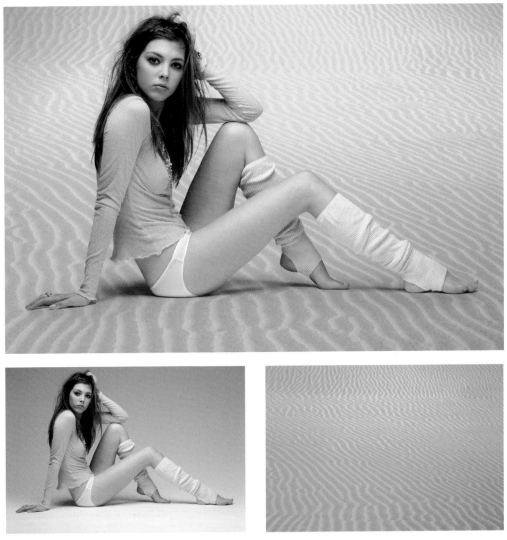

Studio photograph by Rahel Weiss

Replacing a studio background – Project 6

This project combines the skills learned from both the hair extraction project (Project 3) and the shadow preservation project in the Basic Retouching chapter. The purpose of this project is to demonstrate how the model's fine hair and the original shadows from the studio backdrop (cyclorama or 'cyc') can be preserved after creating a composite image using a new location image. The ideal background color for extracting hair for composite image is level 255 white or level 0 black, but when the model is standing or sitting on the studio 'cyc' it may not always be possible to render the background absolute white or black due to the limitations of lighting and the size of the backdrop available. The techniques in this project show you how to work around these issues.

1. Open the Raw file in Adobe Camera Raw. Select the White Balance Tool and click on neutral tone in the image such as the white backdrop (the modeling lights of the studio flash used to capture this image confused the auto white balance setting in the camera). Then open the image in Photoshop. A JPEG image is supplied on the DVD with this step already completed. Go to the Channels panel to start the process of creating a mask. The following steps summarize the hair extraction techniques from Project 3. Find the channel with the highest contrast between the hair and the background by clicking on each one in turn. Duplicate the channel with the highest contrast by dragging it to the New Channel icon. Increase the contrast of the copy channel to further refine the mask. Use a Brightness/Contrast adjustment (Image > Adjustments > Brightness/Contrast) and raise the Contrast to +100 and the Brightness slider to a level just before you start to lose detail in the fine hairs.

2. Choose the Brush Tool, set the foreground color to black and set the mode to Overlay in the Options bar. Choose a soft-edged brush and be careful NOT to paint over fine strands of hair where the background is also visible. Move close to the edge of the hair but do not paint where any background is visible. Switch the mode of the Brush Tool back to Normal in the Options bar and paint with black to fill in any areas of white around the face. The first step of the mask is complete when the head and hair appears as a silhouette. The rest of the subject that has a more defined edge will be selected in the next step.

3. Create a path around the outline of the body excluding the hair (see Project 2). A finished path has been supplied with the tutorial image for your convenience. Hold down the Ctrl key (PC) or Command key (Mac) and click on the path you created to load the path as a selection. The edge of a vector path is not suitable for masking photographs. The path has to be converted to a selection so that the edge can be refined. Go to the Channels panel and click on the 'Save selection as channel' icon. You will now have a Blue copy channel and an Alpha 1 channel. The two of these channels will provide you with the mask you need to hide the studio backdrop. Choose Select > None.

4. The background of the Blue copy Alpha channel is still too light so must be modified further. Select the Gradient Tool and choose White as the foreground color and the Foreground to Transparent and Linear options in the Options bar. Set the Opacity to 100%. Drag a series of gradients from the bottom, left and right sides of the hair that fall short of the hair to lighten all of the tones surrounding the hair. The Gradient Tool is a useful way of introducing a smooth transition. Using the Brush Tool to lighten the background may introduce harsh edges that may be detected later so this approach should be avoided.

5. Darken any remaining gray tones by going to Image > Adjustments > Levels. Drag the central gamma slider beneath the histogram to the left. Do not go beyond 1.5 gamma so that you can preserve the fine detail in the hair. Drag the shadows slider to level 10 to clip any dark gray tones present in the body of the hair to black.

6. Click on RGB in the Channels panel. Open the M6_Sand image file and drag the background thumbnail from the Layers panel into your project image. Double click the name of the new layer and call it New-Location. In this example a fairly abstract location has been used, but you can use any location providing the vantage point or angle of view and lighting is consistent with the subject photographed in the studio. Make sure you are in the Channels panel. Hold down the Ctrl key (PC) or Command key (Mac) and click on the Blue copy channel first to load it as a selection. Now hold down the Alt/Option key as well as the Ctrl/Command key and click on the Alpha 1 channel to add this to the selection. All of the area around the model should now be selected.

Note > The modifier keys control how a second Alpha channel is loaded as a selection (add, subtract or intersect). The order in which you load the channels may also make a difference to the resulting selection.

7. Go to the Layers panel and click on the 'Add layer mask' icon at the base of the Layers panel. Go to the blending options and choose Multiply from the menu. Using Multiply will improve the fine detail in the hair and restore the shadows to the image. The new location will appear darker due to the gray tone of the white studio background on the background layer. This will be rectified later.

8. There should be no active selection now that it has been converted into a layer mask. Go to Select > Refine Edge (we are now refining the edges of the mask and not the selection). Select the On Layers preview option from the View mode in the Refine Mask dialog. Set the Radius, Smooth and Contrast sliders to zero. Raise the Feather slider to a setting between 0.5 and 2.0 pixels and raise the Shift Edge slider to hide any haloes that may appear around your subject. Zoom in to 100% and take a look at both the smooth edges and the hair to choose appropriate values for both of these sliders. Choose the Layer Mask option in the Output section of the Refine Mask dialog and then select OK.

9. Hold down the Alt/Option key and click on the layer mask to view the contents. Look for any holes in the mask that may have appeared as a result of using the Refine Edge command. Set the brush mode to Normal and paint with black if you see any areas of gray in the main body of the mask. Do not paint in the areas of fine detail at the edge of the mask. If you have any haloes along the sharp edges of the mask make a selection of the problem area with the Lasso Tool. Go to Image > Adjustments > Levels and move the gamma slider to the right or left to perfect this localized portion of the mask. Moving the black or white sliders towards the center will increase the contrast of the mask in this area and may help you to perfect the edge.

10. Hold down the Ctrl key (PC) or Command key (Mac) and click on the layer mask to load it as a selection. This selection will create its own mask when we create an adjustment layer. This will enable us to work on the tonality of the studio backdrop while protecting the tonality of the model. Select the background layer and create a Levels adjustment layer from the Adjustments panel. Set the mode of the adjustment layer to Luminosity. Drag the white input slider beneath the right side of the histogram to the left to clip the background tones to white. Stop dragging the slider when you notice it impacting on the fine detail in the hair. As the shadow tones are darker they should be some of the last tones that would be rendered white using this technique. If the shadow tones become too light move the middle gamma slider to the right. Select the Brush Tool in the Tools panel. Select Black as the foreground color and the Opacity as 50%. Paint over the cast shadows in the adjustment layer mask to restore the shadows to their original darkness.

11. Invariably the color and tone of the subject and the new location image will need to be matched for consistency of contrast and white point. In this project the color of the sand is matched to the clothing the model is wearing. In the Tools panel choose the 'Color Sampler' Tool (behind the Eyedropper Tool) and set the Sample Size to a 5 by 5 Average in the Options bar. Set the Second Color Readout to HSB in the Info panel options by clicking on the small triangle underneath the eyedropper. Click once on the clothing, take a note of the Brightness value, and then move the Color Sampler to the sand and take a second color sample of the sand that is approximately as bright as the clothing sample taken.

12. Select the New-Location layer and then choose a Curves adjustment layer from the adjustments panel. Go to each of the three RGB channels in turn and click anywhere on the curve to set an adjustment point. In the Input field in the Curves panel type in the value that appears in the first set of values in the #2 sample RGB information in the Info dialog (in the illustration above, level 106 that appears in the Info panel has been typed into the Input field in the Curves dialog). Each of the output values is then changed so that they are the same as the #1 color sample values. By matching the output values in the Curves dialog to the values of the first color sample point we have effectively made the color of the sand the same color as the clothing prior to adding this Curves adjustment layer. Ignore the fact that the model and the clothing have turned magenta at this point!

13. In the Curves panel click on the overlapping circles icon to clip the Curves adjustment layer to the sand layer. This restricts the color adjustments to just this layer and restores the original color of the model. To tidy the file you can remove the color samplers by holding down the Alt/Option key and the Shift key and click on each color sample target in turn to remove them.

14. Create a second Curves adjustment layer and clip it to the layers below. Raise the RGB curve so that the sand is much brighter than before. Drag a Black, White linear gradient into the adjustment layer mask so that the bottom half of the sand is shielded from this adjustment. Just replace the contents of the sand layer with another background to transport the model around the world.

Chris Mollison

Let's sea
a world of change!

WWF

Every year, governments pour billions into subsidies for
their fishing fleets. But details of how these billions are
spent remain locked in government files.
With subsidies increasingly linked to overfishing,
it's time for greater transparency and accountability.

advanced retouching

Haydn Cattach

essential skills

- Create a monochrome or black and white image from an RGB master.
- Manipulate tonality and split-tone an image.
- Enhance detail and depth to create a dramatic effect.
- Create an image with reduced depth of field.
- Create a 'Faux' style by manipulating focus and color.
- Use professional techniques to enhance the facial features of a portrait image.
- Create smooth tone and exaggerate midtone contrast to create a signature style.
- Merge bracketed exposures to create high dynamic range images.
- Create a time lapse video using an image sequence.

Black and white – Project 1

When color film arrived over half a century ago the pundits who presumed that black and white film would die a quick death were surprisingly mistaken. Color is all very nice but sometimes the rich tonal qualities that we can see in the work of the photographic artists are something certainly to be savored. Can you imagine an Ansel Adams masterpiece in color? If you can – read no further.

Creating fabulous black and white photographs from your color images is a little more complicated than hitting the 'Convert to Grayscale mode' or 'Desaturate' buttons in your image-editing software (or worse still, your camera). Ask any professional photographer who has been raised on the film medium and you will discover that crafting tonally rich images requires both a carefully chosen color filter during the capture stage and some dodging and burning in the darkroom. Color filters for black and white? Now there is an interesting concept! Well as strange as it may seem, screwing on a color filter for capturing images on black and white film has traditionally been an essential ingredient in the recipe for success. The most popular color filter in the black and white photographer's kit-bag, that is used for the most dramatic effect, is the 'red filter'. The effect of the red filter is to lighten all things that are red and darken all things that are not red in the original scene. The result is a print with considerable tonal differences compared to an image shot without a filter. Is this a big deal? Well yes it is – blue skies are darkened and skin blemishes are lightened. That's a winning combination for most landscape and portrait photographers wanting to create black and white masterpieces.

Note > The more conservative photographers of old (those not big on drama) would typically invest in a yellow or orange filter rather than the 'full-on' effects that the red filter offers.

The Black & White adjustment offers a quick and controlled method for controlling tonality – just click in the main image window and drag left or right to darken or lighten the tonal value of this color range.

Traditional Black and White

Now just before you run out to purchase your red filter and 'Grayscale image sensor' you should be reminded that neither is required by the digital photographer with access to Photoshop. Shooting digitally in RGB (red, green, blue) means that you have already shot the same image using the three different filters. If you were to selectively favor the goodies in the red channel, above those to be found in the green or blue channels, you would, in effect, be creating a Grayscale image that would appear as if it had been shot using the red filter from the 'good old days'. You can see the different tonal information by using the 'Channels panel' to view the individual channels (turn off the visibility of all but one channel). Then you can selectively control the information using the Black & White adjustment layer feature.

Black & White adjustment in Photoshop

The Black & White adjustment feature is now the easiest and most versatile way to convert images to black and white. No more juggling sliders in Channel Mixer to prevent clipping. The adjustment feature is a breeze to use and very versatile. You can use the color sliders if you like or simply click on a color within the image window and drag to the right to make the color lighter, or to the left to make it darker. How easy is that! In fact, this technique is so easy to use it hardly warrants a project to master the technique. The adjustment feature does, however, have its limitations. Dragging the sliders to their extreme values in the Black & White adjustment feature can introduce image artifacts and haloes around adjusted colors and the image adjustment feature has no contrast adjustment within the dialog box. Total control over tonality still requires some additional and essential skills using the information from the individual channels in conjunction with the contrast blend modes such as Overlay and Soft Light. The skill of controlled black and white conversions is a foundation for most of the color toning projects that follow.

1. Optimize the project file in Adobe Camera Raw making sure that there is no clipping in either the shadows or highlights. Hold down the Alt/Option key as you drag the Blacks and Exposure sliders to set the Black and White points in the image. The Recovery slider has been raised to allow the Exposure slider to be raised to +1.20. The project image also has to be straightened using the Straighten Tool before it is opened in the main editing space.

Note > It is possible to render the image as a Grayscale image in the HSL/Grayscale tab of the ACR dialog box. It is also possible, using the Grayscale Mix sliders, to brighten the rocks by raising the Yellows slider and darken the sky by lowering the Blues slider. You may notice, however, that such an aggressive adjustment introduces both noise and haloes. The haloes around the edges of the rocks (the transition between the darkened blues and lightened yellows) are most noticeable when viewed at 100%. This is where a manual conversion to Grayscale in the main editing space can provide the user with superior results.

2. Open the project file into Adobe Camera Raw and set the Workflow Options to 16 Bits/ Channel and check the Open in Photoshop as Smart Objects preference. Select OK and click on the Open Object button (formerly the Open Image button). This will ensure we embed the Raw file into the project file and allow us to make large changes in tonality and reduce the risk of introducing image artifacts and banding into the edited image.

3. Open the Channels panel and click on the Blue channel thumbnail (not the visibility icon). Note how this channel offers the best contrast between the sky and the rocks (blue sky will be lighter in the Blue channel and opposite colors, such as the yellow rocks, will be darker in the Blue channel). We can use this channel to create a quick and effective mask for this project. This mask will allow us to work on the sky and the foreground separately to achieve optimum tonality and contrast in both areas. This technique is called channel masking and is a commonly used advanced technique for professional retouchers to save time. Drag the Blue channel to the New Channel icon to copy it. From the Image > Adjustments submenu choose 'Levels'. Drag the shadow slider in the Levels dialog box to the right until the dark rocks are mostly black. Drag the highlight slider to the left until the sky is mostly white (you should be left with a few gray clouds). Click OK to apply the adjustment. Although not perfect, this mask can be optimized in the next step.

4. Painting in Photoshop is not an easy skill to acquire. There is, however, a clever brush technique when masking that makes it a far less painful procedure. Switch the blend mode of the Brush Tool to 'Overlay' in the Options bar and set the foreground color to white. When you paint over the clouds with a white brush in Overlay mode all the gray tones are progressively rendered lighter. The magic of the Overlay mode lies in the fact that white has little or no effect on the darkest tones and black has little or no effect on the lightest tones. Switching the foreground color to black and painting over the dark gray tones on the rocks will help to expand the contrast of the Alpha channel.

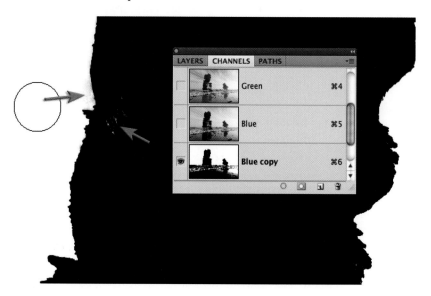

Switch the mode of the brush back to Normal for final clean-up work in the sky (away from the edges of the rocks). There is no need to work on the water or beach at this stage. Zoom in to 100% (Actual Pixels) and check the mask for any holes in the rocks that need painting with black.

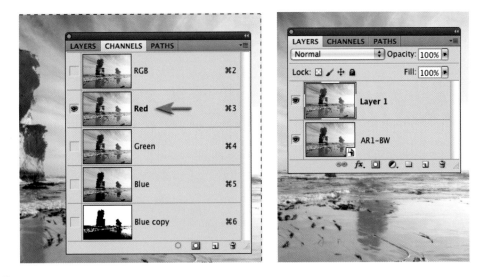

5. Go to the Channels panel and click on the Red channel thumbnail (not the visibility icon). This channel offers the best contrast in the sky. To copy the Red copy channel to the clipboard, choose All from the Select menu (Ctrl/Command + A) and then Copy from the Edit menu (Ctrl/Command + C). Click on the RGB channel and then go to the Layers panel and create a new layer by choosing Paste from the Edit menu (Ctrl/Command + V).

6. From the Image > Adjustments menu choose Levels. Hold down the Alt/Option key as you drag the black slider to the right. Stop moving the slider only when you see the darker areas of the sky clipping. Move the slider back a little until no clipping is visible in the sky. Drag the central gamma slider underneath the histogram to the left to brighten the sky. You have now expanded the contrast of the sky to the maximum possible before clipping occurs. The tonality of the beach and rocks will be used from the underlying Smart Object and will not be damaged by this step.

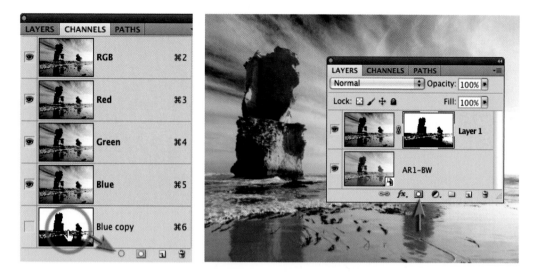

7. Drag the Blue copy channel to the 'Load channel as selection' icon at the base of the Channels panel to load the channel as a selection. The keyboard shortcut to load a channel as a selection is to hold down the Command key on a Mac or the Ctrl key on a PC and click on the channel thumbnail. Click on Layer 1 (the information from your Red channel) to make sure it is the active layer. Click on the 'Add layer mask' icon at the base of the Layers panel. The mask will require further work to ensure the modified sky is seamless and the immediate foreground (waves and sand) does not appear a little strange.

8. Click on the 'Create a new layer' icon to create a new empty layer. From the Edit menu choose Fill and then select 50% Gray from the contents menu of the Fill dialog box before selecting OK. Drag the gray layer beneath the Smart Object. Change the blend mode of the smart object (the AR1-BW layer) to Luminosity. This blend mode will allow only the Luminance values to be visible and is a non-destructive way of removing the color from view.

9. Click on the layer mask thumbnail on Layer 2 to make it active and then go to Filter > Blur > Gaussian Blur and apply a 1-pixel blur to soften the edge of the mask a little. Select OK and then zoom in and take a close look around the edges of the rocks. If you notice a halo around any section select that portion using the Lasso Tool. Go to Image > Adjustments > Levels. Drag the central gamma slider underneath the histogram to the left or right to reduce the width of the halo.

10. Haloes around edges can be removed or substantially reduced using the technique in the previous step. Sometimes, however, an additional step may be required to remove the halo completely. Create an empty new layer by clicking on the 'Create a new layer' icon. Set the mode of the layer to Darken and select the Clone Stamp Tool in the Tools panel. Make sure All Layers is selected in the Options bar, hold down the Alt/Option key and click to select a clone source point just next to the lighter edge. Click and drag the Clone Stamp Tool over the light edge to replace these pixels with the darker pixels from the source point. This will continue to work only if the source point is selecting darker pixels as you paint. Next, so that you can keep track of what each layer is doing, double-click on the layer names you have created to rename the layers, e.g. Layer 1 can be renamed 'Sky', Layer 2 can be renamed Gray and layer 3 can be renamed 'Darken edge'.

11. As we only require the tonality of the sky on this layer we will need to mask the water and beach using the Gradient Tool from the Tools panel. Choose the Black, White gradient and the Linear options and set the Opacity to 100% in the Options bar. Set the mode to Multiply to add information rather than replace information in the layer mask. Make sure the sky layer mask is selected then drag a short gradient, while holding the Shift key down, from just below the horizon line to just above the horizon line to mask the foreground.

Note > An alternative to the Black, White gradient in Multiply mode is to set the Foreground color to Black and then use the Foreground to Transparent gradient in Normal mode.

12. This step will add contrast to the waves and beach to match the expanded contrast in the sky. We can do this in one of two ways. The first way is to double-click the Smart Object thumbnail and increase the Contrast and Clarity in the Adobe Camera Raw dialog box. Click Done in ACR to close the dialog box and update the Smart Object.

Alternatively we can choose Select > All, then Edit > Copy Merged and then Edit > Paste. These three commands can be combined into a single command which is commonly referred to as Stamp Visible by professional retouchers. This command has an unlisted shortcut which is to hit the letter E while holding down the Ctrl + Alt + Shift keys (PC) or Command + Option + Shift keys (Mac). This will create a copy of what you see on the screen and paste it as a new layer. Switch the blend mode of this layer to Overlay (a contrast blend mode) and then add a layer mask. Add a short Black to White gradient to this mask from just above the horizon line to just below the horizon line.

Note > Toggle the layer visibility on and off to see the actual effect this has on the image.

13. This step will darken the sky on the right side of the image. Click on the New Layer icon at the base of the Layers panel and set the mode to Overlay. Choose Black as the Foreground color and select a Foreground to Transparent gradient. Drag a gradient (while holding the Shift key down) from the right side of the image to a position just short of the larger dominant rock in the sea. Hold down the Alt/Option key and drag a copy of the layer mask on the Sky layer to the Gradient layer. Lower the opacity of the Gradient layer to reduce the effect and create a balance of sky tones within the image.

14. This step will create a subtle vignette that is designed to darken the corners without darkening the brighter highlights of the image. Add another new layer and set the mode to Overlay. Select the Elliptical Marquee Tool from the Tools panel (behind the Rectangular Marquee Tool). Drag a selection from the top-left corner to the bottom-right corner of the image. Choose Inverse from the Select menu. Press the Q key to turn this selection into a 'Quick Mask'. Go to Filter > Blur > Gaussian Blur and apply a 200-pixel blur to this mask. Press Q on the keyboard to return to the selection. Be sure the foreground color is set to black and fill the selection with black using the keyboard shortcut Alt + Backspace (PC) or Option + Delete (Mac). Lower the opacity of the layer to around 35%. Finally, don't forget to choose Select > Deselect before going on to the next step.

15. Create a 'Dodge & Burn' layer (create a new layer and fill with 50% gray and then set the mode to Overlay). Select the Brush Tool from the Tools panel and then choose a soft-edged brush, Opacity 10% and Normal mode from the Options bar. Set the foreground color to white to dodge or black to burn, then paint over the rock on the right to darken and increase its localized contrast. Paint several times until you are happy with the effect. It does not matter if the brushwork spills into the background sky, because we will apply a layer mask to hide any spill. Hold down the Alt/Option key and drag the layer mask from the Gradient layer to the Dodge & Burn layer. Holding down the Alt/Option key will copy the mask. Invert this mask using the Invert shortcut Ctrl + I (PC) or Command + I (Mac).

Reintroducing color and sharpening

The original color can be reintroduced in a way that preserves the tonal values we have just created. Copy the Apostles layer by holding down the Alt/Option key and dragging it to the top of the Layers stack. Right-click on the layer and choose Rasterize if you need to reduce the overall files size and then change the mode of this copy layer to Color. Adjust the opacity until an appropriate balance between tonality and color is achieved. This Color layer does not affect the underlying luminance values that we have created in the previous steps.

Note > The ability to modify color and tonality separately and then reunite them later in the editing process can be a powerful technique for creating information-rich images where luminance values have the priority over color values.

All of the detail in this project is on the first Smart Object above the gray layer. To sharpen this project for printing apply the Unsharp Mask filter. Raising the Threshold slider in the Unsharp Mask dialog box to 3 or 4 will prevent image artifacts from being sharpened. The sky and gradients will not be sharpened using this procedure. As the layer is a Smart Object the filter will automatically be applied as a Smart Filter allowing subsequent adjustments to the sharpening settings.

Manipulating tone and color – Project 2

This is an exercise in injecting the drama that photographers witness, but cameras often fail to capture. Ansel Adams was the master of previsualization (the ability to see his final image in his mind's eye when he was looking at the scene in front of his camera lens). When I stood in front of this grand vista in Monument Valley, Arizona I previsualized a scene of full of drama. When I saw the Raw image in ACR I realized the camera had interpreted a completely different outcome to the one that I had imagined – was the camera really looking at the same scene as me?

IMAGE ON DVD

Monument Valley at dawn from Artist's Point, Arizona, USA.

Ansel Adams said that if the negative was his music score then work in the darkroom was his performance. I knew that this was going to take one hell of a performance if the outcome was going to match my expectations for this image. So starts this monumental project. The vertical format seems too long and the distance between the foreground drama and the background rock formations seems too great. Compressing the information without distorting the subject matter, I feel, would help the composition. I also want to bring out the drama from the directional lighting (if I was only interested in the color I wouldn't have bothered getting up before dawn). And that sky is contributing nothing – yes it's blue but it is also disappointingly empty. We need something to mirror the drama of the desert in the foreground. So let the show begin.

Stage 1

1. Open the Project file into Adobe Camera Raw (ACR). The aim here is raise the contrast but retain shadow detail. Raise the Contrast slider to +70, the Fill Light Slider to +20 and the Clarity slider to +25. The color temperature has been lowered slightly from the 'As Shot' setting. Use the Targeted Adjustment Tool to both increase the saturation and decrease the luminance of the blue sky (select Saturation from the Targeted Adjustment Tool menu drag up to raise the saturation and then select Luminance and drag down to darken the sky).

2. Select the Graduated Filter (press the G key) and set the Exposure to –1.00. Raise the Contrast to +30 and then drag a gradient from just above the central rock formation to the lower half of the image. This will balance the exposure and contrast within the image. From the Workflow options set the Bit Depth to 16 Bits/Channel. Then click on the Open Image button (this project does not require that you open the image as a Smart Object as all of the remaining tonal and color adjustments will be made in the main editing space of Photoshop.

Content-Aware Scale meets its match

It is possible to use the Content-Aware Scale feature, that was first introduced with Photoshop CS4, to change the shape of the image from the long 2:3 aspect ratio to the squarer 4:5 aspect ratio, without losing any of the foreground detail. This would be a simple case of first duplicating the background layer and then making a rectangular selection of the top of the image and then, while holding down the Shift key, make an additional selection of the bottom of the image. In the Channels panel the user would then click the Save selection as channel icon to create an Alpha channel that can be used to protect the detail in these areas. From the Edit menu the user would then choose Content-Aware Scale and in the Options bar select the Alpha 1 channel from the Protect menu. The Image can then be scaled while protecting both the top and bottom of the image. The problem with this technique in this particular image is that if you were to zoom in to 100% (Actual Pixels) you would see the fault lines or 'stress fractures' where Photoshop has been sacrificing detail. The detail in this area of the image cannot be compressed without sacrificing quality when using this feature. This is a task where the Auto-Blend Layers feature comes into its own to create a seamless compression.

3. Select the Rectangular Marquee Tool from the Tools panel and set the Feather to 0 px. Make a selection of the top of the image that just includes the two tiny white houses. Copy the pixels (Ctrl + C for a PC or Command + C for a Mac) and then Paste the pixels to a new layer (Ctrl + V for a PC or Command + V for a Mac). Select the Background layer and copy and paste the bottom of the image so that you now have three layers. Switch off the visibility of the Background layer. Select the Move Tool from the Tools panel (press the V key) and then, while holding the Shift key down, move Layer 1 and Layer 2 closer so that they overlap. Drop the Opacity of the two layers in the Layers panel to see the extent of the overlap. Move Layer 2 to the top of the layers stack and add a layer mask to Layer 2 by clicking the Add layer mask icon at the base of the Layers panel. Select the Brush Tool from the Tools panel and paint with black at 100% Opacity in the region of the two tiny white houses in the zone of the overlap. This action will force Photoshop to retain the houses in the composite view. Return Layer 1 and Layer 2 to 100% opacity, select both layers (Shift + Click) and then go to Edit > Auto-Blend Layers. Select the Panorama and Seamless Tones and Colors option and then select OK.

4. Zoom in to make sure Photoshop has done a seamless job of blending these two layers together. Save the project file as a 'stage 1' file and then from the Layers fly-out menu choose Flatten Image. We have no further use for the individual layers in this project.

5. Select the Crop Tool from the Tools panel and then in the Options bar enter in the new 4:5 aspect ratio. If you don't know the size of the image you require for your output device just leave the Resolution field in the Options bar blank to ensure Photoshop does not interpolate the image. If you are not sure of the composition at this stage, i.e. you are not sure whether you want to crop away the top or bottom of the image, just drag the lock icon on the background layer to the trash can in the Layers panel and select the Hide rather than the Delete option in the Options bar.

6. In this step we will create an alpha channel that can be used as a mask for the sky later in this project. Go to the Channels panel and click on each channel in turn. You will notice that the blue channel has the best contrast between the sky and the land. This is confirmed by reviewing the Blue channel in the Histogram panel. Duplicate the Blue channel by dragging it to the Create new channel icon at the base of the Channels panel.

7. Use the keyboard shortcut Ctrl + L (PC) or Command + L (Mac) to open the Levels dialog. Drag the Black and White Input Levels sliders towards the histogram to render the sky almost white and the foreground almost black. Be careful not to drag the White input Levels slider too far as you may clip some of the foreground tones to white. We can increase the contrast of this alpha channel in the next step.

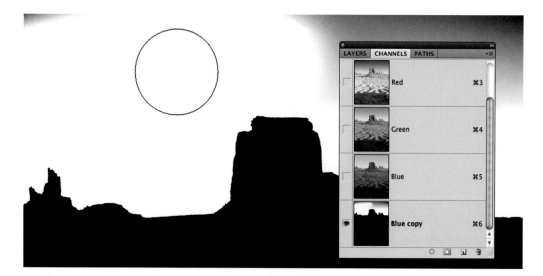

8. Select the Brush Tool from the Tools panel and set the mode of the Brush Tool to Overlay in the Options bar. Choose a large soft-edged brush and make sure that white is the foreground color in the Tools panel. Paint over any gray areas that you can see in the sky to render them white. Painting in Overlay mode will protect any tones that are already black in the image. Switch the foreground and background colors so that black is now the foreground color. Paint over any areas near the horizon line that are not absolutely black (the white sky will be protected by the blend mode). If any areas are slow to render black switch the blend mode to Normal, reduce the size of the brush, zoom in and carefully paint these black (the two white houses in the middle-distance will require this last treatment).

9. Select the Red Channel in the Channels panel as this has the best contrast for the desert landscape. From the Select menu choose Select All (Ctrl or Command + A) and then from the Edit menu choose Copy (Ctrl or Command + C). Click on the master RGB composite view and then return to the Layer panels. Choose Paste from the Edit menu (Ctrl or Command + V) to paste the information from the Red channel into a new layer.

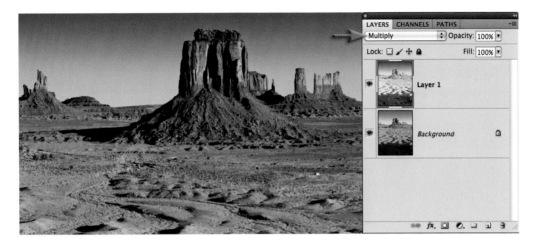

10. Set the mode of this new layer to Multiply. This will darken the shadows in the composite view. We will next create softer shadows by blurring them slightly using the Gaussian Blur filter. If carefully controlled this will increase the apparent depth of the image but retain the all-important detail within the image.

Note > I would love to be able to say that I pioneered the technique that follows but it actually emulates a classic Black & White darkroom technique that utilizes a silk-stocking placed over the enlarger lens (applied to the high contrast stage of a split-grade printing technique made famous by Max Ferguson).

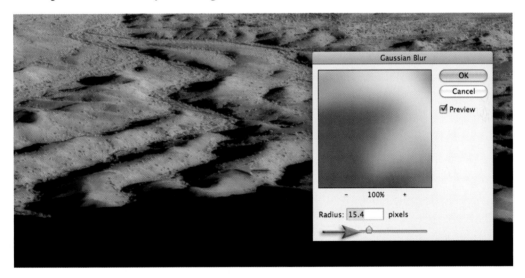

11. Go to Filter > Blur > Gaussian Blur. Zoom in to the image to take a close look at the shadows as we try to find the most appropriate Radius value for the image we are working on (it varies from image to image). The idea is to blur the shadows so that the tone extends or 'bleeds' into the midtone regions of the image. If the shadows extend too far they will muddy the all-important highlights. In this project I have decided to use a Radius of around 15 pixels. Select OK to apply the blur.

12. To prevent the blur bleeding into the smooth tone of the sky we will add a mask to this layer. Go to the Channels panel and while holding down the Ctrl key (PC) or Command key (Mac) click on the Blue Channel copy thumbnail to load it as a selection. Return to the Layers panel and click on the Add layer mask icon at the base of the panel to add a mask to Layer 1. Go to Filter > Blur > Gaussian Blur and add a 2.0 pixel blur to this layer mask to soften the hard edge.

13. This step will seek to increase the effect of the shadows while keeping the highlights free from the effect. Go to the Adjustments panel and choose a Levels adjustment. Clip the Levels layer to the blur layer using the icon at the base of the Adjustments panel. Move the Black Outputs Levels slider so that it reads 50 in the Output Levels field to ensure the shadows do not become too dark (a result of the Multiply mode of the layer below). Now increase the intensity of the bleed by moving the central gamma slider (directly underneath the histogram) to the right (a value of 0.6 gamma). Move the White Input Levels slider to the left (a value of around 200) so that the highlights remain clean. Hold down the Alt/Option key as you move this slider so you can see which highlight tones are being clipped on the blur layer below thereby allowing the highlight detail from the background layer to be the sole contributor to the final outcome.

Note > Do not confuse the Blacks Input Levels slider for the Blacks Output levels slider in this step otherwise you may render the shadows too dark to print with detail. Do not move the Black Outputs levels slider too far otherwise the effect will be removed.

14. Any shadows that may be too dark to print with detail (take a look at the Histogram panel to see if tones are bunching up against the left hand wall of the histogram) can be lightened in this step. Merge the visible elements of this project to a single new layer by holding down the modifier keys Ctrl + Alt + Shift (PC) or Command + Option + Shift (Mac) and then pressing the E key. Go to Image > Adjustments > Shadows/Highlights. Check the Show More Options box and then raise the Amount and Tonal Width sliders to 30 in the Shadows section (the Radius slider has been left at 60 px). Select OK to apply this adjustment. Hold down the Shift key and select all layers except the background layer and then use the keyboard shortcut Ctrl + G (PC) or Command + G (Mac) to place these layers into a group. Double-click on the group name to rename the group 'Blur Shadows'.

Stage 2

15. Go to File > Place and then browse to the desert sky image. Select Place to open this image in Adobe Camera Raw. Increase the contrast of this image. Set the Exposure slider to +1.75 and lower the Brightness slider to –28. Raise both the Contrast and Clarity sliders to +100. Raise the Temperature slider to 5900 and lower the Tint slider to –8. As this contrast adjustment will raise the apparent noise within the image go to the Detail Tab and raise the Noise Reduction slider slightly. Select OK to place the file.

16. The large cross you see on the file is inviting you to scale the image. Move the lower central anchor point on the bounding box upwards to compress the information. Right-click in the bounding box and select Flip Horizontal. Hit the Commit icon in the Options bar or press the Return/Enter key to commit the scaling operation. You will notice a small icon on the thumbnail of this layer indicating that this is a Smart Object.

17. Hold down the Alt/Option key and drag the layer mask from the Gaussian Blur layer to copy the layer mask to the Smart Object layer (the new sky). Invert the mask (Ctrl or Command + I) so that the sky is masked behind the rocks on the horizon line. If the sky needs moving or scaling a second time click on the link icon between the layer thumbnail and the layer mask so that the sky layer can be moved independently of the mask. Check that the image and not the layer mask is the active component of the layer and then use the Free Transform command to re-scale the image (Ctrl or Command + T).

18. If you zoom in and take a look at the horizon line you will notice a small white halo. This can be eliminated by going to Select > Refine Mask. Raise the Contrast and Shift Edge sliders to the right until the thin white line disappears.

19. For the sky to look at home it needs to be lighter where it meets the horizon line. To make these changes go to the Adjustments panel and choose a Curves adjustment. Raise the curve so that the highlights are much brighter. Then select the Gradient Tool from the Tools panel and select the Black, White option in the Options bar. Set the Opacity to 100% and drag a gradient from a position just higher than the top of the central rock to a position just above the horizon line in order to restore the tonality to the top portion of the sky.

20. The sky can be made warmer by either double-clicking the Smart Object thumbnail and adjusting the Temperature in ACR or by simply adding a Warming Filter by going to the Adjustments panel and choosing the Warming Filter from the Photo Filter adjustment options. If you elect to add the Photo Filter then ensure that you clip this adjustment to the clipping group below by clicking the clipping icon at the base of the Adjustments panel.

21. To darken and add contrast to the sky, at the top of the image, add a new layer by clicking the Create new layer icon at the base of the Layers panel. Set the mode of this new layer to Overlay and clip this layer to the clipping group below (from the Layer menu choose Create Clipping Mask). Select the Gradient Tool and choose the new Neutral Density preset from the Gradient Presets. Drag a gradient from the top of the image towards the horizon line. This step completes the second stage of the editing procedure so it would be considered good housekeeping if you save your work in progress. You can then proceed to hold down the Shift key and click the Neutral Density gradient layer and the Smart Object containing the sky and then using the keyboard shortcut, Ctrl or Command + G, place these layers into a group and rename the group 'Sky'.

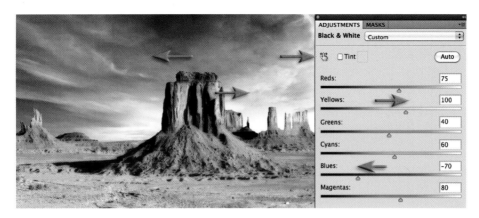

Stage 3

22. Although we have certainly lifted the drama in the first two stages of this project, converting the image to Black and White will give us additional opportunities to really increase localized contrast. Go to the Adjustments panel and choose a Black & White adjustment. Move the Reds and Yellows to the right and the Blues to the left to increase the contrast slightly. Use the Targeted Adjustment Tool to make fast work of this step.

23. In this step we will increase localized contrast by painting tonal adjustments. This is called dodging (making tones lighter) and burning (making tones darker). As the tones are distributed over many different layers we will dodge and burn on a new layer that is set to a contrast blend mode. Select the Blur Shadows group and then click on the Create new layer icon at the base of the Layers panel and set the mode of this new layer to Overlay. Placing the Dodge & Burn layer beneath the Sky group will ensure we don't darken or lighten the sky. Overlay is a good blend mode for dodging and burning Black and White images (better contrast) but Soft Light is usually superior when dodging and burning color images (better saturation control). Choose the Brush Tool from the Tools panel and set the Opacity to 10% and set the Brush Hardness to 0. Paint with Black as the foreground color to darken selected areas of the image and paint with white to lighten selected areas of the image. There is no right or wrong about where you paint. I have decided to lighten the right side of the central rock formation and darken the left side. I have also decided to darken the area of land between the foreground and background. Use the Eraser Tool if you want to remove any of your handiwork.

24. To introduce color into this image you can either lower the opacity of the Black and White adjustment layer (you may need to switch the blend mode of the Dodge & Burn layer to Soft Light if you do this) or you can create a new Curves adjustment layer to tone this image with colors of your own choosing. With this latter option select the top layer in the Layers panel and then go to the Adjustments panel and select a Curves adjustment. Go to the Blue channel and create an inverse 'S' curve, i.e. pulling the curve down in the highlights and up in the shadows. I have anchored the curve in the center so that midtones stay neutral. In the Red channel make a shallow 'S' curve so that the highlights appear warm and the shadows cool. A slight tweak to the highlights in the RGB composite view completes the toning procedure. If the saturation of the colors appears too high then lower the opacity of this Curves adjustment layer. Select the Black and White and Curves adjustment layers and place these in a new group called Toning.

25. Some images that are captured in relatively flat light can benefit enormously from a High Pass layer that can be used to increase localized contrast and create more depth in the image. This project does not require too much extra depth but the sky and immediate foreground can stand a little extra. Merge the visible elements to a new layer (Ctrl + Alt + Shift + E for PC users and Command + Option + Shift + E for Mac users) set the mode to Soft Light and then go to Filter > Other > High Pass. Raise the Radius slider until you achieve maximum depth (around 80 pixels for this image). Hold down the Alt/Option key and click the Add layer mask icon in the Layers panel to add a layer mask filled with black. Paint with white to apply the High Pass adjustment where required.

26. To sharpen this image for your intended output device you need to open the Blur Shadows group and select the Merge Visible layer. This is the layer that you created after blurring the shadows so that you could apply the Shadows/Highlights adjustment feature. Go to Filter > Convert for Smart Filters and then go to Filter > Sharpen > Smart Sharpen. Use a high Amount setting and low Radius setting to achieve some crisp detail in the rock formations and desert detail.

27. After reviewing the file more fine-tuning can occur. This is where good housekeeping of naming layers and layer groups becomes very useful. I have returned to the Curves layer that is clipped to the Sky and lowered the white point so that the bright clouds are not the brightest highlights in the overall image.

28. To complete the project a vignette is added to darken the edges. Select the top layer in the Layers panel, the rectangular Marquee Tool from the Tools panel and set a feather Radius of 250 pixels in the Options bar. Click and drag from near the top left-hand side of the image to the lower right-hand side of the image to select the central portion of the image and then go to Select > Inverse so that only the edges of the image are selected. From the Edit menu choose Copy Merged and then from the Edit menu again, choose Paste.

29. Set the mode of the new layer to Multiply to darken the edges and use the keyboard shortcut Ctrl + Shift + U (PC) or Command + Shift + U (Mac) to desaturate the layer (this prevents a rise in saturation at the edges of the image). Click on the Add layer mask icon at the base of the Layers panel and then select the Gradient Tool from the Tools panel. Choose the Neutral Density gradient preset and drag from the lower edge to a position just above where the dark foreground shadows end. This will help protect these dark edges from further darkening. The project is complete but the flexibility of the workflow will allow you to modify and fine-tune any aspect of the visual outcome.

Enhancing detail and depth – Project 3

Images captured in flat light can sometimes lack detail, depth and drama. It is possible, however, to unleash the hidden potential of an image using post-production techniques. The secret to success lies in the contrast blend modes together with filters and adjustment features that can detect and enhance edge contrast. This depth charge technique is designed to inject the drama that the start image lacks.

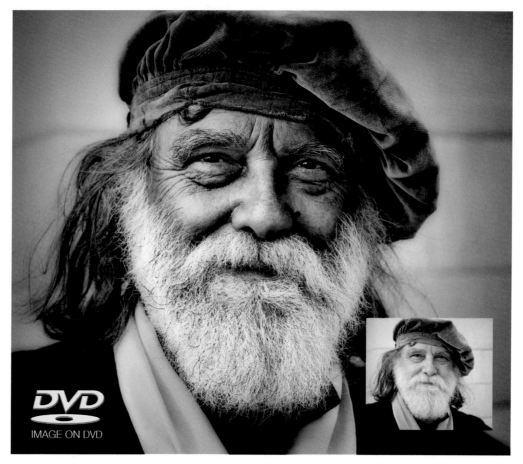

Piergiorgio Brusegan (Venetian artist) – Mark Galer

The technique that follows uses a Gaussian Blur 'smooth tone technique' to smooth the broader areas of tone while the fine detail will be preserved and sharpened. The application of a blur filter in a project where the fine detail is preserved may, at first, sound strange, but if it is applied in conjunction with a blend mode the sharp detail within the subject can be made to interact with the smoother surface tones. The steps that follow enhance the localized contrast and fine detail and the balance between the resulting smooth contours and the sharp detail creates the drama that is required. The luminance or brightness values are optimized independently of the color values in this tutorial and the color is reunited with the image in the last step as an optional alternative.

1. Open the project image in Adobe Camera Raw (ACR) and select the Crop Tool. Crop the image to increase the impact of the image and remove any distracting detail from the edges of the image. Move the mouse cursor to a position just outside one of the corner handles of the crop marquee and rotate the marquee counter-clockwise slightly to straighten the image.

2. Only minor adjustments are required to optimize this file in the default settings of the Basic panel. Drag the Fill Light slider to +30 so that we are not clipping any of the shadow tones.

3. Our eyes are normally drawn to the brightest tones in the image (currently the white silk scarf the artist is wearing). Select the Adjustment Brush and slide the exposure setting to −1.00 stop. Adjust the size of the brush and then paint over this scarf so that the beard becomes the dominant highlight. The overlay color in the illustration above shows where I have painted this adjustment. The overlay color or mask is highlighted when you click on the Show Mask checkbox or move your mouse cursor over the pin as is the case in the illustration above. If you need to remove any of the adjustment hold down the Alt/Option key and paint again to erase.

4. We can remove the dandruff on the artist's shoulder using the Spot Removal Tool. Set the Radius to 4 and click on each spot you can see on the shoulder. Zoom in if you need to take a closer look. You can click and move the source point (green circle) if necessary. Click on either the Hand Tool or the Zoom Tool to exit the Spot Removal Tool panel.

5. We can draw the viewer's eye into this image by darkening the background slightly. Only limited Lens Vignetting can be applied to this image because the edges of each side of the image have been cropped away, but we will take whatever we can get in the ACR space. Go to the Lens Corrections tab and take the Amount slider in the Lens Vignetting section down to –80.

Post Crop Vignetting

In Photoshop CS5 (ACR 6) we have new and improved Post Crop vignetting. We can now darken down highlights much more effectively than we could in Photoshop CS4 (ACR 6) now that we have a Highlight Priority option. The Post Crop Vignette has been moved to the new Effects tab. Although the Highlight Priority option is much friendlier to highlights than when using Post Crop Vignetting in CS4, it is not possible to achieve a vignette that does not clip the dark tones of the artist's jacket and infringe on the artist's beard (there is still no option to offset the vignette). When working in the main editing space of Photoshop, there is a risk of banding or stepping the tones when a vignette is applied to a background with a flat even tone or color (as in this image). Working in ACR is much more forgiving, the next few steps attempts to resolve this problem by creating an offset vignette using smart objects. Set the amount back to zero if you have experimented with the Post Crop Vignetting.

6. Open the image as a Smart Object by holding down the Shift key so that you can access the Open Object button (holding down the Shift key will not be necessary if you have already checked the 'Open in Photoshop as Smart Objects' option in the Workflow Options dialog). We will copy this layer and use it to darken the background. Right click the Smart Object layer in the Layers panel and choose New Smart Object via Copy (you will not get this option of you right-click on the thumbnail instead of the layer itself). Double click on the Smart Object copy thumbnail to open the image in Adobe Camera Raw.

7. When the Raw file opens in ACR lower the exposure slider to −1.50 and then click the OK button to change the Raw settings of this new smart object layer.

8. To restrict the darkening to the edges of the file, choose the Rectangular Marquee Tool from the Tools panel, enter 250 px in the Feather field in the Options bar. Click and drag to make a selection of the central portion of the image. Invert the selection so that the edges are selected by going to Select > Inverse. Click on the Add Layer mask at the base of the Layers panel and then press the D key to select the default values for the Foreground and Background. Lower the opacity of this smart object copy layer to fine-tune the process.

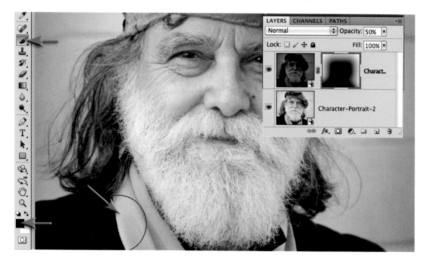

9. Select the Brush Tool in the Tools panel and set the brush hardness to zero and the Opacity to 100%. Press the x key to make Black the foreground color and then paint over the artist's shoulders and beard to ensure the darkening does not effect these parts of the image. If a halo appears over the shoulders switch the foreground and background colors and paint with white to remove the halo.

10. To convert to black and white choose a Black & White adjustment layer from the Adjustments panel. Moving the Reds and Yellows sliders to the left slightly will increase localized contrast in the artist's skin. We could have converted to Black & White in Adobe Camera Raw (Convert to Grayscale) but this would not allow us to feed the color back into the image later in the project.

11. To create the smoother tones in the areas of low contrast, we need to merge the visible pixels to a new layer. Hold down the modifier keys Ctrl + Alt + Shift (PC) or Command + Option + Shift (Mac) and then press the E key. Set the mode of this 'merge visible' layer to Multiply. The image will appear darker (courtesy of the blend mode) until we complete the next three steps. The luminance values will be rectified using two adjustment layers.

Note > You may find it useful to rename the layers as we go in this project so that we can quickly recognize and return to layers later to modify them to optimize the visual appearance of the end-result.

12. To create the softer smooth tones go to Filter > Blur > Gaussian Blur. Choose a Radius value that gives the image smoother tones but also retains depth. A value around 26 pixels suits the project image. Select OK to apply the blur to this layer.

13. From the Adjustments panel choose a Levels adjustment. Clip the adjustment layer to the Merge-Visible layer using the clipping icon at the base of the Adjustments panel. Move the black 'Output Levels' slider to a value of 90 to lighten the darkest tones in the image.

14. Click on the Return to adjustment list icon in the Adjustments panel and then select another Levels adjustment layer. Set the mode of this layer to Screen and then move the white Output Levels slider to 190 to protect the brightest tones from becoming too light.

15. To increase the apparent depth in this image we will accentuate the light and shade using a Dodge & Burn layer. Hold down Alt/Option key and click on the Create a new layer icon in the Layers panel. Name the layer 'Dodge & Burn'. Select Overlay as the mode and check the 'Fill with overlay-neutral color (50% gray) checkbox. Select OK to create the layer.

16. Select the Brush Tool in the Tools panel and set the foreground color to black. Choose a soft-edged brush and lower the opacity to between 10 and 20%. Paint around the edges of the cheeks (over the shaded areas). Paint multiple times, if required, to build up the shadows, which will in turn, increase the apparent depth and volume of the face. Zoom in and work with a smaller brush on the lower eyelids in a similar fashion as you did with the cheeks. The same can be achieved by painting over the shaded portions of the artist's hat.

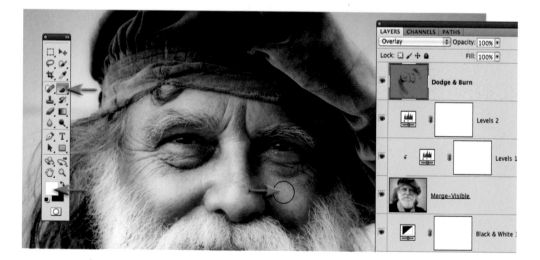

17. Switch the foreground color to white and paint over the highlight areas within the image. Do not paint over the beard as this is already light enough and requires no further modelling.

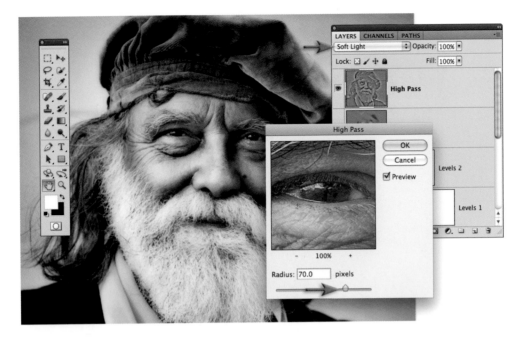

18. The High Pass filter we use in this step will continue the process of increasing localized contrast. Merge the visible pixels to a new layer. Hold down the modifier keys Ctrl + Alt + Shift (PC) or Command + Option + Shift (Mac) and then press the E key. Set the mode of this 'merge visible' layer to Soft Light. Go to Filter > Other > High Pass and then adjust the Radius to a high setting that gives maximum apparent depth to the image. Rename the layer High Pass.

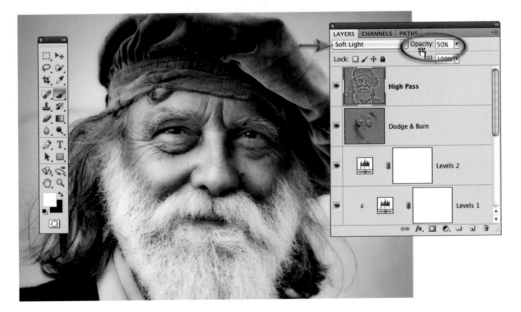

19. If the depth added to this image is too much then simply lower the opacity of the High Pass layer to achieve the desired outcome. In this tutorial I have lowered the opacity to 50%.

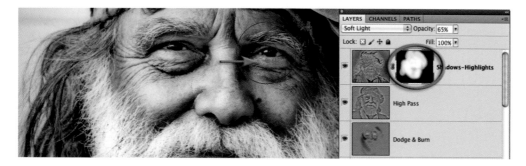

20. This step will increase apparent detail in the image. Merge the Visible elements once again and set the mode of this new layer to Soft Light (as we did in the previous step). Name this layer Shadows-Highlights and then go to Image > Adjustments > Shadows/Highlights. Click on the Show More Options checkbox. Raise the Amount slider in the Shadows and Highlights sections to 100%. Set the Tonal Width in the Shadows and Highlights sections to 50%. Now raise the Midtone Contrast slider in the Adjustments section to raise localized contrast. The effect is likely to be too heavy when applied globally to the whole image but this can be corrected in the next step.

21. If the effect of the Shadows/Highlights adjustment is too strong, lower the opacity of the layer. Use a layer mask to restrict the effect to localized areas of the image. Hold down the Alt/Option key as you click on the 'Add layer mask' icon in the Layers panel to create a black layer mask. Select the Brush Tool and set white as the Foreground color. Paint with a soft-edged brush with the opacity set to around 50% to paint in the adjustment gradually. In this tutorial project the adjustment is restricted to just the face.

22. Even though we have been using the Merge Visible command in this project we are still able to optimize layers at the base of the layers stack if required, and have these changes affect the visual outcome. This is due to the blend modes and layer masks we have been using throughout the project. To darken, and add texture to the vignette, double-click on the Smart Object copy (Character Portrait copy). When the file opens in ACR, go to the Effects tab and increase the Grain amount to 50, the Size to 30 and the Roughness to 50.

23. In the Basic panel lower the Exposure to –2.00 stops and the Brightness to –50. Select OK in the bottom right-hand corner of the ACR dialog to update the changes to the Smart Object in the multi-layered project file. This in turn will darken the vignette.

24. In this step we will apply the final sharpening to the image. Select the top layer in the Layers panel and then Merge the visible pixels to a new layer. Hold down the modifier keys Ctrl + Alt + Shift (PC) or Command + Option + Shift (Mac) and then press the E key. Set the mode of this 'merge visible' layer to Luminosity. Normally we don't need to set a sharpening layer to Luminosity when working with black and white images but in this instance the Luminosity mode will allow us to restore color to the image in the step that follows. In the Unsharp Mask dialog the Amount slider has been raised to 150, the Radius slider reduced to 0.5 and the Threshold slider raised to 5.

25. Select the Black and White adjustment layer in the Layers panel and lower the opacity to restore some color to the image. If you lower the opacity of the Black & White adjustment layer too much, the color may look excessive when combined with the increased contrast and detail. A balance can be achieved where the color and tone sit comfortably together.

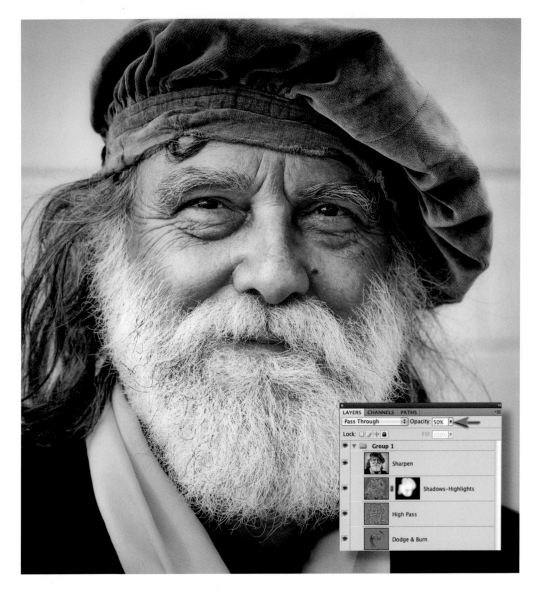

26. It is often very easy to get carried away and inject too much drama with this workflow (I have used multiple techniques to increase depth and detail where only one or two may be required on images that you are working on), so if your image is looking like it has had one too many pokes with the ugly stick try the following. Select the top Sharpen layer and then holding down the Shift key select the Smart Object copy layer. Use the keyboard shortcut Ctrl + G (PC) or Command + G (Mac to group the layers into a layer set. Set the opacity of this layer set to between 50 and 60%. Also try turning off the visibility of the Black and White layer inside the layer set to feed more of the original color back into the file now that the contrast has been lowered.

Lens Blur – Project 4

Most digital cameras achieve greater depth of field (more in focus) at the same aperture when compared to their 35 mm film cousins due to their comparatively small sensor size. Greater depth of field is great in some instances but introduces unwelcome detail and distractions when the attention needs to be firmly fixed on the subject.

Photography by Dorothy Connop

Sometimes when capturing a decisive moment with a camera the most appropriate aperture or shutter speed for the best visual outcome often gets overlooked. Photoshop can, however, come to the rescue and drop a distracting background into smooth out-of-focus colors. A careful selection to isolate the subject from the background and the application of a blur filter usually does the trick. Problems with this technique arise when the resulting image, all too often, looks manipulated rather than realistic. The Gaussian Blur filter will usually require some additional work if the post-production technique is not to become too obvious. A more realistic shallow depth of field effect, however, is created by using the 'Lens Blur filter'.

Lens Blur or Gaussian Blur?

The Gaussian Blur filter has a tendency to 'bleed' strong tonal differences and saturated colors from around your subject into the background fog, making the background in the image look more like a watercolor painting rather than a photographic image. The Lens Blur filter (when used with a mask) introduces none of the bleed that is associated with the Gaussian Blur technique. The filter is extremely sophisticated, allowing you to choose different styles of aperture and control the specular highlights to create a more realistic camera effect.

1. The first step in the process is to isolate the subjects that you would like to keep in sharp focus. The people in this project file cannot be selected quickly using any of the selection tools or by using the channel masking techniques. The Pen Tool was used to create paths around each of the children and the two parents holding hands. The three paths have been retained in the project file to fast-track the process of adjusting the focus. Hold down the Command key (Mac) or the Ctrl key (PC) and click on the Parents path in the Paths panel to load it as a selection.

2. In this step we will clear the background of some distracting elements before we move on to adjusting the focus. Go to the Layers panel and click on the 'Create a new layer' icon to create an empty new layer. Double-click on the layer name and name the layer 'Clone'. From the Select menu choose Inverse so that the background is selected instead of the people. Go to Select > Modify > Feather and choose 1 pixel. From the Tools panel choose the Clone Stamp Tool and in the Options bar choose a soft-edged brush and select the All Layers option. Hold down the Option/Alt key and set the clone source point in the sea to the left of the woman's legs. Proceed to clone out the legs of the child playing in front of the mother.

3. With the Clone Stamp Tool still selected proceed to clone out the man in the ocean just above the father's shoulder and boy on the body board just above the breaking wave on the right side of the image. The preview inside the clone stamp cursor allows you to line up the waves and the soft edge of the brush makes the cloning seamless.

4. When you have finished cleaning up the background go to the Channels panel and click on the 'Save selection as channel' icon at the base of the panel. Go to Select > Deselect and you will now have an Alpha 1 channel which will act as a saved selection and allow us to create a depth map that can be used by the Lens Blur filter.

5. The mask will require further work to create an area of sharp focus in the background for positioning or anchoring the subject realistically in its environment. The subject will need to be planted firmly on an area of ground that is not blurred to prevent the subject from floating above the background. A simple gradient will allow us to anchor the subject and allow the background to fade gradually from focus to out-of-focus. Set the Foreground Color to black and then select the Gradient Tool from the Tools panel. Choose the 'Foreground to Transparent', 'Reflected Gradient' and 'Opacity: 100%' options in the Options bar. Drag the Gradient Tool (while holding down the Shift key to constrain the gradient vertically) from the base of the feet to the bottom of the shorts. The darker areas of this Alpha channel will help retain the focus in this part of the image.

6. We will now add the children to this depth map but as they are a little further away from the camera they will not be as sharp as the parents. Go to the Paths panel and Command or Ctrl + click the Younger Child path to load it as a selection. Go to Select > Modify > Feather and choose a 1-pixel feather.

7. Sample the tone next to the child's feet using the Eyedropper Tool. This tone will become the Foreground color in the Tools panel. Go to Edit > Fill. In the Use menu in the Contents section of the Fill dialog box choose Foreground Color and select OK. The child should be slightly lighter than the parents and match the tone of the gradient at the feet. Go to Select > Deselect to clear the selection.

8. Repeat Steps 6 and 7 using the path of the older child. When filled with the Foreground Color the older child will be a slightly lighter gray than the younger child. The depth map is now complete and the channel is renamed DOF-Map (by double-clicking on the name) so that it can be easily identified later. This depth map simulates the depth of field that would have been created if the image had been captured using an extremely wide aperture. Using a longer initial gradient would give you a greater depth of field in the final result. The plane of focus is falling away from the camera towards the horizon. A subject that stands vertically from this horizontal plane of focus must adopt the focus at that point in the gradient for the depth of field to appear realistic.

9. In the Layers panel stamp the visible elements from the two layers into a new layer. Hold down the Command, Option and Shift keys on a Mac or Ctrl, Alt and Shift keys on a PC and type the letter E. Rename the layer 'Stamp Visible'. Go to Filter > Blur > Lens Blur to open the Lens Blur dialog box.

10. From the 'Depth Map' section of this dialog box choose the DOF-Map. Choose the depth of field required by moving the Radius slider. The Blade Curvature, Rotation, Brightness and Threshold sliders fine-tune the effect. Zoom in to 100% before applying a small amount of noise (1 or 2% Gaussian Monochromatic is usually sufficient) to replicate the noise of the rest of the image. Select OK to apply the Lens Blur and return to the main workspace.

11. If part of the background along the edge of the subject is sharp when it should be blurred then this can be corrected using the Clone Stamp Tool. Create a new layer and name it Repair Edges. Load an appropriate path as a selection. From the Select menu choose Inverse and feather the selection by 1 pixel (Select > Modify > Feather). Expand the selection by 1 pixel also (Select > Modify > Expand). Select the Clone Stamp Tool from the Tools panel and choose the All Layers option from the Sample menu. Hide the selection edges by going to the View > Extras. Hold down the Alt/Option key and take a source point for the Clone Stamp Tool just next to the area to be corrected. Cloning away sharp pixels with blurred pixels will correct any minor errors that may exist. Remember to go to Select > Deselect to remove the hidden active selection before proceeding.

Note > Zoom in to 100% (Actual Pixels) and navigate around the edges. If part of the image that should have been sharp has accidentally been blurred (due to an inaccuracy with the original depth map) then add a layer mask to the Stamp Visible layer and paint with black to reveal the sharp image below.

12. To complete this project we need to correct one minor flaw and add some finishing touches. There is a small amount of pin-cushion distortion in the image that needs correcting. Stamp the Visible layers to another new layer (see Step 9) and name it 'Stamp Visible-Warp'. Go to View > Rulers (Command or Ctrl + R). Drag a guide from the rule onto the horizon line. You will notice the horizon line curls up at each side of the image.

13. Make sure the Stamp Visible-Warp layer is selected. Go to Edit > Transform > Warp. Move your mouse cursor onto one end of the horizon line in the image window and click and drag down slowly until the horizon aligns with the guide. Move your mouse cursor to the other end of the horizon line and repeat the process until the horizon line is straight. Hit the Enter key when you are done to commit the changes.

14. To breathe a little more life into that washed out sky we can add a simple gradient. Click on the 'Create a new layer' icon in the Layers panel to add a new layer named 'Gradient-Sky'. Set the mode to Multiply. Select the Gradient Tool from the Tools panel. Hold down the Alt/Option key and sample some of the dark blue water just below the horizon line. Select the Foreground to Transparent gradient, set to Linear gradient and drag a gradient from the top of the image down the horizon line (hold down the Shift key to constrain the line to a vertical).

15. Hold down the Alt/Option key again and this time sample a color from the sand. Using a Reflected gradient drag a short gradient from a position just below the feet to the edge of the water. Drag a second gradient in the same position if the sand needs darkening further.

16. All that remains to finish the project is to sharpen the image. Click on the top Stamp Visible-Warp layer in the Layers panel (the one that was warped straight). Go to Filter > Convert for Smart Filters. Next go to Filter > Sharpen > Unsharp Mask. Sharpen the image using a generous amount (180 or more) and a small radius setting (between 0.5 and 1.0 pixel). There is no need to sharpen the gradients as there is no detail in this layer that requires sharpening.

17. If the edges around the subject appear too sharp, select the Smart Filters mask thumbnail in the Layers panel, go to the Channels panel and Command or Ctrl + click on your depth map to load it as a selection. Fill the selection with Black (Edit > Fill > Black) and then go to Filter > Other > Minimum and choose a Radius of 3 or 4 pixels to expand the mask and protect the edge from the sharpening filter.

Faux styles – Project 5

Getting tired of pin-sharp, noise-free, character-free images from your 24 Megapixel Pro DSLR? Try this grunge effect to give your images the toy camera aesthetic – think WEIRD – think GRUNGE, think ART!

IMAGE ON DVD

Brooklyn Bridge, New York – before and after.

The Holga is a cheap (US $30) plastic medium format film camera mass-produced in China. Originally manufactured in the early 80s for the home consumption, it has now gained cult status amongst bohemian western photographers who are drawn to the grunge 'art' aesthetic. The camera represents the antithesis of everything that the modern digital camera manufacturers are striving to achieve. If you are looking for edge-to-edge sharpness and color-fidelity then give the Holga a very wide berth. If, however you are looking to create images that are full of 'character', but without the hassle of going back to film, then you may like to look into the wonderful, and weird, world of Holga-style imagery and give this Photoshop workflow a spin (no Holga required).

To see images captured with a real Holga take a look at this Flickr gallery: http://www.flickr.com/photos/microabi

1. Open the JPEG project image from the supporting DVD, or process your own 8 Bits/ Channel starting image from the Raw image supplied. Images produced by the Holga camera are square so grab the Crop Tool from the Tools panel, hold down the Shift key to constrain the crop marquee to a perfect square and drag over the central portion of the start image. Hit the Commit icon or Return/Enter key to get rid of the unwanted pixels.

2. Duplicate the background layer using the keyboard shortcut Ctrl+J (PC) or Command+J (Mac). The background layer will serve as a resource to tone down the final effect in localized areas (if required). The next few steps will start to degrade the sharpness of your image (the Holga camera has a single simple lens element). With Layer 1 selected in the Layers panel go to Filter > Blur > Radial Blur.

3. In the Radial Blur dialog box set the Amount to 3 and then select the Zoom and Best options. Click where you would like to preserve maximum sharpness in the Blur Center control box (to the right of the Zoom and Best options). There is an element of guesswork in this step but sharpness can be restored later in the process. I have selected the region in the lower center (where I estimate the pedestrians to be crossing the bridge in the actual image). Select OK to apply the blur to Layer 1.

4. Go to Filter > Blur > Gaussian Blur. Select a Radius of 1.0 pixel and then select OK to apply the blur to Layer 1. Set the Foreground and Background Colors to their Default setting (either click on the small Black and White box icon in the Tools panel or press the D key on the keyboard). Setting the Foreground and Background colors to their default settings will ensure the next blur filter will have a diffuse glow that is white and not any other color.

5. Go to Filter > Distort > Diffuse Glow. Try setting the Graininess and Glow Amounts to 4 and the Clear Amount to 17 as a starting point. You can increase the Graininess to simulate a high ISO film. Alternatively the grain can be set low in this dialog as we will have more control over how the grain looks if we apply it to a separate layer. Select OK to apply the Diffuse Glow to Layer 1.

6. To create a Grain layer, hold down the Alt key (PC) or Option key (Mac) and click on the Create a new layer icon at the base of the Layers panel. Holding down the Alt/Option key while clicking on the icon will open the New Layer dialog. Name the layer 'Grain', set the mode to Overlay and check the Fill with overlay-neutral color (50% gray) checkbox. Select OK to create the Layer. The effects of the layer will be invisible at this point in time (courtesy of the blend mode) until the grain is added in the next step.

7. Go to Filter > Noise > Add Noise. In the Add Noise dialog set the Amount to 7% for a 12-Megapixel image (adjust it higher or lower if you are using a higher- or lower-resolution image). Choose the Gaussian option and select the Monochromatic checkbox before selecting OK to apply the Noise to the Grain layer. Adjust the opacity of the layer if the noise is too prominent.

8. We will now replicate the dark vignette that is a characteristic of Holga images. Select the Rectangular Marquee Tool and set the Feather to 150-pixels (adjust this higher or lower if you are using a higher- or lower-resolution image). Drag a selection so that the central portion of the image is selected (this will leave a border around the edge of the image that is not selected. Hold down the spacebar as you are making the selection if you need to reposition the selection. From the Select menu choose Inverse and from the Edit menu choose Copy Merged to copy the edge pixels to the clipboard. From the Edit menu choose Paste.

9. The pixels will be pasted to a new layer (Layer 2). At the moment they are identical to the pixels on Layer 1 but when we select the Multiply mode from the Layers panel they can be used to darken down the edges of the image.

10. Another characteristic of the Holga image is the surreal color-palette that is present in many (but not all) Holga images. This is a result of either poor processing or cross processing of the film (cross processing intentionally uses the wrong chemicals for the film stock used). We can replicate this look with just a few Adjustment layers. From the Adjustments panel choose a Levels adjustment layer.

11. Clip the shadow and highlight tones by setting the Black input slider to 30 and the White input slider to 225 (these sliders are located directly underneath the histogram). Select the Blue Channel from the drop-down menu in the Levels dialog and then drag the Output Levels sliders to 64 and 190. The Output Levels sliders are located directly underneath the Input sliders. This action will weaken the blacks, render the whites slightly dull and introduce a color cast in both. Select the Green Channel and set the Output sliders to 40 and 230 to increase this effect. Finally, select the Red channel and drag the central gamma slider (directly underneath the histogram) to the left so that it reads 1.10. Select OK to apply these Levels adjustments. Click on the return to adjustments button.

12. We can alter the color and tone using a Levels adjustment but we will need to use a Hue/Saturation adjustment layer to alter global saturation levels and target specific colors for further attention. Start by raising the Saturation level to +24 in the Master channel. In the red channel Adjust the hue to −10 and raise the saturation to +20. In the Cyan and Blue channels raise the Saturation to +10 for both.

Note > Use these target values as a starting point only. When applying this technique to your own images you may like to try experimenting by raising the saturation levels of key colors within a specific image.

13. To increase the overall contrast you can add another Levels adjustment layer and set the Mode to Overlay. There is no need to make any changes to the levels themselves as the change of blend mode alone will increase the contrast. If the colors become too 'intense' (increased saturation is a by-product of increasing the contrast), either lower the opacity of the Hue/Saturation layer below or change the mode of this second Levels adjustment layer to Soft Light. If this contrast adjustment layer compromises shadow detail, raise the Levels Output slider to a value of approximately +25.

14. Many aspects of the final result can be fine-tuned by going back to the individual layers and adjusting either the settings or the opacity. Paint with black as the foreground color into any of the adjustment layer masks to reduce the effects in a localized region of the image. Add a layer mask to Layer 1 and paint with black to restore small amounts of detail for important parts of the subject matter.

15. Some Holga images 'suffer' (or are 'blessed with' – depending how you look at it) from serious edge clipping and/or light leaks. The corner clipping can be unevenly distributed and more severe than your typical vignette. The corner clipping can be replicated by first making another edge selection using the Rectangular Marquee Tool with a 150-pixel feather as we did in Step 8. Choose Inverse from the Select menu.

16. Go to Select > Transform Selection. Zoom out so that you can see the corner handles of the Transform bounding box. Hold down the Ctrl key (PC) or Command key (Mac) and drag two of the four corner handles out in a diagonal direction. Commit the transformation by hitting the Return/Enter key.

17. Click on the Create a new layer icon in the Layers panel and then go to Edit > Fill and choose Black as the contents before selecting OK. Lower the opacity of the layer depending on how severe or subtle you want the effect to appear.

18. Light leaks in Holga camera's appear as light orange patches on some frames (some Holga camera owners use black tape around the film loading area of the camera in an attempt to minimize this problem. These light leaks (if required) can be simulated by adding a new empty layer and setting the mode to Screen. Go to Select > Deselect. Click on the Foreground color swatch in the Tools panel to open the Color Picker. Select an orange color (around Hue 35°) and lower opacity to between 65 and 70%. Select OK and then select the Gradient Tool in the Tools panel. Choose the Foreground to Transparent gradient and the Linear Gradient options in the options bar and then drag a diagonal gradient across one of the corners of the image. Lower the opacity of the layer if you need more subtlety – although to be honest, subtlety is not the name of the game here.

Surface Blur – Project 6

The craft of professional skin retouching is the ability to render perfect skin without giving your model the appearance of a plastic-fantastic shop window mannequin. A 12-megapixel DSLR with a professional grade lens at point blank range is a very cruel combination for showing every minor imperfection in the skin's surface.

Image by Shane Monopoli of Exclusive Photography

The technique in this tutorial can be used at full throttle to render the skin suitable for use in a skin care advertisement, or toned down a little to return the skin to something approaching normal (rather than how the camera lens captured it).

Ozgurdonmaz (www.iStockphoto.com – image number 4875147)

Adjustments in Adobe Camera Raw

Many of the basic image adjustments carried out in the main editing space can now be performed much faster in Adobe Camera Raw (ACR). In Adobe Camera Raw 5 we now have the option to use a 'Negative Clarity' adjustment. This is useful to soften and suppress detail and texture. In the example above the Clarity slider has been dropped to −50 to illustrate how the adjustment can be used to reduce the excessive detail in the model's skin. Negative Clarity can also be painted with the Adjustment Brush to avoid haloes around high-contrast edges.

Angelika Stern (www.iStockphoto.com – image number 4244581)

Aldra (www.iStockphoto.com – image number 919547)

The Adjustment Brush can be accessed from the Tools bar and can be programmed to apply multiple adjustments at the same time, e.g. it can lighten the whites of the eyes and the teeth at the same time as lowering the saturation so that eyes look clean and bright (rather than dark and bloodshot) and teeth look white rather than yellow. The Adjustment Brush can also be used to quickly add depth and detail to eyelashes and eyebrows by using a positive clarity together with some sharpening. The adjustments that follow in this project are best carried out in the main editing space.

1. Open the Surface-Blur Raw file and create a tighter crop for this image. Select either the Hand Tool or the Zoom Tool to apply this crop. Select the White Balance Tool and click on the neutral background tone to remove the color cast present in this image.

2. Create a slightly warmer skin tone for this image by raising the Temperature to 4500 and lowering the Tint to –8. Optimize the color and tonality of this image by raising the Fill Light slider to +10 and the Brightness slider to +60. Lower the Vibrance slider to –10 to keep the saturation levels in check.

3. Select the Graduated Filter option and set the Exposure setting to +0.60. Drag a gradient upward from the base of the image to just above the chin to balance the exposure and lighten the skin tones in this area. Select the Hand Tool or the Zoom Tool to return to the Basic tab.

4. Lower the Exposure slider to –0.25 to remove any highlight clipping that resulted from the Gradient Filter. Open the image into the main editing space as a Smart Object (set this option in the Workflows Panel or hold down the Shift key to access the Open Object button).

5. Start the process of smoothing the skin by going to Filter > Blur > Surface Blur. This filter, unlike the Gaussian Blur filter, has a 'Threshold' slider that, if used correctly, will leave edges crisp and sharp while blurring the surfaces inside the edges. This will ensure there are no nasty haloes around the edges of your subject as a result of the blurring process.

6. It is important to get the balance right between the Radius and the Threshold slider settings for each and every image (there is no one 'perfect recipe' that suits every image). To get a feel for what these two sliders do, set them both to a value between 20 and 25. Now move the Radius slider lower until you detect the surface tone becoming 'mottled' or 'blotchy' and then move it higher again until the surface appears very smooth. Finding the minimum radius that renders the surface smooth is your goal here. I have used a Radius of 40 with this project image.

7. Now drag the Threshold slider higher until you see haloes appear around the edges of your subject. Back the slider off to a point where all, or most, of the haloes disappear. If you continue to move the slider lower, after the haloes have disappeared, you will start to reintroduce the finer detail that was removed by the Radius slider. A Threshold setting of 70 has been used with this project image. Try to make the surface of the brow as smooth as possible at this stage as we will reintroduce the texture of the skin in a later step.

8. Select OK to apply the Surface Blur filter. Select the Smart Filters layer mask in the Layers panel. Use the keyboard shortcut Alt + Backspace (PC) or Option + Delete (Mac) to fill the layer mask with black to conceal the surface blur. Select white as the foreground color in the Tools panel (press the x key) and then choose a soft-edged brush. Set the brush opacity to 50–80% in the Options bar. Make sure the layer mask is selected and then paint to reveal the blur in the areas of the skin only. Paint a second time to reveal additional softening where needed. Switch the foreground to Black and reduce the size of the brush to restore any detail that may have been affected by the Surface Blur, e.g. the eyebrows.

Note > It is possible to reduce the effect of this smart filter (if you think the surface blur is excessive) by double-clicking on the Smart Filter blending Options icon and reducing the Opacity in the Blending Options dialog.

9. In this step we will eliminate minor imperfections in the skin that the Surface Blur filter could not smooth over. Go to Select > All and then Edit > Copy Merged and then Edit Paste to merge the visible pixels to a new layer. Go to Filter > Noise > Dust & Scratches and set the Threshold slider to 0. Raise the Radius slider just enough to remove the imperfections from the nose (between 5 and 10 pixels). Don't worry about the lack of texture at this point in time as we will be adjusting the Threshold slider in the next step.

10. Raise the Threshold slider to reintroduce surface texture but stop just short of the point where the larger skin imperfections start to reappear. Select OK to apply the filter. Then hold down the Alt/Option key and click on the 'Add layer mask' icon at the base of the Layers panel to conceal the effects of this layer.

Note > Do not attempt to remove large skin imperfections with the Dust & Scratches filter. These are best removed using the Healing Brush Tool later.

11. Select the Brush Tool and white as the foreground color in the Tools panel and set the Opacity to 70% in the Options bar. Zoom in to 200%, be sure the layer mask is selected and paint to remove any imperfections from the nose and around the eyes. Hold down the Spacebar and click and drag to move the image in the image window so that you can navigate around the surface of the skin to look for additional imperfections. Paint multiple times if required. The skin should now be rendered smooth but with realistic surface texture and free from all minor imperfections. Rename the layer 'Dust & Scratches' by double-clicking on the name of the layer.

12. To remove larger imperfections click on the Create a new layer icon in the Layers panel. Select the Healing Brush Tool from the Tools panel (behind the Spot Healing Brush) and select All Layers from the Sample menu in the Options bar. Hold down the Alt/Option key and click the mouse button to select an area of good skin texture close to the imperfection you wish to remove. Adjust the size of the brush so that it is just bigger than the skin imperfection, move your mouse cursor over the defect and then click once again to heal the area. Rename the layer 'Heal' by double-clicking on the name of the layer. Renaming all the layers as we go will help us quickly identify what each is contributing to the overall effect.

Note > If you work close to an area that is very different in tone or color you will need to make the brush harder so that the heal area does not get contaminated with the adjacent color or tone. If the heal area continues to become contaminated try making a selection that excludes the nearby color or tone and try again or use the Lighten and Darken painting techniques that follow.

13. New for Photoshop CS5 is the Content-Aware option for the Spot Healing Brush. This feature may prove useful for removing long wrinkles. There is no need to select a source point when using the Spot Healing Brush as this is done automatically as you paint. An alternative to painting freehand is to click once at the start of the wrinkle, then hold down the shift key and click again at the end of the wrinkle. Photoshop will draw a heal stroke between the two points.

Note > These healing actions will remove blemishes and wrinkles completely. To restore some reality to the face (a face without any wrinkles looks unnatural) it is recommended that you lower the opacity of this Heal layer slightly.

14. Click on the Create a new layer icon and set the mode to Darken. Select the Eyedropper Tool and set the Sample Size to 5 by 5 average and select All Layers from the Sample menu in the Options bar. Click your mouse button over an area of skin that is representative of the skin color that is neither in the shaded nor in the highlight areas of the face to take a sample.

Note > Once these Eyedropper settings have been established you can take different color samples when working with the Brush Tool without having to select the Eyedropper Tool first.

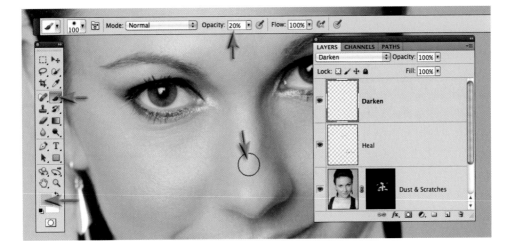

15. This step is useful to reduce excessive shine (skin with excessive amounts of shine will appear oily). Select the Brush Tool in the Tools panel and set the opacity to 20% in the Options bar. Set the brush Hardness to zero so that we will not see the edges of the brush strokes as we paint. Limit the painting to one or two strokes in the same region only, otherwise the skin will appear as if it has been airbrushed and we will lose the skin texture.

Note > The darken blend mode will protect dark areas such as the hair, eyebrows and eyelashes from the painting action as these areas will be darker than the paint color you are working with. You will, however have to be careful when working close to areas such as the whites of the eyes that are lighter than the paint color.

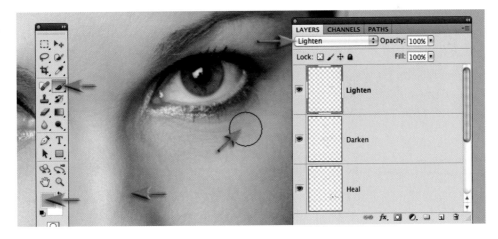

16. Create another empty layer and this time set the mode to Lighten. This time we will lighten areas that are too dark. Hold down the Alt/Option key and click an area of skin that is adjacent to a dark crease or wrinkle under the eye. Then paint one or two strokes underneath each eye to lighten these areas. The bridge of the nose can also be straightened in this fashion by reducing the impact of the darker shadow that invades the central highlight. Take a sample of the highlight (Option/Alt + Click) above this shadow and then paint one or two strokes as before. Other areas that can be worked on are the shadows underneath the lower lip.

17. The line of the lower lip is not even towards the center. To correct this make a selection just to the right hand side of this area. Use the Lasso Tool with 5 pixels entered in the Feather field in the Options bar. Select Copy Merged from the Edit menu to float this selection and then choose Paste from the Edit menu to paste this selection to a new layer and name it Lip Patch. Use the Keyboard shortcut Ctrl + T (PC) or Command + T (Mac) to move and transform this selection. Click inside the Free Transform bounding box and drag the pixels to the left. Move your cursor to a position just outside one of the corner handles of the Free Transform bounding box so that you can rotate and align the pixels. Use the arrow keys on the keyboard to nudge the patch into position. Select the Return/Enter key to apply the transformation. Add a layer mask and paint with black if some of the peripheral colors of the patch do not match. Once this adjustment is complete hold down the Shift key and select the Heal layer in the layers panel so that the Heal, Darken, Lighten and Lip Patch layers are all selected. Use the keyboard shortcut Ctrl + G (PC) or Command + G (Mac) to group these layers together (good housekeeping for projects where lots of layers are used). Rename this group of layers 'Paint & Patch'.

18. In this step we will brighten the whites of the eyes. Select a Curves adjustment layer from the Adjustments panel and select the targeted adjustment tool icon in the upper left-hand corner of the Curves dialog box (the one that looks like a scrubby slider icon). Click once on the black eyelashes and a second time on the iris of the eye to set adjustment points. These adjustment points will anchor these tones when we adjust the whites of the eye. Move your mouse cursor over the white of the eye and click and drag upwards (do not let go of the mouse button as you drag) to raise the brightness of the whites of the eye. Set the blending mode of the adjustment layer to Luminosity to remove the shift in color saturation that this curve has created.

19. In the Masks panel select the Invert option to fill the layer mask with black. Make sure you still have white as the foreground color and select the Brush Tool in the Tools panel. Set the Opacity to 50% in the Options bar and then paint over the eye to lighten the white of the eye. If you accidentally brush over the eyelashes or eyeliner you will probably not see any change to these darker tones as the darker tones have been locked down by the initial adjustment points you entered into the Curves dialog.

Note > Zoom out to review if the eyes are now too bright (a common mistake) and drop opacity of the Curves adjustment layer if required.

20. In this step we will reduce any redness in the eyes. Select a Hue/Saturation adjustment from the Adjustments panel. Lower the saturation to −100 and then invert the layer mask as we did in the last step. Zoom in and paint carefully in the whites of the eyes with a hard-edged brush so that you do not accidentally paint over the iris or eyelids of each eye. If any blood vessels are still obvious in each eye you can return to the 'Lighten' layer (in the Paint and Scratch Group) to lighten these further (sample a bright white next to the blood vessel and paint with the Brush Tool set to a low opacity). Rename this adjustment layer 'Desaturate Whites'.

21. In this step we can increase the vibrancy of the iris in each eye and also the lips. Select a Vibrance adjustment layer from the Adjustments panel and then set the Vibrance to +100 and invert the mask as before. Paint over each eye and the lips with a soft-edged brush set at 50% opacity. Paint multiple times to increase the effect if required.

22. Skin can be rendered a little warmer by adding a Warming Filter from the Adjustments panel. Lower the density slider to 10–15%. This will, however, impact on the neutral gray background as the effects of this adjustment, and the white balance correction we did in Adobe Camera Raw, are global adjustments. We could invert the mask and paint with white over the skin to make this a localized adjustment, but to render the background truly neutral we will have to desaturate these tones.

23. Create a Hue/Saturation adjustment layer. Use the targeted adjustment tool and then click and drag left on the background to desaturate the target color only. Invert the mask and then paint the background area with a large soft-edged brush set to 100% opacity to render the background completely neutral. Select all of the adjustment layers in the layers panel and then use the keyboard shortcut Ctrl + G (PC) or Command + G (Mac) to place them all in a group. Rename this group 'Adjustments'.

24. With the project nearly complete you may need to review the file and make subtle adjustments where required, e.g. adjusting opacity of individual layers or layer groups etc. In this project we have used quite a heavy Radius in the Surface Blur filter to render the forehead contour smooth. This can give the forehead an unnatural airbrushed appearance. We can add texture to this area of the image with a texture layer that simulates skin. Hold down the Alt/Option key and click on the Create a new layer icon in the Layers panel. Name the layer 'Add texture' set the mode to Overlay and select the Fill with Overlay-neutral color (50% gray) option. Select OK to create the layer. The layer will not, of course, have any texture until we add it.

25. Start by going to Filter > Noise > Add Noise. For this file we will choose 20 as the Amount and then select the 'Uniform' and 'Monochromatic' options. The Amount will vary from file to file, depending on resolution and the coarseness of the skin texture you require. After applying the Noise to the layer go to Filter > Blur > Gaussian Blur and select a radius of 2 pixels. Go to Filter > Stylize > Emboss and set the height to 3 pixels and the Amount to 100%.

Note > You can create a pattern of this texture to fast-track this step in the future. Switch the blend mode of the layer back to Normal and then go to Edit > Define Pattern. You will then be able to fill these gray layers with this texture quickly in the future.

26. Hold down the Alt/Option key and click the Add layer mask option in the Layers panel to add a black layer mask to this layer. Select the Brush Tool and with a large soft-edge brush set to 50% opacity paint into the layer mask to reveal texture in areas of the skin that appear too smooth. If you overdo the texture just lower the opacity of the layer slightly until you strike an effective balance.

27. To finish the project we need to Sharpen the image for the intended output device. The problem with sharpening the base layer (the Surface-Blur smart object) is that the layer mask that accompanies the smart filter has already been optimized for the Surface Blur we applied in the early stages of this project. We will need to obtain a clean layer mask that is dedicated to the Sharpen filter if we want to sharpen the eyes only. This can be achieved by going to Layer > Smart Objects > Convert to Smart Object. This may sound a little strange as the layer is already a Smart Object but this action will place the original smart object inside another smart object and give us the option to apply a new smart filter with a new layer mask.

28. Go to Filter > Sharpen > Smart Sharpen and apply sharpening to make the eyes appear crisp. Select OK to apply the sharpening. Select the Layer mask on the smart filter layer and then invert the mask (Amount 180 and Radius 0.5). Use the keyboard shortcut Ctrl + I (PC) or Command + I (Mac) or hit the Invert button in the Masks panel. Paint with a soft-edged brush to reveal sharpness in the eyes.

29. In some instances you may want to apply additional Gaussian softening to the Surface Blur techniques, in order to achieve a romantic or dreamy mood. This Gaussian blur will, unlike the Surface Blur filter, bleed tones beyond the edges of the subject matter. To try this, load the 'Blur-STT' action from the supporting DVD (double-click the action to load it). Before playing the action, merge the visible pixels to a new layer by holding down the modifier keys Ctrl + Alt + Shift (PC) or Command + Option + Shift (Mac) and then press the E key. Place all of the layers that are created using this action in a group and lower the opacity of the group to see how this technique can interact with the Surface Blur technique used in this project.

Before and after – Skin should still hold surface texture when examined closely.

Photograph by Jennifer Stephens

Pixel surgery

The Liquify filter can reshape facial features, if this does not present an ethical dilemma for the retoucher or model. The various tools in the Liquify filter dialog box can be used to modify the shape or size of the sitter's features. The Pucker Tool and Bloat Tool can be used to contract or expand various features, e.g. grow eyes or lips and shrink noses. Perhaps the most useful of the Liquify tools, however, is the Shift Pixels Tool. This tool can be used to move pixels to the left when stroking down and to the right when stroking up. This tool is ideal for trimming off unsightly fat or reshaping features. In the illustration the brush pressure is dropped to 25%. The side of the face and the top of the lips have been frozen using the Freeze Mask Tool so that the side of the face and lips are not moved along with the nose. If things start to get ugly just remember the keyboard shortcut Ctrl/Command + Z (undo)!

Note > It is important to exercise great restraint when using the Liquify filter, as the face can quickly become a cartoon caricature of itself when taken too far. The filter also softens detail that becomes obvious when overdone.

457

Motion Blur and Radial Blur (spin)

We have looked at Gaussian Blur, Surface Blur and Motion Blur in the preceding projects. The Motion Blur and Radial Blur filters help to extend the creative possibilities. The Motion Blur rather than the Radial Blur filter dominates the effect in the image above. The Radial Blur filter is, however, used to spin the wheels. When the wheels appear as an ellipse the following technique must be used to ensure a quality result.

To get the best result from the Radial Blur filter we must present the wheel on the same plane to the one in which the filter works, i.e. front on. Make a selection with the Circular Marquee Tool using a small amount of feather. Copy the wheel and paste it into a new layer. Use the Free Transform command and drag the side handle of the bounding box until the wheel appears as a circle instead of an ellipse. From the Blur group of Filters choose the Radial Blur filter. When you have applied the filter choose the Transform command again and return the wheel to its original elliptical shape. You can then leave this as a separate layer or merge down.

iStock_000001143384 (Endless Highway 2 by ra-photos)
iStock_000001300100 (BMW 318i by felixR)

Radial Blur (zoom)

When the movement is towards the camera the illusion of movement can be created by using the Radial Blur filter instead of the Motion Blur filter. To reduce the effects of the blur in the distance the filter can first be applied to a duplicate layer and this duplicate layer can then be grouped with an adjustment layer that contains a radial gradient. The sky was also masked using a linear gradient in Multiply mode.

The car in this illustration came from a separate image and was masked using the techniques outlined in the chapter Montage Projects in this book. The original shadow was preserved using the techniques outlined in the Retouching Projects chapter.

Smooth tone and tonal mapping – Project 7

In commercial photography the post-production treatment is discussed early in the pitch to the agency or client. One of the cutting-edge treatments in commercial photography, that is all the rage at the moment, is where maximum detail and surface texture are expanded along with midtone contrast. The final effect is one where the image seems to be part photograph/part illustration. Take a look at http://www.davehillphoto.com to get an idea of how this treatment is being applied by one popular photographer in the USA. This treatment can now be created in Photoshop CS5 using an adjustment feature (go to Image > Adjustments > HDR Toning) or by adjustment features that have been around for a while.

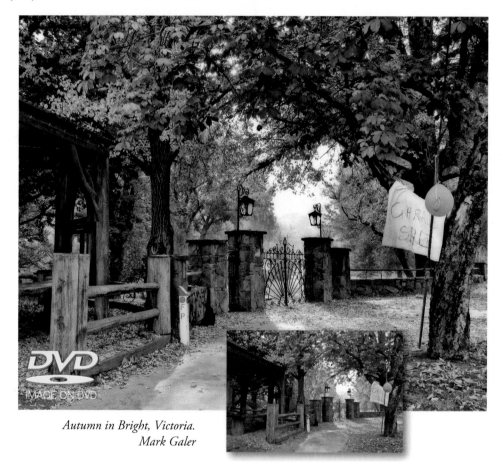

Autumn in Bright, Victoria.
Mark Galer

The treatment works best when there is directional light falling across the subject. Use either low directional sunlight or introduce photographic lights to create the optimal effect. In this project we will take a brief look at the HDR Toning adjustment that is new to CS5 and then combine two other techniques in order to create this signature style. The first technique is designed to smooth the overall tones of the image while the second exaggerates midtone contrast and creates greater depth within the finished image. The project culminates with localized saturation control, a vignette and sharpening to create a look that is part photographic and part illustration.

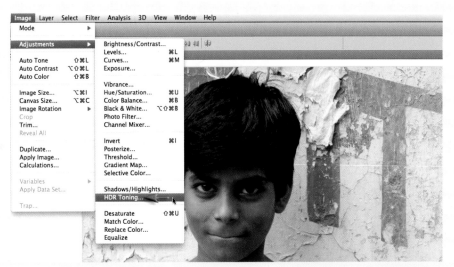

Photograph by Dorothy Connop

HDR Toning

The HDR Toning adjustment only works on a flattened or single layer image file. The dialog that opens is very similar to the one that is used by the new Merge to HDR Pro dialog. It is recommended that you first duplicate your file given that you cannot duplicate the layer (Image > Duplicate) before applying the HDR Toning adjustment. This will allow you to make a composite file of the before and after versions after the adjustment has been applied so that you can apply the treatment to localized areas of the image to 'tone down' the treatment by dropping the opacity of the treated layer.

Go to Image > Adjustments > HDR Toning. Most of the sliders in this dialog are designed for merging multiple exposures, so don't have to be moved. Drag the Detail slider to the right to increase surface texture and then adjust the Radius and Strength sliders to give the image more 'volume'. These last two sliders will create halos around the high contrast edges but if unadjusted the image will look very flat. As the detail is raised the saturation of the colors will also increase, so you may need to lower the Vibrance or Saturation before selecting OK.

After applying the HDR Toning you can combine the before and after versions to create a composite file. In the Layer panel drag the background thumbnail into the image preview of your duplicate file.

Adjust the opacity of the treated layer to decrease the overall effect if required. Click the Add layer mask icon at the base of the Layers panel, select the Brush from the Tools panel and set the Foreground color to black. Set the brush hardness to 0% and lower the opacity of the brush in the Options bar. Paint over any areas where you need to tone down the effect further and then add an adjustment layer to fine tune the overall effect.

Tonal Mapping using Shadows/Highlights

1. Open the .dng project image and protect the highlight tones in Adobe Camera Raw. The Raw file on the DVD has had the exposure of the brightest highlights lowered using both the Adjustments Brush and the Recovery slider (see Raw Processing) and the Brightness slider has been raised to increase the luminance of the midtone values.

2. In the next three steps we will create some smooth tones before we expand the midtone contrast and surface texture. Start by duplicating the background layer by dragging it to the 'Create a new layer' icon in the Layers panel. Set the mode to Multiply. Next, go to Filter > Blur > Gaussian Blur. Use a Radius of around 15 pixels for high resolution images (10 megapixels and over).

3. From the Adjustments panel choose a Levels adjustment and click on the 'clip to layer' icon at the base of the Adjustments panel. Raise the Output slider to a value of around 90 Levels to protect the shadows from becoming too dark.

4. Return to the Adjustments list and create a second Levels adjustment and name the layer 'screen'. Do NOT clip this to the previous Levels adjustment as we need to lighten all tones (not just the ones on the background copy layer). Set the layer mode to Screen and drag the highlight slider to the left to a value of around 165 to protect the brightest highlights in the image.

Note > The first adjustment layer is designed to preserve the shadow detail and the second adjustment layer (the one set to Screen mode) controls the highlight brightness. Experiment with adjusting these sliders to achieve the correct balance using different images.

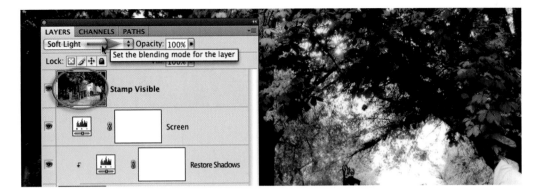

5. Rename the first Levels adjustment layer 'Restore Shadows' and the second adjustment layer 'Screen'. Hold down the Ctrl, Alt and Shift keys on a PC or Command, Option and Shift keys on a Mac and press the letter E to stamp the visible layers to a new layer (name the layer Stamp Visible). Set the layer mode to Soft Light and then desaturate the color from the layer using the keyboard shortcut (Command + Shift + U on a Mac or Ctrl + Shift + U on a PC).

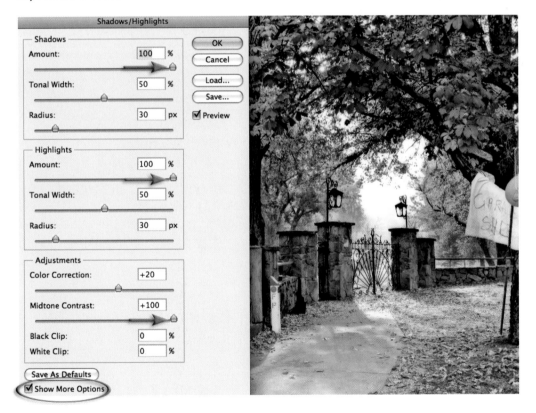

6. With the desaturated layer selected, go to Image > Adjustments > Shadows/Highlights and click on the Show More Options checkbox to expand the dialog box. Set the Amount for the Shadows, Highlights and Midtone Contrast to +100. Set the Tonal Width for the Shadows and the Highlights to +50 and then select OK to apply the changes.

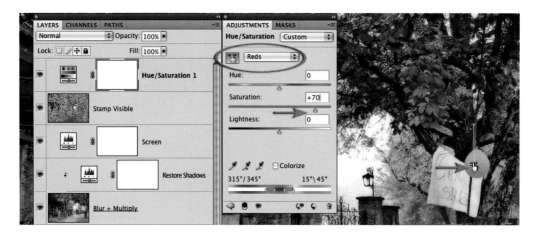

7. In this step we will selectively target just a few colors to remain fully saturated while the others can be subdued. From the Adjustments panel select a Hue/Saturation adjustment. Lower the overall saturation to −20 and then click on the targeted adjustment tool and click on the balloon and drag to the right to increase the saturation of the Reds to around +70. The targeted adjustment tool will automatically target the reds when you click on the balloon.

8. You may need to check that you still have a good spread of tones before signing off on the project. In the illustration above I have painted with black into the layer mask of the Screen layer to ensure those very bright highlights are not clipped to white. Finally the base layer is converted for Smart Filters and an Unsharp Mask is applied using the approximate settings of 180 for the Amount, 0.5 for the Radius and 3 for the Threshold.

High Dynamic Range (HDR) – Project 8

Contrary to popular opinion – what you see is not what you always get. You may be able to see the detail in those dark shadows and bright highlights when the sun is shining – but can your CCD or CMOS sensor? Contrast in a scene is often a photographer's worst enemy. Contrast is a sneak thief that steals away the detail in the highlights or shadows (sometimes both). A wedding photographer will deal with the problem by using fill flash to lower the subject contrast; commercial photographers diffuse their own light source or use additional fill lighting and check for missing detail using the 'Histogram'.

St Peter bridge over the Adige River, Verona. Italy. Mark Galer

Landscape photographers, however, have drawn the short straw when it comes to solving the contrast problem. For the landscape photographer there is no 'quick fix'. A reflector that can fill the shadows of the Grand Canyon has yet to be made and diffusing the sun's light is only going to happen if the clouds are prepared to play ball.

Note > The dynamic range of camera sensors and film cannot compete with the dynamic range of human vision so high contrast has always been a problem for photographers. When the Subject Brightness Range (SBR) exceeds the Dynamic Range (DR) of the sensor, the excessive contrast can result in a loss of detail in the highlights and/or shadows. HDR photography uses techniques to resolve this problem and/or enhance detail throughout the contrast range of the image.

Ansel Adams (the famous landscape photographer) developed 'The Zone System' to deal with the high-contrast vistas he encountered in California. By careful exposure and processing he found he could extend the film's ability to record high-contrast landscapes and create a black and white print with full detail. Unlike film, however, the latitude of a digital imaging sensor (its ability to record a subject brightness range) is fixed. In this respect the sensor is a straitjacket for our aims to create tonally rich images when the sun is shining – or is it? Here is a post-production 'tone system' that will enrich you and your images.

Note > To exploit the full dynamic range that your image sensor is capable of, it is recommended that you capture in Raw mode. JPEG processing in-camera may clip the shadow and highlight detail (see Adobe Camera Raw).

If we can't fit all the goodies in one exposure, then we'll just have to take two or more. The idea is to montage, or merge, the best of both worlds (the light and dark side of the camera's not quite all seeing eye). To make the post-production easier we need to take a little care in the pre-production. We need to 'bracket' five exposures. Capture an image using the meter-indicated exposure (MIE) from the camera and then take two shots underexposing by first one stop, then two stops and repeat the process overexposing by one stop and then two stops from the MIE. Two stops either side of the meter-indicated exposure should cover most high-contrast situations. Using a tripod helps the process but is not essential.

Note > If you intend to use the new 'Automate > Merge to HDR Pro' (High Dynamic Range) feature Adobe recommends that you use the shutter speed rather than the aperture to bracket the exposures. This will ensure the depth of field is consistent between the exposures.

Bracketing exposures

If you use a tripod (you do not want to trust to Auto Aligning the images) you have the option of setting your camera to 'auto bracket exposure mode'. This means that you don't have to touch the camera between exposures, thereby ensuring the exposures can be exactly aligned with the minimum of fuss. Use a cable release or the camera's timer to allow any camera vibration to settle. The only other movement to be aware of is something beyond your control. If there is a gale blowing (or even a moderate gust) you are not going to get the leaves on the trees to align perfectly in post-production. This also goes for fast-moving clouds and anything else that is likely to be zooming around in the fraction of a second between the first and second exposures. There is now a Remove Ghosts option in the new Merge to HDR Pro feature that may work in some instances to reduce or eliminate ghosts from moving people or objects.

1. Open the five Raw project files in Adobe Camera Raw (ACR) by holding down the Shift key as you select the range of images. The first image was captured using the Meter Indicated Exposure user the Aperture Priority exposure mode. A further four exposures were captured during the bracketing burst. The images for this project were all captured hand-held. The aim of opening these files in ACR is so that we can optimize the images prior to merging them.

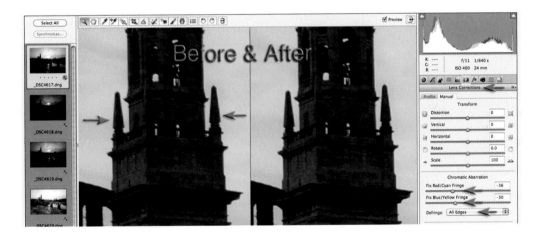

2. Zoom in to 200% and use the Hand Tool to locate the bell tower in the preview window. No Auto lens correction was available for the lens used to capture the project images at the time of writing this book (a Nikon 24mm f/2.8 lens) so the chromatic aberration may have to be fixed manaully. Go to the Lens Corrections tab and in the Chromatic Aberration section, in the Manual tab in ACR 6.1 and later, move the Fix Red/Cyan Fringe and Fix Blue/Yellow Fringe sliders to the left to reduce the chromatic aberration. Holding down the Alt/Option key as you move each of the sliders will switch the preview to show you only those colors that each slider can fix (for those users who may have trouble recognizing Blue from Cyan). Selecting the All Edges option from the Defringe drop-down menu may also help to clean up the edges of this file.

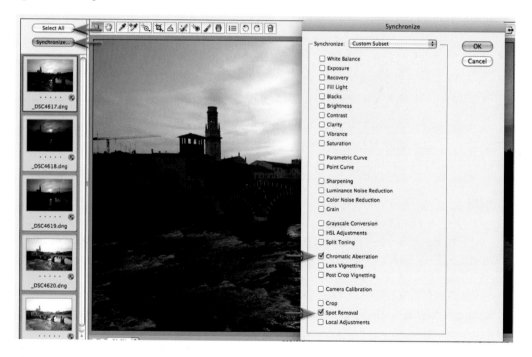

3. Select the Spot Removal Tool, raise the Radius slider to 5 and click on a couple of blemishes that appear in the sky to the left of the bell tower. Click on the Hand Tool to exit the Spot Removal panel.

4. Click the Select All button in the top left-hand corner of the ACR dialog and then click the Synchronize button. In the Synchronize dialog choose Lens Corrections from the drop-down Synchronize menu and then check the Spot Removal checkbox before selecting OK. Click the Done button in the bottom right-hand corner of the ACR dialog to commit these settings to the Raw files and close the ACR dialog.

5. Go to File > Automate > Merge to HDR Pro. From the dialog that opens click the Browse button and locate the same five files that you just finished optimizing in ACR. Make sure the Attempt to Automatically Align Source Images is checked and then select OK to start the HDR processing. The process may take some time, so be prepared to wait a while.

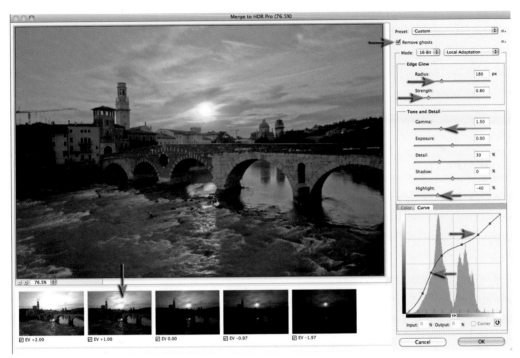

6. The five files will appear in the Merge to HDR Pro dialog along with a large preview of the merged version. This preview will appear a little flat until we optimize the settings using the sliders and the tone curve to the right of the image preview. Increase the brightness by moving the Gamma slider to the left. To increase the contrast of the file we need to click on the Curve tab in the bottom right-hand corner of the dialog. To protect the highlights from the contrast adjustment click two points on the straight diagonal line towards the top right-hand corner of the curve. Increase the steepness of the curve through the shadow section of the histogram and flatten the curve off as it approaches the midtones. Check the Remove Ghosts option so that the ghosts are removed from the canoeists on the river (click on a different thumbnail if you need Photoshop to select alternate detail). Set the Mode to 16 Bit and raise the Radius slider to 180 pixels and the Strength slider to 0.80 in the Edge Glow section. This action will add depth to the file. Increase the vibrance of the colors using the slider in the Color tab. It is recommended to save all of these settings as a Preset before selecting OK. This will ensure that you can return to these settings at a later date and fine-tune the process a second time if required. The Preset used in this project is available from the supporting DVD in the ESP_Presets folder.

7. This step will darken the sky to balance the overall exposure. Click the Create a new layer icon at the base of the Layers panel and set the mode to Soft Light. Select the Gradient Tool from the Tools panel and choose the Neutral Density gradient from the Gradient Presets. Select the Linear Gradient option and set the Opacity to 100%. Drag a gradient from the top of the image to a position just below the setting sun in order to darken the sky. Hold down the Shift key as you drag to constrain the gradient to a perfect vertical.

8. This step will increase midtone contrast while protecting the darkest shadows and brightest highlights. From the Adjustment panel choose a Levels adjustment and set the mode to Soft Light (one of the contrast blend modes). Drag the black Output Levels slider to a value of 80 and the white Output Levels slider to a value of 200.

9. To increase shadow detail we can use the Shadows/Highlights adjustment feature as a smart filter. Merge the visible elements of this project to a new layer. Hold down the modifier keys Ctrl + Alt + Shift (PC) or Command + Option + Shift (Mac) and then press the E key. From the Filter menu choose Convert for Smart Filters and then go to Image > Adjustments > Shadows/Highlights. Check the Show More Options checkbox and then set the amount to 50% and the Tonal Width to 25% in the Shadows section of the dialog. Select OK to apply this adjustment. As this will be applied as a smart filter we have the option to return to the Shadows/Highlights adjustment dialog at any time to optimize the settings.

10. Go to the Adjustments panel and choose a Brightness/Contrast adjustment layer in order to complete the tonal adjustments. Raise the Brightness slider to +40 and the Contrast slider to +10. Select the Merge Visible layer that you converted to a Smart Object and apply sharpening to this layer to complete the project.

HDR – problems and solutions

There is additional HDR software that has been popular in recent times such as Photomatix Pro and EnfuseGUI. EnfuseGUI uses the Enfuse technology developed by sourceforge.net that produces very realistic results with good localized contrast. The downside to EnfuseGUI is that it does not have an auto align option. The Photomatix pro has an Alignment option and an Attempt to Reduce ghosting artefacts option but these are generally not as effective as the Remove Ghosting feature in Adobe's Merge to HDR Pro.

In some Images where the movement is coming towards the camera, even Photoshop may not be able to remove ghosting completely (there is no single image in the bracket set where the contours of the moving shape or object are separated from the other images). In the illustration above we can see how, with or without the Remove Ghosting option selected, the outcome is less than perfect. In this project we will look how we can use the Auto-Align feature in Photoshop to align bracketed images (shot hand-held), merge the exposures using EnfuseGUI and then fix the ghosting and minor exposure errors in Photoshop using the Auto-Blend Layers option.

Note > EnfuseGUI is available for Windows and Mac operating systems and is available for a donation (the website suggests a $10 donation or any amount you like!).

Photomatix Pro is a standalone application that also has a tonal mapping component. It can create natural looking images or you can set the 'Smoothing' low to enhance/exaggerate detail and localized contrast. This graphic 'illustrative' look has become very popular as a stylized treatment and can be replicated in Photoshop's Merge to HDR Pro by raising the Detail slider.

Note > If you look in the Loupe view in the top right-hand corner of the illustration above you will notice edge artefacts that appear due to misalignment of the source images (even though the auto align option in Photomatix Pro was checked) and the tonal mapping that has been carried out.

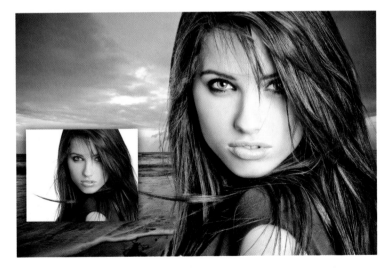

A 'Faux HDR' look (where exaggerated tonal mapping is applied to single exposure) can be created by going to Image > Adjustments > HDR Toning. The look can also be created in Adobe Camera Raw be raising the Fill Light, Recovery, Contrast and Clarity sliders very aggressively. This look can also be created in the main editing space of Photoshop using the Shadows/Highlights adjustment feature (see the previous project).

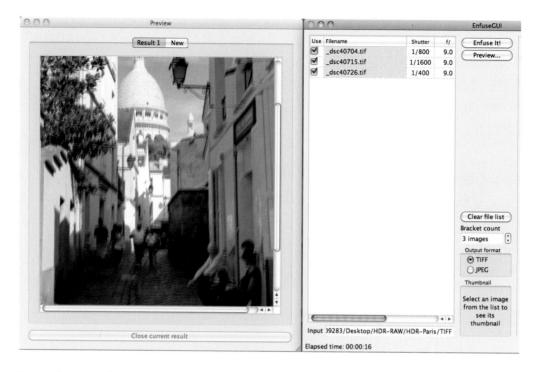

For enthusiasts of HDR imaging EnfuseGUI is an excellent alternative to Photoshop for merging bracketed images. The Enfuse technology from sourceforge.net is also available in a Mac only GUI called Bracketeer that does have an alignment option (although very slow). Unfortunately the cost-effective EnfuseGUI software has no alignment option and cannot process Raw files. These shortcomings are, however, easily overcome.

1. Although this project uses EnfuseGUI to merge the exposures the processing starts in Photoshop. Process and export the bracketed Raw files from Adobe Camera Raw as 16 Bit TIFF files (see Raw Processing). The images can then be aligned in Photoshop by going to File > Scripts > Load Files into Stack. Check the Attempt to Automatically Align Source Images and then select OK in the Load Layers dialog.

2. Crop the multi-layered file that opens in Photoshop so that there is no transparency at the edges. The file will contain all of the bracketed images that have now been aligned. Go to File > Scripts > Export Layers as Files. Select the destination using the Browse button and TIFF as the File Type and then hit the Run button.

3. The nice thing about Enfuse technology is that it gets it nearly right just about every time without adjusting any sliders or tone curves. Localized contrast is very good and alignment is not an issue if Photoshop has handled this part of the process first. The three files exported from Photoshop have been dragged over the EnfuseGUI window to load them and then the 'Enfuse It!' button has been clicked.

4. If you check the histogram after Merge to HDR Pro or EnfuseGUI has 'done-its-stuff' you may notice that minor clipping of highlights may have occurred. Although this not ideal for a process which is designed to maximize tonality, the error can be fixed quite easily using the following technique.

5. In this case scenario, the brightest highlight tones have become blown out or 'clipped'. If we drag the background layer thumbnail from the Layers panel in the underexposed file (from the bracketed images) into the enfused version we can use the highlights from this file to restore detail in the background layer.

Layer Style

Styles	Blending Options	
Blending Options: Custom	**General Blending**	

Blend Mode: Normal

Opacity: ———————○ 100 %

Advanced Blending

Fill Opacity: ————————○ 100 %

Channels: ☑ R ☑ G ☑ B

Knockout: None

☐ Blend Interior Effects as Group
☑ Blend Clipped Layers as Group
☑ Transparency Shapes Layer
☐ Layer Mask Hides Effects
☐ Vector Mask Hides Effects

Blend If: Gray

This Layer: 0 255

Underlying Layer: 200 / 245 255

Styles list:
- ☐ Drop Shadow
- ☐ Inner Shadow
- ☐ Outer Glow
- ☐ Inner Glow
- ☐ Bevel and Emboss
  - ☐ Contour
  - ☐ Texture
- ☐ Satin
- ☐ Color Overlay
- ☐ Gradient Overlay
- ☐ Pattern Overlay
- ☐ Stroke

OK
Reset
New Style...
☑ Preview

6. If you have used Merge to HDR Pro you will first need to select both layers and run the Auto-Align Layers feature from the Edit menu. If you have used EnfuseGUI the layers will already be aligned. Double-click the top layer to open the Layer Style dialog. In the Blend If section drag the black slider under the bottom left-hand side of the Underlying Layer ramp to a position where the readout is 200. This will effectively render all levels darker than Level 200 on this layer transparent. Hold down the Alt key (PC) or Command key (Mac) and separate the two sides of the black triangle and drag the right hand side to a position of level 245. This will ensure that the transparency on this layer fades in gradually between level 200 and 245.

This will resolve the issue of the blown out highlights, but not the problem of the mismatched detail due to the subject movement in the image. Even the Remove Ghosting option in Merge to HDR Pro cannot resolve the problem in this image (the example above was merged using EnfuseGUI). Choose Flatten Image from the Layers menu.

7. Open the image that is closest in exposure to the mismatched detail (in this case it is the overexposed image). Select the Rectangular Marquee Tool from the Tools panel and set a Feather value of 0 in the Options bar. Make a selection around the area where ghosting occurs. It is important to make a selection that is generous enough so that the selection edge is set back from the mismatched detail. From the Edit menu choose Copy. We will use these copied pixels to patch the enfused image with detail that has no ghosting.

8. Go to the enfused image and choose Paste from the Edit menu. Set the mode to Difference in the Layers panel and using the Move Tool from the Tools panel move this layer into alignment with the detail on the background layer. Once this has been achieved set the mode of the layer back to Normal.

Note > If you have used Merge to HDR Pro to align and merge the exposures you will once again have to use the Auto-Align Layers option to create alignment between these two layers.

9. Hold down the Ctrl key (PC) or Command key (Mac) and click the layer thumbnail to load the pixels on this layer as a selection. Switch off the visibility of this layer. Before we blend this patch with the background layer we must delete the pixels on the background layer.

10. We need to create an overlap between the patch on the top layer and the pixels we delete on the background layer. This will create a smooth transition when the patch is blended with the underlying layer. In order to create this overlap we must contract the selection. Go to Select > Modify > Contract and enter in a value of 60 pixels. Select OK to apply this adjustment to the selection.

11. Select the background layer in the Layers panel so that it is the active layer. Drag the lock on the background layer to the trash can in the Layers panel to covert the background layer into a regular layer. Hit the delete key to delete the selected pixels on this layer.

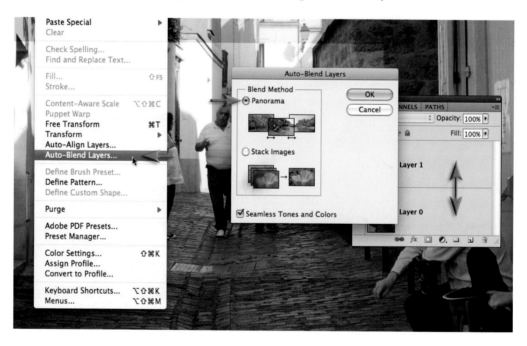

12. Switch on the visibility of the top layer and then hold down the Shift key and click on the top layer in the Layers panel so that both layers are now selected. Go to Edit > Auto-Blend Layers and in the Auto-Blend Layers dialog select the Panorama radio button and the Seamless Tones and Colors checkbox and then select OK.

13. Choose Flatten Image from the Layers menu or merge the visible elements into a new layer by holding down the modifier keys Ctrl + Alt + Shift (PC) or Command + Option + Shift keys (Mac) and then press the E key.

As you can see from the merged version (now complete with highlight detail and no ghosting) the EnfuseGUI software offers another alternative to Merge to HDR Pro. There are pros and cons to both workflows but each workflow offers slightly different management of localized contrast, color and tonality.

Time Lapse Photography – Project 9

All compact digital cameras and the latest Digital SLR cameras offer movie capture (some are even capable of 1080p HD movie capture). It is, however, possible to create High Definition Time-Lapse movies using any camera by capturing still images over an extended period of time and then playing them back over a short period of time.

Since the arrival of Photoshop CS3 Extended we have had the capability of opening, editing and exporting movie files. We are also able to create a movie from a sequence of still images (called an Image Sequence). For a stills photographer the advantage of creating a movie using Photoshop (rather than Adobe Premiere) is that they can work with all of their familiar adjustment layers and filters they know and love, in order to create some spectacular results at the highest video quality possible.

Examples of time-lapse and stop motion

The first problem to be resolved is how often to take a still image. Here are a few ideas:

- Fast Change, e.g. people exiting station, or busy street scene – try using one frame every second.

- Medium Change, e.g. a city lighting up at night – try using one frame every 10 seconds.

- Slow Change, e.g. Growth or decay – try using one frame every minute.

- Stop-Motion – Capture one frame after each time the subject has moved. The interval between frames is variable depending on how quickly or slowly it takes for the subject to move into a new position. Think claymation animations.

Tips for capturing the still images

To ensure that the highest quality still images have been captured follow these guidelines:

- Use the same white balance for all images, i.e. Auto White balance is not recommended. Use a custom white-balance in camera or sync the white balance in Adobe Camera Raw.

- Use 'Auto Exposure' mode for images that are captured over an extended period of time, e.g. where the level of ambient light changes significantly. Use a 'Manual Exposure' setting for a short duration time-lapse movie where the level of lighting is consistent.

- Mount the camera on a sturdy tripod and ensure the tripod is protected from excessive vibration and wind.

- Use a remote shutter release or look for an Interval Timer Shooting mode in your camera's menu. This interval option may also be available when you have tethered the camera to your computer via a USB cable and you are using tethered capture software (this software is sometimes shipped with the camera or available as a separate purchase).

- Consider using manual focus in situations where the subject matter may move in and out of view.

- Remember not to use the portrait/vertical format!

Note > You can create time-lapse movies from JPEG images but my recommendation is to capture images in the Raw file format whenever possible for increased control over the dynamic range, tone and color.

Note > Due to the limitations of storage capacity on the supporting DVD only the first five files are supplied in the Raw format. All files required to complete the time lapse movie are, however, available as processed JPEGs on the supporting DVD.

1. To optimize the Raw images select them all in Bridge or go to File > Open in Photoshop. Select the folder on your hard drive where the images have been stored, select the first image in the folder and then use the keyboard shortcut Ctrl + A (PC) or Command + A (Mac) to select all images in this folder. Then select OK to open all of the Raw files into Adobe Camera Raw (ACR).

Important > Do not attempt to open hundreds of high-resolution JPEG images into Photoshop at the same time if you are using the Raw file format. See Step 10 for instructions on how to use JPEG images to create a time-lapse image sequence.

2. Click and hold on the Crop Tool to reveal the crop menu and then select Custom. From the Crop pull-down menu in the Custom Crop dialog choose pixels. Enter in a value of 1920 by 1080 (1080p HD TV size) or 1280 by 720 for standard HD proportions (720p). Then crop your image.

3. Create a custom white balance setting for the first image (if you did not already do so in camera). Photographers choosing to shoot in the JPEG format must select a custom white balance in camera, i.e. not auto white balance. In this project you can click on the gray car that is passing through the intersection in the first image file.

4. Adjust the global tonality and color in the 'Basic' tab. In this image the Recovery and Fill Light sliders have been raised to 25 to restore detail in this sunlit street scene. The Blacks slider has been lowered to +2 and the 'Vibrance' slider has been raised to +30.

5. Target and optimize colors in the first image of the sequence. If you are using ACR 5.2 or later you will be able to use the Targeted Adjustment Tool. In this image I have selected the Hue option and then clicked and dragged on the yellow tones (the building in the center of the image) to make them slightly less orange. I have then selected the Saturation option and again clicked and dragged on the yellow tones to make them slightly more saturated. I have then selected the Luminance option and dragged left to lower the luminance (brightness) of the yellow tones within this image.

6. Click on the Workflow Options at the base of the ACR dialog and set the depth to 8 Bits/Channel. You also have the option in the latest versions of ACR to sharpen images for screen or print as part of the Workflow Options.

7. Click on the 'Select All' button in the top right-hand corner of the ACR dialog. Choose 'Everything' from the Synchronize menu and select 'OK' to apply the changes to the rest of the images.

Removing Frames from an Image Sequence

If there are any frames you wish to remove from the final movie it is easier to remove them in ACR now rather than later. Hold down the Ctrl key (PC) or Command key (Mac) and click on any frames you wish to exclude (there are a couple of frames where pedestrians have walked in front of the camera). Click on the Trash icon in the Tools bar or hit the Delete or Backspace key.

8. Click on the 'Save' button. In the Save Options dialog select a location and folder you want to save your processed images to. Rename the files so that the file numbering is sequential (no gaps due to files removed from the original sequence in ACR) otherwise you will see black flashes in the final video. Choose either the TIFF or JPEG format. If using JPEG use a High or Maximum quality setting.

9. In Photoshop select Open from the File menu. Browse to the folder you just saved the images to (the processed images from ACR). Select the first file in the folder and then select the Image Sequence option in the Open dialog.

Important > Do not select all the images in the folder – just the first. If you were using the JPEG file format in your camera this is where the process of movie making would begin.

10. Before the image sequence opens you will be asked to nominate a frame rate for the project. Choosing a frame rate slower than 30 frames per second (fps) will slow down the final movie when it plays back. For this project I have selected 10 fps. The image sequence is contained in a single 'movie' layer and the motion can be started and stopped using the controls in the Animation panel (select Motion in the Application bar or go to Window > Animation).

Note > Playback in Photoshop will usually be very slow.

11. Convert the layer into a Smart Object (Filter > Convert for Smart Filters). Now the movie can be optimized, enhanced or manipulated just as if it were a regular Smart Object in Photoshop (with a few exceptions). If you want to apply lens correction to the movie use the Transform controls rather than the 'Lens Correction' filter. I have used the keyboard shortcut Command + T (Mac) or Ctrl + T (PC) and then holding down the Command/Ctrl key move the anchor points to correct the converging verticals.

12. Now that the layer is a Smart Object you can also apply filters as Smart Filters to edit the look and feel of your time lapse video. These adjustments get applied to each and every frame in the sequence. Here I have applied a 10 pixel Gaussian Blur filter and set the Blending Options to Soft Light (double-click the Blending Options icon on the smart filter in the Layers panel).

13. The Shadows/Highlights adjustment can also be applied as if it were a filter (go to Image > Adjustments > Shadows/Highlights). In this example the shadows have been rendered lighter to deal with the high-contrast lighting, and the effect of the soft light blend mode, in this sequence of images.

14. Adjustment layers can be added above the image layer. In this example a Black & White adjustment layer in Luminosity mode has been added and the luminosity of the blue sky lowered. Although it is not essential I have used the Luminance preset available from the Essential Skills DVD to ensure the luminance values of all the colors in the image are accurately preserved when the Luminosity mode is applied to the adjustment layer.

15. As we are working with a timeline it is possible to create a transition from one effect to another. In this project a black and white version of the image will transition to color. Add a second Black & White adjustment layer, but this time do not use the Luminosity mode. Use the adjustment panel to render the tones of the building lighter and the blue sky darker.

16. Make sure the Current Time is set to zero (click on the 'selects first frame' icon in the bottom left-hand corner of the animation panel if necessary). Expand the Black & White timeline control and click on the little alarm clock (Time-Vary stop watch) in the opacity control. This adds a 'keyframe' (small yellow diamond icon) on the timeline at the start of the sequence.

17. Double-click on the current time (top left of panel) or Current Time Indicator on the Time Ruler to advance to a new position in the sequence. Click between the arrows to add another keyframe at this location. Adjust the opacity of the Black & White adjustment layer to 0% in the Layers panel to restore the color to the image.

Note > The color will fade in gradually between the first and second keyframe.

18. At this time in the project it is worth saving the multi-layered Photoshop file to a project folder that contains the folder of TIFF or JPEG files used for the Image sequence and also any sound file that you may be adding to this project. This will ensure that the Photoshop file will always be able to locate the 'footage' and the sound files that have been used to build the movie.

Note > The master still images and any sound file used in this project are only linked to the Photoshop file and not embedded.

19. Add sound to the movie by going to File > Open (Mac) or File > Open As (PC). Browse to your audio file (copy your audio file to your project folder if you intend to continue this project on another computer). Choose 'All Documents' in the Enable menu when working on a Mac. Select the Audio file and then choose 'QuickTime Movie' in the Format menu. Then click on the Open button.

Note > Photoshop converts Audio Files to the QuickTime format before they can be used. Make sure you have the current version of QuickTime installed in your computer.

20. You may have to navigate the Missing Profile warning (just select 'OK') before the file will open in Photoshop, i.e. ignore the warning as you can't color-manage sound.

21. The Audio file will open as an empty layer with a movie icon. Drag the thumbnail of this layer from the Layers panel into your project image to add audio to your image sequence.

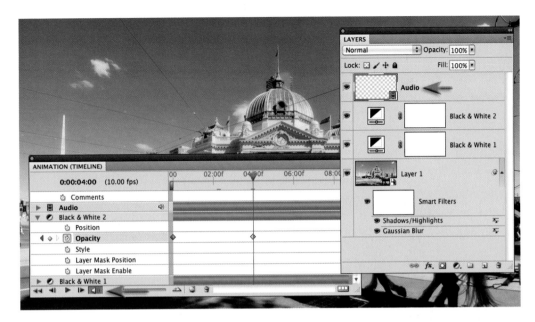

22. You may find it useful to rename the layer as 'Audio' to help you remember what this empty layer adds to the project.

Note > The Audio will only play if you click on the Audio icon in the Animation panel.

Removing frames in Photoshop rather than ACR

For speed of editing it is advisable to remove frames before an Image Sequence is opened in the main editing space of Photoshop (remember to renumber the files if you have done this). It is possible, however, to remove frames from a movie or Image Sequence at this stage of the editing. First add keyframes either side of the frames you want to remove.

Select Layer 1 in the Animation panel. Move the current time to the first keyframe and then from the Animation fly-out menu choose 'Split Layer'. Select the Layer 1 copy that was created when you split the original layer. Move the current time to the second keyframe (click on the forward arrow, next to the stop-watch, to quickly advance the current time to the next keyframe), and then from the Animation fly-out menu choose 'Trim Layer Start to Current Time'.

Click on the back arrow next to the stop-watch to return to the first keyframe and then from the Animation fly-out menu choose 'Move Layer In Point to Current Time'. Move the time-line to the end of the Layer 1 copy and then from the fly-out menu choose Trim Document Duration to Work Area.

Note > You may remember that I said in Step 8 that it was faster to delete problem frames in ACR.

23. To make a movie from your project file go to File > Export > Render Video).

Note > Save the master project file as a Photoshop or PSD file to your project folder that contains the images folder and sound file).

24. In the render Video dialog check the size is 1920 x 1080 (the Document Size or HDTV options will ensure the movie is the correct size. Click on the Settings button to open the Movie Settings dialog. Click on the Settings button in the Movie Settings dialog to access the 'compression settings' (no changes are made in the Movie Settings dialog). Select the H.264 Compression Type setting for a high quality movie that can be compressed to a comparatively small size. Select 'High' or 'Maximum' in the Compressor section of the dialog if quality is paramount above size. Click OK in the Compression Settings and Movie Settings dialog and then click on Render.

Connecting missing footage

Photoshop does not embed the still images or sound file in the layers (the component images needed to render a video are still residing in their respective folders). If you open the Photoshop file on another computer you may get warning dialogs when opening it if you did not use a master project folder for all your files. If this is the case you will be invited to 'reconnect' the missing footage.

In this project we converted the Image Sequence layer into a Smart Object (Convert for Smart Filters). The warning about missing footage will only occur if you were to double-click the Smart Object to view the Image Sequence layer. Note in the example above how the file is remembering the original location of the Image Sequence folder (a project folder was not created so the file is looking for a location that cannot be found on the new computer).

Go to Layer > Video Layer > Replace Footage. Select the first image in the Image Sequence folder and select OK to fix the problem.

Haydn Cattach

Mark Galer

align and blend projects

Rory Gardiner- rorygardiner.com.au

essential skills

- Create a fixed-position montage where different elements are combined to create an image where the lighting and action has been optimized.
- Create a wide panoramic image and correct parallax error.
- Create a vertical panorama and control the converging verticals to retain a realistic end-result.

Rory Gardiner – rorygardiner.com.au

Composite lighting and action – Project 1

The lighting of a studio set is often compromised by either limitations of time or the complexity of the lighting that is required for the creative outcome. Take, for instance, the example above, where the ideal lighting required for the liquid and the label is different. Perfect the lighting for one and the quality of the other is compromised. The solution is remarkably simple of course. Perfect the lighting for one at a time and then create a composite image in post-production. The drama is further enhanced by adding a splash, ripples and the perfect background. Prior to CS3, pin-registering each exposure in-camera using a sturdy tripod was an essential requirement for the success of this technique. Small differences in camera position (such as knocking the tripod between exposures) can now be corrected using the new Auto-Align Layers command.

1. Open the two bottle images and make a composite image by dragging the background thumbnail (in the Layers panel) from the label image into the beer image. Shift-click both layers to select them. Select Auto-Align Layers from the Edit menu and in the dialog box, select the Reposition option before selecting OK. Hold down the Ctrl key (PC) or Command key (Mac) and then click on the 'Create a new layer' icon at the base of the Layers panel to create an empty new layer below Layer 0. Fill this new layer with white (Edit > Fill).

2. Make one path around the bottle and another path around the labels using the Pen Tool (see the Selections chapter and Project 2 in this chapter). Hold down the Command key (Mac) or Ctrl key (PC) and click on a Path thumbnail to load it as a selection. In the Layers panel select the corresponding layer, e.g. the label path for the label layer and then click on the 'Add layer mask' icon at the base of the Layers panel. Apply a 1-pixel Gaussian Blur to each layer mask (Edit > Blur > Gaussian Blur). Select the top two layers and use the keyboard shortcut to load them into a group (Command or Ctrl + G) and name the group 'Bottle'.

3. Open the Ripples and Background files. In Adobe Camera Raw, the Ripples file has had a +1.15 exposure increase and the Contrast slider has been raised to +75 so that the tones match the background image. Make a composite image from these two files by dragging the background thumbnail (in the Layers panel) from the ripples image into the background image. Drag the lock on the background layer of the background image to the trash in the Layers panel. Add a layer mask to the top layer (the ripples) and lower the Opacity to 50%. Select Layer 0 and go to Edit > Free Transform. Drag the bottom-center handle of the bounding box down to increase the height of this layer so that a clean background extends behind the ripples and commit the transformation (use the keyboard shortcut Ctrl + 0 (PC) or Command + 0 (Mac) to access the edges of the Transform bounding box).

4. Select the Gradient Tool and choose the Black, White and Linear options and set the Opacity to 100% (make sure the Reverse option is deselected). Select the layer mask and drag a short gradient to hide the top of the tray containing the ripples and create a smooth transition between the new background below. Set the Opacity of Layer 1 back to 100%.

5. Select the Brush Tool and black as the foreground color. Choose a large soft-edged brush (0% hardness) and lower the Opacity to around 50%. Paint over any remaining signs of the top of the tray to remove them from view. Several strokes of the brush my be required to complete this task.

6. If you would like to make the ripples more symmetrical, duplicate the ripples layer and then go to Edit > Transform > Flip Horizontal. Select the Gradient Tool again, choose Multiply as the mode and drag a gradient from the right side of the bottle to the left side of the bottle. Stamp the visible elements of all the layers into a new layer (Command + Option + Shift + E for a Mac and Ctrl + Alt + Shift + E for a PC). This composite layer will enable you to warp the ripples into better shape (Edit > Transform > Warp). Drag down on the base of the bounding box to create a better shape for the ripples before committing the transformation. The background should now be ready to accept the bottle that we prepared earlier. Hold down the Shift key and select the top and bottom layers in the Layers panel and then use the keyboard shortcut Ctrl or Command + G to load the layers into a group. Name the group 'Background'.

7. Drag the bottle group into the background image and apply the Free Transform (Edit > Free Transform) so that you can move the bottle into position and scale if required. Zoom in and check the edge of the bottle against the new background at 100%. If required, refine the edge of the bottle mask in Layer 0 of the bottle group (Select > Refine Edge). Add the splash image to the composite file, lower the opacity of the layer and repeat the transformation process to position and scale the splash. Return the layer to 100% Opacity when finished.

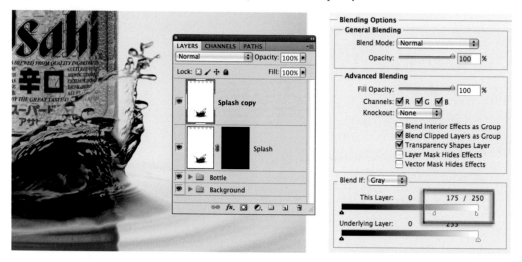

8. To mask the white background behind the splash we will need to duplicate the splash layer and add a black layer mask to the first splash layer (hold down the Alt/Option key as you click the 'Add a layer mask' icon in the Layers panel). Double-click the top splash layer away from the name of the layer so that the Layer Style dialog opens (if you double-click near the name of the layer you will be given the option to rename the layer instead). In the Blending Options section of the dialog drag the white slider on the This Layer slider to 250. Hold down the Alt/Option key and drag the left side of the slider again to split the slider. Drag this left side of the slider to 175 to create a smooth transition that will render the white background mostly transparent.

9. Select OK to apply the Advanced Blending options and then add a layer mask to this layer. Select the Brush Tool and black as the foreground color. Lower the Opacity in the Options bar to 50% and start to mask any traces of the white background that may still be visible. On the right side of the image mask the splash so that it appears to be going around the bottle rather than in front of the bottle. Adjust the size and hardness of the brush as required.

10. The previous two steps will have hidden the white background but also rendered the brightest highlights on the water droplets transparent as well. If you want to replace these bright highlights select the layer mask on the layer below and choose white as the foreground color. Select a small soft-edged brush and 100% Opacity and paint in the image to reveal these bright highlights.

11. The final steps required in this project are to optimize the brightness and contrast of the bottle. Select the label layer in the Bottle group of layers and then create a Curves adjustment layer. Clip this Curves layer to the layer below and increase the brightness of the highlights while maintaining the tone of the black lettering.

12. Create a second Brightness/Contrast adjustment layer to modify the tonality of the bottle cap. Raise both the Brightness and Contrast sliders and then fill the layer mask with black. Select the Brush Tool and paint with white to paint in the adjustment on the bottle cap as required. Sharpen the completed image by selecting the Bottle group and the splash layer and converting for Smart Filters (Filter > Convert for Smart Filters). Apply either the Unsharp Mask or Smart Sharpen filter.

Haydn Cattach

Fixed position montage

The composite lighting technique used for Project 1 (the beer bottle) does not have to be confined to the studio. Working with the camera in a fixed position the photographer is free to light aspects of a large or complex scene with a single light source – one piece or frame at a time. Masking is relatively simple when most of the subject matter is not moving.

Photomerge – Project 2

Photomerge is capable of aligning and blending images without any signs of banding in smooth areas of transition. The new and improved Photomerge first made its appearance back in Photoshop CS3 and the stitching is usually seamless. This project, however, takes a look at how we can correct minor errors when things don't quite match up. This is usually a result of using a wide-angle lens that includes a lot of foreground subject matter but without using a specialized tripod head to eliminate parallax error. The ease with which Photoshop can stitch these panoramas will be improved if you capture vertical images with a 50% overlap using manual exposure, manual focus and a manual White Balance setting (or process the images identically in Camera Raw). With a little know how, Photomerge is an excellent way of widening your horizons or competing with your best friend's 60 Megapixel Hasselblad H4D.

DVD
images on DVD

Note > The Raw files on the DVD have already been optimized for the reader for use in this project. No additional processing in Adobe Camera Raw is required. The information on this page highlights the work already carried out.

Lowering the Exposure slider and raising the Recovery slider has recovered the highlights, while raising the Fill Light slider lightened the shadow detail. If the subject brightness range or contrast of the scene had been any higher it would have been necessary to bracket the exposure for each of the component shots and then use Merge to HDR Pro to create an image with full detail for each of the five component images (see High Dynamic Range).

To balance the exposure the Raw files were further optimized using the Graduated Filter in ACR. The sky was darkened using one graduated filter and the Foreground was lightened using another. In some instances a third Graduated Filter was added to even the exposure from left to right.

1. Select and open the five project images (the JPEG or TIFF images on the DVD have already been processed from the Raw files). Go to File > Automate and choose Photomerge.

Note > The files for this project were captured on a 12 Megapixel DSLR using the Camera Raw file format and then scaled down to 6 Megapixel images to speed up the processing. If you have less than 2 Gigabytes of RAM on your computer you would be advised to do the same when stitching your own images or be prepared to be very patient.

2. In the Photomerge dialog box click on the Add Open Files button and select the Auto radio button in the Layout options. Select OK and let Photoshop do all of the work – and what a lot of work it has to do, aligning and blending all of these images.

3. Prior to Photoshop CS3 many more steps of manual techniques were required to circumnavigate the shortcomings of Photomerge – but as you can see from the results in this project we just about have perfection handed to us on a plate. Fantabulous! (I know that's not in the dictionary but neither is Photomerge – yet.) If you have used the full-resolution images you probably had to go and make a cup of coffee while Photoshop put this one together (all 60 megapixels of it) and will now be considering downsampling your file – but wait, we have a couple of small glitches in this result.

Performance Tip 1

Now the only limitation you may run up against when handholding the camera, or placing the camera on a standard tripod head, is Photoshop's ability to align and blend strong geometric lines that come close to the camera lens. If you have not used a specialized tripod head designed for professional panoramic stitching work, then the problem of aligning both foreground and distant subject matter is a big problem for any software (Photoshop handles it better than most). The camera should ideally be rotated around the nodal point of the lens to avoid something called parallax error. You will probably not encounter any problems with the new Photomerge feature unless you are working with strong lines in the immediate foreground.

Performance Tip 2

If you downsample before you flatten your file you will probably encounter hairline cracks after reducing the image size. The solution to this problem is to either flatten the file or stamp the visible content to a new layer (Ctrl/Command + Shift + Alt/Option and then type the letter E) before you reduce the size of the image.

If you hold down the Alt/Option key and click on each layer mask in turn you will notice that Photoshop uses hard-edged layer masks to hide or reveal the piece of the jigsaw puzzle that makes up the final panorama. The panorama has seamless joins because Photoshop has adjusted or 'blended' the color and tonality of the pixels on each layer. Any pixels concealed by the layer masks have not been subjected to these color and tonal adjustments. This, in effect, means that the user cannot override which bit of each layer is visible as the hidden pixels have not been color-matched.

4. Merge the visible elements to new a new layer (Ctrl + Shift + Alt and then type the letter E on a PC or Command + Shift + Option and then type the letter E on a Mac). Crop away that which is surplus to requirements before flattening the file, be sure to leave the Width and Height fields blank. It is OK to leave a small area of transparency in the top right-hand corner of the image when cropping if this helps the composition as we can fix this using the techniques outlined in the next step. This is a big image (especially if you used the full-resolution files) so don't be surprised if things are a little slower in computer land right now.

5. There is a small area of transparency at the top of the frame that will need cloning (I did not want to crop too tight at the top of the frame). Select the Clone Stamp tool from the Tools panel and then clone in some new sky from immediately below the transparent area. I have created an empty new layer to clone into and have checked the Sample All Layers option in the Options bar. Only when I am happy with the patch job will I select Merge Down from the Layers fly-out menu.

6. When stitching just two or three images Photomerge Panorama gets it right pretty much all of the time. When stitching much wider panoramas where there is a good deal of foreground detail you may find a couple of alignment errors. These images were captured using a wide-angle lens and the foreground rocks are just in front of the tripod. If I had used a specialized panorama tripod head the effects of parallax error would not be a problem. Photomerge in this instance, however, has met its match. The foreground rocks all match perfectly but that horizon line has a small break and is undulating. We can fix this. Zoom in to the horizon line, select the Rectangular Marquee tool and make a selection that just touches the horizon line at the lowest point. Make sure the feather option in the Options bar is set to 0. From the Select menu choose Inverse.

Note > The stitching errors may change depending on the resolution (pixel dimensions) of the files you choose for Photomerge to align and blend.

7. Go to Filter > Liquify. Choose the Warp Tool to nudge the horizon line down towards the red frozen area (created from the selection you made in the last step). Increase the size of the brush to 500 pixels and decrease the Brush Pressure to a lowly 10 pixels. When using the Warp tool just click and drag to push the pixels into alignment. When the horizon line is sitting on top of the red rectangle click OK to apply the changes to the image.

8. Pushing the pixels down onto the selection in Liquify will create an unnaturally hard edge to the horizon. This can be fixed by selecting the Blur tool in the Tools panel and a Strength setting of 50% in the Options bar. Zoom in so you can see the effects of your painting and then paint along the edge to soften it.

9. If you find a physical break in the horizon line or on the rocks either side of it you can create a patch to hide the awkward break. Use the Rectangular Marquee Tool with a Feather radius of 10 pixels and make a small selection just next to the break. Choose Copy and then Paste from the Edit menu to put the patch onto its own layer. Then go to Edit > Free Transform. You can now slide and rotate the patch into position. Hold down the Ctrl key (PC) or Command key (Mac) and pull any of the bounding box handles to distort the shape of the patch so that you can achieve a seamless fix.

Note > An alternative to this technique would be to use the Clone Stamp Tool and clone to an empty new layer (see Project 4 from the Retouching chapter).

10. Click on the Add layer mask icon at the base of the Layers panel. Select the Brush Tool from the Tools panel and set the foreground color to black. Set the Brush hardness low and then mask any areas of the patch that may be affecting the rocks. You may need to zoom in to check that your work does not leave any brush strokes.

11. If the Patch does not match the color of the tones then you can create an empty new layer and set the mode of this layer to Color. Select the Brush tool in the Tools panel, hold down the Alt or Option key and click on a more appropriate color to load this into the Foreground Color Swatch in the Tools panel. Then paint over the area that needs adjusting to further perfect the patched area.

Note > If the Foreground Color does not change when you hold down the Alt/Option key and click in the image window make sure the Eyedropper Tool options are set to All Layers from the Sample pull-down menu in the Options bar.

12. To create a Faux HDR (High Dynamic Range) effect that enhances localized contrast, go to Image > Duplicate and check the Duplicate Merged Layers Only option in the Duplicate Image dialog. It is not possible to apply the HDR Toning Adjustment to a multi-layered file so we will apply the toning to a flattened duplicate version of this file and then reimport the layer.

13. In order to apply the HDR Toning the image Photoshop has to temporarily convert the image into a 32 Bits/Channel file (hence the reason we have a single layer). Go to Image > Adjustments and select HDR Toning. When the HDR Toning dialog opens expand the Tone and Detail section and raise the Detail slider to +150. You may need to decrease the Highlight slider to restore the highlight detail in the image and raise the Radius slider in the Edge Glow section to make a smoother transition between the rocks and sky. Adjust the Vibrance and Saturation sliders to taste and select OK.

14. This Faux HDR effect may look a little bit too edgy for most photographers. We can, however, dial in just the right amount of the effect after we have placed this file as a layer above the multi-layered file. Hold down the Shift key and drag the layer thumbnail from the duplicate image (the HDR Toned image) into the panorama image.

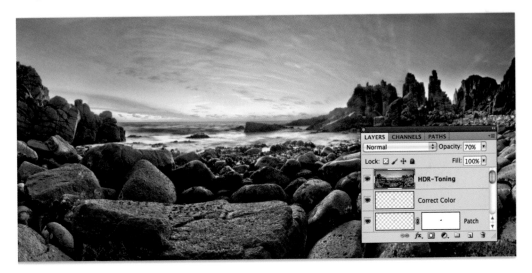

15. Lower the opacity of this new layer until you achieve a good balance between the panorama image and the HDR toned image.

Note > The bottom five layers holding the original component images and layer masks are no longer required and can be deleted before saving the master Photoshop file.

Perspective or Cylindrical

When we select Auto in the Layout section of the Photomerge dialog, Photoshop elected to use the Cylindrical option. This option is usually preferable and is usually selected by Auto when you are stitching wide panoramas. When stitching two or three images together you may find that Photoshop decides to use the Perspective option or you can choose this option to override the Cylindrical option if it is chosen by Auto. The Perspective option creates a bow-tie effect when stitching three images and is useful for creating a realistic perspective with straight horizon lines. When this option is used for more than three images, however, the distortion required to create the effect tends to be extreme for the images on the edge of the panorama and cannot, therefore, be considered as a usable option.

Auto-Align for pin-registering images

The Auto Align feature is an invaluable tool for photographers who need to be able to pin-register images that have been captured hand-held. This is, however, only recommended for those photographers who use a custom or manual white balance rather than auto white balance in-camera. In the illustration above the boy is blinking in one image and the dog is looking away in the second. The images were captured a split second apart but the best elements of each image can be combined to create one image even though the camera was hand-held. The two images have been combined by dragging the background layer from one file onto the image window of the other (hold down the Shift key as you let go of the mouse button). Dropping the Opacity of the top layer reveals the misalignment even though the boy was still.

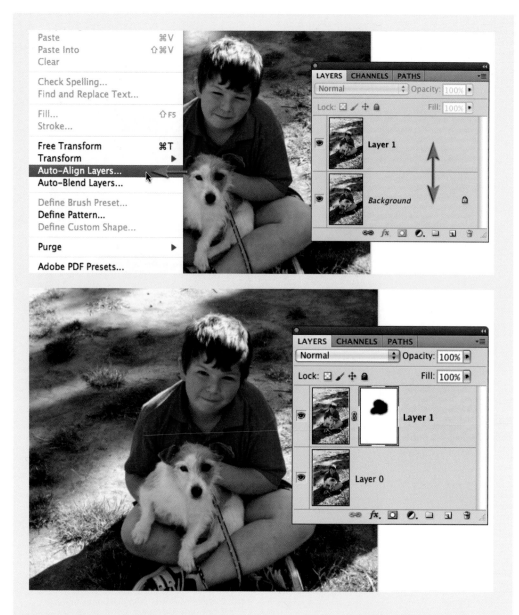

Select both layers in the Layers panel. From the Edit menu choose Auto-Align Layers. Now select only the top layer and click on the 'Add a layer mask' icon in the Layers panel. Choose the Brush Tool in the Tools panel and paint with black into the mask to shield any of the pixels you do not want to see on this layer. Painting over the boy's head will reveal the head with the open eyes on the layer below. You will need to crop the image to finish your project. If you can see the value of this technique then you will quickly realize that taking multiple shots the next time you are presented with a group (or even just one man and his best friend) ensures the decisive moment is history (sorry Henri).

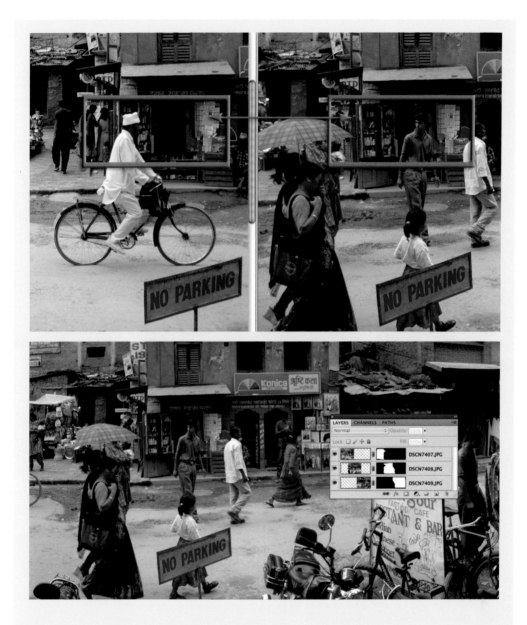

Aligning images with moving content

When creating a panorama with moving subject matter the information in the images may change in the region of the 50% overlap as subjects move out of, or into, the frame. The difference in content forces Photoshop to mask around the moving subject matter during the blending process (to avoid cutting subjects in two). This is not always successful as Photoshop finds it difficult to distinguish between different subjects when they overlap. In the illustration above Photoshop has successfully blended images where the subject matter is very different in the region of the overlap. Photoshop has completely ignored the moving bicycle in the resulting blend.

We cannot paint into the layer masks of these layers to adjust visible content after the blend is complete as the differences in tone and color between these two images are significant due to the auto exposure and auto white balance used. In the illustration above (top image) I have switched off the layer mask to illustrate how the colors that have been blended do not extend beyond the hard-edged layer mask (the mask is only used to define visible content). To prevent Photoshop from using content in a blend we need to hide it by adding a layer mask and painting into this mask prior to blending (there is no need to be too precise about the painting). Painting in both layers in the area of transition, however, could result in transparency when the layers are blended.

After repeating the blending process we can see that we have now prioritized the bicycle instead of the pedestrians in the region of the overlap. We have, however, created new problems as Photoshop cannot distinguish between the rear end of the bicycle and a nearby pedestrian as the objects overlap. If we undo and add a little more paint into that mask before blending again we can finally resolve the problem in this region. If we turn our attention to the No Parking sign and parked bicycle in front of the restaurant sign we will see that all is not yet fixed. Going backwards and forwards like this can be time-consuming if we have a large number of high-resolution files to be blended each time. Avoid problems with editing by shooting in manual white balance and manual exposure (color and tone on the individual layers will be consistent). This allow us to fix up minor errors by painting into the mask, safe in the knowledge that the color and tone will not change.

Vertical panoramas – Project 3

In the image above if I had moved any further back there would have been power lines, telephone lines and tram lines between me and the front of this old theme park. Capturing a building so close will inevitably lead to aggressive converging verticals due to a combination of the wide-angle lens and the angle of view required to capture the top of the structure. If you allow the Photomerge to take control of the stitching you will end up with the result above left. Capture images using the horizontal (landscape) format for a vertical panorama. You can then achieve a more professional result by intercepting the automated process by aligning and blending the images as separate tasks, rather than using the automated Photomerge feature.

1. Optimize the color and tonality of the Raw files in Adobe Camera Raw and then choose Select All and Synchronize before opening. Go to File > Scripts > Load Files into Stack. Select the Open files but do not select the Attempt to Automatically Align Source Images option in the dialog. When the files have been loaded into one image select the layer with the subject matter that is closest to the ground (the one with the least amount of converging verticals). Go to the Lock options in the Layers panel and click on the 'Lock all' icon to lock this layer. This action will force Photoshop to respect the perspective of this layer (the other layers will be forced to adopt the perspective of this layer when we align the images). Select all three layers in the Layers panel (Shift-click the top and bottom layers).

2. Go to File > Edit > Auto-Align Layers. In the dialog select the Perspective option and also select the Lens Correction options. Select OK to process the layers. After the images have been Auto Aligned make sure all three layers are still selected and then go to Edit > Auto-Blend Layers. Select the Panorama and Seamless Tones and Colors options and select OK to process the layers. In the Layers panel select only the top layer and unlock this layer before proceeding with the next step.

3. Select all three layers in the Layers panel again and then go to Filter > Convert for Smart Filters. Select the Crop Tool and crop the image to remove the transparency that surrounds this composite image. If you look at the image closely you will notice that there is a small amount of barrel distortion in this image (the sides of the building balloon or bow out). This defect cannot be accurately fixed using the Lens Correction filter as the distortions are not central to the cropped image. We can, however, use the Warp feature but first we need to create a perspective grid that we can work with. Click on the 'Create a new layer' icon to create an empty new layer.

4. Go to Filter > Vanishing Point and select the Render Grids to Photoshop in the options. Using the Create Plane Tool click in each corner of the entrance to create a perspective plane. Zoom in to make sure you do this accurately. Select OK to export this grid back to Photoshop.

5. The grid is not very dark but can be made more prominent by going to Filter > Other > Minimum. Choose 1 pixel and select OK. From the Image > Adjustments menu choose Levels and drag the shadows slider underneath the histogram to the right to darken the grid.

6. Now we can set about correcting the perspective of all three layers at the same time (one of the advantages of working with layers nested inside a Smart Object). Click on the Smart Object in the Layers panel and go to Edit > Transform > Warp. The barrel distortion can be very accurately fixed by dragging the four corner handles of the Warp grid outwards and tucking the sides in until they align with the grid. Zoom in to ensure you have fixed the problem accurately. Go to Edit > Transform > Distort and then drag the top two corner handles out to reduce the extent of the converging verticals. The verticals of the building cannot be aligned to the sides of the image or vertical guides otherwise the shape of the building at the top appears misshapen. Click on the Commit Transform option in the Options bar and hide or delete the grid layer you have used as a reference grid.

Michelle lee

Exported grids

Grids exported from Vanishing Point can help the photographer capture additional elements that must conform to the perspective of the first image. The layer containing the grid can be dragged onto subsequent images to ensure 100% accuracy.

Abhijit Chattaraj

Glossary

ACR	Adobe Camera Raw.
Additive color	A color system where the primaries of red, green and blue mix to form the other colors.
Adjustment layer	Image adjustment placed on a layer.
Adobe Camera Raw	Adobe's own Raw conversion utility.
Adobe gamma	A calibration and profiling utility supplied with Photoshop.
Adobe Photo Downloader	Adobe's download utility used for transferring photos from card or camera to computer. The utility ships with Bridge.
Algorithm	A sequence of mathematical operations.
Aliasing	The display of a digital image where a curved line appears jagged due to the square pixels.
Alpha channel	Additional channel used for storing masks and selections.
Analyze/Analysis	To examine in detail.
Anti-aliasing	The process of smoothing the appearance of a curved line in a digital image.
APD	Adobe Photo Downloader.
Aperture	A circular opening in the lens that controls light reaching the film.
Area array	A rectangular pattern of light-sensitive sensors alternately receptive to red, green or blue light.
Artifacts	Pixels that are significantly incorrect in their brightness or color values.
Aspect ratio	The ratio of height to width. Usually in reference to the light-sensitive area or format of the camera.
Bit	Short for binary digit, the basic unit of the binary language.
Bit depth	Number of bits (memory) assigned to recording color or tonal information.
Bitmap	A one-bit image, i.e. black and white (no shades of gray).
Black and White	A color to grayscale adjustment feature. As well as customized mapping of colors to gray the feature can tint monochromes as well.
Blend mode	The formula used for defining the mixing of a layer with those beneath it.
Bridge	Adobe's sophisticated file browsing and organization program that ships with Photoshop.
Brightness	The value assigned to a pixel in the HSB model to define the relative lightness of a pixel.
Byte	Eight bits. The standard unit of binary data storage containing a value between 0 and 255.
Captured	A record of an image.

CCD	Charge Coupled Device. A solid-state image pick-up device used in digital image capture.
Channels	The divisions of color data within a digital image. Data is separated into primary or secondary colors.
Charge Coupled Device	See *CCD*.
CIS	Contact Image Sensor. A single row of sensors used in scanner mechanisms.
Clipboard	The temporary storage of something that has been cut or copied.
Clipping group	Two or more layers that have been linked. The base layer acts as a mask, limiting the effect or visibility of those layers clipped to it.
Cloning Tool	A tool used for replicating pixels in digital photography.
CMOS	Complementary Metal Oxide Semiconductor. A chip used widely within the computer industry, now also frequently used as an image sensor in digital cameras.
CMYK	Cyan, Magenta, Yellow and black (K). The inks used in four-color printing.
Color fringes	Bands of color on the edges of lines within an image.
Color fringing	See *Color fringes*.
Color gamut	The range of colors provided by a hardware device, or a set of pigments.
Color Picker	Dialog box used for the selection of colors.
Color space	An accurately defined set of colors that can be translated for use as a profile.
ColorSync	System level software developed by Apple, designed to work together with hardware devices to facilitate predictable color.
Complementary metal oxide semiconductor	See *CMOS*.
Composition	The arrangement of shape, tone, line and color within the boundaries of the image area.
Compression	A method for reducing the file size of a digital image.
Constrain proportions	Retains the proportional dimensions of an image when changing the image size.
Contact image sensor	See *CIS*.
Context	The circumstances relevant to something under consideration.
Continuous tone	An image containing the illusion of smooth gradations between highlights and shadows.
Contrast	The difference in brightness between the darkest and lightest areas of the image or subject.
CPU	Central Processing Unit, used to compute exposure.
Crash	The sudden operational failure of a computer.
Crop	Reduce image size to enhance composition or limit information.
Curves	Control for adjusting tonality and color in a digital image.
DAT	Digital Audio Tape. Tape format used to store computer data.
Default	The settings of a device as chosen by the manufacturer.

Defringe	The action of removing the edge pixels of a selection.
Density	The measure of opacity of tone on a negative.
Depth of field	The zone of sharpness variable by aperture, focal length or subject distance.
Descreen	The removal of half-tone lines or patterns during scanning.
Device	An item of computer hardware.
Device dependent	Dependent on a particular item of hardware. For example, referring to a color result unique to a particular printer.
Device independent	Not dependent on a particular item of hardware. For example, a color result that can be replicated on any hardware device.
Digital audio tape	See *DAT*.
Digital image	A computer-generated photograph composed of pixels (picture elements) rather than film grain.
Digital Negative format	Adobe's open source Raw file format.
DNG	Adobe's Digital Negative format.
Download	To copy digital files (usually from the Internet).
Dpi	Dots per inch. A measurement of resolution.
Dummy file	To go through the motions of creating a new file in Photoshop for the purpose of determining the file size required during the scanning process.
Dye sublimation print	A high-quality print created using thermal dyes.
Dyes	Types of pigment.
Edit	Select images from a larger collection to form a sequence or theme.
Editable text	Text that has not been rendered into pixels.
Eight-bit image	A single-channel image capable of storing 256 different colors or levels.
Evaluate	Assess the value or quality of a piece of work.
Exposure	Combined effect of intensity and duration of light on a light-sensitive material or device.
Exposure compensation	To increase or decrease the exposure from a meter-indicated exposure to obtain an appropriate exposure.
Feather	The action of softening the edge of a digital selection.
File format	The code used to store digital data, e.g. TIFF or JPEG.
File size	The memory required to store digital data in a file.
Film grain	See *Grain*.
Film speed	A precise number or ISO rating given to a film or device indicating its degree of light sensitivity.
F-numbers (f-stops)	A sequence of numbers given to the relative sizes of aperture opening. F-numbers are standard on all lenses. The largest number corresponds to the smallest aperture and vice versa.
Format	The size of the camera or the orientation/shape of the image.
Frame	The act of composing an image. See *Composition*.

Freeze	Software that fails to interact with new information.
FTP software	File Transfer Protocol software is used for uploading and downloading files over the Internet.
Galleries	A managed collection of images displayed in a conveniently accessible form.
Gaussian Blur	A filter used for defocusing a digital image.
GIF	Graphics Interchange Format. An 8-bit format (256 colors) that supports animation and partial transparency.
Gigabyte	A unit of measurement for digital files, 1024 megabytes.
Grain	Tiny particles of silver metal or dye that make up the final image. Fast films give larger grain than slow films. Focus finders are used to magnify the projected image so that the grain can be seen and an accurate focus obtained.
Gray card	Card that reflects 18% of incident light. The resulting tone is used by light meters as a standardized midtone.
Grayscale	An 8-bit image with a single channel used to describe monochrome (black and white) images.
Half-tone	A system of reproducing the continuous tone of a photographic print by a pattern of dots printed by offset litho.
Hard copy	A print.
Hard drive	Memory facility that is capable of retaining information after the computer is switched off.
HDR	High Dynamic Range image.
High Dynamic Range	A picture type that is capable of storing 32 bits per color channel. This produces a photo with a much bigger possible brightness range than found in 16- or 8-bit per channel photos. Photoshop creates HDR images with the Merge to HDR feature.
Highlight	Area of subject receiving highest exposure value.
Histogram	A graphical representation of a digital image indicating the pixels allocated to each level.
Histories	The memory of previous image states in Photoshop.
History Brush	A tool in Photoshop with which a previous state or history can be painted.
HTML	HyperText Markup Language. The code that is used to describe the contents and appearance of a web page.
Hue	The name of a color, e.g. red, green or blue.
Hyperlink	A link that allows the viewer of a page to navigate or 'jump' to another location on the same page or on a different page.
ICC	International Color Consortium. A collection of manufacturers including Adobe, Microsoft, Agfa, Kodak, SGI, Fogra, Sun and Taligent who came together to create an open, cross-platform standard for color management.

ICM	Image Color Management. Windows-based software designed to work together with hardware devices to facilitate predictable color.
Image Color Management	See *ICM*.
Image setter	A device used to print CMYK film separations used in the printing industry.
Image size	The pixel dimensions, output dimensions and resolution used to define a digital image.
Infrared film	A film that is sensitive to the wavelengths of light longer than 720 nm, which are invisible to the human eye.
Instant capture	An exposure that is fast enough to result in a relatively sharp image free of significant blur.
International Color Consortium	See *ICC*.
Interpolated resolution	Final resolution of an image arrived at by means of interpolation.
Interpolation	Increasing the pixel dimensions of an image by inserting new pixels between existing pixels within the image.
ISO	International Standards Organization. A numerical system for rating the speed or relative light sensitivity of a film or device.
ISP	Internet Service Provider, allows individuals access to a web server.
Jaz	A storage disk capable of storing slightly less than 2 GB, manufactured by Iomega.
JPEG (.jpg)	Joint Photographic Experts Group. Popular image compression file format.
Jump	To open a file in another application.
Juxtapose	Placing objects or subjects within a frame to allow comparison.
Kilobyte	1024 bytes.
LAB mode	A device-independent color model created in 1931 as an international standard for measuring color.
Lasso Tool	Selection Tool used in digital editing.
Latent image	An image created by exposure onto light-sensitive silver halide ions, which until amplified by chemical development is invisible to the eye.
Latitude	Ability of the film or device to record the brightness range of the subject.
Layer	A feature in digital editing software that allows a composite digital image where each element is on a separate layer or level.
Layer mask	A mask attached to a layer that is used to define the visibility of pixels on that layer.
Layer Stacks	A group of Photoshop layers that have to be converted into a Smart Object for the purposes of performing image analysis on the differences between the picture content of each layer.

LCD	Liquid Crystal Display.
LED	Light-Emitting Diode. Used in the viewfinder to inform the photographer of exposure settings.
Lens	An optical device usually made from glass that focuses light rays to form an image on a surface.
Levels	Shades of lightness or brightness assigned to pixels.
Light cyan	A pale shade of the subtractive color cyan.
Light magenta	A pale shade of the subtractive color magenta.
LiOn	Lithium ion. Rechargeable battery type.
Lithium ion	See *LiOn*.
LZW compression	A lossless form of image compression used in the TIFF format.
Magic Wand Tool	Selection Tool used in digital editing.
Magnesium lithium	See MnLi.
Marching ants	A moving broken line indicating a digital selection of pixels.
Marquee Tool	Selection Tool used in digital editing.
Maximum aperture	Largest lens opening.
Megabyte	A unit of measurement for digital files, 1024 kilobytes.
Megapixels	More than a million pixels.
Memory card	A removable storage device about the size of a small card. Many technologies available result in various sizes and formats. Often found in digital cameras.
Merge to HDR	Photoshop's feature for creating HDR images from a series of photos with bracketed exposures.
Metallic silver	Metal created during the development of film, giving rise to the appearance of grain. See *Grain*.
Minimum aperture	Smallest lens opening.
MnLi	Magnesium lithium. Rechargeable battery type.
Mode (digital image)	RGB, CMYK, etc. The mode describes the tonal and color range of the captured or scanned image.
Moiré	A repetitive pattern usually caused by interference of overlapping symmetrical dots or lines.
Motherboard	An electronic board containing the main functional elements of a computer upon which other components can be connected.
Multiple exposure	Several exposures made onto the same frame of film or piece of paper.
Negative	An image on film or paper where the tones are reversed, e.g. dark tones are recorded as light tones and vice versa.
NiCd	Nickel cadmium. Rechargeable battery type.
Nickel cadmium	See *NiCd*.
Nickel metal hydride	See *NiMH*.
NiMH	Nickel metal hydride. Rechargeable battery type.
Noise	Electronic interference producing white speckles in the image.

Non-destructive editing	An editing approach that doesn't alter the original pixels in a photo throughout the enhancement process. Typically used for Raw processing or in techniques that make use of Smart Object technology.
Non-imaging	To not assist in the formation of an image. When related to light it is often known as flare.
ODR	Output Device Resolution. The number of ink dots per inch of paper produced by the printer.
Opacity	The degree of non-transparency.
Opaque	Not transmitting light.
Optimize	The process of fine-tuning the file size and display quality of an image or image slice destined for the web.
Out of gamut	Beyond the scope of colors that a particular device can create.
Output device resolution	See *ODR*.
Path	The outline of a vector shape.
PDF	Portable Document Format. Data format created using Adobe software.
Pegging	The action of fixing tonal or color values to prevent them from being altered when using Curves image adjustment.
Photomerge	Adobe's own panoramic stitching utility.
Photo multiplier tube	See *PMT*.
Photoshop Document	The native file format used by Photoshop.
Piezoelectric	Crystal that will accurately change dimension with a change of applied voltage. Often used in inkjet printers to supply microscopic dots of ink.
Pixel	The smallest square picture element in a digital image.
Pixelated	An image where the pixels are visible to the human eye and curved lines appear jagged or stepped.
PMT	Photo Multiplier Tube. Light-sensing device generally used in drum scanners.
Portable Document Format	See *PDF*.
Pre-press	Stage where digital information is translated into output suitable for the printing process.
Primary colors	The three colors of light (red, green and blue) from which all other colors can be created.
Processor speed	The capability of the computer's CPU measured in megahertz.
PSD	Photoshop Document format.
Quick Mask mode	Temporary alpha channel used for refining or making selections.
Quick Selection Tool	A selection tool added to Photoshop in version CS3 that tries to predict the shape of the selection as you draw. The feature takes into account tone, color, texture and shape of the underlying photo as it creates the selection.

RAID	Redundant Array of Independent Disks. A type of hard disk assembly that allows data to be simultaneously written.
RAM	Random Access Memory. The computer's short-term or working memory.
Redundant array of independent disks	See *RAID*.
Reflector	A surface used to reflect light in order to fill shadows.
Refraction	The change in direction of light as it passes through a transparent surface at an angle.
Resample	To alter the total number of pixels describing a digital image.
Resolution	A measure of the degree of definition, also called sharpness.
RGB	Red, Green and Blue. The three primary colors used to display images on a color monitor.
Rollover	A web effect in which a different image state appears when the viewer performs a mouse action.
Rubber Stamp	A tool used for replicating pixels in digital imaging. Also called Clone Stamp Tool.
Sample	To select a color value for analysis or use.
Saturation (color)	Intensity or richness of color hue.
Save a Copy	An option that allows the user to create a digital replica of an image file but without layers or additional channels.
Save As	An option that allows the user to create a duplicate of a digital file but with an alternative name, thereby protecting the original document from any changes that have been made since it was opened.
Scale	A ratio of size.
Scratch disk memory	Portion of hard disk allocated to software such as Photoshop to be used as a working space.
Screen real estate	Area of monitor available for image display that is not taken up by palettes and toolbars.
Screen redraws	Time taken to render information being depicted on the monitor as changes are being made through the application software.
Secondary colors	The colors cyan, magenta and yellow, created when two primary colors are mixed.
Sharp	In focus. Not blurred.
Single lens reflex	See *SLR camera*.
Slice	Divides an image into rectangular areas for selective optimization or to create functional areas for a web page.
Slider	A sliding control in digital editing software used to adjust color, tone, opacity, etc.
SLR camera	Single Lens Reflex camera. The image in the viewfinder is essentially the same image that the film will see. This image, prior to taking the shot, is viewed via a mirror that moves out of the way when the shutter release is pressed.

Smart Filter	An extension of the Smart Object technology that allows the non-destructive application of Photoshop filters to an image.
Smart Object	Technology first introduced in Photoshop CS2 that maintains the original form of an embedded image but stills allows it to be edited and enhanced. Smart Objects are used in many non-destructive editing or enhancement techniques.
Snapshot	A record of a history state that is held until the file is closed.
Soft proof	The depiction of a digital image on a computer monitor used to check output accuracy.
Software	A computer program.
Stack	Several photos grouped together in the Bridge workspace.
Subjective analysis	Personal opinions or views concerning the perceived communication and aesthetic value of an image.
Subtractive color	A color system where the subtractive primary colors yellow, magenta and cyan mix to form all other colors.
System software	Computer operating program, e.g. Windows or Mac OS.
Tagging	System whereby a profile is included within the image data of a file for the purpose of helping describe its particular color characteristics.
Thematic images	A set of images with a unifying idea or concept.
TIFF	Tagged Image File Format. Popular image file format for desktop publishing applications.
Tone	A tint of color or shade of gray.
Transparent	Allowing light to pass through.
Tri-color	A filter taking the hue of either one of the additive primaries red, green or blue.
True resolution	The resolution of an image file created by the hardware device, either camera or scanner, without any interpolation.
TTL meter	Through-The-Lens reflective light meter. This is a convenient way to measure the brightness of a scene as the meter is behind the camera lens.
Tweening	Derived from the words in betweening – an automated process of creating additional frames between two existing frames in an animation.
UCR	Under Color Removal. A method of replacing a portion of the yellow, magenta and cyan ink, within the shadows and neutral areas of an image, with black ink.
Under color removal	See UCR.
Unsharp Mask	See USM.
Unsharp Mask filter	A filter for increasing apparent sharpness of a digital image.
URL	Uniform Resource Locator. The unique web address given to every web page.
USM	Unsharp Mask. A process used to sharpen images.

Vanishing Point	A Photoshop feature designed to allow the manipulation of photos within a three-dimensional space.
Vector graphic	A resolution-independent image described by its geometric characteristics rather than by pixels.
Video card	A circuit board containing the hardware required to drive the monitor of a computer.
Video memory	Memory required for the monitor to be able to render an image.
Virtual memory	Hard drive memory allocated to function as RAM.
Visualize	To imagine how something will look once it has been completed.
Workflow	Series of repeatable steps required to achieve a particular result within a digital imaging environment.
Zip	An older style storage disk manufactured by Iomega, available in either 100 MB or 250 MB capacity.
Zoom Tool	A tool used for magnifying a digital image on the monitor.

Keyboard Shortcuts

⌥ = Option ⇧ = Shift ⌘ = Command ⌫ = Delete/Backspace

Action	Keyboard Shortcut
Navigate and view	
Fit image on screen	Double-click Hand Tool or ⌘/Ctrl + 0 (zero)
View image at 100%	Double-click Zoom Tool or ⌥/Alt + ⌘/Ctrl + 0
Zoom Tool (magnify)	⌘/Ctrl + Spacebar + click image
Zoom Tool (reduce)	⌥/Alt + ⌘/Ctrl + click image
Full/Standard/Maximized screen mode	F
Show/hide rulers	⌘/Ctrl + R
Show/hide guides	⌘/Ctrl + ;
Hide panels	Tab key
File commands	
Open	⌘/Ctrl + O
Close	⌘/Ctrl + W
Save	⌘/Ctrl + S
Save As	⇧ + ⌘/Ctrl + S
Undo/Redo	⌘/Ctrl + Z
Step Backward	⌥/Alt + ⌘/Ctrl + Z
Step Forward	⌘/Ctrl + ⇧ + Z
Selections	
Add to selection	Hold ⇧ key and select again
Subtract from selection	Hold ⌥/Alt key and select again
Copy	⌘/Ctrl + C
Cut	⌘/Ctrl + X
Paste	⌘/Ctrl + V
Paste Into	⌘/Ctrl ⇧ + V
Free Transform	⌘/Ctrl + T
Distort image in Free Transform	Hold ⌘ key + move handle
Feather	⌘/Ctrl + ⌥/Alt + D
Select All	⌘/Ctrl + A
Deselect	⌘/Ctrl + D
Reselect	⇧ + ⌘/Ctrl + D
Inverse selection	⌘/Ctrl + I
Edit in Quick Mask mode	Q

Painting

Set default foreground and background colors	D
Switch between foreground and background color	X
Enlarge brush size (with Paint Tool selected)	]
Reduce brush size (with Paint Tool selected)	[
Make brush softer	[+ Shift
Make brush harder	] + Shift
Change opacity of brush in 10% increments (with Brush Tool selected)	Press number keys 0–9
Fill with foreground color	⌥/Alt ⌫
Fill with background color	⌘/Ctrl ⌫

Adjustments

Levels	⌘/Ctrl + L
Curves	⌘/Ctrl + M
Hue/Saturation	⌘/Ctrl + U

Layers and masks

Add new layer	⇧ ⌘/Ctrl + N
Load selection from layer mask or channel	⌘/Ctrl + click thumbnail
Change opacity of active layer in 10% increments	Press number keys 0–9
Add layer mask – Hide All	⌥/Alt + click 'Add layer mask' icon
Move layer down/up	⌘/Ctrl + [or]
Stamp Visible	⌘/Ctrl + ⌥/Alt + ⇧ then type E
Group selected layers	⌘/Ctrl + G
Create Clipping Mask	⌘/Ctrl + ⌥/Alt + G
Disable/enable layer mask	⇧ + click layer mask thumbnail
Preview contents of layer mask	⌥/Alt + click layer mask thumbnail
Preview layer mask and image	⌥/Alt + ⇧ + click layer mask thumbnail
Group or clip layer	⌘/Ctrl + G
Blend modes	⌥/Alt + ⇧ + (N, K, M, G, S, O, F, Y, C) Normal, Darken, Multiply, Lighten, Screen, Overlay, Soft Light, Luminosity, Color

Crop

Enter crop	Return key
Cancel crop	Esc key
Constrain proportions of crop marquee	Hold ⇧ key
Turn off magnetic guides when cropping	Hold ⌥/Alt ⇧ keys + drag handle

Web Links

Information and blogs

Essential Skills	http://www.photoshopessentialskills.com
Photoshop Support	http://www.photoshopsupport.com
Adobe Digital Imaging	http://www.adobe.com/digitalimag/main.html
Martin Evening	http://www.martinevening.com
Luminous Landscape	http://www.luminous-landscape.com
Digital Photography Review	http://www.dpreview.com
Digital Dog	http://www.digitaldog.net
Epson	http://www.epson.com
Photoshop Blog	http://www.photoshopblog.net/
John Nack	http://blogs.adobe.com/jnack/
Photoshop News	http://www.photoshopnews.com/

Tutorials

Adobe	http://www.adobe.com/designcenter/
Essential Skills	http://www.photoshopessentialskills.com
Russell Brown	http://www.russellbrown.com
Photoshop Support	http://www.photoshopsupport.com
Planet Photoshop	http://www.planetphotoshop.com
Photoshop Workshop	http://www.psworkshop.net

Illustrators

iStockphoto	www.iStockphoto.com
Magdelena Bors	www.magdalenabors.com
Samantha Everton	www.samanthaeverton.com
Rory Gardiner	www.rorygardiner.com.au
Chis Mollison	www.chrismollison.com.au
Chris Neylon	www.chrisneylon.net
Serap Osman	www.seraposman.com.au
Rod Owen	www.owenphoto.com.au
Ed Purnomo	www.edpurnomo
Craig Shell	www.craigshell.com
Daniel Stainsby	www.danstainsby.com
Victoria Verdon Roe	www.victoriaverdonroe.com

Index